MW00985968

Additional praise for

STILLNESS IS THE KEY

"Some authors give advice. Ryan Holiday distills wisdom. This book is a must read."   —CAL NEWPORT, *NEW YORK TIMES* BESTSELLING AUTHOR OF *DIGITAL MINIMALISM*

"Don't be fooled. Within the pages of this unassuming little book lie a life-changing idea: that in order to move forward, we must learn to be still. Ryan Holiday has done it again."   —SOPHIA AMORUSO, COFOUNDER AND CEO, GIRLBOSS

"In the world today the dangers are many—most notably, the endless distractions and petty battles that make us act without purpose or direction. In this book, through his masterful synthesis of Eastern and Western philosophy, Ryan Holiday teaches us all how to maintain our focus and presence of mind amid the sometimes overwhelming conflicts and troubles of twenty-first-century life."

—ROBERT GREENE, *NEW YORK TIMES* BESTSELLING AUTHOR OF *THE 48 LAWS OF POWER*

"Ryan Holiday is one of the brilliant writers and minds of our time. In *Stillness Is the Key* he gives us the blueprint to clear our minds, recharge our souls, and reclaim our power."   —JON GORDON, BESTSELLING AUTHOR OF *THE ENERGY BUS*

"Ryan Holiday is a national treasure and a master in the field of self-mastery. In his most compelling book yet, he has mined both the classical literature of the ancient world and cultural touchstones from Mister Rogers to Tiger Woods, and brought his learnings to us in terms that the frantic, distracted, overcaffeinated modern mind can understand and put to use. Highly recommended."

—STEVEN PRESSFIELD, BESTSELLING AUTHOR OF *THE WAR OF ART* AND *THE ARTIST'S JOURNEY*

Praise for Ryan Holiday

"[Ryan is a] self-help sage, who is now a sought-after guru to NFL coaches, Olympians, hip-hop stars, and Silicon Valley entrepreneurs… [he] translates Stoicism, which had counted emperors and statesmen among its adherents during antiquity, into pithy catchphrases and digestible anecdotes for ambitious, twenty-first-century life hackers." —ALEXANDRA ALTER, *NEW YORK TIMES*

"Holiday is an out-of-the-box thinker who likes to take chances."
—*NEW YORK TIMES BOOK REVIEW*

"I don't have many rules in life, but one I never break is: If Ryan Holiday writes a book, I read it as soon as I can get my hands on it."
—BRIAN KOPPELMAN, SCREENWRITER AND DIRECTOR,
ROUNDERS, OCEAN'S THIRTEEN, AND *BILLIONS*

"Ryan Holiday is one of the most promising young writers of his generation." —GEORGE RAVELING, HALL OF FAME BASKETBALL COACH,
NIKE'S DIRECTOR OF INTERNATIONAL BASKETBALL

STILLNESS IS THE KEY

STILLNESS

IS THE KEY

RYAN HOLIDAY

PORTFOLIO/PENGUIN

Portfolio/Penguin
An imprint of Penguin Random House LLC
penguinrandomhouse.com

Copyright © 2019 by Ryan Holiday
Penguin supports copyright. Copyright fuels creativity, encourages diverse voices, promotes free speech, and creates a vibrant culture. Thank you for buying an authorized edition of this book and for complying with copyright laws by not reproducing, scanning, or distributing any part of it in any form without permission. You are supporting writers and allowing Penguin to continue to publish books for every reader.

Most Portfolio books are available at a discount when purchased in quantity for sales promotions or corporate use. Special editions, which include personalized covers, excerpts, and corporate imprints, can be created when purchased in large quantities. For more information, please call (212) 572-2232 or e-mail specialmarkets@penguinrandomhouse.com. Your local bookstore can also assist with discounted bulk purchases using the Penguin Random House corporate Business-to-Business program. For assistance in locating a participating retailer, e-mail B2B@penguinrandomhouse.com.

Library of Congress Cataloging-in-Publication Data

Names: Holiday, Ryan, author.
Title: Stillness is the key / Ryan Holiday.
Description: New York : Portfolio/Penguin, [2019] | Includes bibliographical references.
Identifiers: LCCN 2019018368 (print) | LCCN 2019021767 (ebook) |
ISBN 9780525538592 (ebook) | ISBN 9780525538585 (hardcover)
Subjects: LCSH: Quietude.
Classification: LCC BJ1533.Q5 (ebook) | LCC BJ1533.Q5 H65 2019 (print) |
DDC 128/.4—dc23
LC record available at https://lccn.loc.gov/2019018368

Printed in the United States of America

18th Printing

While the author has made every effort to provide accurate telephone numbers, internet addresses, and other contact information at the time of publication, neither the publisher nor the author assumes any responsibility for errors or for changes that occur after publication. Further, the publisher does not have any control over and does not assume any responsibility for author or third-party websites or their content.

The struggle is great, the task divine—to gain mastery, freedom, happiness, and tranquility.

—EPICTETUS

CONTENTS

PREFACE

It was the late first century AD and Lucius Annaeus Seneca, Rome's most influential power broker, its greatest living playwright, and its wisest philosopher, was struggling to work.

The problem was the ear-shattering, soul-rattling noise that poured in from the street below.

Rome had always been a loud city—think New York City construction loud—but the block where Seneca was staying was a deafening cacophony of disturbances. Athletes worked out in the gymnasium underneath his suite of rooms, dropping heavy weights. A masseuse pummeled the backs of old fat men. Swimmers splashed in the water. At the entrance of the building, a pickpocket was being arrested and making a scene. Passing carriages rumbled over the stone streets, while carpenters hammered away in their shops and vendors shouted their wares. Children laughed and played. Dogs barked.

And more than the noise outside his window, there was the simple fact that Seneca's life was falling apart. It was crisis upon crisis upon crisis. Overseas unrest threatened his finances. He was getting older and could feel it. He had been pushed out of politics by his enemies, and, now on the outs with Nero, he could easily—at the emperor's whim—lose his head.

It was not, we can imagine from the perspective of our own busy lives, a great environment for a human to get anything done. Unconducive to thinking, creating, writing, or making good decisions. The noise and distractions of the empire were enough "to make me hate my very powers of hearing," Seneca told a friend.

Yet for good reason, this scene has tantalized admirers for centuries. How does a man, besieged by adversity and difficulty, not only *not* go out of his mind, but actually find the serenity to think clearly and to write incisive, perfectly crafted essays, some in that very room, which would reach millions upon millions and touch on truths that few have ever accessed?

"I have toughened my nerves against all that sort of thing," Seneca explained to that same friend about the noise. "I force my mind to concentrate, and keep it from straying to things outside itself; all outdoors may be bedlam, provided that there is no disturbance within."

Ah, isn't that what we all crave? What discipline! What focus! To be able to tune out our surroundings, to access one's full capabilities at any time, in any place, despite every difficulty? How wonderful that would be! What we'd be able to accomplish! How much happier we would be!

To Seneca and to his fellow adherents of Stoic philosophy, if a person could develop peace within themselves—if they could achieve *apatheia,* as they called it—then the whole world could be at war, and they could still think well, work well, and be well. "You may be sure that you are at peace with yourself," Seneca wrote, "when no noise reaches you, when no word shakes you out of yourself, whether it be flattery or a threat, or merely an empty sound buzzing about you with unmeaning sin." In this state, nothing could touch them (not even a deranged emperor), no emotion could disturb them, no threat could interrupt them, and every beat of the present moment would be theirs for living.

It's a powerful idea made all the more transcendent by the remarkable fact that nearly every other philosophy of the ancient world—no matter how different or distant—came to the exact same conclusion.

It wouldn't have mattered whether you were a pupil at the feet of Confucius in 500 BC, a student of the early Greek philosopher Democritus one hundred years later, or sitting in Epicurus's garden a generation after that—you would have heard equally emphatic calls for this imperturbability, unruffledness, and tranquility.

The Buddhist word for it was *upekkha.* The Muslims spoke of *aslama.* The Hebrews, *hishtavut.* The second book of the Bhagavad Gita, the epic poem of the warrior Arjuna, speaks of *samatvam,* an "evenness of mind—a peace that is ever the same." The Greeks, *euthymia* and *hesychia.* The Epicureans, *ataraxia.* The Christians, *aequanimitas.*

In English: *stillness.*

To be steady while the world spins around you. To act without frenzy. To hear only what needs to be heard. To possess quietude—exterior and interior—on command.

To tap into the *dao* and the *logos*. The Word. The Way.

Buddhism. Stoicism. Epicureanism. Christianity. Hinduism. It's all but impossible to find a philosophical school or religion that does not venerate this inner peace—this *stillness*—as the highest good and as the key to elite performance and a happy life.

And when basically *all* the wisdom of the ancient world agrees on something, only a fool would decline to listen.

STILLNESS IS THE KEY

INTRODUCTION

The call to stillness comes quietly. The modern world does not.

In addition to the clatter and chatter and intrigue and infighting that would be familiar to the citizens of Seneca's time, we have car horns, stereos, cell phone alarms, social media notifications, chainsaws, airplanes.

Our personal and professional problems are equally overwhelming. Competitors muscle into our industry. Our desks pile high with papers and our inboxes overflow with messages. We are always reachable, which means that arguments and updates are never far away. The news bombards us with one crisis after another on every screen we own—of which there are many. The grind of work wears us down and seems to never stop. We are overfed and undernourished. Overstimulated, overscheduled, and lonely.

Who has the power to stop? Who has time to think? Is there anyone not affected by the din and dysfunctions of our time?

While the magnitude and urgency of our struggle is modern,

it is rooted in a timeless problem. Indeed, history shows that the ability to cultivate quiet and quell the turmoil inside us, to slow the mind down, to understand our emotions, and to conquer our bodies has always been extremely difficult. "All of humanity's problems," Blaise Pascal said in 1654, "stem from man's inability to sit quietly in a room alone."

In evolution, distinct species—like birds and bats—have often evolved similar adaptations in order to survive. The same goes for the philosophical schools separated by vast oceans and distances. They developed unique paths to the same critical destination: The stillness required to become master of one's own life. To survive and thrive in any and every environment, no matter how loud or busy.

Which is why this idea of stillness is not some soft New Age nonsense or the domain of monks and sages, but in fact desperately necessary to all of us, whether we're running a hedge fund or playing in a Super Bowl, pioneering research in a new field or raising a family. It is an attainable path to enlightenment and excellence, greatness and happiness, performance as well as presence, for *every kind of person.*

Stillness is what aims the archer's arrow. It inspires new ideas. It sharpens perspective and illuminates connections. It slows the ball down so that we might hit it. It generates a vision, helps us resist the passions of the mob, makes space for gratitude and wonder. Stillness allows us to persevere. To succeed. It is the key that unlocks the insights of genius, and allows us regular folks to understand them.

The promise of this book is the location of that key . . . and a call not only for possessing stillness, but for radiating it outward like a star—like the sun—for a world that needs light more than ever.

The Key to Everything

In the early days of the American Civil War, there were a hundred competing plans for how to secure victory and whom to appoint to do it. From every general and for every battle there was an endless supply of criticism and dangerous passions—there was paranoia and fear, ego and arrogance, and very little in the way of hope.

There is a wonderful scene from those fraught first moments when Abraham Lincoln addressed a group of generals and politicians in his office at the White House. Most people at that time believed the war could only be won through enormous, decisively bloody battles in the country's biggest cities, like Richmond and New Orleans and even, potentially, Washington, D.C.

Lincoln, a man who taught himself military strategy by poring over books he checked out from the Library of Congress, laid out a map across a big table and pointed instead to Vicksburg, Mississippi, a little city deep in Southern territory. It was a fortified town high on the bluffs of the Mississippi River, held by the toughest rebel troops. Not only did it control navigation of that important waterway, but it was a juncture for a number of other important tributaries, as well as rail lines that supplied

Confederate armies and enormous slave plantations across the South.

"Vicksburg is the key," he told the crowd with the certainty of a man who had studied a matter so intensely that he could express it in the simplest of terms. "The war can never be brought to a close until that key is in our pocket."

As it happened, Lincoln turned out to be exactly right. It would take years, it would take incredible equanimity and patience, as well as ferocious commitment to his cause, but the strategy laid out in that room was what won the war and ended slavery in America forever. Every other important victory in the Civil War—from Gettysburg to Sherman's March to the Sea to Lee's surrender—was made possible because at Lincoln's instruction Ulysses S. Grant laid siege to Vicksburg in 1863, and by taking the city split the South in two and gained control of that important waterway. In his reflective, intuitive manner, without being rushed or distracted, Lincoln had seen (and held fast to) what his own advisors, and even his enemy, had missed. Because he possessed the key that unlocked victory from the rancor and folly of all those early competing plans.

In our own lives, we face a seemingly equal number of problems and are pulled in countless directions by competing priorities and beliefs. In the way of everything we hope to accomplish, personally and professionally, sit obstacles and enemies. Martin Luther King Jr. observed that there was a violent civil war raging within each and every person—between our good and bad impulses, between our ambitions and our principles, between what we can be and how hard it is to actually get there.

In those battles, in that war, stillness is the river and the railroad junction through which so much depends. *It is the key . . .*

To thinking clearly.

To seeing the whole chessboard.

To making tough decisions.

To managing our emotions.

To identifying the right goals.

To handling high-pressure situations.

To maintaining relationships.

To building good habits.

To being productive.

To physical excellence.

To feeling fulfilled.

To capturing moments of laughter and joy.

Stillness is the key to, well, just about everything.

To being a better parent, a better artist, a better investor, a better athlete, a better scientist, a better human being. To unlocking all that we are capable of in this life.

This Stillness Can Be Yours

Anyone who has concentrated so deeply that a flash of insight or inspiration suddenly visited them knows stillness. Anyone who has given their best to something, felt pride of completion, of knowing they left absolutely nothing in reserve—that's stillness. Anyone who has stepped forward with the eyes of the crowd upon them and then poured all their training into a single moment of performance—that's stillness, even if it involves active movement. Anyone who has spent time with that special, wise person, and witnessed them solve in two seconds the problem that had vexed us for months—stillness. Anyone who has walked out alone on a quiet street at night as the snow fell, and watched as the light fell softly on that snow and is warmed by the contentment of being alive—that too is stillness.

Staring at the blank page in front of us and watching as the words pour out in perfect prose, at a loss for where they came from; standing on fine white sand, looking out at the ocean, or really any part of nature, and feeling like part of something bigger than oneself; a quiet evening with a loved one; the satisfaction of having done a good turn for another person; sitting, alone with our thoughts, and seizing for the first time the ability to think about them as we were thinking them. *Stillness*.

Sure, there is a certain ineffableness to what we're talking about, to articulating the stillness that the poet Rainer Maria Rilke described as "full, complete" where "all the random and approximate were muted."

"Although we speak of attaining the *dao*," Lao Tzu once said, "there is really nothing to obtain." Or to borrow a master's reply to a student who asked where he might find Zen: "You are seeking for an ox while you are yourself on it."

You have tasted stillness before. You have felt it in your soul. And you want more of it.

You *need* more of it.

Which is why the aim of this book is simply to show how to uncover and draw upon the stillness we already possess. It's about the cultivation of and the connection to that powerful force given to us at birth, the one that has atrophied in our modern, busy lives. This book is an attempt to answer the pressing question of our time: If the quiet moments are the best moments, and if so many wise, virtuous people have sung their praises, why are they so rare?

Well, the answer is that while we may naturally possess stillness, accessing it is not easy. One must really listen to hear it speaking to us. And answering the call requires stamina and mastery. "To hold the mind still is an enormous discipline," the late comedian Garry Shandling reminded himself in his journal as he struggled to manage fame and fortune and health problems, "one which must be faced with the greatest commitment of your life."

The pages that follow tell the stories and strategies of men and women who were just like you, who struggled as you struggle amid the noise and responsibilities of life, but managed to succeed in finding and harnessing stillness. You will hear stories of the triumphs and trials of John F. Kennedy and Fred Rogers,

Anne Frank and Queen Victoria. There will be stories about Jesus and Tiger Woods, Socrates, Napoleon, the composer John Cage, Sadaharu Oh, Rosanne Cash, Dorothy Day, Buddha, Leonardo da Vinci, and Marcus Aurelius.

We will also draw on poetry and novels, philosophical texts and scientific research. We will raid every school and every era we can to find strategies to help us direct our thoughts, process our emotions, and master our bodies. So we can do less . . . and do more. Accomplish more but need it less. Feel better and *be* better at the same time.

To achieve stillness, we'll need to focus on three domains, the timeless trinity of mind, body, soul—the head, the heart, the flesh.

In each domain, we will seek to reduce the disturbances and perturbations that make stillness impossible. To cease to be at war with the world and within ourselves, and to establish a lasting inner and outer peace instead.

You know that is what you want—and what you deserve. That's why you picked up this book.

So let us answer the call together. Let us find—let us lock into—the stillness that we seek.

PART I

MIND • SPIRIT • BODY

The mind is restless, Krishna, impetuous, self-willed, hard to train: to master the mind seems as difficult as to master the mighty winds.

—THE BHAGAVAD GITA

THE DOMAIN OF THE MIND

The entire world changed in the few short hours between when John F. Kennedy went to bed on October 15, 1962, and when he woke up the following morning.

Because while the president slept, the CIA identified the ongoing construction of medium- and long-range Soviet ballistic nuclear missile sites on the island of Cuba, just ninety miles from American shores. As Kennedy would tell a stunned American public days later, "Each of these missiles is capable of striking Washington, D.C., the Panama Canal, Cape Canaveral, Mexico City, or any other city in the southeastern part of the United States, in Central America, or in the Caribbean."

As Kennedy received his first briefing on what we now know as the Cuban Missile Crisis—or simply as the Thirteen Days— the president could consider only the appalling stakes. As many as seventy million people were expected to die in the first strikes between the United States and Russia. But that was just a guess— no one actually knew how terrible nuclear war would be.

What Kennedy knew for certain was that he faced an unprecedented escalation of the long-brewing Cold War between the United States and the USSR. And whatever factors had contributed to its creation, no matter how inevitable war must have appeared, it fell on him, at the very least, to just *not make things worse.* Because it might mean the end of life on planet Earth.

Kennedy was a young president born into immense privilege, raised by an aggressive father who hated to lose, in a family whose motto, they joked, was "Don't Get Mad, Get Even." With almost no executive leadership experience under his belt, it's not a surprise, then, that the first year and half of Kennedy's administration had not gone well.

In April 1961, Kennedy had tried and failed—embarrassingly so—to invade Cuba and overthrow Fidel Castro at the Bay of Pigs. Just a few months later, he was diplomatically dominated by Soviet premier Nikita Khrushchev in a series of meetings in Vienna. (Kennedy would call it the "roughest thing in my life.") Sensing his adversary's political weakness, and likely aware of the chronic physical frailty he endured from Addison's disease and back injuries suffered during World War II, Khrushchev repeatedly lied to Kennedy about any weapons being placed in Cuba, insisting that they would be for defensive purposes only.

Which is to say that during the Missile Crisis, Kennedy faced, as every leader will at some point in their tenure, a difficult test amid complicating personal and political circumstances. There were many questions: Why would Khrushchev do this? What was his endgame? What was the man possibly trying to accomplish? Was there a way to solve it? What did Kennedy's advisors think? What were Kennedy's options? Was he up to this task? Did he have what it took?

The fate of millions depended on his answers.

The advice from Kennedy's advisors was immediate and emphatic: The missile sites must be destroyed with the full might of the country's military arsenal. Every second wasted risked the safety and the reputation of the United States. After the surprise attack on the missiles, a full-scale invasion of Cuba by American troops would need to follow. This, they said, was not only more than justified by the actions of the USSR and Cuba, but it was Kennedy's *only* option.

Their logic was both primal and satisfying: Aggression must be met with aggression. Tit replied to with tat.

The only problem was that if their logic turned out to be wrong, no one would be around to account for their mistake. Because everyone would be dead.

Unlike in the early days of his presidency, when Kennedy allowed the CIA to pressure him into supporting the Bay of Pigs fiasco, this time he surprised everyone by pushing back. He had recently read Barbara Tuchman's *The Guns of August,* a book about the beginning of World War I, which imprinted on his mind the image of overconfident world leaders rushing their way into a conflict that, once started, they couldn't stop. Kennedy wanted everyone to slow down so that they could really think about the problem in front of them.

This is, in fact, the first obligation of a leader and a decision maker. Our job is not to "go with our gut" or fixate on the first impression we form about an issue. No, we need to be strong enough to resist thinking that is too neat, too plausible, and therefore almost always wrong. Because if the leader can't take the time to develop a clear sense of the bigger picture, who will? If the leader isn't thinking through all the way to the end, who is?

We can see in Kennedy's handwritten notes taken during the crisis, a sort of meditative process by which he tried to do precisely this. On numerous pages, he writes "Missile. Missile. Missile," or "Veto. Veto. Veto. Veto," or "Leaders. Leaders. Leaders." On one page, showing his desire to not act alone or selfishly: "Consensus. Consensus. Consensus. Consensus. Consensus. Consensus." On a yellow legal pad during one meeting, Kennedy drew two sailboats, calming himself with thoughts of the ocean he loved so much. Finally, on White House stationery, as if to clarify to himself the only thing that mattered, he wrote one short sentence: "We are *demanding* withdrawal of the missiles."

Perhaps it was there, as Kennedy sat with his advisors and doodled, that he remembered a passage from another book he'd read, by the strategist B. H. Liddell Hart, on nuclear strategy. In Kennedy's review of Hart's book for the *Saturday Review of Literature* a few years before, he quoted this passage:

> Keep strong, if possible. In any case, keep cool. Have unlimited patience. Never corner an opponent, and always assist him to save face. Put yourself in his shoes—so as to

see things through his eyes. Avoid self-righteousness like the devil—nothing is so self-blinding.

It became Kennedy's motto during the Missile Crisis. "I think we ought to think of why the Russians did this," he told his advisors. *What is the advantage they are trying to get?* he asked, with real interest. "Must be some major reason for the Soviets to set this up." As Arthur Schlesinger Jr., Kennedy's advisor and biographer, wrote, "With his capacity to understand the problems of others, the President could see how threatening the world might have looked to the Kremlin."

This understanding would help him respond properly to this unexpected and dangerous provocation—and give him insight into how the Soviets would react to that response.

It became clear to Kennedy that Khrushchev put the missiles in Cuba because he believed Kennedy was weak. But that didn't mean the Russians believed their own position was particularly strong. Only a desperate nation would take such a risk, Kennedy realized. Armed with this insight, which came through long discussions with his team—designated as ExComm—he began to formulate an action plan.

Clearly, a military strike was the most irrevocable of all the options (nor, according to his advisors, was it likely to be 100 percent effective). What would happen after that, Kennedy wondered? How many soldiers would die in an invasion? How would the world respond to a larger country invading a smaller one, even if it was to deter a nuclear threat? What would the Russians do to save face or protect their soldiers on the island?

These questions pointed Kennedy toward a blockade of Cuba. Nearly half of his advisors opposed this less aggressive move, but he favored it precisely because it preserved his options.

The blockade also embodied the wisdom of one of Kennedy's favorite expressions: It *used time as a tool*. It gave both sides a chance to examine the stakes of the crisis and offered Khrushchev the opportunity to reevaluate his impression of Kennedy's supposed weakness.

Some would later attack Kennedy for this choice, too. Why challenge Russia at all? Why were the missiles such a big deal? Didn't the United States have plenty of their own pointed at the Soviets? Kennedy was not unsympathetic to this argument, but as he explained to the American public in an address on October 22, it wasn't possible to simply back down:

> The 1930s taught us a clear lesson: Aggressive conduct, if allowed to go unchecked and unchallenged, ultimately leads to war. This nation is opposed to war. We are also true to our word. Our unswerving objective, therefore, must be to prevent the use of these missiles against this or any other country, and to secure their withdrawal or elimination from the Western Hemisphere. . . . We will not prematurely or unnecessarily risk the costs of worldwide nuclear war in which even the fruits of victory

would be ashes in our mouth—but neither will we shrink
from that risk at any time it must be faced.

What's most remarkable about this conclusion is how calmly
Kennedy came to it. Despite the enormous stress of the situation, we can hear in tapes and see in transcripts and photos
taken at the time just how collaborative and open everyone was.
No fighting, no raised voices. No finger-pointing (and when
things did get tense, Kennedy laughed it off). Kennedy didn't let
his own ego dominate the discussions, nor did he allow anyone
else's to. When he sensed that his presence was stifling his advisors' ability to speak honestly, he left the room so they could debate and brainstorm freely. Reaching across party lines and past
rivalries, he consulted openly with the three still-living ex-
presidents and invited the previous secretary of state, Dean
Acheson, into the top-secret meetings as an equal.

In the tensest moments, Kennedy sought solitude in the
White House Rose Garden (afterward, he would thank the gar-
dener for her important contributions during the crisis). He
would go for long swims, both to clear his mind and to think. He
sat in his specially made rocking chair in the Oval Office, bathed
in the light of those enormous windows, easing the pain in his
back so that it might not add to the fog of (cold) war that had
descended so thickly over Washington and Moscow.

There is a picture of Kennedy with his back to the room,
hunched over, leaning both fists on the big desk he had been

chosen by millions of voters to occupy. This is a man with the fate of the world on his shoulders. He has been provoked by a nuclear superpower in a surprise act of bad faith. Critics are questioning his courage. There are political considerations, personal considerations, there are more factors than any one person should be able to weigh at one time.

Yet he lets none of this rush him. None of it will cloud his judgment or deter him from doing the right thing. He is the stillest guy in the room.

Kennedy would need to stay that way, because simply *deciding* on the blockade was only the first step. Next came announcing and enforcing this five-hundred-mile no-go zone around Cuba (which he brilliantly called a "quarantine" to underplay the more aggressive implications of a "blockade"). There would be more belligerent accusations from the Russians and confrontations at the UN. Congressional leaders voiced their doubts. One hundred thousand troops still had to be readied in Florida as a contingency.

Then there would be the actual provocations. A Russian tanker ship approached the quarantine line. Russian submarines surfaced. An American U-2 spy plane was shot down over Cuba, and the pilot killed.

The two biggest and most powerful countries in the world were "eyeball to eyeball." It was actually scarier and more dire than anyone knew—some of the Soviet missiles, which had been previously thought to be only partly assembled, were armed and ready. Even if this wasn't known, the awful danger could be *felt*.

Would Kennedy's emotions get the best of him? Would he blink? Would he break?

No. He wouldn't.

"It isn't the first step that concerns me," he said to his advisors as much as to himself, "but both sides escalating to the fourth and fifth step—and we don't go to the sixth because there is no one around to do so. We must remind ourselves we are embarking on a very hazardous course."

The space Kennedy gave Khrushchev to breathe and think paid off just in time. On October 26, eleven days into the crisis, the Soviet premier wrote Kennedy a letter saying that he now saw that the two of them were pulling on a rope with a knot in the middle—a knot of war. The harder each pulled, the less likely it would be that they could ever untie it, and eventually there would be no choice but to cut the rope with a sword. And then Khrushchev provided an even more vivid analogy, one as true in geopolitics as it is in everyday life: "If people do not display statesmanlike wisdom," he said, "they will eventually reach the point where they will clash, like blind moles, and then mutual annihilation will commence."

Suddenly, the crisis was over as quickly as it began. The Russians, realizing that their position was untenable and that their test of U.S. resolve had failed, made signs that they would negotiate—that they would remove the missiles. The ships stopped dead in the water. Kennedy was ready too. He pledged that the United States would not invade Cuba, giving the Russians and their allies a win. In secret, he also let the Russians know that he was willing to remove American missiles in Turkey, but would do so in several months' time so as not to give the impression that he could be pressured into abandoning an ally.

With clear thinking, wisdom, patience, and a keen eye for the root of a complex, provocative conflict, Kennedy had saved the world from a nuclear holocaust.

We might say that Kennedy, if only for this brief period of a little less than two weeks, managed to achieve that stage of clarity spoken about in the ancient Chinese text *The Daodejing*. As he stared down nuclear annihilation, he was:

> *Careful as someone crossing an iced-over stream.*
> *Alert as a warrior in enemy territory.*
> *Courteous as a guest.*
> *Fluid as melting ice.*
> *Shapable as a block of wood.*
> *Receptive as a valley.*
> *Clear as a glass of water.*

The Daoists would say that he had stilled the muddied water in his mind until he could see through it. Or to borrow the image from the emperor Marcus Aurelius, the Stoic philosopher who himself had stared down countless crises and challenges, Kennedy had been "like the rock that the waves keep crashing over. It stands, unmoved and the raging of the sea falls still around it."

Each of us will, in our own lives, face crisis. The stakes may be lower, but to us they will matter. A business on the brink of

THE DOMAIN OF THE MIND

collapse. An acrimonious divorce. A decision about the future of our career. A moment where the whole game depends on us. These situations will call upon all our mental resources. An emotional, reactive response—an unthinking, half-baked response—will not cut it. Not if we want to get it right. Not if we want to perform at our best.

What we will need then is that same stillness that Kennedy drew upon. His calmness. His open-mindedness. His empathy. His clarity about what really mattered.

In these situations we must:

- Be fully present.
- Empty our mind of preconceptions.
- Take our time.
- Sit quietly and reflect.
- Reject distraction.
- Weigh advice against the counsel of our convictions.
- Deliberate without being paralyzed.

We must cultivate mental stillness to succeed in life and to successfully navigate the many crises it throws our way.

It will not be easy. But it is essential.

For the rest of his short life, Kennedy worried that people would learn the wrong lessons from his actions during the Missile Crisis. It wasn't that he had stood up to the Soviets and threatened them with superior weapons until they backed down. Instead, calm and rational leadership had prevailed over rasher, reckless voices. The crisis was resolved thanks to a mastery of his own thinking, and the thinking of those underneath him— and it was these traits that America would need to call on repeatedly in the years to come. The lesson was one not of *force* but of the power of patience, alternating confidence and humility, foresight and presence, empathy and unbending conviction, restraint and toughness, and quiet solitude combined with wise counsel.

How much better would the world be with more of this behavior? How much better would your own life be?

Kennedy, like Lincoln, was not born with this stillness. He was a defiant troublemaker in high school, a dilettante for most of college and even as a senator. He had his demons and he made plenty of mistakes. But with hard work—work you are capable of doing too—he overcame those shortcomings and developed the equanimity that served him so well over those terrifying thirteen days. It was work in just a few categories that nearly everyone else neglects.

Which is where we will now turn our focus—toward mastering what we will call in this section "the domain of the mind"— because everything we do depends on getting that right.

BECOME PRESENT

Trust no future, howe'er pleasant!
Let the dead Past bury its dead!
Act,—act in the living present!
Heart within, and God o'erhead!

—HENRY WADSWORTH LONGFELLOW

The decision in 2010 to title Marina Abramović's four-decade retrospective at MoMA in New York City *The Artist Is Present* all but preordained the monumental performance that would come out of it. Naturally, Marina would have to be present in one way or another.

But no one would have dared think that she would literally be there . . . for all of it.

Who could conceive that a human could sit silently in a chair, completely still, for a total of 750 hours over 79 days directly across from 1,545 strangers, without aid, without distraction, without so much as a way to go to the bathroom? That she would want to do this? That she would pull it off?

As her former lover and collaborator Ulay said when he was asked what he thought of the possibility, "I have no thoughts. Only respect."

The performance was as simple as it was straightforward. Marina, aged sixty-three, her long hair braided and over her shoulder, walked into the cavernous room, sat down in a hard wooden chair, and simply stared at the person across from her. One after another they came, hour after hour, day in and day out, for nearly three months. Each time, she looked down, gathered herself, and then looked up afresh at the new face.

As Marina would say of her art, "The proposition here is just to empty the self. To be able to be present."

Is it really that hard—to be present? What's so special about that?

No one who was in the audience, who sat across from her, would ask such questions. For those souls lucky enough to see the performance in person, it was a near religious experience. To experience another person fully in the moment is a rare thing. To feel them engage with you, to be giving all their energy to you, as though there is nothing else that matters in the world, is rarer still. To see them do it for so long, so intensely?

Many viewers cried. Each one said the hours in line were worth it. It was like looking in a kind of mirror, where they could feel their own life for the first time.

Imagine: If Marina's mind drifted, if she daydreamed, the

person across from her could immediately sense that she was somewhere else. If she slowed her mind and body down too much, she might have fallen asleep. If she allowed for normal bodily sensations—hunger, discomfort, pain, the urge to go to the bathroom—it would be impossible not to move or get up. If she began to think of how much time was left in the day's performance, time would slow to an intolerable crawl. So with monklike discipline and warriorlike strength she ignored these distractions to exist exclusively in the present moment. She had to be where her feet were; she had to care about the person across from her and the experience they were sharing more than anything else in the world.

"People don't understand that the hardest thing is actually doing something that is close to nothing," Abramović said about the performance. "It demands all of you . . . there is no object to hide behind. It's just you."

Being present demands all of us. It's not nothing. It may be the hardest thing in the world.

As we stand on the podium, about to give a speech, our mind is focused not on our task but on what everyone will think of us. How does that not affect our performance? As we struggle with a crisis, our mind repeats on a loop just how unfair this is, how insane it is that it keeps happening and how it can't go on. Why are we draining ourselves of essential emotional and mental energies right when we need them most?

Even during a quiet evening at home, all we're thinking about is the list of improvements that need to be made. There may be a beautiful sunset, but instead of taking it in, we're *taking a picture of it.*

We are not present . . . and so we miss out. On life. On being our best. On *seeing* what's there.

Many of the people in line to see Marina Abramović's performance accidentally illustrate this phenomenon. Rushing in as the doors opened, they zoomed past equally impressive pieces from her career so that they could be first for the "special" one. In line, they fidgeted endlessly and chatted with each other, trying to kill time as the hours ticked by. They napped, leaning up against one another. They checked their phones . . . and then checked them again. They planned what they would do when it was their turn and speculated about what it would be like. Some of them worked in secret on little stunts they hoped would bring them fifteen seconds of fame.

How much ordinary wonderfulness they closed their minds to.

It makes you wonder: After they had their transcendent experience with Marina—coming face-to-face with real presence—when they left the museum and walked out into the busy New York City street, did they breathe in anew the vibrant rhythm of the urban jungle, or, more likely, did they immediately resume their busy lives, full of distractions, anxiety, dreams, insecurities, and ego?

In short, did they do exactly what all of us do most of every single day?

We do not live in *this* moment. We, in fact, try desperately to get out of it—by thinking, doing, talking, worrying, remembering, hoping, whatever. We pay thousands of dollars to have a device in our pocket to ensure that we are never bored. We sign up for endless activities and obligations, chase money and accomplishments, all with the naïve belief that at the end of it will be happiness.

Tolstoy observed that love can't exist off in the future. Love is only real if it's happening right now. If you think about it, that's true for basically everything we think, feel, or do. The best athletes, in the biggest games, are completely *there*. They are within themselves, within the now.

Remember, there's no greatness in the future. Or clarity. Or insight. Or happiness. Or peace. There is only this moment.

Not that we mean literally sixty seconds. The real present moment is what we choose to exist in, instead of lingering on the past or fretting about the future. It's however long we can push away the impressions of what's happened before and what we worry or hope might occur at some other time. Right now can be a few minutes or a morning or a year—if you can stay in it that long.

As Laura Ingalls Wilder said, *now is now.* It can never be anything else.

Seize it!

Who is so talented that they can afford to bring only part of themselves to bear on a problem or opportunity? Whose relationships are so strong that they can get away with not showing up? Who is so certain that they'll get another moment that they can confidently skip over this one? The less energy we waste re-gretting the past or worrying about the future, the more energy we will have for what's in front of us.

We want to learn to see the world like an artist: While other people are oblivious to what surrounds them, the artist really *sees*. Their mind, fully engaged, notices the way a bird flies or the way a stranger holds their fork or a mother looks at her child. They have no thoughts of the morrow. All they are thinking about is how to capture and communicate this experience.

An artist is *present*. And from this stillness comes brilliance.

This moment we are experiencing right now is a gift (that's why we call it *the present*). Even if it is a stressful, trying experience—it could be our last. So let's develop the ability to be in it, to put everything we have into appreciating the plentitude of the now.

Don't reject a difficult or boring moment because it is not exactly what you want. Don't waste a beautiful moment because you are insecure or shy. Make what you can of what you have been given. Live what can be lived. That's what excellence is. That's what presence makes possible.

In meditation, teachers instruct students to focus on their breath. *In and out. In and out.* In sports, coaches speak about "the process"—this play, this drill, this rep. Not just because this mo-ment is special, but because you can't do your best if your mind is elsewhere.

We would do well to follow this in our own lives. Jesus told his disciples not to worry about tomorrow, because tomorrow will take care of itself. Another way of saying that is: You have plenty on your plate right now. Focus on that, no matter how small or insignificant it is. Do the very best you can right now. Don't think about what detractors may say. Don't dwell or needlessly complicate. Be here. Be *all* of you.

Be present.

And if you've had trouble with this in the past? That's okay.

That's the nice thing about the present. It keeps showing up to give you a second chance.

LIMIT YOUR INPUTS

A wealth of information creates a poverty of attention.

—HERBERT SIMON

As a general, Napoleon made it his habit to delay responding to the mail. His secretary was instructed to wait three weeks before opening any correspondence. When he finally did hear what was in a letter, Napoleon loved to note how many supposedly "important" issues had simply resolved themselves and no longer required a reply.

While Napoleon was certainly an eccentric leader, he was never negligent in his duties or out of touch with his government or his soldiers. But in order to be active and aware of what actually mattered, he had to be selective about who and what kind of information got access to his brain.

In a similar vein, he told messengers never to wake him with *good news*. Bad news, on the other hand—that is to say, an unfolding crisis or an urgent development that negatively impacted his campaign—was to be brought to him immediately. "Rouse me instantly," he said, "for then there is not a moment to be lost."

These were both brilliant accommodations to the reality of life for a busy person: There is way too much coming at us. In order to think clearly, it is essential that each of us figures out how to filter out the inconsequential from the essential. It's not enough to be inclined toward deep thought and sober analysis; a leader must create time and space for it.

In the modern world, this is not easy. In the 1990s, political scientists began to study what they called the "CNN Effect." Breathless, twenty-four-hour media coverage makes it considerably harder for politicians and CEOs to be anything but reactive. There's too much information, every trivial detail is magnified under the microscope, speculation is rampant—and the mind is overwhelmed.

The CNN Effect is now a problem for everyone, not just presidents and generals. Each of us has access to more information than we could ever reasonably use. We tell ourselves that it's part of our job, that we have to be "on top of things," and so we give up precious time to news, reports, meetings, and other forms of feedback. Even if we're not glued to a television, we're still surrounded by gossip and drama and other distractions.

We must stop this.

"If you wish to improve," Epictetus once said, "be content to appear clueless or stupid in extraneous matters."

Napoleon was content with being behind on his mail, even if

it upset some people or if he missed out on some gossip, because it meant that trivial problems had to resolve themselves without him. We need to cultivate a similar attitude—give things a little space, don't consume news in real time, be a season or two behind on the latest trend or cultural phenomenon, don't let your inbox lord over your life.

The important stuff will still be important by the time you get to it. The unimportant will have made its insignificance obvious (or simply disappeared). Then, with stillness rather than needless urgency or exhaustion, you will be able to sit down and give what deserves consideration your *full* attention.

There is ego in trying to stay up on everything, whether it's an acclaimed television show, the newest industry rumor, the smartest hot take, or the hottest crisis in [the Middle East, Africa, Asia, the climate, the World Bank, the NATO Summit, ad infinitum]. There is ego in trying to appear the most informed person in the room, the one with all the gossip, who knows every single thing that's happening in everyone's life.

Not only does this cost us our peace of mind, but there's a serious opportunity cost too. If we were stiller, more confident, had the longer view, what truly meaningful subject could we dedicate our mental energy to?

In her diary in 1942, Dorothy Day, the Catholic nun and social activist, admonished herself much the same. "Turn off your radio," she wrote, "put away your daily paper. Read one review of events and spend time reading." *Books,* spend time reading books—that's what she meant. Books full of wisdom.

Though this too can be overdone.

The verse from John Ferriar:

What wild desires, what restless torments seize
The hapless man, who feels the book-disease.

The point is, it's very difficult to think or act clearly (to say nothing of being happy) when we are drowning in information. It's why lawyers attempt to bury the other side in paper. It's why intelligence operatives flood the enemy with propaganda, so they'll lose the scent of the truth. It's not a coincidence that the goal of these tactics is casually referred to as analysis *paralysis*.

Yet we do this to ourselves!

A century and a half after Napoleon, another great general and, later, head of state, Dwight D. Eisenhower, struggled to manage the torrent of facts and fiction that was thrown at him. His solution was strict adherence to the chain of command when it came to information. No one was to hand him unopened mail, no one was to just throw half-explored problems at him. Too much depended on the stillness within that he needed to operate to allow such haphazard information flow. One of his innovations was to organize information and problems into what's now called the "Eisenhower Box," a matrix that orders our priorities by their ratio of urgency and importance.

Much that was happening in the world or on the job, Eisenhower found, was urgent but not important. Meanwhile, most of what was truly important was not remotely time-sensitive.

Categorizing his inputs helped him organize his staff around what was important versus what *seemed* urgent, allowed them to be strategic rather than reactive, a mile deep on what mattered rather than an inch on too many things.

Indeed, the first thing great chiefs of staff do—whether it's for a general or a president or the CEO of a local bank—is limit the amount of people who have access to the boss. They become gatekeepers: no more drop-ins, tidbits, and stray reports. So the boss can see the big picture. So the boss has time and room to think.

Because if the boss doesn't? Well, then nobody can.

In his *Meditations,* Marcus Aurelius says, "Ask yourself at every moment, 'Is this necessary?'"

Knowing what not to think about. What to ignore and not to do. It's your first and most important job.

Thich Nhat Hanh:

> Before we can make deep changes in our lives, we have to look into our diet, our way of consuming. We have to live in such a way that we stop consuming the things that poison us and intoxicate us. Then we will have the strength to allow the best in us to arise, and we will no longer be victims of anger, of frustration.

It's as true of food as it is of information.

There's a great saying: *Garbage in, garbage out.* If you want good output, you have to watch over the inputs.

This will take discipline. It will not be easy.

This means fewer alerts and notifications. It means blocking incoming texts with the Do Not Disturb function and funneling emails to subfolders. It means questioning that "open door" policy, or even *where you live*. It means pushing away selfish people who bring needless drama into our lives. It means studying the world more *philosophically*—that is, with a long-term perspective—rather than following events second by second.

The way you feel when you awake early in the morning and your mind is fresh and as yet unsoiled by the noise of the outside world—that's space worth protecting. So too is the zone you lock into when you're really working well. Don't let intrusions bounce you out of it. Put up barriers. Put up the proper chuting to direct what's urgent and unimportant to the right people.

Walker Percy, one of the last great southern novelists, has a powerful passage in *Lancelot,* based on Percy's own struggle with idleness and addiction to entertainment. In the book, the harried narrator walks outside of his Mississippi mansion and, for the first time in years, simply stops. He steps outside his bubble and experiences the moment. "Can a man stand alone, naked, and at his ease, wrist flexed at his side like Michelangelo's David, without assistance, without diversion . . . in silence?" he asks.

> Yes. It was possible to stand. Nothing happened. I listened.
> There was no sound: no boats on the river, no trucks on
> the road, not even cicadas. What if I didn't listen to the

news? I didn't. Nothing happened. I realized I had been afraid of the silence.

It is in this stillness that we can be present and finally see truth. It is in this stillness that we can hear the voice inside us.

How different would the world look if people spent as much time listening to their conscience as they did to chattering broadcasts? If they could respond to the calls of their convictions as quickly as we answer the dings and rings of technology in our pockets?

All this noise. All this information. All these inputs.

We are afraid of the silence. We are afraid of looking stupid. We are afraid of missing out. We are afraid of being the bad guy who says, "Nope, not interested."

We'd rather make ourselves miserable than make ourselves a priority, than be our best selves.

Than be still . . . and in charge of our own information diet.

EMPTY THE MIND

> To become empty is to become one with the divine—
> this is the Way.
>
> —AWA KENZO

Shawn Green began his third season with the Los Angeles Dodgers in 2002 in the worst slump of his Major League Baseball career. The media was out for blood, and so were the fans, who booed him at the plate. Dodgers management began to doubt him too. The man was making $14 million a year and he could not hit.

After *weeks* of intense hitting famine, would he be benched? Traded? Sent down to the minors?

All this was racing through Green's mind, as it would race through the mind of anyone struggling at work. That little voice: *What's wrong with you? Why can't you get this right? Did you lose your touch?*

Hitting a baseball is already a nearly inconceivable feat. It requires the batter to see, process, decide, swing at, and connect with a tiny ball traveling at speeds north of 90 miles per hour from an elevated position sixty feet away. *Four hundred milliseconds.* That's how long it takes for the ball to travel from the mound to the batter. To be able to swing and hit it literally defies physics—it's the single hardest act in all of sports.

The anxiety and doubts in a slump make it even harder. Yogi Berra's warning: "It's impossible to hit and think at the same time."

For Green, the ball began to look smaller and smaller the longer he went without a hit. But it was Buddhism, which he had long practiced, that Shawn leaned on to prevent this vicious cycle from destroying his career. Instead of giving in to those churning thoughts—instead of trying harder and harder—he tried to clear his mind entirely. Instead of fighting the slump, he was going to try not to think about it at all.

It seems crazy, but it isn't. "Man is a thinking reed," D. T. Suzuki, one of the early popularizers of Buddhism in the West, once said, "but his great works are done when he is not calculating and thinking. 'Childlikeness' has to be restored with long years of training in the art of self-forgetfulness. When this is attained, man thinks yet he does not think."

The way out of the slump wasn't to consult experts or redesign his swing. Shawn Green knew he had to get rid of the toxic thinking that had knocked him off his game in the first place—the thinking about his big contract, the expectations for how he wanted the season to go, the stress at home, or the critics in the media.

He had to push all that out of his mind. He had to let his training take over.

On May 23, 2002, Green was struggling to do exactly that. It was the rubber match in a series against the Brewers. The Dodgers had eked out a 1–0 victory the night before, and lost the night before that. Green's own hitting was sporadic and discouraging. So when he got to the ballpark that morning, he worked to give himself a fresh start. First in the batting cage, and then at the batting tee, he slowly, patiently, quietly cleared his mind. With each swing, he tried to focus on the mechanics, the placement of his feet, really planting himself where his feet were—not thinking of the past, not worrying about what was coming in the future, not thinking about the fans or how he wanted to hit the ball. Really, he wasn't thinking at all. Instead, he repeated an old Zen proverb to himself: *Chop wood, carry water. Chop wood, carry water. Chop wood, carry water.*

Don't overanalyze. Do the work.

Don't think. *Hit.*

In his first at bat on that day, Green took two strikes in the first two pitches. His mind burbled a bit—*Is the slump going to keep going, is this ever going to end, why can't I get this right?*—but he let those wild horses run right on by, waiting for the dust they kicked up to settle. He breathed in, emptied his mind again—as empty as the seats in the stadium during his pregame ritual.

Then he got back to work. On the third pitch—*CRACK!* A solid double down the right-field line.

In the second inning, Green got an inside fastball. He planted his front foot and focused only on that, on the feeling of being nailed to the ground. He watched the pitch, and swung. The ball was soon going back out the other direction, high up over the right-field wall. Three runs came in along with it. In the fourth inning, he hit another homer up in the walkway over right-center field. In the fifth inning, he hit a home run deep into left field. Opposite field, a sign that a hitter is really starting to dial in. In the eighth inning, he hit a long single.

The slump was no more.

Five for five in his at bats, and the manager wanted to send him home for the day. Green asked for another at bat.

Now his mind was tempted to race in a different direction, his brain filled with congratulations instead of doubts. *You're killing it. How exciting is this? Are you going to get another hit? You could set a record!*

Just like the overactive voice in a slump, the voice in a streak is an equally deleterious racing mental loop. Both get in the way. Both make a hard thing harder.

As Shawn Green stepped into the batter's box for the sixth and final time, he said to himself, "There's no sense in thinking now." He cleared his mind, and enjoyed himself like a kid at a Little League game.

No pressure. Just presence. Just happy to be there.

On the third pitch, he got a dipping cutter that sank low and inside, below knee level. For lefties, like Green, when they are in a slump, that area of the hitting zone is like a black hole. When they're locked in, it's the wheelhouse. Green connected, with a swing that even one of the coaches said looked like it was happening in slow motion. Every part of the batter was behind the bat, mentally and physically—and the ball was launched deep, deep into right-center field. He hit it a mile. It slammed high off the back wall of the enclosed stadium and bounced back onto the field.

As Green's teammates went nuts in the dugout, he kept his head down and rounded the bases with the same calm, deliberate trot as in his previous three home runs. You couldn't tell from the lack of celebrating, but he was in that moment only the fourteenth player in history ever to hit four home runs in a single game. Six for six, with nineteen total bases and seven runs batted in, perhaps the single greatest one-game performance in baseball. The entire crowd of 26,728 people—at an away game— rose for a standing ovation. But Green was already clearing that all away, and coming back to his routine. He took off his batting gloves and swept the experience from his mind, keeping it empty to use in the next game.*

Shawn Green is hardly the first Buddhist baseball player. Sadaharu Oh, the greatest home run hitter in the history of

---

*In his next two games, Green would hit three more home runs. He was 11 for 13 in three games with seven home runs. On the last home run he broke his bat, which now sits in the Baseball Hall of Fame.

baseball, was one too. The goal of Zen, his master taught him, was to "achieve a void . . . noiseless, colorless, heatless void"—to get to that state of emptiness, whether it was on the mound or in the batter's box or at practice.

Before that, Zhuang Zhou, the Chinese philosopher, said, "Tao is in the emptiness. Emptiness is the fast of the mind." Marcus Aurelius once wrote about "cutting free of impressions that cling to the mind, free of the future and the past," to become the "sphere rejoicing in its perfect stillness." But if you saw those words in the first paragraph of the write-up for the Dodgers-Brewers game in the *Los Angeles Times* the next day, they would have made perfect sense. Epictetus, Marcus's philosophical pre-decessor, was in fact speaking about sports when he said, "If we're anxious or nervous when we make the catch or throw, what will become of the game, and how can one maintain one's composure; how can one see what is coming next?"

As is true in athletics, so too in life.

Yes, thinking is essential. Expert knowledge is undoubtedly key to the success of any leader or athlete or artist. The problem is that, unthinkingly, we think too much. The "wild and whirling words" of our subconscious get going and suddenly there's no room for our training (or anything else). We're overloaded, over-whelmed, and distracted . . . by our own mind!

But if we can clear space, if we can consciously empty our mind, as Green did, insights and breakthroughs happen. The perfect swing connects perfectly with the ball.

There is a beautiful paradox to this idea of *void*.

The Daodejing points out that when clay is formed around emptiness, it becomes a pitcher that can hold water. Water from the pitcher is poured into a cup, which is itself formed around emptiness. The room this all happens in is itself four walls formed around emptiness.

Do you see? By relying on what's not there, we actually have something worth using. During the recording of her album *Interiors,* the musician Rosanne Cash posted a simple sign over the doorway of the studio. "Abandon Thought, All Ye Who Enter Here." Not because she wanted a bunch of unthinking idiots working with her, but because she wanted everyone involved—included herself—to go deeper than whatever was on the surface of their minds. She wanted them to be present, connected to the music, and not lost in their heads.

Imagine if Kennedy had spent the Cuban Missile Crisis obsessing over the Bay of Pigs. Imagine if Shawn Green had tried frantically to re-create his swing because it wasn't working, or if he had faced those pitchers with a racing mind, filled with insecurities and desperation. We've all experienced that—*Don't mess up. Don't mess up. Don't forget,* we say to ourselves—and what happens? We do exactly what we were trying *not* to do!

Whatever you face, whatever you're doing will require, first and foremost, that you don't defeat yourself. That you don't make it harder by overthinking, by needless doubts, or by second-guessing.

That space between your ears—that's yours. You don't just have to control what gets in, you also have to control what goes on *in* there. You have to protect it from yourself, from your own thoughts. Not with sheer force, but rather with a kind of gentle, persistent sweeping. Be the librarian who says "Shhh!" to the rowdy kids, or tells the jerk on his phone to please take it outside.

Because the mind is an important and sacred place.

Keep it clean and clear.

SLOW DOWN, THINK DEEPLY

With my sighted eye I see what's before me, and with
my unsighted eye I see what's hidden.

—ALICE WALKER

In the intro sequence of the beloved children's show *Mister
Rogers' Neighborhood*, the first interior shot does not show
the host. Instead, in the beat before Fred Rogers appears on the
screen singing his cheerful song about being a good neighbor,
viewers see a traffic light, blinking yellow.

For more than thirty years and for nearly a thousand episodes, this subtle piece of symbolism opened the show. If as a
hint, it went over the heads of most people watching, viewers
were still primed to get the message. Because whether Fred Rogers was speaking on camera, playing in the Neighborhood of
Make-Believe with King Friday the Puppet, or singing one of his
trademark songs, just about every frame of the show seemed to
say: *Slow down. Be considerate. Be aware.*

As a child at Latrobe Elementary School in Pennsylvania, Fred Rogers had been a victim of vicious bullying. Kids picked on him because of his weight and because he was sensitive about it. It was a horrible experience, but this pain spurred his groundbreaking work in public television. "I began a lifelong search for what is essential," he said about his childhood, "what it is about my neighbor that doesn't meet the eye." He even framed a print of that idea on the wall of his production studio in Pittsburgh, a snippet from one of his favorite quotes: *L'essentiel est invisible pour les yeux.*

What's essential is invisible to the eye.

That is: Appearances are misleading. First impressions are too. We are disturbed and deceived by what's on the surface, by what others see. Then we make bad decisions, miss opportunities, or feel scared or upset. Particularly when we don't slow down and take the time to really look.

Think about Khrushchev on the other side of the Cuban Missile Crisis. What provoked his incredible overreach? A poor reading of his opponent's mettle. A rush to action. Shoddy thinking about how his own actions would be interpreted on the world stage. It was a nearly fatal miscalculation, as most rush jobs are.

Epictetus talked about how the job of a philosopher is to take our impressions—what we see, hear, and think—and put them to the test. He said we needed to hold up our thoughts and examine them, to make sure we weren't being led astray by appearances or missing what couldn't be seen by the naked eye.

Indeed, it is in Stoicism and Buddhism and countless other schools that we find the same analogy: The world is like muddy water. To see through it, we have to let things settle. We can't be disturbed by initial appearances, and if we are patient and still, the truth will be revealed to us.

That's what Mr. Rogers taught children to do—starting a crucial habit as early as possible in their lives. In countless episodes, Rogers would take a topic—whether it was self-worth or how crayons were made, divorce or having fun—and walk his young viewers through what was really happening and what it meant. He seemed to naturally know how a kid's mind would process information, and he'd help them clear up understandable confusion or fears. He taught empathy and critical reasoning skills. He reassured his viewers that they could figure just about anything out if they took the time to work through it—with him, together.

It's a message he shared with adults too. "Just think," Rogers once wrote to a struggling friend. "Just be quiet and think. It'll make all the difference in the world."

There is, on the surface, a contradiction here. On the one hand, the Buddhists say we must empty our minds to be fully present. We'll never get anything done if we are paralyzed by overthinking. On the other hand, we must look and think and study deeply if we are ever to truly *know* (and if we are to avoid falling into the destructive patterns that harm so many people).

In fact, this is not a contradiction at all. It's just life.

We have to get better at thinking, deliberately and intentionally, about the big questions. On the complicated things. On understanding what's really going on with a person, or a situation, or with life itself.

We have to do the kind of thinking that 99 percent of the population is just not doing, and we have to stop doing the destructive thinking that they spend 99 percent of their time doing.

The eighteenth-century Zen master Hakuin was highly critical of teachers who believed that enlightenment was simply a matter of thinking *nothing*. Instead, he wanted his students to think really, really hard. This is why he assigned them perplexing *kōans* like "What is the sound of one hand clapping?" and "What did your face look like before you were born?" and "Does the dog have the Buddha nature?"

These questions defy easy answers, and that's the point. By taking the time to meditate on them deeply, in some cases for days and weeks or even years, students put their mind in such a clarified state that deeper truths emerge, and enlightenment commences (and even if they don't get all the way there, they are stronger for having tried).

"Suddenly," Hakuin promised his students, "unexpectedly your teeth sink in. Your body will pour with cold sweat. At the instant, it will all become clear." The word for this was *satori*—an illuminating insight when the inscrutable is revealed, when an essential truth becomes obvious and inescapable.

Couldn't we all use a bit more of that?

Well, no one gets to *satori* going a million miles a minute. No one gets there by focusing on what's obvious, or by sticking with the first thought that pops into their head. To see what matters, you really have to look. To understand it, you have to really think. It takes real work to grasp what is invisible to just about everyone else.

This will not only be advantageous to your career and your business, but it will also help you find peace and comfort.

There is another great insight from Fred Rogers, which now goes viral each time there is another unspeakable tragedy. "Always look for the helpers," he explained to his viewers who were scared or disillusioned by the news. "There's always someone who is trying to help.... The world is full of doctors and nurses, police and firemen, volunteers, neighbors and friends who are ready to jump in to help when things go wrong."

Make no mistake—this was not some glib reassurance. Rogers, building on advice from his own mother when he was a child, had managed to find comfort and goodness inside an event that would provoke only pain and anger and fear in other people. And he figured out how to communicate it in a way that continues to make the world a better place long after his death.

So much of the distress we feel comes from reacting instinctually instead of acting with conscientious deliberation. So much of what we get wrong comes from the same place. We're reacting to shadows. We're taking as certainties impressions we have yet to test. We're not stopping to put on our glasses and really *look*.

Your job, after you have emptied your mind, is to slow down and think. To really think, on a regular basis.

... Think about what's important to you.

... Think about what's actually going on.

... Think about what might be hidden from view.

... Think about what the rest of the chessboard looks like.

... Think about what the meaning of life really is.

The choreographer Twyla Tharp provides an exercise for us to follow:

> Sit alone in a room and let your thoughts go wherever they will. Do this for one minute.... Work up to ten minutes a day of this mindless mental wandering. Then start paying attention to your thoughts to see if a word or goal materializes. If it doesn't, extend the exercise to eleven minutes, then twelve, then thirteen ... until you find the length of time you need to ensure that something interesting will come to mind. The Gaelic phrase for this state of mind is "quietness without loneliness."

If you invest the time and mental energy, you'll not only find what's interesting (or your next creative project), you'll find truth. You'll find what other people have missed. You'll find solutions to the problems we face—whether it's insight to the logic of the Soviets and their missiles in Cuba, or how to move your business forward, or how to make sense of senseless violence.

These are answers that must be fished from the depths. And what is fishing but slowing down? Being both relaxed and highly attuned to your environment? And ultimately, catching hold of what lurks below the surface and reeling it in?

START JOURNALING

Keep a notebook. Travel with it, eat with it, sleep with it. Slap into it every stray thought that flutters up into your brain.

—JACK LONDON

For her thirteenth birthday, a precocious German refugee named Anne Frank was given a small red-and-white "autograph book" by her parents. Although the pages were designed to collect the signatures and memories of friends, she knew from the moment she first saw it in a store window that she would use it as a journal. As Anne wrote in her first entry on June 12, 1942, "I hope I will be able to confide everything to you, as I have never been able to confide in anyone, and I hope you'll be a great source of comfort and support."

No one could have anticipated just how much comfort and support she'd need. Twenty-four days after that first entry, Anne and her Jewish family were forced into hiding, in the cramped attic annex over her father's warehouse in Amsterdam. It's where they would spend the next two years, hoping the Nazis would not discover them.

Anne Frank had wanted a diary for understandable reasons. She was a teenager. She had been lonely, scared, and bored before, but now she was cooped up in a set of cramped, suffocating rooms with six other people. It was all so overwhelming, all so unfair and unfamiliar. She needed somewhere to put those feelings.

According to her father, Otto, Anne didn't write every day, but she always wrote when she was upset or dealing with a problem. She also wrote when she was confused, when she was curious. She wrote in that journal as a form of therapy, so as not to unload her troubled thoughts on the family and compatriots with whom she shared such unenviable conditions. One of her best and most insightful lines must have come on a particularly difficult day. "Paper," she said, "has more patience than people."

Anne used her journal to reflect. "How noble and good everyone could be," she wrote, "if at the end of the day they were to review their own behavior and weigh up the rights and wrongs. They would automatically try to do better at the start of each new day, and after a while, would certainly accomplish a great deal." She observed that writing allowed her to watch herself as if she were a stranger. At a time when hormones usually make teenagers more selfish, she regularly reviewed her writings to challenge and improve her own thinking. Even with death lurking outside the doors, she worked to make herself a better person.

The list of people, ancient and modern, who practiced the art of journaling is almost comically long and fascinatingly diverse. Among them: Oscar Wilde, Susan Sontag, Marcus Aurelius, Queen Victoria, John Quincy Adams, Ralph Waldo Emerson, Virginia Woolf, Joan Didion, Shawn Green, Mary Chesnut, Brian Koppelman, Anaïs Nin, Franz Kafka, Martina Navratilova, and Ben Franklin.

All journalers.

Some did it in the morning. Some did it sporadically. Some, like Leonardo da Vinci, kept their notebooks on their person at all times. John F. Kennedy kept a diary during his travels before World War II, and then as president was more of a notetaker and a doodler (which is shown in studies to improve memory) on White House stationery both to clarify his thinking and to keep a record of it.

Obviously this is an intimidating list of individuals. But Anne Frank was thirteen, fourteen, and fifteen years old. If she can do it, what excuse do we have?

Seneca, the Stoic philosopher, seems to have done his writing and reflection in the evenings, much along the lines of Anne Frank's practice. When darkness had fallen and his wife had gone to sleep, he explained to a friend, "I examine my entire day and go back over what I've done and said, hiding nothing from myself, passing nothing by." Then he would go to bed, finding that "the sleep which follows this self-examination" was particularly sweet. Anyone who reads him today can feel him reaching for stillness in these nightly writings.

Michel Foucault talked of the ancient genre of *hupomnemata* (notes to oneself). He called the journal a "weapon for spiritual combat," a way to practice philosophy and purge the mind of agitation and foolishness and to overcome difficulty. To silence the barking dogs in your head. To prepare for the day ahead. To reflect on the day that has passed. Take note of insights you've heard. Take the time to feel wisdom flow through your fingertips and onto the page.

This is what the best journals look like. They aren't for the reader. They are for the *writer.* To slow the mind down. To wage peace with oneself.

Journaling is a way to ask tough questions: Where am I standing in my own way? What's the smallest step I can take toward a big thing today? Why am I so worked up about this? What blessings can I count right now? Why do I care so much about impressing people? What is the harder choice I'm avoiding? Do I rule my fears, or do they rule me? How will today's difficulties reveal my character?*

While there are plenty of people who will anecdotally swear to the benefits of journaling, the research is compelling too. According to one study, journaling helps improve well-being after traumatic and stressful events. Similarly, a University of Arizona

---

*Check out *The Daily Stoic Journal,* published by Portfolio, if you're looking for a journal with prompts.

study showed that people were able to better recover from divorce and move forward if they journaled on the experience. Keeping a journal is a common recommendation from psychologists as well, because it helps patients stop obsessing and allows them to make sense of the many inputs—emotional, external, psychological—that would otherwise overwhelm them.

That's really the idea. Instead of carrying that baggage around in our heads or hearts, we put it down on paper. Instead of letting racing thoughts run unchecked or leaving half-baked assumptions unquestioned, we force ourselves to write and examine them. Putting your own thinking down on paper lets you see it from a distance. It gives you objectivity that is so often missing when anxiety and fears and frustrations flood your mind.

What's the best way to start journaling? Is there an ideal time of day? How long should it take?

Who cares?

How you journal is much less important than *why* you are doing it: To get something off your chest. To have quiet time with your thoughts. To clarify those thoughts. To separate the harmful from the insightful.

There's no right way or wrong way. The point is *just to do it*.

If you've started before and stopped, start again. Getting out of the rhythm happens. The key is to carve out the space again, *today*. The French painter Eugène Delacroix—who called Stoicism his consoling religion—struggled as we struggle:

I am taking up my Journal again after a long break. I think it may be a way of calming this nervous excitement that has been worrying me for so long.

Yes!

That is what journaling is about. It's spiritual windshield wipers, as the writer Julia Cameron once put it. It's a few minutes of reflection that both demands and creates stillness. It's a break from the world. A framework for the day ahead. A coping mechanism for troubles of the hours just past. A revving up of your creative juices, for relaxing and clearing.

Once, twice, three times a day. Whatever. Find what works for you.

Just know that it may turn out to be the most important thing you do all day.

CULTIVATE SILENCE

All profound things, and emotions of things are preceded and attended by Silence. . . . Silence is the general consecration of the universe.

—HERMAN MELVILLE

The fascination with silence began early in life for the composer John Cage. In 1928, in a speech contest for Los Angeles High School, he tried to persuade his fellow students and the judges that America should institute a national day of quiet. By observing silence, he told the audience, they would finally be able to "hear what other people think."

It was the beginning of Cage's lifelong exploration and experimentation with what it means to be quiet and the opportunities for listening that this disciplined silence creates.

Cage wandered after high school. He toured Europe. He studied painting. He taught music. He composed classical music. He was an avid observer. Born in 1915 in California, he was just old enough to remember what premechanized life was like, and as the century became modern—and technology remade every industry and occupation—he began to notice just how loud everything had become.

"Wherever we are, what we hear is mostly noise," he would say. "When we ignore it, it disturbs us. When we listen to it, we find it fascinating."

To Cage, silence was not necessarily the absence of all sound. He loved the sound of a truck at 50 miles an hour. Static on the radio. The hum of an amplifier. The sound of water on water. Most of all, he appreciated the sounds that were missed or overwhelmed by our noisy lives.

In 1951, he visited an anechoic chamber, the most advanced soundproof room in the world at the time. Even there, with his highly sensitive musician's ear, he heard sounds. Two sounds, one high and one low. Speaking with the engineer afterward, he was amazed to discover that the source of those sounds was his own nervous system and the pumping of his blood.

How many of us have ever come close to this kind of quiet? Reducing the noise and chatter around you to the degree that you can literally hear your own life? Can you imagine? What you could *do* with that much silence!

It was a reaction against unnecessary noise that inspired Cage's most famous creation, *4'33"*, which was originally conceived with the title *Silent Prayer*. Cage wanted to create a song identical to the popular music of the day—it'd be the same length, it'd be performed live and played on the radio like every other song. The only difference was that *4'33"* would be a "piece of un-interrupted silence."

Some people saw this as an absurd joke, a Duchampian send-up of what constitutes "music." In one sense, it was. (Cage thought it would be funny to sell the "song" to Muzak Co. to be played in elevators.) But it was also inspired by his lifelong study of Zen philosophy, a philosophy that finds fullness in emptiness. The performance instructions for the song are themselves a beautiful contradiction: "In a situation provided with maximum amplification, perform a disciplined action."

In fact, *4'33"* was never about achieving perfect silence—it's about what happens when you stop contributing to the noise. The song was first performed at Woodstock, New York, by the pianist David Tudor.* "There's no such thing as silence," Cage said of that first performance. "What they thought was silence, because they didn't know how to listen, was full of accidental sounds. You could hear the wind stirring outside during the first move-ment. During the second, raindrops began pattering the roof, and during the third the people themselves made all kinds of interesting sounds as they talked or walked out."

We were given two ears and only one mouth for a reason, the philosopher Zeno observed. What you'll notice when you stop to listen can make all the difference in the world.

Too much of our lives is defined by noise. Headphones go in (noise-*canceling* headphones so that we can better hear . . .

*In 2015, a late-night talk show recorded a version performed by a cat.

noise). Screens on. Phones ringing. The quiet metal womb of a jumbo jet, traveling at 600 miles per hour, is filled with nothing but people trying to avoid silence. They'd rather watch the same bad movies again and again, or listen to some inane interview with an annoying celebrity, than stop and absorb what's happening around them. They'd rather close their mind than sit there and have to use it.

"Thought will not work except in silence," Thomas Carlyle said. If we want to think better, we need to seize these moments of quiet. If we want more revelations—more insights or breakthroughs or new, big ideas—we have to create more room for them. We have to step away from the comfort of noisy distractions and stimulations. We have to start listening.

In downtown Helsinki, there is a small building called the Kamppi Chapel. It's not a place of worship, strictly speaking, but it's as quiet as any cathedral. Quieter, in fact, because there are no echoes. No organs. No enormous creaking doors. It is, in fact, a Church of Silence. It's open to anyone and everyone who is interested in a moment of quiet spirituality in a busy city.

You walk in and there is just silence.

Glorious, sacred silence. The kind of silence that lets you really start *hearing*.

Randall Stutman, who for decades has been the behind-the-scenes advisor for many of the biggest CEOs and leaders on Wall Street, once studied how several hundred senior executives of major corporations recharged in their downtime. The answers were things like sailing, long-distance cycling, listening quietly to classical music, scuba diving, riding motorcycles, and fly-fishing. All these activities, he noticed, had one thing in common: *an absence of voices.*

These were people with busy, collaborative professions. People who made countless high-stakes decisions in the course of a day. But a couple hours without chatter, without other people in their ear, where they could simply think (or not think), they could recharge and find peace. They could be still—even if they were moving. They could finally hear, even if over the sounds of a roaring river or the music of Vivaldi.

Each of us needs to cultivate those moments in our lives. Where we limit our inputs and turn down the volume so that we can access a deeper awareness of what's going on around us. In shutting up—even if only for a short period—we can finally hear what the world has been trying to tell us. Or what we've been trying to tell ourselves.

That quiet is so rare is a sign of its value. Seize it.

We can't be afraid of silence, as it has much to teach us. Seek it.

The ticking of the hands of your watch is telling you how time is passing away, never to return. Listen to it.

SEEK WISDOM

Imperturbable wisdom is worth everything.

—DEMOCRITUS

In Greece in 426 BC, the priestess of Delphi answered a question posed to her by a citizen of Athens: Was there anyone wiser than Socrates?

Her answer: No.

This idea that Socrates could be the wisest of them all was a surprise, to Socrates especially.

Unlike traditionally wise people who knew many things, and unlike pretentious people who claimed to know many things, Socrates was intellectually humble. In fact, he spent most of his life sincerely proclaiming his lack of wisdom.

Yet this was the secret to his brilliance, the reason he has stood apart for centuries as a model of wisdom. Six hundred years after Socrates's death, Diogenes Laërtius would write that what made Socrates so wise was that "he knew nothing except just the fact of his ignorance." Better still, he was aware of what he did *not* know and was always willing to be proven wrong.

Indeed, the core of what we now call the Socratic method comes from Socrates's real and often annoying habit of going around asking questions. He was constantly probing other people's views. *Why do you think that? How do you know? What evidence do you have? But what about this or that?*

This open-minded search for truth, for *wisdom,* was what made Socrates the most brilliant and challenging man in Athens—so much so that they later killed him for it.

All philosophical schools preach the need for wisdom. The Hebrew word for wisdom is חכמה (*chokmâh*); the corresponding term in Islam is *ḥikma,* and both cultures believe that God was an endless source of it. The Greek word for wisdom was *sophia,* which in Latin became *sapientia* (and why man is called *Homo sapiens*). Both the Epicureans and the Stoics held *sophia* up as a core tenet. In their view, wisdom was gained through experience and study. Jesus advised his followers to be as wise as snakes and as innocent as doves. Proverbs 4:7 holds acquiring wisdom to be the most important thing people can do.

The Buddhists refer to wisdom as *prajñā,* and took wisdom to mean the understanding of the true nature of reality. Confucius and his followers spoke constantly of the cultivation of wisdom, saying that it is achieved in the same way that a craftsman develops skill: by putting in the time. Xunzi was more explicit: "Learning must never cease. . . . The noble person who studies widely and examines himself each day will become clear in his knowing and faultless in his conduct."

Each school has its own take on wisdom, but the same themes appear in all of them: The need to ask questions. The need to study and reflect. The importance of intellectual humility. The power of experiences—most of all failure and mistakes—to open our eyes to *truth* and *understanding*. In this way, wisdom is a sense of the big picture, the accumulation of experience and the ability to rise above the biases, the traps that catch lazier thinkers.

The fact that you are sitting here reading a book is a wonderful step on the journey to wisdom. But don't stop here—this book is only an introduction to classical thinking and history. Tolstoy expressed his exasperation at people who didn't read deeply and regularly. "I cannot understand," he said, "how some people can live without communicating with the wisest people who ever lived on earth." There's another line, now cliché, that is even more cutting: People who don't read have no advantage over those who cannot read.

There's little advantage to reading with arrogance or to confirm preexisting opinions either. Hitler, spent his short prison sentence after World War I reading the classics of history. Except instead of learning anything, he found in those thousands of pages only that, as he said, "I recognized the correctness of my views."

That's not wisdom. Or even stupidity. That's insanity.

We must also seek mentors and teachers who can guide us in our journey. Stoicism, for instance, was founded when Zeno, then a successful merchant, first heard someone reading the teachings of Socrates out loud in a bookstore. But that wasn't enough. What he did *next* was what put him on the path to wisdom, for he walked up to the person reading and said, "Where can I find a man like that?" In Buddhism, there is the idea of *pabbajja,* which means "to go forth" and marks the serious beginning of one's studies. That's what Zeno was doing. Answering the call and going forth.

Zeno's teacher was a philosopher named Crates, and Crates not only gave him many things to read, but like all great mentors helped him address personal issues. It was with Crates's help that Zeno overcame his crippling focus on what other people thought of him, in one case by dumping soup on Zeno and pointing out how little anyone cared or even noticed.

Buddha's first teacher was an ascetic named Alara Kalama, who taught him the basics of meditation. When he learned everything he could from Kalama, he moved on to Uddaka Ramaputta, who was also a good teacher. It was during Ramaputta's time that Buddha started to realize the limitations of the existing schools and consider striking out on his own.

If Zeno and Buddha needed teachers to advance, then we will *definitely* need help. And the ability to admit that is evidence of not a small bit of wisdom!

Find people you admire and ask how they got where they are. Seek book recommendations. Isn't that what Socrates would do?

Add experience and experimentation on top of this. Put yourself in tough situations. Accept challenges. Familiarize yourself with the unfamiliar. That's how you widen your perspective and your understanding. The wise are still because they have *seen it all*. They know what to expect because they've been through so much. They've made mistakes and learned from them. And so must you.

Wrestle with big questions. Wrestle with big ideas. Treat your brain like the muscle that it is. Get stronger through resistance and exposure and training.

Do not mistake the pursuit of wisdom for an endless parade of sunshine and kittens. Wisdom does not immediately produce stillness or clarity. Quite the contrary. It might even make things less clear—make them darker before the dawn.

Remember, Socrates looked honestly at what he didn't know. That's hard. It's painful to have our illusions punctured. It's humbling to learn that we are not as smart as we thought we were.

It's also inevitable that the diligent student will uncover disconcerting or challenging ideas—about the world and about themselves. This will be unsettling. How could it not be?

But that's okay.

It's better than crashing through life (and into each other) like blind moles, to borrow Khrushchev's analogy.

We want to sit with doubt. We want to savor it. We want to follow it where it leads.

Because on the other side is truth.

FIND CONFIDENCE, AVOID EGO

> Avoid having your ego so close to your position that
> when your position falls, your ego goes with it.
>
> —COLIN POWELL

In 1000 BC in the Valley of Elah, the people of Israel and Philistia were locked in terrible war. No end was in sight until the towering Goliath offered a bold challenge to end the stalemate between the armies. "This day I defy the armies of Israel! Give me a man and let us fight each other," he shouted.

For forty days, not a single soldier stepped forward, not even the king of Israel, Saul. If Goliath was driven by ego and hubris, the Israelites were paralyzed by fear and doubt.

Then came young David, a visiting shepherd with three brothers in the army. David heard Goliath's challenge, and unlike the entire army, cowering in fear, he was *confident* that he could fight Goliath and win. Was he crazy? How could he possibly think he could beat someone so big?

"When a lion or a bear came and carried off a sheep from the flock," David said to his brothers, "I went after it, struck it, and rescued the sheep from its mouth. When it turned on me, I seized it by its hair, struck it, and killed it. Your servant has killed both the lion and the bear; this Philistine will be like one of them."

David's confidence arose from experience, not ego. He had been through worse and done it with his bare hands.

David knew his strengths, but he also knew his weaknesses. "I cannot go in these," he said after trying on a soldier's armor, "because I am not used to them." He was ready to proceed with what we could call true self-awareness (and of course, his faith).

How did Goliath respond to his tiny challenger? Like your typical bully: He laughed. "Am I a dog, that you come at me with sticks?" Goliath shouted. "Come here," he said, "and I'll give your flesh to the birds and the wild animals!"

This arrogance would be short-lived.

David came at Goliath at a full sprint, a sling in one hand and a few stones from the river in the other. In those few quick seconds, Goliath must have seen the confidence in David's eyes and been afraid for the first time—and before he could do anything, he was dead. Felled by the stone flung expertly from David's sling. His head cut off by his own sword.

The story of these two combatants may be true. It may be a fable. But it remains one of the best stories we have about the perils of ego, the importance of humility, and the necessity of confidence.

STILLNESS IS THE KEY

There is perhaps no one less at peace than the egomaniac, their mind a swirling miasma of their own grandiosity and insecurity. They constantly bite off more than they can chew. They pick fights everywhere they go. They create enemies. They are incapable of learning from their mistakes (because they don't believe they make any). Everything with them is complicated, everything is *about* them.

Life is lonely and painful for the man or woman driven by ego. Donald Trump in the White House at night, his wife and son far away, in his bathrobe, ranting about the news. Alexander the Great, drunk again, fighting and killing his best friend over a stupid argument, thinking of nothing but the next conquest. Howard Hughes, trapped in his mansion, manically excited about some crazy project (which he will inevitably sabotage).

Successful, yes, but would you want to trade places with them?

This toxic form of ego has a less-assuming evil twin—often called "imposter syndrome."

It's a nagging, endless anxiety that you're not qualified for what you're doing—and you're about to be found out for it. Shakespeare's image for this feeling was of a thief wearing a stolen robe he knows is too big. The writer Franz Kafka, the son of an overbearing and disapproving father, likened imposter syndrome to the feeling of a bank clerk who is cooking the books. Frantically trying to keep it all going. Terrified of being discovered.

Of course, this insecurity exists almost entirely in our heads.

People aren't thinking about you. They have their own problems to worry about!

What is better than these two extremes—ego and imposter syndrome—but simple confidence? Earned. Rational. Objective. *Still.*

Ulysses S. Grant had an egotistical, self-promoting father, who was always caught up in some scheme or scandal. Grant knew that wasn't who he wanted to be. In response, he developed a cool and calm self-confidence that was much closer to his mother's quiet but strong personality. It was the source of his greatness.

Before the Civil War, Grant experienced a long chain of setbacks and financial difficulties. He washed up in St. Louis, selling firewood for a living—a hard fall for a graduate of West Point. An army buddy found him and was aghast. "Great God, Grant, what are you doing?" he asked. Grant's answer was simple: "I am solving the problem of poverty."

That's the answer of a confident person, a person at peace even in difficulty. Grant wouldn't have chosen this situation, but he wasn't going to let it affect his sense of self. Besides, he was too busy trying to fix it where he could. Why hate himself for working for a living? What was shameful about that?

Observers often commented on Grant's unshakable confidence in battle. When other generals were convinced that defeat was imminent, Grant never was. He knew he just needed to stay the course. He also knew that losing hope—or his cool—was unlikely to help anything.

With similar equanimity, he was equally unchanged by his success and power in later years, not just leading a powerful army but spending eight years as a world leader. (Charles Dana observed of Grant that he was an "unpretending hero, whom no ill omens could deject and no triumph unduly exalt.") After his presidency, Grant visited the old cabin where he and his wife had lived in those hard days. One of his aides pointed out what an incredible rags-to-riches story his life was—almost like the plot of an epic poem—to go from that cabin to the presidency. Grant shrugged. "Well I never thought about it in that light."

This is also confidence. Which needs neither congratulations nor glory in which to revel, because it is an honest understanding of our strengths and weakness that reveals the path to a greater glory: inner peace and a clear mind.

Confident people know what matters. They know when to ignore other people's opinions. They don't boast or lie to get ahead (and then struggle to deliver). Confidence is the freedom to set your own standards and unshackle yourself from the need to prove yourself. A confident person doesn't fear disagreement and doesn't see change—swapping an incorrect opinion for a correct one—as an admission of inferiority.

Ego, on the other hand, is unsettled by doubts, afflicted by hubris, exposed by its own boasting and posturing. And yet it will not probe itself—or allow itself to be probed—because it knows what might be found.

But confident people are open, reflective, and able to see

themselves without blinders. All this makes room for stillness, by removing unnecessary conflict and uncertainty and resentment.

And you? Where are you on this spectrum?

There are going to be setbacks in life. Even a master or a genius will experience a period of inadequacy when they attempt to learn new skills or explore new domains. Confidence is what determines whether this will be a source of anguish or an enjoyable challenge. If you're miserable every time things are not going your way, if you cannot enjoy it when things *are* going your way because you undermine it with doubts and insecurity, life will be hell.

And sure, there is no such thing as full confidence, or everpresent confidence. We will waver. We will have doubts. We will find ourselves in new situations of complete uncertainty. But still, we want to look inside that chaos and find that kernel of calm confidence. That was what Kennedy did in the Cuban Missile Crisis. He had been in tough situations before, like when his PT boat sank in the Pacific and all appeared to be lost. He learned then that panic solved nothing, and that salvation rarely came from rash action. He also learned that he could count on himself and that he could get through it—if he kept his head. Whatever happened, he told himself early in the crisis, no one would write *The Guns of October* about his handling of it. That was something he could control, and so in that he found confidence.

This is key. Both egotistical and insecure people make their flaws central to their identity—either by covering them up or by brooding over them or externalizing them. For them stillness is impossible, because stillness can only be rooted in strength.

That's what we have to focus on.

Don't feed insecurity. Don't feed delusions of grandeur.

Both are obstacles to stillness.

Be confident. You've earned it.

LET GO

Work done for a reward is much lower than work
done in the Yoga of wisdom. Set thy heart upon thy
work, but never on its reward. Work not for the
reward; but never cease to do thy work.

—THE BHAGAVAD GITA

The great archery master Awa Kenzo did not focus on teaching technical mastery of the bow. He spent almost no time instructing his students on how to deliberately aim and shoot, telling them to simply draw a shot back until it "fell from you like ripe fruit."

He preferred instead to teach his students an important mental skill: detachment. "What stands in your way," Kenzo once told his student Eugen Herrigel, "is that you have too much willful will." It was this willful will—the desire to be in control and to dictate the schedule and the process of everything we're a part of—that held Herrigel back from learning, from *really* mastering the art he pursued.

What Kenzo wanted students to do was to put the thought of hitting the target out of their minds. He wanted them to detach even from the idea of an outcome. "The hits on the target," he would say, "are only the outward proof and confirmation of your purposelessness at its highest, of your egolessness, your self-abandonment, or whatever you like to call this state."

That state is *stillness*.

But detachment and purposelessness don't exactly sound like productive attitudes, do they? That was exactly the kind of vexing predicament Kenzo wanted to put his students in. Most of his pupils, like us, wanted to be told what to do and shown how to do it. We're supposed to care, *a lot*. Willful will should be a *strength*. That's what's worked for us since we were kids who wanted to excel in school. How can you improve without it? How can this be the way to hitting a bull's-eye?

Well, let's back up.

Have you ever noticed that the more we want something, the more insistent we are on a certain outcome, the more difficult it can be to achieve it? Sports like golf and archery are the perfect examples of this. When you try to hit the ball *really* hard, you end up snap-hooking it. If you look up to follow the ball, you jerk the club and slice it into the woods. The energy you're spending aiming the arrow—particularly early on—is energy *not* spent developing your form. If you're too conscious of the technical components of shooting, you won't be relaxed or smooth enough. As marksmen say these days, "Slow is smooth, smooth is fast."

Stillness, then, is actually a way to superior performance. Looseness will give you more control than gripping tightly—to a method or a specific outcome.

Obviously an archery master like Kenzo realized that by the early twentieth century the skills he was teaching were no longer matters of life and death. Nobody needed to know how to shoot an arrow for survival. But other skills required to master archery remained essential: focus, patience, breathing, persistence, clarity. And most of all, the ability to let go.

What we need in life, in the arts, in sports, is to loosen up, to become flexible, to get to a place where there is nothing in our way—including our own obsession with certain outcomes. An actor doesn't become his character by *thinking* about it; he has to let go, dispense with technique and sink into the role. Entrepreneurs don't walk the streets deliberately looking for opportunities—they have to open themselves up to noticing the little things around them. The same goes for comedians or even parents trying to raise a good kid.

"Everyone tries to shoot naturally," Kenzo wrote, "but nearly all practitioners have some kind of strategy, some kind of shallow, artificial, calculating technical trick that they rely on when they shoot. Technical tricks ultimately lead nowhere."

Mastering our mental domain—as paradoxical as it might seem—requires us to step back from the rigidity of the word "mastery." We'll get the stillness we need if we focus on the individual steps, if we embrace the process, and give up *chasing*. We'll think better if we aren't thinking so *hard*.

Most students, whether it's in archery or yoga or chemistry, go into a subject with a strong intention. They are outcome-focused. They want to get the best grade or the highest score. They bring their previous "expertise" with them. They want to skip the unnecessary steps and get right to the sexy stuff. As a result, they are difficult to teach and easily discouraged when the journey proves harder than expected. They are not present. They are not open to experience and cannot learn.

In Kenzo's school, it was only when a student had fully surrendered, when they had detached themselves from even the idea of aiming, having spent months firing arrows into a hay bale just a few feet in front of them, that he would finally announce, "Our new exercise is shooting at a target." And even then, when they would hit the target, Kenzo wouldn't shower the archer with praise.

On the contrary, after a bull's-eye, Kenzo would urge them to "go on practicing as if nothing happened." He'd say the same after a bad shot. When the students asked for extra instruction, he'd reply, "Don't ask, *practice!*"

He wanted them to get lost in the process. He wanted them to give up their notions of what archery was supposed to look like. He was demanding that they be present and empty and open—so they could *learn*.

In Hinduism, Buddhism, Sikhism, and Jainism, the lotus

flower is a powerful symbol. Although it rises out of the mud of a pond or a river, it doesn't reach up towering into the sky—it floats freely, serenely on top of the water. It was said that wherever Buddha walked, lotus flowers appeared to mark his footprints. In a way, the lotus also embodies the principle of letting go. It's beautiful and pure, but also attainable and lowly. It is simultaneously attached and detached.

This is the balance we want to strike. If we aim for the trophy in life—be it recognition or wealth or power—we'll miss the target. If we aim too intensely for the target—as Kenzo warned his students—we will neglect the process and the art required to hit it. What we should be doing is practicing. What we should be doing is pushing away that willful will.

The closer we get to mastery, the less we care about specific results. The more collaborative and creative we are able to be, the less we will tolerate ego or insecurity. The more at peace we are, the more productive we can be.

Only through stillness are the vexing problems solved. Only through reducing our aims are the most difficult targets within our reach.

ON TO WHAT'S NEXT . . .

> If the mind is disciplined, the heart turns quickly
> from fear to love.
>
> —JOHN CAGE

The stakes of what each of us is trying to do are too high to allow ourselves to be riven by the chatter of the news or the noise of the crowd. The insights we seek are often buried and rarely obvious—to find them, we need to be able to look deeply, to perceive what others are unable to.

So we ignore the noise. We zero in on what's essential. We sit with presence. We sit with our journals. We empty our minds.

We try, in the words of Marcus Aurelius, to "shrug it all off and wipe it clean—every annoyance and distraction—and reach utter stillness." To build a kind of mental vault or stronghold that no distraction or false impression can breach. For brief moments, we are able to get there. And when we're there, we find ourselves capable of things we didn't even know were possible: Superior performance. Awesome clarity. Profound happiness.

Yet that stillness is often fleeting. Why?

Because it is undermined by disturbances elsewhere—not just the expected turbulence of the surrounding world, but also inside us. In our spirit and our physical bodies.

"The mind tends toward stillness," Lao Tzu said, "but is opposed by craving." We are like the audience at Marina Abramović's performance. Present for a moment. Moved to stillness for a moment. Then back out into the city, back to the old routines and pulled by endless desires and bad habits, as if that experience never happened.

A flash of stillness is not what we're after. We want consistent focus and wisdom that can be called upon in even the most trying situations. Getting there will require more work. It's going to require some holistic self-examination, treating the disease and not just the symptoms.

The premise of this book is that our three domains—the mind, the heart, and the body—must be in harmony. The truth is that for most people not only are these domains out of sync, but they are at war with each other. We will never have peace until that civil war Dr. King described is settled.

History teaches us that peace is what provides the opportunity to build. It is the postwar boom that turns nations into superpowers, and ordinary people into powerhouses.

And so we must go onward to fight the next battle, to pacify the domain of the spirit and purify our hearts, our emotions, our drives, our passions.

PART II

MIND ◆ **SPIRIT** ◆ BODY

Most of us would be seized with fear if our bodies went numb, and would do everything possible to avoid it, yet we take no interest at all in the numbing of our souls.

—EPICTETUS

THE DOMAIN OF THE SOUL

In retrospect, it was one of the finest moments in golf, perhaps in all of sports. In June 2008, Tiger Woods birdied the final hole of the U.S. Open at Torrey Pines, just north of San Diego, to force an eighteen-hole playoff. He took an early three-stroke lead but surrendered it, only to come charging back, to birdie again and force forty-six-year old Rocco Mediate into a head-to-head, sudden-death round. On that 488-yard par-four, Tiger Woods would birdie a final time to win his third U.S. Open and his fourteenth major. The second most major victories in the history of the game.

And Woods was certainly the first person and likely the last golfer in history to win such a roller-coaster match on a torn ACL and a leg *broken* in two places. To call it a triumph of grit and determination almost undersells Woods's performance, because he did it with such poise that no one watching even knew the extent of his injuries.

Woods himself knew only of the fractures, not the fact that his knee joint was basically gone. Yet somehow, with nearly inhuman mental and physical discipline, he transcended every limit the complex and crushing game of golf had tried to place on him, and he did it with little more than an occasional grimace.

We could call this moment the high-water mark of Tiger Woods's career. He took a six-month leave to recover from emergency knee surgery. Not long after, his mistress, Rachel Uchitel, was caught at his hotel in Australia, and suddenly the secrets of his personal life were no longer secret.

When he was confronted by his wife, Tiger tried to lie his way out of it, but the lies stopped working. Within minutes, Tiger was sprawled out in a neighbor's driveway, his SUV crashed into a nearby fire hydrant and the back windows smashed by a golf club. Unconscious, his wife weeping over him, he was, for a moment, *still,* in a way he had not been perhaps since he was a baby.

It did not last long.

The tabloid nightmare of all tabloid nightmares would ensue—twenty-one consecutive covers of the *New York Post.* The text messages. The affairs with porn stars and Perkins waitresses, frantic sex in church parking lots, sex even with the twenty-one-year-old daughters of family friends, all made public. The stint in sex rehab, the loss of his sponsors, and the $100 million divorce—it all nearly broke him, as it would break anyone.

He wouldn't win another major for a decade.

"On the surface of the ocean there is stillness," the monk Thich Nhat Hanh has said of the human condition, "but underneath there are currents." So it was for Tiger Woods. This man who had become an icon for his ability to be calm and focused in moments of intense stress, a man with the physical discipline to pump the emergency brake on his 129-mile-per-hour swing if he wanted to start over, the champion of the "stillest" of sports, was at the mercy of insatiable riptides that lurked beneath his placid demeanor. And as any seasoned captain of the seas of life can tell you, what's happening on the surface of the water doesn't matter—it's what's going on below that will kill you.

Tiger Woods could stare down opponents and unimaginable pressure, persevere through the countless obstacles in his career. He just couldn't do the same for his own spiritual demons.

The seeds of Tiger's undoing were sown early. His father, Earl, was a complicated man. Born into poverty, Earl Woods lived through the worst of American racism and segregation. He managed to put himself through college and join the army, where he became a Green Beret in Vietnam. Beneath the surface of this accomplishment there were also currents—of narcissism, egotism, dishonesty, and greed. A simple example: Earl Woods returned from his second tour in Vietnam with a new wife . . . a fact he neglected to mention to the wife and three children he already had.

When Tiger was born of that second marriage, Earl Woods was forty-three years old and not particularly excited to become a father again. For the first year of Tiger's life, fatherhood mostly involved strapping the baby in a high chair while hitting golf balls in the garage. It was in fact in watching his father play golf—instead of being able to play like a regular kid—that Tiger developed his almost unnatural obsession with the game. According to family legend, at nine months old Tiger slid down from his chair, picked up a club, and hit a golf ball.

It's a story that is both cute and utterly abnormal. At age two, Tiger Woods appeared on *The Mike Douglas Show* to show off his golf skills. The audience loved it, but Jimmy Stewart, the other guest that day, was not amused. "I've seen too many precious kids like this sweet little boy," he told Douglas backstage, "and too many starry-eyed parents."

Still, his parents' dedication is undoubtedly what allowed Tiger Woods to become a great golfer. Thousands of hours in the garage watching his father hit seared the beautiful mechanics of a swing into his mind. The thousands more hours they spent at the driving range and playing golf—thanks in part to the discounted rates Earl Woods got at the military course near their home—were instrumental. His parents sacrificed for him, drove him to tournaments, and hired the best coaches.

They didn't stop there. Earl Woods knew that golf was a mental game, so he worked to prepare his son for the unforgiving world of sports. Starting when Tiger was about seven, Earl took active measures to develop his son's concentration. Whenever Tiger teed off, Earl would cough. Or jingle change in his pocket. Or drop his clubs. Or throw a ball at him. Or block his line of sight. "I wanted to teach him mental toughness," Earl recounted. "If he got distracted by the little things I did, he'd never be able to handle the pressure of a tournament."

But as Tiger got older, the training became, even by Earl's admission, an increasingly brutal finishing school. It was a boot camp of "prisoner-of-war interrogation techniques" and "psychological intimidation" that no civilized person ought to inflict on another. "He constantly put me down," Tiger said later. "He would push me to the breaking point, then back off. It was wild."

Yeah. *Wild.*

That's what it is for a child to hear his father taunt him as he tries to play a sport, to call him a "motherfucker" while he's trying to concentrate. Imagine how painful it would be to have your dad tell you to "fuck off," or to ask, "How do you feel being a little nigger?" to try to get a rise out of you. Earl Woods even cheated when they played together, supposedly to keep his son humble and on his game. As Tiger reflected, this was all deliberate training to become what his father wanted him to be: a "'cold-blooded assassin' on the course."

Now, Tiger, who clearly loved his father, said that they had a code word he could use if his father ever pushed too far—in either their mental or physical training—and that all Tiger had to do was say it and Earl would stop. Tiger says he never did, because he needed and enjoyed the training, but even the word itself is illustrative. It wasn't a cute inside joke or some silly word that meant nothing. The word that Tiger could utter to get his father to stop bullying him, to get him to treat him like a normal child, was, if you can believe it: *enough.*

And not only was it never uttered, but the two of them came to refer to it almost as an expletive: the "e-word."

The e-word was something quitters said, that only losers believed in.

Are we surprised, then, that this talented boy would go on to win so much? But that those wins didn't make him happy? He was imperturbable on the golf course and utterly miserable inside.

Tiger's mother taught him lessons too. She told him, "You will never, ever ruin my reputation as a parent because I will beat you." Notice the threat of physical violence and what it was over—not doing *wrong* but *embarrassing* her. Earl Woods, as a husband, showed Tiger early on how to balance this razor's edge too. He cheated on his wife when he traveled with his son. He drank to excess. He even, likely in violation of amateur sporting rules, accepted a secret $50,000-a-year stipend from IMG, the sports agency that would eventually represent Tiger Woods.

The lesson there? Appearances are the only thing that matters. Do whatever it takes to win—just don't get caught.

A less talented and dedicated athlete would have been crippled by this abuse. But Tiger Woods was not just naturally gifted, he truly loved golf and he loved the work of it. So he got better and better.

By the time he was three, he was beating ten-year-olds. By eleven years old, he could beat his father regularly on eighteen-hole courses. By seventh grade, he was being recruited by Stanford. At Stanford, where he spent two years, Tiger was an All-American and the number one player in the country. By the time he went pro at twenty, it was already obvious that he might become the greatest golfer who ever lived. The richest too. His first contracts with Nike and Titleist were worth a combined $60 million.

Tiger Woods's first decade and a half as a pro stand as possibly the most dominant reign ever, in any sport. He won everything that could be won. Fourteen majors, 140 tournaments. He was ranked the number one golfer in the world for *281 consecutive weeks.* He won more than $115 million in PGA Tour winnings. He won on every continent except Antarctica.

There were, for those who were looking, signs of sickness: the thrown clubs after a bad hole—and the lack of concern for the fans this occasionally imperiled. The way he'd broken up with his longtime high school girlfriend by packing her suitcase and sending it to her parents' hotel room with a letter. The way he responded when Steve Scott saved him from accidentally scratching in their epic head-to-head match, not even thanking him, not even acknowledging the incredible sportsmanship of it—treating it like the weakness of inferior prey.* The way he'd left his college golf team to go pro without even saying goodbye to his teammates, the way after he finished eating with family or friends he'd simply get up and leave without saying a word. The way he could just cut people out of his life.

Woods's golf coach Hank Haney would say that over time Tiger began to understand that "anyone who was brought into his world was lucky and would be playing by his rules." This was

---

*After the match, Steve Scott would marry his caddy and they would live happily ever after.

what he had been taught by his parents, who raised him both as a kind of prince and a prisoner in a psychological experiment. Fame and wealth only added to this. "I felt I had worked hard my entire life and deserved to enjoy all the temptations around me," Tiger would say later. "I felt I was entitled. Thanks to money and fame, I didn't have to go far to find them."

We can imagine Tiger Woods, like so many successful people, getting less happy the more he achieved. Less freedom. Less and less sleep, until it came only with medication. Even with a beautiful, brilliant wife whom he loved, even with two children, whom he also loved, even as the undisputed champion of his craft, he was miserable, tortured by a spiritual malady and a crushing anxiety from which there was no relief.

His mind was strong but his soul ached. It ached over his tragic relationship with his father. It ached over the childhood he had lost. It ached because it *ached—Why am I not happy,* he must have thought, *don't I have everything I ever wanted?*

It's not simply that Tiger loved to win. It's that for so long winning was not nearly enough and never could be enough (the *e*-word). He would tell Charlie Rose, "Winning was fun. Beating someone's even better." Tiger said this *after* his public humiliation, after his multiyear slump, after his stint in sex rehab. He still had not learned. He still could not see what this attitude had cost him.

Everybody's got a hungry heart—that's true. But how we choose to feed that heart matters. It's what determines the kind of person we end up being, what kind of trouble we'll get into, and whether we'll ever be *full,* whether we'll ever really be still.

When Tiger Woods's father died in 2006, Tiger's extramarital affairs went into overdrive. He spent time in clubs, partying, instead of at home with his family. His behavior on the course grew worse, more standoffish, angrier. He also began to spend unusual amounts of time with Navy SEALS, indulging in an impossible fantasy that he might quit golf and join the Special Forces, despite being in his early thirties (and one of the most famous people in the world). In one weekend in 2007, Tiger Woods reportedly jumped out of a plane ten times. In fact, the injuries that plague him to this day are likely a result of that training, not golf—including an accident where his knee was kicked out from under him in a military exercise "clearing" a building.

There he was—rather than enjoying his wealth, success, and family—cheating on his wife, playing a soldier in some sort of early midlife crisis. "Mirror, mirror on the wall, we grow up like our daddy after all," a friend of Earl and Tiger's would say of the situation. Like so many of us, Tiger had unconsciously replicated the most painful and worst habits of his parents.

Some have looked at those fruitless years after Tiger's return to golf as evidence that the selfishness of his previous life helped his game. Or that somehow the work he did in rehab opened up wounds better left bound up.

As if Tiger Woods, a *human being,* did not deserve happiness and existed solely to win trophies and entertain us on television. "For what is a man profited," Jesus asked his disciples, "if he shall gain the whole world, and lose his own soul?"

It's a question we must ask ourselves. Cheating and lying never helped anyone in the long run, whether it was done at work or at home. In Tiger's case, it was that he was so talented, he could get away with it . . . until he couldn't.

Eventually one has to say the e-word, *enough*. Or the world says it for you.

In one sense, his father's training had succeeded. Tiger Woods was mentally tough. He was cold-blooded and talented. But in every other part of his life, he was weak and fragile— bankrupt and unbalanced. That stillness existed only on the golf course; everywhere else he was at the mercy of his passions and urges. As he worked to crowd out distractions—anything that would get in the way of his concentration addressing each shot—he was also crowding out so many other essential elements of life: An open heart. Meaningful relationships. Selflessness. Moderation. A sense of right and wrong.

These are not just important elements of a balanced life; they are sources of stillness that allow us to endure defeat and enjoy victory. Mental stillness will be short-lived if our hearts are on fire, or our souls ache with emptiness. We are incapable of seeing what is essential in the world if we are blind to what's going on within us. We cannot be in harmony with anyone or anything if the need for more, more, more is gnawing at our insides like a maggot.

"When you live a life where you're lying all the time, life is no fun," Tiger would say later. When your life is out of balance, it's not fun. When your life is solely and exclusively about yourself, it's worse than not fun—it's empty and awful. Tiger Woods wasn't just a solitary man; he was, like so many of us in the modern world, *an island*. He might have been famous, but he was a stranger to himself. No one who reads about his endless affairs gets the sense that he was enjoying it or that they brought him much pleasure. In fact, it almost feels like he wanted to get caught. So he could get help.

We don't need to judge Tiger Woods. We need to learn from him, from both his fall and his long and valiant journey back to winning the Masters in 2019 at forty-three years old with a fused back, with his own young son cheering him on. Because we share the same flaws, the same weaknesses—and have the same potential for greatness, if we are willing to put in the work.

Marcus Aurelius would ask himself, "What am I doing with my soul? Interrogate yourself, to find out what inhabits your so-called mind and what kind of soul you have now. A child's soul? An adolescent's? . . . A tyrant's soul? The soul of a predator—or its prey?"

We need to ask ourselves these questions, too, especially as we become successful.

One of the best stories in Zen literature is a series of ten poems about a farmer and his trouble with a bull. The poems are an allegory about conquering the self, and the titles of each one map out the journey that each of us must go on: We search for the bull, we track the footprints, we find it, we catch it, we tame it, we ride it home.

At first the beast is untamable, it's wild and impossible to contain. But the message is that with struggle and perseverance, with self-awareness and patience—with *enlightenment,* really—eventually we can tame the emotions and the drives inside us. As one of the poems reads:

> *Being well-trained, he becomes*
> *naturally gentle.*
> *Then, unfettered, he obeys his master.*

The narrator is in a state of serenity and peace. He has tamed his wild spirit.

That's what we're trying to do. Since ancient times, people have strived to train and control the forces that reside deep inside them so that they can find serenity, so that they can preserve and protect their accomplishments. What good is it to be rational at work if our personal lives are a hot-blooded series of disasters? How long can we keep the two domains separate anyway? You might rule cities or a great empire, but if you're not in control of yourself, it is all for naught.

The work we must do next is less cerebral and more spiritual. It's work located in the *heart* and in the *soul,* and not in the mind. Because it is our soul that is the key to our happiness (or our unhappiness), contentment (or discontent), moderation (or gluttony), and stillness (or perturbation).

That is why those who seek stillness must come to . . .

- Develop a strong moral compass.
- Steer clear of envy and jealousy and harmful desires.
- Come to terms with the painful wounds of their childhood.
- Practice gratitude and appreciation for the world around them.
- Cultivate relationships and love in their lives.
- Place belief and control in the hands of something larger than themselves.
- Understand that there will never be "enough" and that the unchecked pursuit of more ends only in bankruptcy.

Our soul is where we secure our happiness and unhappiness, contentment or emptiness—and ultimately, determine the extent of our greatness.

We must maintain a good one.

CHOOSE VIRTUE

The essence of greatness is the perception that virtue is enough.

—RALPH WALDO EMERSON

Marcus Aurelius famously described a number of what he called "epithets for the self." Among his were: Upright. Modest. Straightforward. Sane. Cooperative. These were, then, the traits that served him well as emperor.

There are many other traits that could be added to this list: Honest. Patient. Caring. Kind. Brave. Calm. Firm. Generous. Forgiving. Righteous.

There is one word, however, under which all these epithets sit: virtue.

Virtue, the Stoics believed, was the highest good—the *summum bonum*—and should be the principle behind all our actions. Virtue is not holiness, but rather moral and civic excellence in the course of daily life. It's a sense of pure rightness that emerges from our souls and is made real through the actions we take.

The East prized virtue as much as the West. *The Daodejing,* for instance, actually translates as *The Way of Virtue.* Confucius, who advised many of the rulers and princes of his day, would have agreed with Marcus that a leader was well served by the pursuit of virtue. His highest compliment would have been to call a ruler a *junzi*—a word that translators still have trouble finding equivalents for in English but is roughly understood as a person who emanates integrity, honor, and self-control.

If the concept of "virtue" seems a bit stuffy to you, consider the evidence that a virtuous life is worthwhile for *its own sake.* No one has less serenity than the person who does not know what is right or wrong. No one is more exhausted than the person who, because they lack a moral code, must belabor every decision and consider every temptation. No one feels worse about themselves than the cheater or the liar, even if—often especially if—they are showered with rewards for their cheating and lying. Life *is* meaningless to the person who decides their choices have no meaning.

Meanwhile, the person who knows what they value? Who has a strong sense of decency and principle and behaves accordingly? Who possesses easy moral self-command, who leans comfortably upon this goodness, day in and day out? This person has found stillness.

A sort of soul power they can draw on when they face challenges, stress, even scary situations.

Look at the response of Canadian politician Jagmeet Singh to an angry protester during a campaign stop. When the agitated woman came up and started shouting at him about Islam (despite the fact that he is Sikh), he replied with two of his own epithets for the self: "Love and courage." Soon, the crowd began to chant along with him: "Love and courage. Love and courage. Love and courage."

He could've stood there and yelled back. He could have run away. It could have made him cruel and mean, in the moment or forever after. He may well have been prodded in those directions. But instead he remained cool, and those two words helped him recenter in the midst of what not only was a career-on-the-line situation, but probably felt like a life-threatening one.

Different situations naturally call for different virtues and different epithets for the self. When we're going into a tough assignment, we can say to ourselves over and over again, "Strength and courage." Before a tough conversation with a significant other: "Patience and kindness." In times of corruption and evil: "Goodness and honesty."

The gift of free will is that in this life we can choose to be good or we can choose to be bad. We can choose what standards to hold ourselves to and what we will regard as important, honorable, and admirable. The choices we make in that regard determine whether we will experience peace or not.

Which is why each of us needs to sit down and examine ourselves. What do we stand for? What do we believe to be essential and important? What are we really *living* for? Deep in the marrow of our bones, in the chambers of our heart, we know the answer. The problem is that the busyness of life, the realities of pursuing a career and surviving in the world, come between us and that self-knowledge.

Confucius said that virtue is a kind of polestar. It not only provides guidance to the navigator, but it attracts fellow travelers too. Epicurus, who has been unfairly branded by history as a hedonist, knew that virtue was the way to tranquility and happiness. In fact, he believed that virtue and pleasure were two sides of the same coin. As he said:

> It is impossible to live the pleasant life without also living sensibly, nobly, and justly, and conversely it is impossible to live sensibly, nobly, and justly without living pleasantly. A person who does not have a pleasant life is not living sensibly, nobly, and justly, and conversely the person who does not have these virtues cannot live pleasantly.

Where virtue is, so too are happiness and beauty.

Confucius wrote that the "gentleman is self-possessed and relaxed, while the petty man is perpetually full of worry." It's worth a look at Seneca, another Stoic philosopher, who, like Marcus, made his living in politics. Like us, Seneca was full of contradictions. On the one hand, his writings contain some of the most beautiful meditations on morality and self-discipline ever written, and they are obviously the result of incredible concentration and mental clarity. On the other, Seneca was a striver—an ambitious writer-politician who aspired to be remembered as much for his prose as for his policies.

At the height of his career, he could be found working as a fixer for the emperor, Nero. Nero, although he had begun as a promising student of Seneca, did not make his teacher's job easy. He was deranged, selfish, distractible, paranoid, and coldhearted. Imagine that you spend your evenings writing about the importance of doing the right thing, of temperance and wisdom, and then by day you have to help your all-powerful boss justify trying to assassinate his mother. Seneca knew he should walk away; he probably wanted to, but he never did.

What is virtue? Seneca would ask. His answer: "True and steadfast judgment." And from virtue comes good decisions and happiness and peace. It emanates from the soul and directs the mind and the body.

Yet when we look at Seneca's life, we get the sense that he was the type of man whose ambition did not provide much peace, but instead skewed his decision making. Seneca wrote eloquently of the meaninglessness of wealth, yet came to possess an enormous fortune through questionable means. He believed in mercy, kindness, and compassion, but he willingly served two different emperors who were probably psychopaths. It was as if he didn't believe in his own philosophy enough to put it wholly into practice—he couldn't quite accept that virtue would provide enough to live on.

Money, power, fame just seemed a little more urgent.

Seneca knew of the virtuous path, but chased the prizes that drew him away from it. This choice cost him many sleepless nights and forced him into ethically taxing dilemmas. In the end, it cost him his life. In AD 65, Nero turned on his former teacher and forced him to commit suicide—the evil Seneca had rationalized for so long, it eventually cost him everything.

There's no question it's possible to get ahead in life by lying and cheating and generally being awful to other people. This may even be a quick way to the top. But it comes at the expense of not only your self-respect, but your security too.

Virtue, on the other hand, as crazy as it might seem, is a far more attainable and sustainable way to succeed.

How's that? Recognition is dependent on other people. Getting rich requires business opportunities. You can be blocked from your goals by the weather just as easily as you can by a dictator. But virtue? No one can stop you from knowing what's right. Nothing stands between you and it . . . but yourself.

Each of us must cultivate a moral code, a higher standard that we love almost more than life itself. Each of us must sit down and ask: *What's important to me? What would I rather die for than betray? How am I going to live and why?*

These are not idle questions or the banal queries of a personality quiz. We must have the answers if we want the stillness (and the strength) that emerges from the citadel of our own virtue.

It is for the difficult moments in life—the crossroads that

Seneca found himself on when asked to serve Nero—that virtue can be called upon. Heraclitus said that character was fate. He's right. We develop good character, strong epithets for ourselves, so when it counts, we will not flinch.

So that when everyone else is scared and tempted, we will be virtuous.

We will be still.

HEAL THE INNER CHILD

The child is in me still ... and sometimes not so still.

—FRED ROGERS

There was always something childlike about Leonardo da Vinci. Indeed, this is what made him such a brilliant artist— his mischievousness, his curiosity, his fascination with inventing and creating. But behind this playfulness was a deep sadness, pain rooted in the events of his early life.

Leonardo was born in 1452, an illegitimate son from a prosperous family of notaries. Though in time his father would invite his bastard son to come live with him, and would help secure Leonardo's first artistic apprenticeship, a distance between them never closed.

At the time, it was customary that the oldest son of a prominent tradesman like Leonardo's father would be chosen to take up his father's profession and eventually take over his business. While the notary guild technically did not recognize *non legittimo* heirs, it's surprising that Leonardo's father never even attempted to appear before a local magistrate and present a petition to legitimate his son.

Leonardo's father would go on to have twelve more children, nine of whom were sons. When he died, he left no specific will, an act that for a notary, familiar with the law, meant one thing: He was legally disinheriting Leonardo in favor of his "real" children. As Leonardo's biographer Walter Isaacson would later write, by excluding Leonardo and never fully accepting him, Piero da Vinci's "primary bequest to his son was to give him an insatiable drive for an unconditional patron."

Indeed, all of Leonardo's artistic life exhibits an almost childlike search for love and acceptance from the powerful men he worked for. He devotedly served his first mentor, Andrea del Verrocchio, for more than eleven years—until Leonardo was twenty-five—an incredibly long time for such a prodigal talent (Michelangelo broke out on his own at sixteen). What could have attracted a sweet soul like Leonardo to Cesare Borgia, a murderous psychopath? Borgia was the only patron who was willing to look at and consider Leonardo's military inventions—a longtime passion project. From Milan to France and to the Vatican itself, Leonardo traveled far and wide in his career, looking for the financial support and artistic freedom he thought would make him whole.

Nearly half a dozen times, he uprooted himself and his workshop in a huff, leaving unfinished commissions behind him. Sometimes it was over a slight. Usually it was because the patron couldn't quite be everything Leonardo wanted. The subtext of his angry letters and half-completed work speaks as loudly to us today as any angry teenager: *You're not my dad. You can't tell me what to do. You don't really love me. I'll show you.*

Many of us carry wounds from our childhood. Maybe someone didn't treat us right. Or we experienced something terrible. Or our parents were just a little too busy or a little too critical or a little too stuck dealing with their own issues to be what we needed.

These raw spots shape decisions we make and actions we take—even if we're not always conscious of that fact.

This should be a relief: The source of our anxiety and worry, the frustrations that seem to suddenly pop out in inappropriate situations, the reason we have trouble staying in relationships or ignoring criticism—it isn't us. Well, it is us, just not *adult* us. It's the seven-year-old living inside us. The one who was hurt by Mom and Dad, the sweet, innocent kid who wasn't seen.

Think of Rick Ankiel, one of the greatest natural pitchers to ever play baseball. He had a brutal childhood in the home of an abusive father and a brother who was a drug dealer. His whole life, he stuffed this pain and helplessness down, focusing on his skill on the mound, eventually becoming the minor leagues' top pitching prospect. Then suddenly, just as his career was starting to go well, in the first game of the playoffs in 2000, in front of millions of people, he lost the ability to control his pitches.

What happened? Just days before, his father and brother had gone to jail on drug charges and Rick had been in the courthouse to see them. He'd been running from that pain and that anger for years, until it finally exploded and shattered the delicate balance that pitching required. It took years of work with Harvey Dorfman, a brilliant, patient sports psychologist, to coax his gifts back. And even then only so far. Ankiel would pitch only five more times in his career, none as a starter. The rest of his career he spent in the outfield—mostly in center field, the position farthest away from the mound.

Sigmund Freud himself wrote about how common it is for deficiencies, big and small, at a young age to birth toxic, turbulent attitudes in adulthood. Because we weren't born rich enough, pretty enough, naturally gifted enough, because we weren't appreciated like other children in the classroom, or because we had to wear glasses or got sick a lot or couldn't afford nice clothes, we carry a chip on our shoulder. Some of us are like Richard III, believing that a deformity entitles us to be selfish or mean or insatiably ambitious. As Freud explained, "We all demand reparation for our early wounds to our narcissism," thinking we are owed because we were wronged or deprived. (This was Tiger Woods to the detail.)

It's dangerous business, though, creating a monster to protect your wounded inner child.

The insecure lens. The anxious lens. The persecuted lens. The prove-them-all-wrong lens. The will-you-be-my-father? lens that Leonardo had. These adaptations, developed early on to make sense of the world, don't make our lives easier. On the contrary.

Who can be happy that way? Would you put a nine-year-old in charge of anything stressful or dangerous or important?

The movie producer Judd Apatow has talked about something he realized after a big fight during the filming of one of his movies. For years, he had seen every note the studio or the executives had for him, every attempt at restrictions or influence, as if it were the obnoxious meddling of his parents. Instinctively, emotionally, he had fought and resisted each intervention. *Who are these idiots to tell me what to do? Why are they always trying to boss me around? Why are they so unfair?*

Each of us on occasion has surprised ourself with a strong reaction to someone's innocuous comments, or thrown a fit when some authority figure tried to direct our actions. Or felt the pull of attraction to a type of relationship that never ends well. Or to a type of behavior that we know is wrong. It's almost primal how deep these feelings go—they're rooted in our infancy.

It took therapy and self-reflection (and probably the observations of his wife) for Apatow to understand that the movie studio was *not his parents.* This was a business transaction and a creative discussion, not another instance of a talented boy being bossed around by otherwise absent parents.

But with that realization came stillness, if only because it deintensified arguments at work. Think about it: How much better and less scary life is when we don't have to see it from the perspective of a scared, vulnerable child? How much lighter will our load be if we're not adding extra baggage on top?

It will take patience and empathy and real self-love to heal the wounds in your life. As Thich Nhat Hanh has written:

> After recognizing and embracing our inner child, the third function of mindfulness is to soothe and relieve our difficult emotions. Just by holding this child gently, we are soothing our difficult emotions and we can begin to feel at ease. When we embrace our strong emotions with mindfulness and concentration, we'll be able to see the roots of these mental formations. We'll know where our suffering has come from. When we see the roots of things, our suffering will lessen. So mindfulness recognizes, embraces, and relieves.

Take the time to think about the pain you carry from your early experiences. Think about the "age" of the emotional reactions you have when you are hurt or betrayed or unexpectedly challenged in some way. That's your inner child. They need a hug from you. They need you to say, "Hey, buddy. *It's okay*. I know you're hurt, but I am going to take care of you."

The functional adult steps in to reassert and reassure. To make stillness possible.

We owe it to ourselves as well as to the people in our lives to do this. Each of us must break the link in the chain of what the Buddhists call *samsara*, the continuation of life's suffering from generation to generation.

The comedian Garry Shandling lost his brother, Barry, at

age ten to cystic fibrosis, and was left for the rest of his life at the mercy of his distraught and controlling mother, who was so disturbed by the loss of her older son that she forbade Garry from attending the funeral for fear that he would see her cry.

But one day, as a much older man, Garry wrote in his diary a formula that might help him overcome that pain and not only heal his own inner child but pass on the lesson to the many surrogate children he had as a mentor and elder in show business.* The formula was simple and is key to breaking the cycle and stilling the deep anguish we carry around with us:

> Give more.
> Give what you didn't get.
> Love more.
> Drop the old story.

> Try it, if you can.

---

*As it happens, Judd Apatow was one of the most successful of these surrogate children.

BEWARE DESIRE

Every man has a passion gnawing away at the bottom
of his heart, just as every fruit has its worm.

—ALEXANDRE DUMAS

John F. Kennedy achieved indisputable greatness through
stillness in those thirteen fateful days in October 1962. The
world is forever in his debt. But we should not allow that shining
moment to obscure the fact that, like all of us, he had demons
that dogged and haunted him and undermined that same
greatness—and as a result, his stillness.

Kennedy grew up in a house where his father often brought
his mistresses home for dinner and on family vacations. It was
a house where anger and rage were common too. "When I hate
some sonofabitch," Joseph Kennedy liked to say, "I hate him
until I die." It's probably not a surprise, then, that his young son
would develop his own bad habits and wrestle with controlling
his urges and appetites.

The first time Kennedy's sex drive got him in trouble was during the early days of World War II, when he began dating Inga Arvad, a beautiful Dutch journalist who many suspected was a Nazi spy. When he was running for president, he had an affair with Judith Exner, who happened to be the girlfriend of Sam Giancana, a Chicago mobster. But instead of suffering any consequences for theses massive lapses of judgment, Kennedy skated away clean each time, a fact that only escalated his risky behavior.

Kennedy was no romantic. Girlfriends would describe his insatiable but joyless sex drive. According to one conquest, sex was "just physical and social activity to him," a way to stave off the boredom, or get a rush. He didn't care about the other person, and in time, he almost didn't care about the pleasure it gave himself either. As Kennedy told the prime minister of Britain in a moment of very uncomfortable honesty, if he went without sex for a few days, he'd get headaches. (His father had told his sons that he couldn't sleep unless he'd "had a lay.") Given Kennedy's terrible back, having sex was probably painful too—but he never let that stop him.

In one shameful moment, as Soviet and American forces teetered on the brink of nuclear war during the Cuban Missile Crisis, Kennedy brought in a nineteen-year-old student from Wheaton College for a rendezvous in a hotel near the White House. Here was a man who had no idea how much longer he would live, who was working with inhuman dedication in that crisis to curb the dangerous impulses of his nation's enemies . . . cheating on his wife, choosing to spend what were potentially his last moments on earth in the sheets with a random girl half his age instead of with his scared and vulnerable family.

That doesn't sound like stillness. It doesn't sound particularly glamorous either.

It sounds like a man who is spiritually broken, at the whims of his worst impulses, unable to think clearly or prioritize. But before we condemn Kennedy as a despicable addict or abuser, we should look at our own failings. Do we not fall prey to various desires in our own personal lives? Do we not know better and do it anyway?

Lust is a destroyer of peace in our lives: Lust for a beautiful person. Lust for an orgasm. Lust for someone other than the one we've committed to be with. Lust for power. Lust for dominance. Lust for other people's stuff. Lust for the fanciest, best, most expensive things that money can buy.

And is this not at odds with the self-mastery we say we want?

A person enslaved to their urges is not free—whether they are a plumber or the president.

How many great men and women end up losing everything—end up, in some cases, literally behind bars—because they freely chose to indulge their endless appetites, whatever they happened to be?

And at least power and sex and attention are pleasurable. The most common form of lust is *envy*—the lust for what other people have, for the sole reason that they have it. Joseph Epstein's brilliant line is: "Of the seven deadly sins, only envy is no fun at all." Democritus, twenty-four hundred years before him: "An envious man pains himself as though he were an enemy."

No one in the sway of envy or jealousy has a chance to think clearly or live peacefully. How can they?

It is an endless loop of misery. We're envious of one person, while they envy somebody else. The factory worker wishes desperately to be a millionaire, the millionaire envies the simple life of the nine-to-five worker. The famous wish they could go back to the private life that so many others would gladly give away; the man or woman with a beautiful partner thinks only of someone a little more beautiful. It's sobering to consider that the rival we're so jealous of may in fact be jealous of us.

There is also a "have your cake and eat it too" immaturity to envy. We don't simply want what other people have—we want to keep everything we have *and* add theirs to it, even if those things are mutually exclusive (and on top of that, we also want them to not have it anymore). But if you had to trade places entirely with the person you envy, if you had to give up your brain, your principles, your proudest accomplishments to live in their life, would you do it? Are you willing to pay the price they paid to get what you covet?

No, you aren't.

Epicurus, again the supposed hedonist, once said that "sex has never benefited any man, and it's a marvel if it hasn't injured him." He came up with a good test anytime he felt himself being pulled by a strong desire: *What will happen to me if I get what I want? How will I feel after?*

Indeed, *most* desires are at their core irrational emotions, and that's why stillness requires that we sit down and dissect them. We want to think ahead to the refractory period, to consider the inevitable hangover before we take a drink. When we do that, these desires lose some of their power.

To the Epicureans real pleasure was about freedom from pain and agitation. If wanting something makes you miserable while you don't have it, doesn't that diminish the true value of the reward? If getting what you "want" has its consequences too, is that really pleasurable? If the same drive that helps you achieve initially also leads you inevitably to overreach or overdo, is it really an advantage?

Those seeking stillness need not become full-fledged ascetics or puritans. But we can take the time to realize how much pull and power desire can have on us, and beyond the momentary pleasure this might provide us, it deprives us of the deeper peace that we seek.

Think about the times when you feel best. It's not when you are pining away. It's not when you get what you pined for either. There is always a tinge of disappointment or loss at the moment of acquisition.

Krishna in the Bhagavad Gita calls desire the "ever-present enemy of the wise . . . which like a fire cannot find satisfaction." The Buddhists personified this demon in the figure of Mara. They said it was Mara who tried to tempt and distract Buddha from the path of enlightenment, from stillness. When Leonardo da Vinci wrote in his notebook about how to portray envy, he said that she should be shown as lean and haggard due to her state of perpetual torment. "Make her heart gnawed by a swelling serpent," he said, "make her ride upon death because Envy never dies." It'd be hard to find a better depiction of lust either, which Leonardo said puts us "on the level of beasts."

None of us are perfect. We have biologies and pathologies that will inevitably trip us up. What we need then is a philosophy and a strong moral code—that sense of virtue—to help us resist what we can, and to give us the strength to pick ourselves back up when we fail and try to do and be better.

We can also rely on tools to help us resist harmful desires. Saint Athanasius of Alexandria wrote in his *Vita Antonii* that one of the benefits of journaling—Confessions, as the Christians called the genre—was that it helped stop him from sinning. By observing and then writing about his own behavior, he was able to hold himself accountable and make himself better:

> Let us each note and write down our actions and impulses of the soul . . . as though we were to report them to each other; and you may rest assured that from utter shame of becoming known we shall stop sinning and entertaining sinful thoughts altogether. . . . Just as we would not give ourselves to lust within sight of each other, so if we were to write down our thoughts as if telling them to each other, we shall so much the more guard ourselves against foul thoughts for shame of being known. Now, then, let the written account stand for the

eyes of our fellow ascetics, so that blushing at writing the same as if we were actually seen, we may never ponder evil.

To have an impulse and to resist it, to sit with it and examine it, to let it pass by like a bad smell—this is how we develop spiritual strength. This is how we become who we want to be in this world.

Only those of us who take the time to explore, to question, to extrapolate the consequences of our desires have an opportunity to overcome them and to stop regrets before they start. Only they know that real pleasure lies in having a soul that's true and stable, happy and secure.

ENOUGH

History relates no instance in which a conqueror has
been surfeited with conquests.

—STEFAN ZWEIG

The writers Kurt Vonnegut, the author of *Slaughterhouse
Five,* and Joseph Heller, the author of *Catch-22,* were once
at a party in a fancy neighborhood outside New York City. Standing in the palatial second home of some boring billionaire, Vonnegut began to needle his friend. "Joe," he said, "how does it feel
that our host only yesterday may have made more money than
your novel has earned in its entire history?"

"I've got something he can never have," Heller replied.

"And what on earth could that be?" Vonnegut asked.

"The knowledge that I've got enough."

Earl Woods called that the e-word, like it was an expletive. In
truth, *enough* is a beautiful thing.

Imagine the stillness that sense of enough brought Joseph

Heller and everyone else who has it. No ceaseless wanting. No insecurity of comparison. Feeling *satisfied* with yourself and your work? What gift!

Saying the word "enough" is not enough. Deeply spiritual, introspective work is required to understand what that idea means—work that may well destroy illusions and assumptions we have held our entire lives.

John Stuart Mill, the philosopher and boy genius who before he hit puberty read and mastered nearly every major classical text in the original Greek or Latin, is an illustration of just how terrifying this process can be. Extremely driven (by his father and by himself), one day, at around twenty years old, Mill stopped to think, for the first time, about what he was chasing. As he writes:

> It occurred to me to put the question directly to myself, "Suppose that all your objects in life were realized; that all the changes in institutions and opinions which you are looking forward to, could be completely effected at this very instant: would this be a great joy and happiness to you?" And an irrepressible self-consciousness distinctly answered, "No!" At this my heart sank within me: the whole foundation on which my life was constructed fell down.

What ensued was a devastating mental breakdown that required years of recovery. Yet Mill was probably lucky to undergo it so early. Most people *never* learn that their accomplishments will ultimately fail to provide the relief and happiness we tell ourselves they will. Or they come to understand this only after so much time and money, so many relationships and moments of inner peace, were sacrificed on the altar of achievement. We get to the finish line only to think: *This is it? Now what?*

It is a painful crossroads. Or worse, one that we ignore, stuffing those feelings of existential crisis down, piling on top of them meaningless consumption, more ambition, and the delusion that doing more and more of the same will eventually bring about different results.

In a way, this is a curse of one of our virtues. No one achieves excellence or enlightenment without a desire to get better, without a tendency to explore potential areas of improvement. Yet the desire—or the need—for more is often at odds with happiness. Billie Jean King, the tennis great, has spoken about this, about how the mentality that gets an athlete to the top so often prevents them from enjoying the thing they worked so hard for. The need for progress can be the enemy of enjoying the *process.*

There is no stillness for the person who cannot appreciate things as they are, particularly when that person has objectively done so much. The creep of more, more, more is like a hydra. Satisfy one—lop it off the bucket list—and two more grow in its place.

The best insights on *enough* come to us from the East. "When you realize there is nothing lacking," Lao Tzu says, "the whole world belongs to you." The verse in *The Daodejing:*

> *The greatest misfortune is to not know contentment.*
> *The word calamity is the desire to acquire.*
> *And so those who know the contentment of contentment*
> *   are always content.*

The Western philosophers wrestled with the balance between getting more and being satisfied. Epicurus: "Nothing is enough for the man to whom enough is too little." Thomas Traherne: "To have blessings and to prize them is to be in Heaven; to have them and not to prize them is to be in Hell. . . . To prize them and not to have them is to be in Hell." And the Stoics who lived in the material world of an empire at its peak knew the truth about money. Seneca had piles of it and he knew how little it correlated with peace. His work is filled with stories of people who drove themselves to ruin and misery chasing money they didn't need and honors beyond their share.

Temperance. That's the key. Intellectually, we know this. It's only in flashes of insight or tragedy that we *feel* it.

In 2010, Marco Rubio was pacing the halls of his home, making fund-raising calls for his surprise Senate bid, when his three-year-old son snuck out the back door and fell into the pool. Rubio had heard the chime of the door opening, assumed someone else was paying attention, and returned to his important phone call. A few minutes later, he found his son floating face-down in their pool, barely breathing.

Even after this near tragedy he returned almost immediately to work—his ambition, like Lincoln's, a "little engine that knew no rest." Only with distance could Rubio begin to see the cost of this drive, what important things we miss when we give ourselves over to it entirely. As he wrote, "I think I understand now that the restlessness we feel as we make our plans and chase our ambitions is not the effect of their importance to our happiness and our eagerness to attain them. We are restless because deep in our hearts we know now that our happiness is found elsewhere, and our work, no matter how valuable it is to us or to others, cannot take its place. But we hurry on anyway, and attend to our business because we need to matter, and we don't always realize we already do."

Have you ever held a gold medal or a Grammy or a Super Bowl ring? Have you ever seen a bank balance nudging up into the seven figures? Maybe you have, maybe you possess these things yourself. If you do, then you know: They are nice but they change nothing. They are just pieces of metal, dirty paper in your pocket, or plaques on a wall. They are not made of anything strong or malleable enough to plug even the tiniest hole in a person's soul. Nor do they extend the length of one's life even one minute. On the contrary, they may shorten it!

They can also take the joy out of the thing we used to love to do. *More* does nothing for the one who feels *less than,* who cannot see the wealth that was given to them at birth, that they have accumulated in their relationships and experiences. Solving your problem of poverty is an achievable goal and can be fixed by earning and saving money. No one could seriously claim otherwise. The issue is when we think these activities can address *spiritual poverty.*

Accomplishment. Money. Fame. Respect. Piles and piles of them will never make a person feel content.

If you believe there is ever some point where you will feel like you've "made it," when you'll finally be *good,* you are in for an unpleasant surprise. Or worse, a sort of Sisyphean torture where just as that feeling appears to be within reach, the goal is moved just a little bit farther up the mountain and out of reach.

You will never feel okay by way of external accomplishments. *Enough* comes from the inside. It comes from stepping off the train. From seeing what you already have, what you've always had.

If a person can do that, they are richer than any billionaire, more powerful than any sovereign.

Yet instead of seizing this path to power, we choose ingratitude and the insecurity of needing more, more, more. "We are here as if immersed in water head and shoulders underneath the great oceans," said the Zen master Gensha, "and yet how piteously we are extending our hands for water." We think we need more and don't realize we already have so much. We work so hard "for our families" that we don't notice the contradiction— that it's because of work that we never see them.

Enough.

Now, there is a perfectly understandable worry that contentment will be the end of our careers—that if we somehow satisfy this urge, all progress in our work and in our lives will come to a screeching halt. *If everyone felt good, why would they keep trying so hard?* First, it must be pointed out that this worry itself is hardly an ideal state of mind. No one does their best work driven by anxiety, and no one should be breeding insecurity in themselves so that they might keep making things. That is not industry, that is slavery.

We were not put on this planet to be worker bees, compelled to perform some function over and over again for the cause of the hive until we die. Nor do we "owe it" to anyone to keep doing, doing, doing—not our fans, not our followers, not our parents who have provided so much for us, not even our families. Killing ourselves does nothing for anybody.

It's perfectly possible to do and make good work from a good place. You can be healthy and still *and* successful.

Joseph Heller believed he had *enough,* but he still kept writing. He wrote six novels after *Catch-22* (when a reporter criticized him by saying he hadn't written anything as good as his first book, Heller replied, "Who has?"), including a number one bestseller. He taught. He wrote plays and movies. He was incredibly productive. John Stuart Mill, after his breakdown, fell in love with poetry, met the woman who would eventually become his wife, and began to slowly return to political philosophy—and ultimately had enormous impact on the world. Indeed, Western democracies are indebted to him for many changes he helped bring about.

The beauty was that these creations and insights came from a better—a *stiller*—place inside both men. They weren't doing it to prove anything. They didn't need to impress anyone. They were in the moment. Their motivations were pure. There was no insecurity. No anxiety. No creeping, painful hope that this would finally be the thing that would make them feel whole, that would give them what they had always been lacking.

What do we want more of in life? That's the question. It's not accomplishments. It's not popularity. It's moments when we feel like we are enough.

More presence. More clarity. More insight. More truth.

More stillness.

BATHE IN BEAUTY

In the face of the Sublime, we feel a shiver . . . something too large for our minds to encompass. And for a moment, it shakes us out of our smugness and releases us from the deathlike grip of habit and banality.

—ROBERT GREENE

O n Wednesday morning, February 23, 1944, Anne Frank climbed up to the attic above the annex where her family had been hiding for two long years to visit Peter, the young Jewish boy who lived with them. After Peter finished his chores, the two of them sat down at Anne's favorite spot on the floor and looked out the small window to the world they had been forced to leave behind.

Staring at the blue sky, the leafless chestnut tree below, birds swooping and diving in the air, the two were entranced to the point of speechlessness. It was so quiet, so serene, so open compared to their cramped quarters.

It was almost as if the world wasn't at war, as if Hitler had not already killed so many millions of people and their families didn't spend each day at risk of joining the dead. Despite it all, beauty seemed to reign. "As long as this exists," Anne thought to herself, "this sunshine and this cloudless sky, and as long as I can enjoy it, how can I be sad?"

She would later write in her diary that nature was a kind of cure-all, a comfort available to any and all who suffer. Indeed, whether it was the blooming of spring or the starkness of winter, even when it was dark and raining, when it was too dangerous to open the window and she had to sit in the stifling, suffocating heat to do it, Anne always managed to find in nature something to boost her spirits and center herself. "Beauty remains, even in misfortune," she wrote. "If you just look for it, you discover more and more happiness and regain your balance."

How true that is. And what a source of peace and strength it can be.

The trackless woods. A quiet child, lying on her belly, reading a book. The clouds cutting over the wing of an airplane, its exhausted passengers all asleep. A man reading in his seat. A woman sleeping. A stewardess resting her feet. The rosy fingertips of dawn coming up over the mountain. A song on repeat. That song's beat, lining up exactly with the rhythm of events. The pleasure of getting an assignment in before a deadline, the temporary quiet of an empty inbox.

This is stillness.

Rose Lane Wilder wrote of looking out over the grassy plateau in Tbilisi, the capital of Georgia:

> Here there was only sky, and a stillness made audible by the brittle grass. Emptiness was so perfect all around me that I felt a part of it, empty myself; there was a moment in which I was nothing at all—almost nothing at all.

The term for this is *exstasis*—a heavenly experience that lets us step outside ourselves. And these beautiful moments are available to us whenever we want them. All we have to do is open our souls to them.

There is a story about the Zen master Hyakujo, who was approached by two students as he began his morning chores on the farm attached to his temple. When the students asked him to teach them about the Way, he replied, "You open the farm for me and I will talk to you about the great principle of Zen." After they finished their labors and walked to the master for their lesson, he simply turned to face the fields, which the sun was just then rising above, extended his arms out in the direction of the serene expanse, and said nothing.

That was the Way. Nature. The cultivated soil. The growing crops. The satisfaction of good hard work. The poetry of the earth. As it was in the beginning, as it will be forever.

Not that all beauty is so immediately beautiful. We're not always on the farm or at the beach or gazing out over sweeping canyon views. Which is why the philosopher must cultivate the poet's eye—the ability to see beauty everywhere, even in the banal or the terrible.

Marcus Aurelius, who is supposedly this dark, depressive Stoic, loved beauty in his own Whitmanesque way. Why else would he write so vividly of the ordinary way that "baking bread splits in places and those cracks, while not intended in the baker's art, catch our eye and serve to stir our appetite," or the "charm and allure" of nature's process, the "stalks of ripe grain bending low, the frowning brow of the lion, the foam dripping from the boar's mouth." Even of dying, he writes, "Pass through this brief patch of time in harmony with nature. Come to your final resting place gracefully, just as a ripened olive might drop, praising the earth that nourished it and grateful to the tree that gave it growth."

The philosopher and the poet, seeing the world the same way, both engaged in the same pursuit, as Thomas Aquinas said, the study of "wonder."

It was Edward Abbey, the environmental activist and writer, who said that even the word *wildness* itself was music. It's music we can listen to anytime we like, wherever we live, whatever we do for a living. Even if we can't visit, we can think of traipsing through the pine-bedded floor of the forest, of drifting down a slow-moving river, of the warmth of a campfire. Or, like Anne Frank, we can simply look out our window to see a tree. In doing this, in *noticing,* we become alive to the stillness.

It is not the sign of a healthy soul to find beauty in superficial things—the adulation of the crowd, fancy cars, enormous estates, glittering awards. Nor to be made miserable by the ugliness of the world—the critics and haters, the suffering of the innocent, injuries, pain and loss. It is better to find beauty in all places and things. Because it does surround us. And will nourish us if we let it.

The soft paw prints of a cat on the dusty trunk of a car. The hot steam wafting from the vents on a New York City morning. The smell of asphalt just as the rain begins to fall. The thud of a fist fitting perfectly into an open hand. The sound of a pen signing a contract, binding two parties together. The courage of a mosquito sucking blood from a human who can so easily crush it. A basket full of vegetables from the garden. The hard right angles that passing trucks cut out of the drooping branches of trees next to a busy road. A floor filled with a child's toys, arranged in the chaos of exhausted enjoyment. A city arranged the same way, the accumulation of hundreds of years of spasmodic, independent development.

Are you starting to see how this works?

It's ironic that stillness is rare and fleeting in our busy lives, because the world creates an inexhaustible supply of it. It's just that nobody's looking.

After his breakdown and nearly two years of struggle and depression resulting from overstimulation and too much study, where did John Stuart Mill find peace again for the first time? In the poetry of William Wordsworth. And what was the inspiration of so much of Wordsworth's poetry? Nature.

Theodore Roosevelt was sent west by his doctor after the

death of his mother and wife to lose himself in the bigness of the Dakota Badlands. Yes, Teddy was a hunter and a rancher and a man's man, but his two greatest passions? Sitting quietly on a porch with a book and *birdwatching*. The Japanese have a concept, *shinrin yoku*—forest bathing—which is a form of therapy that uses nature as a treatment for mental and spiritual issues. Hardly a week passed, even when he was president, that Roosevelt didn't take a forest bath of some kind.

How much cleaner we would feel if we took these baths as often as we took hot showers. How much more present we would be if we *saw* what was around us.

Bathe is an important word. There is something about water, isn't there? The sight of it. The sound of it. The feel of it. Those seeking stillness could find worse ways to wash away the troubles and turbulence of the world than actual water. A dive into a nearby river. The bubbling fountain in a Zen garden. The reflecting pool of a memorial for those we have lost. Even, in a pinch, a sound machine loaded with the noises of the crashing ocean waves.

To those reeling from trauma or a stressful profession as much as to those suffering from the ennui of modern life, Professor John Stilgoe has simple advice:

> Get out now. Not just outside, but beyond the trap of the programmed electronic age so gently closing around so many people. . . . Go outside, move deliberately, then relax, slow down, look around. Do not jog. Do not run. . . .

Instead pay attention to everything that abuts the rural road, the city street, the suburban boulevard. Walk. Stroll. Saunter. Ride a bike and coast along a lot. Explore.

There is peace in this. It is always available to you.

Don't let the beauty of life escape you. See the world as the temple that it is. Let every experience be churchlike. Marvel at the fact that any of this exists—that *you* exist. Even when we are killing each other in pointless wars, even when we are killing ourselves with pointless work, we can stop and bathe in the beauty that surrounds us, always.

Let it calm you. Let it cleanse you.

ACCEPT A HIGHER POWER

Mediocrity knows nothing higher than itself.

—ARTHUR CONAN DOYLE

For nearly a hundred years, one of the most difficult steps in the twelve steps of "recovery" has not been producing a fearless moral inventory of one's failings or the making of amends. It's not admitting you have a problem, finding a sponsor, or attending meetings.

The step that many addicts—particularly the ones who fancy themselves *thinkers*—struggle with intensely is the acknowledgment of the existence of a *higher power*. They just don't want to admit that they "have come to believe a Power greater than themselves could restore them to sanity."

This seemingly simple step is hard, but not because the world has become increasingly secular since Alcoholics Anonymous's founding in 1935. In fact, one of the founders of AA was, in his words, a "militant agnostic." Acknowledging a higher power is difficult because submitting to anything other than their own desires is anathema to what one addict describes as the "pathological self-centeredness" of addiction.

"I don't believe in God" is the most common objection to Step 2. "There's no evidence of a higher power," they say. "Look at evolution. Look at science." Or they might question what the hell any of this has to do with sobriety anyway. Can't they just stop using drugs and follow the other steps? "What does religion or faith have to do with anything?"

These are perfectly reasonable questions. And yet they don't matter.

Because Step 2 isn't really about God. It's about *surrender*. It's about faith.

Remember, the only way to get over the willful will—the force that Awa Kenzo believed was causing everyone, not just addicts, to miss the targets we aim for—is to let go, at the deep, soul level.

While addiction is undoubtedly a biological disease, it is also, in a more practical sense, a process of becoming obsessed with one's own self and the primacy of one's urges and thoughts. Therefore, admitting that there is something bigger than you out there is an important breakthrough. It means an addict finally understands that they are not God, that they are not in control, and really never have been. By the way, *none* of us are.

The twelve-step process is not itself transformative. It's the decision to stop and to listen and to *follow* that does all the work.

If you really look at the teachings, Alcoholics Anonymous

doesn't say you have to believe in Jesus or go to church. Only that you accept "God as we understand him." That means that if you want to believe in Mother Earth, or Providence, or Destiny, or Fate, or Random Luck, that's up to you.

To the Stoics, their higher power was the *logos*—the path of the universe. They acknowledged fate and fortune and the power these forces had over them. And in acknowledging these higher powers, they accessed a kind of stillness and peace (most simply because it meant less fighting battles for control!) that helped them run empires, survive slavery or exile, and ultimately even face death with great poise. In Chinese philosophy, *dao*—the Way—is the natural order of the universe, the way of a higher spirit. The Greeks not only believed in many different gods, but also that individuals were accompanied by a *daemon,* a guiding spirit that led them to their destiny.

The Confucians believed in Tian, 天—a concept of heaven that guided us while we were here on earth and assigned us a role or purpose in life. The Hindus believed that Brahman was the highest universal reality. In Judaism, Yahweh (יהוה) is the word for Lord. Each of the major Native American tribes had their own word for the Great Spirit, who was their creator and guiding deity. Epicurus wasn't an atheist but rejected the idea of an overbearing or judgmental god. What deity would want the world to live in fear? Living in fear, he said, is incongruent with *ataraxia.*

When Krishna speaks of the "mind resting in the stillness of the prayer of Yoga," it is the same thing. The Christians believe that God is that source of stillness in our lives, which extended peace and comfort to us like a river. "Peace! Be still!" Jesus said to the sea, "and the wind ceased and there was a great calm."

There is no stillness to the mind that thinks of nothing but itself, nor will there ever be peace for the body and spirit that follow their every urge and value nothing but themselves.

The progress of science and technology is essential. But for many of us moderns, it has come at the cost of losing the capacity for awe and for acknowledging forces beyond our comprehension. It has deprived us of the ability to access spiritual stillness and piety.

Are we really to say that a simple peasant who piously believed in God, who worshipped daily in a beautiful cathedral that must have seemed a wondrous glory to the greatness of the Holy Spirit, was worse off than us because he or she lacked our technology or an understanding of evolution? If we told a Zen Buddhist from Japan in the twelfth century that in the future everyone could count on greater wealth and longer lives but that in most cases those gifts would be followed by a feeling of utter purposelessness and dissatisfaction, do you think they would want to trade places with us?

Because that doesn't sound like progress.

In his 1978 commencement address to the students of Harvard, Aleksandr Solzhenitsyn spoke of a modern world where all countries—capitalist and communist alike—had been pervaded by a "despiritualized and irreligious humanistic consciousness."

To such consciousness, man is the touchstone in judging everything on earth—imperfect man, who is never free of pride, self-interest, envy, vanity, and dozens of other defects. We are now experiencing the consequences of mistakes which had not been noticed at the beginning of the journey. On the way from the Renaissance to our days we have enriched our experience, but we have lost the concept of a Supreme Complete Entity which used to restrain our passions and our irresponsibility. We have placed too much hope in political and social reforms, only to find out that we were being deprived of our most precious possession: our spiritual life.

Realism is important. Pragmatism and scientism and skepticism are too. They all have their place. But still, you have to believe in *something*. You just have to. Or else everything is empty and cold.

The comedian Stephen Colbert survived a tragic childhood guided by a deep and earnest Catholic faith that he maintains to this day (teaching Sunday school well into his show business career). His mother, who bore the brunt of that tragedy when she lost her husband and two sons in a plane crash, was his example. "Try to look at this moment in the light of eternity," she would tell him. *Eternity.* Something bigger than us. Something bigger than we can possibly comprehend. Something longer than our tiny humanness naturally considers.

We could find a similar story for just about every faith.

It is probably not a coincidence that when one looks back at history and marvels at the incredible adversity and unimaginable difficulty that people made it through, you tend to find that they all had one thing in common: Some kind of belief in a higher deity. An anchor in their lives called faith. They believed an unfailing hand rested on the wheel, and that there was some deeper purpose or meaning behind their suffering even if they couldn't understand it. It's not a coincidence that the vast majority of people who did good in the world did too.

The reformer Martin Luther was called before a tribunal demanding that he recant his beliefs, on threat of denunciation and possibly death. He spent hours in prayer as he waited his turn to testify. He breathed in. He emptied his mind of worry and fear. He spoke. "I cannot and I will not retract, for it is unsafe for a Christian to speak against his conscience. Here I stand, I can do no other; so help me God. Amen."

Is it not interesting that the leaders who end up truly tested by turbulent times end up sincerely relying on some measure of faith and belief to get them through difficult times?

That was the story of Lincoln. Like many smart young people, he was an atheist early in life, but the trials of adulthood, especially the loss of his son and the horrors of the Civil War, turned him into a believer. Kennedy spent most of his life looking down on his parents' Catholicism . . . but you can bet he was praying as he stood up to the threat of nuclear annihilation.

Here I stand, I can do no other; so help me God.

Nihilism is a fragile strategy. It's always the nihilists who seem to go crazy or kill themselves when life gets hard. (Or, more recently, are so afraid of dying that they obsess about living forever.)

Why is that? Because the nihilist is forced to wrestle with the immense complexity and difficulty and potential emptiness of life (and death) with nothing but their own mind. This is a comically unfair mismatch.

Again, when nearly all the wise people of history agree, we should pause and reflect. It's next to impossible to find an ancient philosophical school that does not talk about a higher power (or higher powers). Not because they had "evidence" of its existence, but because they knew how powerful faith and belief were, how essential they were to the achievement of stillness and inner peace.

Fundamentalism is different. Epicurus was right—if God exists, why would they possibly want you to be afraid of them? And why would they care what clothes you wear or how many times you pay obeisance to them per day? What interest would they have in monuments or in fearful pleas for forgiveness? At the purest level, the only thing that matters to any father or mother—or any creator—is that their children find peace, find meaning, find purpose. They certainly did not put us on this planet so we could judge, control, or kill each other.

But this is not the problem most of us are dealing with. Instead we struggle with skepticism, with an egotism that puts us at the center of the universe. That's why the philosopher Nassim

Taleb's line is so spot on: *It's not that we need to believe that God is great, only that God is greater than us.*

Even if we are the products of evolution and randomness, does this not take us right back to the position of the Stoics? As subjects to the laws of gravity and physics, are we not already accepting a higher, inexplicable power?

We have so little control of the world around us, so many inexplicable events created this world, that it works out almost exactly the same way as if there was a god.

The point of this belief is in some ways to override the mind. To quiet it down by putting it in true perspective. The common language for accepting a higher power is about "letting [Him or Her or It] into your heart." That's it. This is about rejecting the tyranny of our intellect, of our immediate observational experience, and accepting something bigger, something beyond ourselves.

Perhaps you're not ready to do that, to let anything into your heart. That's okay. There's no rush.

Just know that this step is open to you. It's waiting. And it will help restore you to sanity when you're ready.

ENTER RELATIONSHIPS

There is no enjoying the possession of anything
valuable unless one has someone to share it with.

—SENECA

After his first marriage fell apart in the 1960s, the song-writer Johnny Cash moved from Southern California to Tennessee. On the first night in his new home, lonely and depressed, he began to pace the length of the ground floor. It was an enormous house, all but empty of furniture, wedged between a steep hill on one side and Old Hickory Lake on the other. As he walked from one end of the floor to the other, from the hill to the lake, he began to feel, almost frantically, that something was absent.

What's missing? he thought. *Where is it?* he repeated, over and over again. Had he forgotten to pack something? Was there something he needed to do? What wasn't right?

Suddenly, it came to him. It wasn't *something,* it was *someone.*

His young daughter, Rosanne. She wasn't there. She was in California with her mother. A house without family is no home. Johnny Cash stopped, began to shout her name as loud as he could, and fell to the ground and wept.

In some sense, it might seem like that is exactly the kind of anguish that philosophy helps us avoid through the cultivation of detachment and indifference to other people. If you don't make yourself dependent on anyone, if you don't make yourself vulnerable, you can never lose them and you'll never be hurt.

There are people who try to live this way. They take vows of chastity or solitude, or, conversely, try to reduce relationships to their most transactional or minimal form. Or because they have been hurt before, they put up walls. Or because they are so talented, they dedicate themselves exclusively to their work. It is necessary, they say, for they have a higher calling. The Buddha, for instance, walked out on his wife and young son without even saying goodbye, because enlightenment was more important.

Yes, every individual should make the life choices that are right for them. Still, there is something deeply misguided—and terribly sad—about a solitary existence.

It is true that relationships take time. They also expose and distract us, cause pain, and cost money.

We are also nothing without them.

Bad relationships are common, and good relationships are hard. Should that surprise us? Being close to and connecting with other people challenges every facet of our soul.

Especially when our inner child is there, acting out. Or we

are pulled away by lust and desire. Or our selfishness makes little room for another person.

The temptations of the world lead us astray, and our tempers hurt the ones we love.

A good relationship requires us to be virtuous, faithful, present, empathetic, generous, open, and willing to be a part of a larger whole. It requires, in order to create growth, real surrender.

No one would say that's easy.

But rising to this challenge—even attempting to rise to it—transforms us . . . if we let it.

Anyone can be rich or famous. Only you can be *Dad* or *Mom* or *Daughter* or *Son* or *Soul Mate* to the people in your life.

Relationships come in many forms. Mentor. Protégé. Parent. Child. Spouse. Best friend.

And even if, as some have argued, maintaining these relationships reduces a person's material or creative success, might the trade be worth it?

"Who is there who would wish to be surrounded by all the riches in the world and enjoy every abundance in life and yet not love or be loved by anyone?" was Cicero's question some two thousand years ago. It echoes on down to us, still true forever.

Even paragons of stillness struggle with what connection and dependence might mean for their careers. Marina Abramović gave a controversial interview in 2016 where she explained her choice to stay single and not to have children. That would have been a disaster for her art, she said. "One only has limited energy in the body, and I would have had to divide it."

Nonsense.

Nonsense that has been internalized by countless driven and ambitious people.

How well they would do to take even a cursory look at history and literature. German chancellor Angela Merkel has been tirelessly supported by her husband, a man she has described as vital to her success, and upon whose advice she depends. Gertrude Stein was tirelessly supported by her life partner, Alice B. Toklas. Madame Curie was long cynical about love, until she met Pierre, whom she married and with whom she collaborated and ultimately won a Nobel Prize. What about the dedication to *On Liberty,* John Stuart Mill's greatest work, where he calls his wife "inspirer, and in part the author, of all that is best in my writings"? The rapper J. Cole has said that the best thing he ever did as a musician was become a husband and a father. "There was no better decision I could have made," he said, "than the discipline I put on myself of having responsibility, having another human being—my wife—that I have to answer to."

Stillness is best not sought alone. And, like success, it is best when shared. We all need someone who understands us better than we understand ourselves, if only to keep us honest.

Relationships are not a productivity hack, though understanding that love and family are not incompatible with *any* career is a breakthrough. It is also true that the single best decision you can make in life, professionally *and* personally, is to find a partner who complements and supports you and makes you better and for whom you do the same. Conversely, choosing partners and friends who do the opposite endangers both career and happiness.

Life without relationships, focused solely on accomplishment, is empty and meaningless (in addition to being precarious and fragile). A life solely about work and doing is terribly out of balance; indeed, it requires constant motion and busyness to keep from falling apart.

The writer Philip Roth spoke proudly late in life about living alone and being responsible or committed to nothing but his own needs. He once told an interviewer that his lifestyle meant he could be always on call for his work, never having to wait for or on anyone but himself. "I'm like a doctor and it's an emergency room," he said. "And I'm the emergency."

That may be just about the saddest thing a person has ever said without realizing it.

Dorothy Day, the Catholic nun, spoke of the *long loneliness* we all experience, a form of suffering to which the only solution is love and relationships. And yet some people inflict this on themselves on purpose! They deprive themselves of the heaven that is having someone to care about and to care about you in return.

The world hurls at us so many hurricanes. Those who have decided to go through existence as an island are the most exposed and the most ravaged by the storms and whirlwinds.

On September 11, 2001, Brian Sweeney was a passenger trapped on hijacked United Airlines Flight 175, which was heading straight for the South Tower of the World Trade Center. He called his wife from one of the plane's seatback phones to say that things were not looking good. "I want you to know that I absolutely love you," he told her voicemail. "I want you to do good, have good times, same with my parents. I'll see you when you get here."

Imagine the terror of that moment, yet when you hear his voice coming through the phone, not a trace of fear. The same serene calmness is found in the final letter written by Major Sullivan Ballou in 1861 in the days before his Federal regiment marched out to Manassas, Virginia, where he seemed to know for certain that he would die in battle. "Sarah," he wrote, "my love for you is deathless. It seems to bind me with mighty cables, that nothing but Omnipotence can break; and yet, my love of country comes over me like a strong wind, and bears me irresistibly on with all those chains, to the battlefield. The memories of all the blissful moments I have spent with you come crowding over me, and I feel most deeply grateful to God and you, that I have enjoyed them so long."

Fyodor Dostoevsky once described his wife, Anna, as a rock on which he could lean and rest, a wall that would not let him fall and protected him from the cold. There is no better description of love, between spouses or friends or parent and child, than that. Love, Freud said, is the *great educator*. We learn when we give it. We learn when we get it. We get closer to stillness through it.

Like all good education, it is not easy. Not easy at all.

It's been said that the word "love" is spelled T-I-M-E. It is also spelled W-O-R-K and S-A-C-R-I-F-I-C-E and D-I-F-F-I-C-U-L-T-Y, C-O-M-M-I-T-M-E-N-T, and occasionally M-A-D-N-E-S-S.

But it is always punctuated by *R-E-W-A-R-D*. Even ones that end.

The stillness of two people on a porch swing, the stillness of a hug, of a final letter, of a memory, a phone call before a plane crash, of paying it forward, of teaching, of learning, of being *together*.

The notion that isolation, that total self-driven focus, will get you to a supreme state of enlightenment is not only incorrect, it misses the obvious: Who will even care that you did all that? Your house might be quieter without kids and it might be easier to work longer hours without someone waiting for you at the dinner table, but it is a hollow quiet and an empty ease.

To go through our days looking out for no one but ourselves? To think that we can or must do this all alone? To accrue mastery or genius, wealth or power, solely for our own benefit? What is the point?

By ourselves, we are a fraction of what we can be.

By ourselves, something is missing, and, worse, we *feel* that in our bones.

Which is why stillness requires other people; indeed, it is *for* other people.

CONQUER YOUR ANGER

He that is slow to anger is better than the mighty; and
he that ruleth his spirit than he that taketh a city.

—PROVERBS 16:32

In 2009, Michael Jordan was inducted into the Basketball
Hall of Fame. It was the crowning achievement of a mag-
nificent career that included six NBA championships, fourteen
trips to the All-Star Game, two Olympic gold medals, and the
highest scoring average in the history of the sport.

Ascending the stage in a silver suit, with his trademark single
hoop earring, Michael was in tears from the start. He joked that
his initial plan had been to simply accept the honor, say thank
you, and then return to his seat. But he couldn't do it.

He had something he wanted to say.

What ensued was a strange and surreal speech where Michael Jordan, a man with nothing to prove and so much to be

thankful for, spent nearly a half hour listing and responding to every slight he'd ever received in his career. Standing at the podium, in a tone that feigned lightheartedness but was clearly deeply felt and deeply angry, he complained of media naysayers, and of how his college coach at North Carolina, Dean Smith, had not touted him as a promising freshman in a 1981 interview with *Sports Illustrated*. He even noted how much he spent on tickets for his children for the ceremony.

After a few sweet remarks about his family, Jordan pointed out a man in the audience named Leroy Smith, the player who had gotten Michael's playing time some thirty-one years earlier. Jordan knew that many people thought that his getting cut in high school was a myth. "Leroy Smith was a guy when I got cut he made the team—on the varsity team—and he's here tonight," Michael explained. "He's still the same six-foot-seven guy—he's not any bigger—probably his game is about the same. But he started the whole process with me, because when he made the team and I didn't, I wanted to prove not just to Leroy Smith, not just to myself, but to the coach that picked Leroy over me, I wanted to make sure you understood—you made a mistake, dude."

It's a remarkable window into Michael's mind, for several reasons. First off, it shows how he had twisted a predictable decision into a major slight about his self-worth. Jordan hadn't been *cut* from any team. He and Leroy had both tried out for a single spot on the varsity team. One had made it. That's not getting "cut"—it's expected that an underclassman won't make the senior class team! Nor had it even been a referendum on his abilities. Leroy was six foot seven. Michael was five foot eleven at the time. It's also so childishly self-absorbed. As if Leroy and his coach weren't their own people, a teammate he could have been happy for, a mentor he could have learned from.

Yet for decades Jordan had chosen to be mad about it.

It's almost palpable how uncomfortable the audience grew as the complaints grew increasingly personal and petty. At one point, Michael mentioned a remark that Jerry Krause made in 1997, supposedly saying that "organizations win championships," not just individual players. Sneering at this minor—but true—observation of the Bulls' general manager, Michael explained that he had specifically not invited Krause to the ceremony in retaliation. He mentioned with pride the time he kicked Pat Riley, the coach of the Lakers, the Knicks, and later the Heat, out of a hotel suite in Hawaii because he wanted to stay in it.

Friends understood that Michael had intended for the speech to be helpful. Instead of uttering a few platitudes, he wanted to show just what it was that created a winning mentality. How tough it was. What it took. He wanted to illustrate how productive anger could be—how as a player each time he was slighted, each time he was underestimated, each time someone didn't do things *his* way, it made him a better player.

The problem is that he delivered almost the exact opposite

message.* Yes, he had shown that anger was powerful fuel. He had also shown just how likely it is to blow up all over yourself and the people around you.

There were undoubtedly moments in Jordan's career when resentment had worked to his advantage and made him play better. It was also a form of madness that hurt him and his teammates (like Steve Kerr and Bill Cartwright and Kwame Brown, whom he physically fought or berated). It had cruelly wrecked the self-confidence of competitors like Muggsy Bogues ("Shoot it, you fucking midget," he'd told his five-foot-three opponent while giving him a free shot in the '95 playoffs). In training camp in 1989, Jordan threw a vicious elbow that knocked a rookie named Matt Brust unconscious, and ended the man's hopes of an NBA career.

Jordan's game was beautiful, but his conduct was often savage and ugly.

Was anger really the secret of Michael Jordan's championships? (Did his anger get him that varsity spot he wanted the next year . . . or did growing four inches help?) Could it have actually been a parasitic by-product that prevented him from enjoying what he accomplished? (Tom Brady wins a lot without being mean or angry.)

If history is any indication, leaders, artists, generals, and

---

*Everyone, that is, but Tiger Woods, who told his golf coach, "I get it. That's what it takes to be as good as MJ. You are always finding ways to get yourself going." It was also Jordan who was partly responsible for introducing Woods to the gambler lifestyle in Las Vegas.

athletes who are driven primarily by anger not only tend to fail over a long enough timeline, but they tend to be miserable even if they don't. It was without a hint of self-awareness that Nixon—who hated Ivy Leaguers, hated reporters, hated Jews and so many other people—said these high-minded words to his loyal staffers in his last hours in the White House: "Always remember, others may hate you, but those who hate you don't win unless you hate them. And then you destroy yourself."

He was right. His own downfall proved it.

The leaders we truly respect, who stand head and shoulders above the rest, have been motivated by more than anger or hate. From Pericles to Martin Luther King Jr., we find that great leaders are fueled by love. Country. Compassion. Destiny. Reconciliation. Mastery. Idealism. Family.

Even in Jordan's case, he was most inspiring not when he was trying to dominate someone but when he was playing for the *love of the game*. And his rings all came under the tutelage and coaching of Phil Jackson, known in basketball as the "Zen Master."

It would be unfair to say that Michael Jordan was as tortured or pained as Richard Nixon, or that he was utterly without joy or happiness. Still, the speech is striking. He had locked so much anger and pain up in a closet in his soul that, at some point, the doors burst open and the mess poured out.

Seneca's argument was that anger ultimately blocks us from whatever goal we are trying to achieve. While it might temporarily help us achieve success in our chosen field, in the long run it is destructive. How excellent is excellence if it doesn't make us feel content, happy, fulfilled? It's a strange bargain that winning, as Jordan illustrated, should require us to constantly think of the times we were made to feel like a loser. The reward for becoming world-class should not be that you are a walking open wound, a trigger that's pulled a thousand times a day.

And what of the people whose anger is more of a hot flash than a slow burn? Seneca once more:

> There is no more stupefying thing than anger, nothing more bent on its own strength. If successful, none more arrogant, if foiled, none more insane—since it's not driven back by weariness even in defeat, when fortune removes its adversary it turns its teeth on itself.

Anger is counterproductive. The flash of rage here, an outburst at the incompetence around us there—this may generate a moment of raw motivation or even a feeling of relief, but we rarely tally up the frustration they cause down the road. Even if we apologize or the good we do outweighs the harm, damage remains—and consequences follow. The person we yelled at is now an enemy. The drawer we broke in a fit is now a constant annoyance. The high blood pressure, the overworked heart, inching us closer to the attack that will put us in the hospital or the grave.

We can pretend we didn't hear or see things that were meant to offend. We can move slowly, giving extreme emotions time to dissipate. We can avoid situations and people (and even entire cities) where we know we tend to get upset or pissed off. When we feel our temper rising up, we need to look for insertion points (the space between stimulus and response). Points where we can get up and walk away. When we can say, "I am getting upset by this and I would like not to lose my cool about it," or "This doesn't matter and I'm not going to hold on to it." We can think even of the Mr. Rogers verse about anger:

> It's great to be able to stop
> When you've planned a thing that's wrong,
> And be able to do something else instead
> And think this song

As silly as those lyrics might seem to us in the moment, as our temper is boiling over, are they any worse than a grown adult losing their cool over some minor slight? Are they worse than saying or doing something that will haunt us, possibly forever?

Not that regret minimization is the point of managing our temper, although it is an important factor. The point is that people who are driven by anger are not happy. They are not still. They get in their own way. They shorten legacies and short-circuit their goals.

The Buddhists believed that anger was a kind of tiger within us, one whose claws tear at the body that houses it. To have a chance at stillness—and the clear thinking and big-picture view that defines it—we need to tame that tiger before it kills us. We have to beware of desire, but *conquer* anger, because anger hurts not just ourselves but many other people as well. Although the Stoics are often criticized for their rigid rules and discipline, that is really what they are after: an inner dignity and propriety that protects them and their loved ones from dangerous passions.

Clearly, basketball was a refuge for Michael Jordan, a game he loved and that provided him much satisfaction. But in the pursuit of winning and domination, he also turned it into a kind of raw, open wound, one that seemed to never stop bleeding or cause pain. One that likely cost him additional years of winning, as well as the simple enjoyment of a special evening at the Hall of Fame in Springfield, Massachusetts.

That can't be what you want. That can't be who you want to be.

Which is why we must choose to drive out anger and replace it with love and gratitude—and purpose. Our stillness depends on our ability to slow down and choose *not* to be angry, to run on different fuel. Fuel that helps us win and build, and doesn't hurt other people, our cause, or our chance at peace.

ALL IS ONE

All that you behold, that which comprises both god
and man, is one—we are the parts of one great body.

—SENECA

In 1971, the astronaut Edgar Mitchell was launched into space.
From 239,000 miles up, he stared down at the tiny blue marble that is our planet and felt something wash over him. It was,
he said later, "an instant global consciousness, a people orienta-
tion, an intense dissatisfaction with the state of the world, and a
compulsion to do something about it."

So far away, the squabbles of the earth suddenly seemed
petty. The differences between nations and races fell away, the
false urgency of trivial problems disappeared. What was left
was a sense of connectedness and compassion for everyone and
everything.

All Mitchell could think of, when he looked at the planet
from the quiet, weightless cabin of his spaceship, was grabbing

every selfish politician by the neck and pulling them up there to point and say, "Look at that, you son of a bitch."

Not that he was angry. On the contrary, he was the calmest and most serene he'd ever been. He wanted them—the leaders, the people who are supposed to work on behalf of their fellow citizens—to have the same realization he was having: the realization that we are all one, that we are all in this together, and that this fact is the *only* thing that truly matters.

The Christian word for this term is *agape*. It is the ecstasy of love from a higher power, the sheer luck and good fortune of being made in that image. If you've ever seen the Bernini statue of Saint Teresa, you can get a sense of this feeling in the physical form. The caring smile of an angel thrusting an arrow into Teresa's heart. The rays of golden sun shooting down from heaven. Teresa's closed eyes and partly opened mouth, realizing, *knowing* the depth of love and connection that exists for her.

Whether it comes from the perspective of space, a religious epiphany, or the silence of meditation, the understanding that we are all connected—*that we are all one*—is a transformative experience.

Such quiet peace follows this . . . such stillness.

With it, we lose the selfishness and self-absorption at the root of much of the disturbance in our lives.

The Greeks spoke of *sympatheia,* the kind of mutual interdependence and relatedness of all things, past, present, and future. They believed that each person on this planet had an important role to play, and should be respected for it. John Cage came to understand something similar as he embraced his own quirky, unique style of music—like that four-minute-and-thirty-three-second song of silence—rather than trying to be like everyone else. "That one sees that the human race as one person," he wrote, with each of us as an individual part of one single body, "enables him to see that originality is necessary, for there is no need for eye to do what hand does so well."

The truly philosophical view is that not only is originality necessary, but *everyone* is necessary. Even the people you don't like. Even the ones who really piss you off. Even the people wasting their lives, cheating, or breaking the rules are part of the larger equation. We can appreciate—or at least sympathize with—them, rather than try to fight or change them.

Robert Greene, known for his amoral study of power and seduction, actually writes in his book *The Laws of Human Nature* about the need to practice *mitfreude,* the active wishing of goodwill to other people, instead of *schadenfreude,* the active wishing of ill will. We can make an active effort to practice forgiveness, especially to those who might have caused those inner-child wounds we have worked to heal. We can seek understanding with those we disagree with. *Tout comprendre c'est tout pardonner.* To understand all is to forgive all. To love all is to be at peace with all, including yourself.

Take something you care about deeply, a possession you cherish, a person you love, or an experience that means a lot to you. Now take that feeling, that radiating warmth that comes up when you think about it, and consider how *every single person,* even murderers on death row, even the jerk who just shoved you in the supermarket, has that same feeling about something in their lives. Together, you share that. Not only do you share it, but you share it with everyone who has ever lived. It connects you to Cleopatra and Napoleon and Frederick Douglass.

You can do the same with your pain. As bad as you might feel in a given moment, this too is a shared feeling, a connection with others. The man stepping outside to take a walk after an argument with his spouse. The mother worrying about her child, the one who seems to always be in trouble. The merchant stressing over where the money will come from—*How will I keep going?* Two siblings grieving the loss of a parent. The average citizen following the news, hoping their country will avoid an unnecessary war.

No one is alone, in suffering or in joy. Down the street, across the ocean, in another language, someone else is experiencing nearly the exact same thing. It has always been and always will be thus.

You can even use this to connect more deeply with yourself and your own life. The moon you're looking at tonight is the same moon you looked at as a scared young boy or girl, it's the same you'll look at when you're older—in moments of joy and in pain—and it's the same that your children will look at in their own moments and their own lives.

When you step back from the enormity of your own immediate experience—whatever it is—you are able to see the experience of others and either connect with them or lessen the intensity of your own pain. We are all strands in a long rope that stretches back countless generations and ties together every person in every country on every continent. We are all thinking and feeling the same things, we are all made of and motivated by the same things. We are all stardust. And no one needs this understanding more than the ambitious or the creative, since they live so much in their own heads and in their own bubble.

Finding the universal in the personal, and the personal in the universal, is not only the secret to art and leadership and even entrepreneurship, it is the secret to centering oneself. It both turns down the volume of noise in the world and tunes one in to the quiet wavelength of wisdom that sages and philosophers have long been on.

This connectedness and universality does not need to stop at our fellow man. The philosopher Martha Nussbaum recently pointed out the narcissism of the human obsession with what it means to be human. A better, more open, more vulnerable, more connected question is to ask what it means to be alive, or to exist, *period*. As she wrote:

> We share a planet with billions of other sentient beings, and they all have their own complex ways of being whatever they are. All of our fellow animal creatures, as Aristotle observed long ago, try to stay alive and reproduce more of their kind. All of them perceive. All of them

desire. And most move from place to place to get what they want and need.

We share much of our DNA with these creatures, we breathe the same air, we walk on the same land and swim in the same oceans. We are inextricably intertwined with each other—as are our fates.

The less we are convinced of our exceptionalism, the greater ability we have to understand and contribute to our environment, the less blindly driven we are by our own needs, the more clearly we can appreciate the needs of those around us, the more we can appreciate the larger ecosystem of which we are a part.

Peace is when we realize that victory and defeat are almost identical spots on one long spectrum. Peace is what allows us to take joy in the success of others and to let them take joy in our own. Peace is what motivates a person to be good, to treat every other living thing well, because they understand that it is a way to treat themselves well.

We are one big collective organism engaged in one endless project together. We are one.

We are the same.

Still, too often we forget it, and we forget ourselves in the process.

ON TO WHAT'S NEXT . . .

Very few go astray who comport themselves with restraint.

—CONFUCIUS

L'*essentiel est invisible pour les yeux.*
What's essential is invisible to the eye.

The quote that hung on Fred Rogers's wall was actually only a partial quote. The rest appears in *The Little Prince,* the beautiful and surreal children's book by the French aviator and World War II hero Antoine de Saint-Exupéry. In it, the fox tells the little boy, "Here is my secret. It is very simple: It is only with the heart that one can see rightly, what is essential is invisible to the eye."

First, we sought mental clarity. But quickly we realized that the soul must be in equally good order if we wish to achieve stillness. In concert with each other—clarity in the mind and in the soul—we find both excellence and unbreakable tranquility. It is with the *heart* and soul that we are able to surface important things that the eyes need to see.

Examining our souls is not as easy as clearing our minds, you'll find. It requires that we peel back what the writer Mark Manson has called the "self-awareness onion" and take responsibility for our own emotions and impulses. Anyone who's done it can tell you that tears and onions often go together.

But it's precisely this soft stuff—getting in touch with ourselves, finding balance and meaning, cultivating virtue—that the volleyball champion Kerri Walsh Jennings has said makes her such a killer on the court.

Some ancient traditions have held that the soul is in the belly, which is fitting for two reasons. Because we've just been through the *belly of the beast* part of our journey, and because it sets up where we go next.

Stillness isn't merely an abstraction—something we only think about or feel. It's also real. It's *in our bodies.* Seneca warned us not to "suppose that the soul is at peace when the body is still." Vice versa. Lao Tzu said that "movement is the foundation of stillness."

What follows then is the final domain of stillness. The literal form that *our form* takes in the course of day-to-day life. Our bodies (where, you must not forget, the heart and the brain are both located). The environment we put those bodies in. The habits and routines to which we subject that body.

A body that is overworked or abused is not only actually not still, it creates turbulence that ripples through the rest of our

ON TO WHAT'S NEXT . . .

lives. A mind that is overtaxed and ill-treated is susceptible to vice and corruption. A spoiled, lazy existence is the manifestation of spiritual emptiness. We can be active, we can be on the move, and still be still. Indeed, we have to be active for the stillness to have any meaning.

Life is hard. Fortune is fickle. We can't afford to be weak. We can't afford to be fragile. We must strengthen our bodies as the physical vessel for our minds and spirit, subject to the capriciousness of the physical world.

Which is why we now move on to this final domain of stillness—the body—and its place in the real world. In real life.

PART III

PART III

MIND · SPIRIT · **BODY**

We are all sculptors and painters, and our material is
our own flesh and blood and bones.

—HENRY DAVID THOREAU

THE DOMAIN OF THE BODY

Winston Churchill had a productive life.

He first saw combat at age twenty-one, and wrote his first bestselling book about it not long after. By twenty-six, he'd been elected to public office and would serve in government for the next six and half decades. He'd write some ten million words and over forty books, paint more than five hundred paintings, and give some twenty-three hundred speeches in the course of his time on this planet. In between all that, he managed to hold the positions of minister of defense, first lord of the admiralty, chancellor of the exchequer, and of course, prime minister of Britain, where he helped save the world from the Nazi menace. Then, to top it off, he spent his twilight years fighting the totalitarian communist menace.

"It is a pushing age," Churchill wrote his mother as a young man, "and we must shove with the rest." It may well be that Winston Churchill was the greatest pusher in all of history. His life spanned the final cavalry charge of the British Empire, which he witnessed as a young war correspondent in 1898, and ended well into the nuclear age, indeed the space age, both of which he helped usher in. His first trip to America was on a steamship (to be introduced on stage by Mark Twain, no less), and his final one on a Boeing 707 that flew at 500 miles per hour. In between he saw two world wars, the invention of the car, radio, and rock and roll, and countless trials and triumphs.

Is there stillness to be found here? Could someone that active, so Herculean in their labors, who embraced so much strife and stress, ever be described as still, or at peace?

Strangely, yes.

As Paul Johnson, one of Churchill's best biographers, would write, "The balance he maintained between flat-out work and creative and restorative leisure is worth study by anyone holding a top position." Johnson as a seventeen-year-old, decades before his own career as a writer, met Churchill on the street and shouted to him, "Sir, to what do you attribute your success in life?"

Immediately, Churchill replied, "Conservation of energy. Never stand up when you can sit down, and never sit down when you can lie down."

Churchill conserved his energy so that he never shirked from a task, or backed down from a challenge. So that, for all this work and pushing, he never burned himself out or snuffed out the spark of joy that made life worth living. (Indeed, in addition to the importance of hard work, Johnson said the other four lessons from Churchill's remarkable life were to aim high; to never allow mistakes or criticism to get you down; to waste no energy on grudges, duplicity, or infighting; and to make room for joy.) Even during the war, Churchill never lost his sense of humor, never lost sight of what was beautiful in the world, and never became jaded or cynical.

Different traditions offer different prescriptions for the good life. The Stoics urged determination and iron self-will. The Epicureans preached relaxation and simple pleasures. The Christians spoke of saving mankind and glorifying God. The French, a certain *joie de vivre*. The happiest and most resilient of us manage to incorporate a little of each of these approaches into our lives, and that was certainly true of Churchill. He was a man of great discipline and passion. He was a soldier. He was a lover of books, a believer in glory and honor. A statesman, a literal bricklayer, and a painter. We are all worms, he once joked to a friend, simple organisms that eat and defecate and then die, but he liked to think of himself as a *glowworm*.

In addition to his impressive mental abilities and spiritual strength, Churchill was also an unexpected—given his portly frame—master of the third and final domain of stillness, the physical one.

Few would have predicted he would distinguish himself here. Born with a frail constitution, Churchill complained as a young man that he was "cursed with so feeble a body that I can hardly support the fatigues of the day." Yet like Theodore Roosevelt before him, he cultivated inside this frail body an indomitable soul and a determined mind that overcame his physical limitations.

It's a balance that everyone aspiring to sustained inner peace must strike. *Mens sana in corpore sano*—a strong mind in a strong body. Remember, when we say that someone "showed so much heart," we don't mean emotion. We mean they had tenacity and grit. The metaphor is actually misleading if you think about it. It's really the *spine*—the backbone of body—that's doing the work.

Young Churchill loved the written word, but, diverging from the traditional path of a writer, he didn't lock himself up with books in a dusty old library. He put his body into action. Serving in or observing three straight wars, he made his name chronicling the exploits of the empire, first as a war correspondent in South Africa during the Boer War, where he was taken prisoner in 1899 and barely escaped with his life.

In 1900, he was elected to his first political office. By age thirty-three, realizing that greatness was impossible alone, he committed his body to another. He married his wife, Clementine, a brilliant, calming influence who balanced out many of his worst traits. It was one of the great marriages of the age—they called each other "Pug" and "Cat"—marked by true affection and love. "My ability to persuade my wife to marry me," he said, was "quite my most brilliant achievement. . . . Of course, it would have been impossible for any ordinary man to have got through what I had to go through in peace and war without the devoted aid of what we call, in England, one's better half."

As busy and ambitious as Churchill was—as much of a pusher as he was—he was rarely frantic and did not tolerate disorganization. It almost ruins the fun to learn that Churchill's infamous bons mots and one-liners were in fact well-practiced and rehearsed. No one knew the effort that went into them, he said, nor the effort that went into making them look effortless. "Every night," he said, "I try myself by court martial to see if I have done anything effective during the day. I don't mean just pawing the ground—anyone can go through the motions—but something really effective."

As a writer, he was gaspingly productive. While holding political office, Churchill managed to publish seven books between 1898 and the end of World War I alone. How did he do it? How did he manage to pull so much out of himself? The simple answer: physical routine.

Each morning, Churchill got up around eight and took his first bath, which he entered at 98 degrees and had cranked up to 104 while he sat (and occasionally somersaulted) in the water. Freshly bathed, he would spend the next two hours reading. Then he responded to his daily mail, mostly pertaining to his political duties. Around noon he'd stop in to say hello to his wife for the first time—believing all his life that the secret to a happy marriage was that spouses should not see each other before noon. Then he tackled whatever writing project he was working on— likely an article or a speech or a book. By early afternoon he would be writing at a fantastic clip and then abruptly stop for lunch (which he would finally dress for). After lunch, he would go for a walk around Chartwell, his estate in the English countryside, feeding his swans and fish—to him the most important and enjoyable part of the day. Then he would sit on the porch and take in the air, thinking and musing. For inspiration and serenity he might recite poetry to himself. At 3 p.m., it was time for a two-hour nap. After the nap, it was family time and then a second bath before a late, seated and formal dinner (after 8 p.m.). After dinner and drinks, one more writing sprint before bed.

It was a routine he would stick to even on Christmas.

Churchill was a hard worker and a man of discipline—but like us, he was not perfect. He often worked more than he should have, usually because he spent more money than he needed to (and it produced a fair bit of writing that would have better remained unpublished). Churchill was impetuous, liked to gamble, and was prone to overcommit. It wasn't from the tireless execution of his wartime duties that he was inspired to depict himself once, in a drawing, as a pig carrying a twenty-thousand-pound weight. It was his indulgences that produced that.

Nor was his life an endless series of triumphs. Churchill made many mistakes, usually lapses of judgment that came from a mind fried by stress. Thus, he emerged from World War I with a mixed record. His service in the wartime administration had been marked by some major failures, but he had redeemed himself by resigning and serving on the front lines with the Royal Scots Fusiliers. After the war, he was called back to serve as secretary of state for war and air and then secretary of state for the colonies.

The mid-1920s saw Churchill serving as chancellor of the exchequer (a position in which he was in way over his head), while having also signed a contract to produce a six-volume, three-thousand-page account of the war, titled *The World Crisis*. Left to his own devices, he might have tried to white-knuckle this incredible workload. But those around him saw the toll that his responsibilities were taking and, worried about burnout, urged him to find a hobby that might offer him a modicum of pleasure and enjoyment and rest. "Do remember what I said about resting from current problems," Prime Minister Stanley Baldwin wrote to him. "A big year will soon begin and much depends on your keeping fit."

In typical Churchillian fashion, he chose an unexpected form of leisure: bricklaying. Taught the craft by two employees at Chartwell, he immediately fell in love with the slow, methodical process of mixing mortar, troweling, and stacking bricks. Unlike his other professions, writing and politics, bricklaying didn't wear down his body, it invigorated him. Churchill could lay as many as ninety bricks an hour. As he wrote to the prime minister in 1927, "I have had a delightful month building a cottage and dictating a book: 200 bricks and 2000 words a day." (He also spent several hours a day on his ministerial duties.) A friend observed how good it was for Churchill to get down on the ground and interact with the earth. This was also precious time he spent with his youngest daughter, Sarah, who dutifully carried the bricks for her father as his cute and well-loved apprentice.

A dark moment in World War I had inspired another hobby—oil painting. He was introduced to it by his sister-in-law, who,

STILLNESS IS THE KEY

sensing that Churchill was a steaming kettle of stress, handed him a small kit of paints and brushes her young children liked to play with. In a little book titled *Painting as a Pastime,* Churchill spoke eloquently of a reliance on new activities that use other parts of our minds and bodies to relieve the areas where we are overworked. "The cultivation of a hobby and new forms of interest is therefore a policy of first importance to a public man," he wrote. "To be really happy and really safe, one ought to have at least two or three hobbies, and they must all be real."

Churchill was not a particularly good painter (his bricklaying was often corrected by professionals too), but even a glance at his pictures reveals how much he enjoyed himself as he worked. It's palpable in the brushstrokes. "Just to paint is great fun," he would say. "The colors are lovely to look at and delicious to squeeze out." Early on, Churchill was advised by a well-known painter never to hesitate in front of the canvas (that is to say, *overthink*), and he took it to heart. He wasn't intimidated or discouraged by his lack of skill (only this could explain the audacity it took for him to add a mouse to a priceless Peter Paul Rubens painting that hung in one of the prime minister's residences). Painting was about expression of joy for Churchill. It was *leisure,* not work.

Painting, like all good hobbies, taught the practitioner to be present. "This heightened sense of observation of Nature," he wrote, "is one of the chief delights that have come to me through trying to paint." He had lived for forty years on planet Earth consumed by his work and his ambition, but through painting, his perspective and perception grew much sharper. Forced to slow down to set up his easel, to mix his paints, to wait for them to dry, he *saw* things he would have previously blown right past.

This was a skill that he actively cultivated—increasing his mental awareness by way of physical exercises. Churchill started going to museums to look at paintings, then he'd wait a day and try to re-create them from memory. Or he'd try to capture a landscape he had seen after he had left it. (This was similar to his habit of reciting poetry aloud.) "Painting challenged his intellect, appealed to his sense of beauty and proportion, unleashed his creative impulse, and . . . brought him peace," remarked his lifelong friend Violet Bonham Carter. It was also, she said, the only thing Churchill ever did silently. His other daughter, Mary, observed that painting and manual labor "were the sovereign antidotes to the depressive element in his nature." Churchill was happy because he got out of his own head and put his body to work.

How necessary this turned out to be, because in 1929 his stunning political career suddenly came to what appeared to be an ignominious end. Driven from political life, Churchill spent a decade in pseudo-exile at Chartwell, while Neville Chamberlain and a generation of British politicians appeased the growing threat of Fascism in Europe.

Life does that to us. It kicks our ass. Everything we work for can be taken away. All our powers can be rendered impotent in a moment. What follows this is not just an issue of spirit or the mind, it's a real physical question: *What do you do with your time? How do you handle the stress of the whiplash?*

Marcus Aurelius's answer was that in these situations one must "love the discipline you know and let it support you." In 1915, reeling from the failure of the Gallipoli campaign, Churchill wrote of feeling like a "sea-beast fished up from the depths, or a diver too suddenly hoisted, my veins threatened to burst from the fall in pressure. I had great anxiety and no means of relieving it; I had vehement convictions and small power to give effect to them." It was then that he picked up painting, and in 1929, experiencing a similar loss in cabin pressure, he returned to his discipline and his hobbies for relief and for reflection.

Churchill didn't know it in the middle of the 1930s, but being out of power during Germany's rearmament was exactly the right place to be. It would take real strength to stay there, to not fight his way back in, but if he had, he would have been sullied by the incompetence of his peers in the government. Churchill was likely one of the only British leaders to take the time to sit through and digest Hitler's *Mein Kampf* (if Chamberlain had, perhaps Hitler could have been stopped sooner). This time allowed Churchill to actively pursue his writing and radio careers, which made him a beloved celebrity in America (and primed the country for its eventual alliance with Britain). He spent time with his goldfish and his children and his oils.

Also, he had to wait. For the first time in his life, excepting those afternoons on the porch, he had to do *nothing*.

Would Churchill have been the outsider called back to lead Britain in its finest hour had he allowed the indignity of his political exile to overwhelm his mind, burrow into his soul, and compel him to fight his way back into the limelight in those years? Could he have had the energy and strength at age sixty-six to put the country on his back and *lead* without that supposedly "lost" decade? If he had kept up his breakneck pace?

Almost certainly not.

Churchill himself would write that every prophet must be forced into the wilderness—where they undergo solitude, deprivation, reflection, and meditation. It's from this physical ordeal he said that "psychic dynamite" is made. When Churchill was recalled, he was ready. He was rested. He could see what no one else could or would. Everyone else cowered in fear of Hitler, but Churchill did not.

Instead, he fought. He stood alone. As he said to the House of Commons:

> Even though large tracts of Europe and many old and famous States have fallen or may fall into the grip of the Gestapo and all the odious apparatus of Nazi rule, we shall not flag or fail. We shall go on to the end, we shall fight in France, we shall fight on the seas and oceans, we shall fight with growing confidence and growing strength in the air, we shall defend our Island, whatever the cost may be, we shall fight on the beaches, we shall fight on the landing grounds, we shall fight in the fields and in the

streets, we shall fight in the hills; we shall never surrender, and even if, which I do not for a moment believe, this Island or a large part of it were subjugated and starving, then our Empire beyond the seas, armed and guarded by the British Fleet, would carry on the struggle, until, in God's good time, the New World, with all its power and might, steps forth to the rescue and the liberation of the old.

Churchill demanded equal courage from those in his own house. When asked by his daughter-in-law what they could possibly do if the Germans invaded Britain, he growled and replied, "You can always get a carving knife from the kitchen and take one with you, can't you?"

The British Empire had been responsible for despicable human rights violations, but Churchill knew irredeemable evil when he saw it, and its name was Nazism. Concentration camps and genocidal extermination still lay off in the future, but Churchill saw that no self-respecting leader, no country of virtue could make a deal with Hitler. Even if that was easier. Even if it might have protected Britain from invasion. At the same time, he was careful to manage the passions that war stirs up. "I hate nobody except Hitler," he said "and that is professional."

Churchill was an indefatigable workhorse from the day Britain declared war on Germany in 1939 until the end of the war in mid-1945. During the war, Clementine designed a special suit her husband could wear *and* sleep in. They were called his "siren

THE DOMAIN OF THE BODY

suits"—though the British public endearingly referred to them as his "rompers"—and they saved him precious minutes getting dressed, allowing him to grab much-needed naps.

So, yes, he was out of balance in those years, working 110-hour weeks, and hardly ever still. It has been estimated that he traveled 110,000 miles by air and sea and car between 1940 and 1943 alone. During the war, it was said that Churchill kept "less schedule than a forest fire and had less peace than a hurricane." But then again, he'd rested up for precisely this moment—and when it was an option, he did maintain his routine, even when he was living like a gopher in the underground bunker that was the Cabinet War Rooms. He didn't have much time for painting during the war—nor many chances to be out in nature—but when he could he did. (One is a beautiful painting of a North African sunset, which he drove an extra five hours to capture after the major war powers met at Casablanca.)

It is unlikely that any single individual has ever done more to save or advance the notions sacred to Eastern or Western civilization. And how was Churchill rewarded for these labors, for all that he had done?

In 1945, he was pushed out of office. Upon hearing the news, Clementine attempted to console him by saying, "Perhaps this is a blessing in disguise." "It must be very well-disguised," Churchill replied. He was wrong. She was right. As usual.

Not only because it allowed Churchill to write his final set of memoirs, *The Second World War,* which firmly established and taught the lessons that have prevented the world from veering toward suicide since, but because it allowed him once again to rest up and balance himself. We can see photos of him painting in Marrakech in 1948, in the south of France in the 1950s. In all he would paint some 550 paintings in his lifetime, 145 of them after the war.

It was, in the end, a life of much struggle and sacrifice, a lot of it thankless and misunderstood. It was productive, but at a high personal cost. The same tasks and responsibilities would have burned out and burned through a dozen normal people.

"Was it worth it?" a wearied hero had asked in Churchill's only novel. "The struggle, the labor, the constant rush of affairs, the sacrifice of so many things that make life easy, or pleasant— for what?" He wrote that when he was young, when he had been busy and ambitious, and but not yet truly engaged in public service. In the future lay fifty-five years in Parliament, thirty-one years as a minister, and nine years as prime minister. The years ahead would show him the true meaning of life and what it meant to really fight for causes that mattered. He experienced both triumph and disaster. And by the end of his life, he came to know that it was all worth it—and certainly all of us alive today are grateful for those labors.

Indeed, Churchill's last words were confirmation of this fact:

The journey has been enjoyable and well worth making— once!

Epicurus once said that the wise will accomplish three

things in their life: leave written works behind them, be financially prudent and provide for the future, and cherish country living. That is to say, we will be reflective, we will be responsible and moderate, and we will find time to relax in nature. It cannot be said that Churchill did not do these things well (even granting that he did live it up when he could afford to).

We compare this description to the three words Aristotle used to describe the lives of slaves in his time: "Work, punishment, and food."

Which of these are we closer to in the modern world? Which of these is the path to happiness and stillness?

No one can afford to neglect the final domain in our journey to stillness. What we do with our bodies. What we put *in* our bodies. Where we dwell. What kind of routine and schedule we keep. How we find leisure and relief from the pressures of life.

If we are to be half as productive as Churchill, and manage to capture the same joy and zest and stillness that defined his life, there are traits we will need to cultivate. Each of us will need to:

- Rise above our physical limitations.
- Find hobbies that rest and replenish us.
- Develop a reliable, disciplined routine.
- Spend time getting active outdoors.
- Seek out solitude and perspective.
- Learn to sit—to do nothing when called for.
- Get enough sleep and rein in our workaholism.
- Commit to causes bigger than ourselves.

As they say, the body keeps score. If we don't take care of ourselves physically, if we don't align ourselves properly, it doesn't matter how strong we are mentally or spiritually.

This will take effort. Because we will not simply *think* our way to peace. We can't pray our soul into better condition. We've got to move and live our way there. It will take our body—our habits, our actions, our rituals, our self-care—to get our mind and our spirit in the right place, just as it takes our mind and spirit to get our body to the right place.

It's a trinity. A holy one. Each part dependent on the others.

SAY NO

The advantages of nonaction.
Few in the world attain these.

—THE DAODEJING

When Fabius was dispatched to lead the Roman legions against Hannibal, he did nothing. He did not attack. He did not race out to drive the terrifying invader out of Italy and back to Africa.

You might think this was a sign of weakness—certainly most of Rome did—but in fact, it was all part of Fabius's strategy. Hannibal was far from home, he was losing men to the elements and could not easily replace them. Fabius believed that if Rome just held out and did not engage in any costly battles, they would win.

But the mob couldn't handle that kind of deliberate restraint. *We're the strongest army in the world,* his critics said. *We don't sit around doing nothing when someone tries to attack us!* So while Fabius was away attending a religious ceremony, they pressured his commander Minucius to attack.

It did not go well. He ran straight into a trap. Fabius had to rush to his rescue. And even then, Minucius was hailed as a hero for *doing something,* while Fabius was labeled a coward for holding himself back. When his term ended, the Roman assemblies voted to abandon what is now known as a "Fabian strategy" of mostly avoiding battle and wearing Hannibal down, in favor of greater aggression and more action.

It didn't work. Only after the bloodbath at the Battle of Cannae, in which the Romans attacked Hannibal and lost nearly their entire army in a horrific rout, did people finally begin to understand Fabius's wisdom. Now they could see that what had looked like an excess of caution was in fact a brilliant method of warfare. He had been buying time and giving his opponent a chance to destroy himself. Only now—and not a moment too soon—were they ready to listen to him.

While most great Romans were given honorific titles that highlighted their great victories or accomplishments in foreign lands, Fabius was later given one that stands out: *Fabius Cunctator.*

The Delayer.

He was special for what he didn't do—for what he *waited* to do—and has stood as an important example to all leaders since. Especially the ones feeling pressure from themselves or their followers to be bold or take immediate action.

In baseball, you make a name for yourself by swinging for the fences. Particularly for players from small, poor countries, showing your power as a home run hitter is how you get noticed by scouts and coaches. As they say in the Dominican Republic, "You don't walk off the island." Meaning, you *hit* your way off.

It's like life. You can't benefit from opportunities you don't try to take advantage of.

But Dr. Jonathan Fader, an elite sports psychologist who has spent nearly a decade with the New York Mets, has talked about just how problematic this lesson is for rookie players in the majors. They built their reputations, and therefore their identities, on swinging at every pitch they thought they could hit . . . and now they're facing the best pitchers in the world. Suddenly, aggression is a weakness, not a strength. Now they have to get up there in front of millions of people, getting paid millions of dollars, and mostly *not* swing the bat. They have to wait for the perfect pitch.

What they have to learn, what the great hitter Sadaharu Oh himself learned in a series of complicated batting exercises designed by his Zen master and hitting coach, Hiroshi Arakawa, was the power of waiting, the power of precision, the power of the void. Because that's what makes for a real pro. A truly great hitter—not just a *swinger*—needs quick hands and powerful hips, to be sure, but they must also possess the power of *wu wei,* or nonaction.

Wu wei is the ability to hold the bat back—waiting until the batter sees the perfect pitch. It is the yogi in meditation. They're *physically* still, so that they can be active on a mental and spiritual level. That was also Kennedy during the Cuban Missile Crisis. It might have seemed like he wasn't doing enough—that he wasn't rushing to destroy his opponent—but he was rightly carving out the space and time to think, and time and space for the Russians to do the same thing. Practicing *wu wei* was precisely what Tiger Woods lost the ability to do as his work and sex addictions took control.

A *disciplined action,* that's what John Cage called doing nothing in the performance instructions on 4′33″.

You don't solve a maze by rushing through. You have to stop and think. You have to walk slowly and carefully, reining in your energy—otherwise you'll get hopelessly lost. The same is true for the problems we face in life.

The green light is a powerful symbol in our culture. We forget what Mr. Rogers was trying to make us see—that the yellow light and the red light are just as important. Slow down. *Stop.* One recent study found that subjects would rather give themselves an electric shock than experience boredom for even a few minutes. Then we wonder why people do so many stupid things.

There is a haunting clip of Joan Rivers, well into her seventies, already one of the most accomplished and respected and talented comedians of all time, in which she is asked why she keeps working, why she is always on the road, always looking for more gigs. Telling the interviewer about the fear that drives her, she holds up an empty calendar. "If my book ever looked like this, it would mean that nobody wants me, that everything I ever tried to do in life didn't work. Nobody cared and I've been totally forgotten."

It's not just that there was never enough for Joan. It's that our best and most lasting work comes from when we take things slow. When we pick our shots and wait for the right pitches.

Somebody who thinks they're nothing and don't matter because they're not doing something for *even a few days* is depriving themselves of stillness, yes—but they are also closing themselves off from a higher plane of performance that comes out of it.

Spiritually, that's hard. Physically, it's harder still. You have to make yourself say no. You have to make yourself *not* take the stage.

A weaker Fabius would not have been able to resist attacking Hannibal, and all of history might have turned out differently. A long-distance runner who can't pace himself. A money manager who can't wait out a bear market. If they can't learn the art of *wu wei* in their professions, they won't succeed. If you can't do it in *your life,* forget about success, you'll burn out your body. And you don't get another one of those!

We should look fearfully, even sympathetically, at the people who have become slaves to their calendars, who require a staff of ten to handle all their ongoing projects, whose lives seem to resemble a fugitive fleeing one scene for the next. There is no stillness there. It's servitude.

Each of us needs to get better at saying no. As in, "No, sorry,

I'm not available." "No, sorry, that sounds great but I'd rather not." "No, I'm going to wait and see." "No, I don't like that idea." "No, I don't need that—I'm going to make the most of what I have." "No, because if I said yes to you, I'd have to say yes to everyone."

Maybe it's not the most virtuous thing to say "No, sorry, I can't" when you really can but just don't want to. But can you really? Can you really afford to do it? And does it not harm other people if you're constantly stretched too thin?

A pilot gets to say, "Sorry, I'm on standby," as an excuse to get out of things. Doctors and firemen and police officers get to use being "on call" as a shield. But are we not on call in our own lives? Isn't there something (or someone) that we're preserving our full capacities for? Are our own bodies not on call for our families, for our self-improvement, for our own work?

Always think about what you're really being asked to give. Because the answer is often *a piece of your life*, usually in exchange for something you don't even want. Remember, that's what time is. It's your life, it's your flesh and blood, that you can never get back.

In every situation ask:

What is it?
Why does it matter?
Do I need it?
Do I want it?
What are the hidden costs?

Will I look back from the distant future and be glad I did it?
If I never knew about it at all—if the request was lost in the
    mail, if they hadn't been able to pin me down to ask me—
    would I even notice that I missed out?

When we know what to say no to, we can say yes to the things
that matter.

TAKE A WALK

It is only ideas gained from walking that have any
worth.

—FRIEDRICH NIETZSCHE

Nearly every afternoon the citizens of Copenhagen were
treated to the strange sight of Søren Kierkegaard walking
the streets. The cantankerous philosopher would write in the
morning at a standing desk, and then around noon would head
out onto the busy streets of the city.

He walked on the newfangled "sidewalks" that had been
built for fashionable citizens to stroll along. He walked through
the city's parks and along the pathways of Assistens Ceme-
tery, where he would later be buried. On occasion, he walked out
past the city's walls and into the countryside. Kierkegaard never
seemed to walk straight—he zigged and zagged, crossing the
street without notice, trying to always remain in the shade.
When he had either worn himself out, worked through what he

was struggling with, or been struck with a good idea, he would turn around and make for home, where he would write for the rest of the day.

Seeing Kierkegaard out walking surprised the residents of Copenhagen, because he seemed, at least from his writings, to be such a high-strung individual. They weren't wrong. Walking was how he released the stress and frustration that his philosophical explorations inevitably created.

In a beautiful letter to his sister-in-law, who was often bedridden, and depressed as a result, Kierkegaard wrote of the importance of walking. "Above all," he told her in 1847, "do not lose your desire to walk: Every day I walk myself into a state of well-being and walk away from every illness; I have walked myself into my best thoughts, and I know of no thought so burdensome that one cannot walk away from it."

Kierkegaard believed that sitting still was a kind of breeding ground for illness. But walking, *movement,* to him was almost sacred. It cleansed the soul and cleared the mind in a way that primed his explorations as a philosopher. Life is a path, he liked to say, we have to walk it.

And while Kierkegaard was particularly eloquent in his writing about walking, he was by no means alone in his dedication to the practice—nor alone in reaping the benefits. Nietzsche said that the ideas in *Thus Spoke Zarathustra* came to him on a long walk. Nikola Tesla discovered the rotating magnetic field, one of the most important scientific discoveries of all time, on a walk through a city park in Budapest in 1882. When he lived in

Paris, Ernest Hemingway would take long walks along the quais whenever he was stuck in his writing and needed to clarify his thinking. Charles Darwin's daily schedule included several walks, as did those of Steve Jobs and the groundbreaking psychologists Amos Tversky and Daniel Kahneman, the latter of whom wrote that "I did the best thinking of my life on leisurely walks with Amos." It was the physical activity in the body, Kahneman said, that got his brain going.

When Martin Luther King Jr. was a seminary student at Crozer, he took an hour walk each day through the campus woods to "commune with nature." Walt Whitman and Ulysses S. Grant often bumped into each other on their respective walks around Washington, which cleared their minds and helped them think. Perhaps it was that experience that Whitman was writing about in this verse of "Song of Myself":

> Know'st thou the joys of pensive thought?
> Joys of the free and lonesome heart, the tender, gloomy heart?
> Joys of the solitary walk, the spirit bow'd yet proud,
>   the suffering and the struggle?

Freud was known for his speedy walks around Vienna's Ringstrasse after his evening meal. The composer Gustav Mahler spent as much as four hours a day walking, using this time to work through and jot down ideas. Ludwig van Beethoven carried sheet music and a writing utensil with him on his walks for the same reason. Dorothy Day was a lifelong walker, and it was on her strolls along the beach on Staten Island in the 1920s that she first began to feel a strong sense of God in her life and the first flickerings of the awakening that would put her on a path toward sainthood. It's probably not a coincidence that Jesus himself was a walker—a *traveler*—who knew the pleasures and the divineness of putting one foot in front of the other.

How does *walking* get us closer to stillness? Isn't the whole point of what we're talking about to reduce activity, not seek it out? Yes, we are in motion when we walk, but it is not frenzied motion or even conscious motion—it is repetitive, ritualized motion. It is deliberate. It is an exercise in peace.

The Buddhists talk of "walking meditation," or *kinhin,* where the movement after a long session of sitting, particularly movement through a beautiful setting, can unlock a different kind of stillness than traditional meditation. Indeed, forest bathing—and most natural beauty—can only be accomplished by getting out of your house or office or car and trekking out into the woods on foot.

The key to a good walk is to be aware. To be present and open to the experience. Put your phone away. Put the pressing problems of your life away, or rather let them melt away as you move. Look down at your feet. What are they doing? Notice how effortlessly they move. Is it you who's doing that? Or do they just sort of move on their own? Listen to the sound of the leaves crunching underfoot. Feel the ground pushing back against you.

Breathe in. Breathe out. Consider who might have walked this very spot in the centuries before you. Consider the person who paved the asphalt you are standing on. What was going on with them? Where are they now? What did they believe? What problems did they have?

When you feel the tug of your responsibilities or the desire to check in with the outside world, push yourself a bit further. If you're on a path you have trod before, take a sudden turn down a street or up a hill where you haven't been before. Feel the unfamiliarity and the newness of these surroundings, drink in what you have not yet tasted.

Get lost. Be unreachable. Go *slowly*.

It's an affordable luxury available to us all. Even the poorest pauper can go for a nice walk—in a national park or an empty parking lot.

This isn't about burning calories or getting your heart rate up. On the contrary, it's not about anything. It is instead just a manifestation, an embodiment of the concepts of presence, of detachment, of emptying the mind, of noticing and appreciating the beauty of the world around you. Walk away from the thoughts that need to be walked away from; walk toward the ones that have now appeared.

On a good walk, the mind is not completely blank. It can't be—otherwise you might trip over a root or get hit by a car or a bicyclist. The point is not, as in traditional meditation, to push *every* thought or observation from your mind. On the contrary, the whole point is to see what's around you. The mind might be active while you do this, but it is still. It's a different kind of thinking, a healthier kind if you do it right. A study at New Mexico Highlands University has found that the force from our footsteps can increase the supply of blood to the brain. Researchers at Stanford have found that walkers perform better on tests that measure "creative divergent thinking" during and after their walks. A study out of Duke University found a version of what Kierkegaard tried to tell his sister-in-law, that walking could be as effective a treatment for major depression in some patients as medication.

The poet William Wordsworth walked as many as 180,000 miles in his lifetime—an average of six and a half miles a day since he was five years old! He did much of his writing while walking, usually around Grasmere, a lake in the English countryside, or Rydal Water, which is not far from Grasmere. On these long walks, as lines of poetry came to him, Wordsworth would repeat them over and over again, since it might be hours until he had the chance to write them down. Biographers have wondered ever since: Was it the scenery that inspired the images of his poems or was it the movement that jogged the thoughts? Every ordinary person who has ever had a breakthrough on a walk knows that the two forces are equally and magically responsible.

In our own search for beauty and what is good in life, we would do well to head outside and wander around. In an attempt to unlock a deeper part of our consciousness and access a high level of our mind, we would do well to get our body moving and our blood flowing.

Stress and difficulty can knock us down. Sitting at our

computers, we are overwhelmed with information, with emails, with one thing after another. Should we just sit there and absorb it? Should we sit there with the sickness and let it fester? No. Should we get up and throw ourselves into some other project—constructive, like cleaning, or cathartic, like picking a fight? No. We shouldn't do any of that.

We should get walking.

Kierkegaard tells the story of a morning when he was driven from his house in a state of despair and frustration—*illness,* in his words. After an hour and a half, he was finally at peace and nearly back home when he bumped into a friendly gentleman who chattered on about a number of his problems. Isn't that how it always seems to go?

No matter. "There was only one thing left for me to do," Kierkegaard wrote, "instead of going home, to go walking again."

And so must we.

Walk.

Then walk some more.

BUILD A ROUTINE

If a person puts even one measure of effort into
following ritual and the standards of righteousness,
he will get back twice as much.

—XUNZI

Each and every morning, Fred Rogers woke up at 5 a.m. to spend a quiet hour in reflection and prayer. Then he would head to the Pittsburgh Athletic Club, where he would swim his morning laps. As he walked out to the pool he would weigh himself—it was important that he always weigh 143 pounds—and as he jumped in, he would sing "Jubilate Deo" to himself. He emerged from that pool as if baptized anew each day, a friend wrote, fresh and fully prepared for the workday ahead.

When he got to the set of his television show, the next part of the ritual began, one that was recorded for posterity in identical fashion over hundreds of episodes, year after year. The theme song starts. The yellow light flashes. The camera pans to the front door. Mr. Rogers enters, singing, and walks down the stairs. He takes off his jacket and neatly hangs it up in the closet. He puts on and zips up his trademark cardigan—the one his mother made him. Then he takes off his shoes and puts on a comfortable pair of boat slippers. Now, and only now, can he begin to speak and teach to his favorite people in the world—the children of his neighborhood.

To some, this might seem monotonous. The same routine, day in and day out, that extended beyond "Cut!" at the end of each show to an afternoon nap, dinner with his family, and a 9:30 bedtime. The same weight. The same food. The same intro-duction. The same close to the day. Boring? The truth is that a good routine is not only a source of great comfort and stability, it's the platform from which stimulating and fulfilling work is possible.

Routine, done for long enough and done sincerely enough, becomes more than routine. It becomes *ritual*—it becomes sanc-tified and holy.

Maybe Mr. Rogers isn't your thing. Perhaps, then, you'd rather look at the perennial all-star point guard Russell West-brook, who begins his own routine *exactly* three hours before tipoff. First, he warms up. Then, one hour before the game, Westbrook visits the arena chapel. Then he eats a peanut butter and jelly sandwich (always buttered wheat bread, toasted, straw-berry jelly, Skippy peanut butter, cut diagonally). At exactly six minutes and seventeen seconds before the game starts, he be-gins the team's final warm-up drill. He has a particular pair of shoes for games, for practice, for road games. Since high school, he's done the same thing after shooting a free throw, walking backward past the three-point line and then forward again to take the next shot. At the practice facility, he has a specific parking space, and he likes to shoot on Practice Court 3. He calls his parents at the same time every day. And on and on.

Sports is filled with stories like Westbrook's. They often feature goalies in hockey, pitchers in baseball, quarterbacks and placekickers in football—the most cerebral positions in their respective games. Players who engage in this kind of behavior are called quirky, and their routines are called superstitions. It's strange to us that these successful people, who are more or less their own boss and are clearly so talented, seem prisoners to the regimentation of their routines. Isn't the whole point of greatness that you're freed from trivial rules and regulations? That you can do whatever you want?

Ah, but the greats know that complete freedom is a nightmare. They know that order is a prerequisite of excellence and that in an unpredictable world, good habits are a safe haven of certainty.

It was Eisenhower who defined freedom as the opportunity for self-discipline. In fact, freedom and power and success *require* self-discipline. Because without it, chaos and complacency move in. Discipline, then, is how we maintain that freedom.

It's also how we get in the right headspace to do our work. The writer and runner Haruki Murakami talks about why he follows the same routine every day. "The repetition itself becomes the important thing," he says, "it's a form of mesmerism. I mesmerize myself to reach a deeper state of mind."

When our thoughts are empty and our body is in its groove, we do our best work.

A routine can be time-based. Jack Dorsey, the founder and CEO of Twitter, gets up at 5 a.m., without fail. The former Navy SEAL Jocko Willink gets up at 4:30 a.m. and posts a picture of his watch to prove it each morning. Queen Victoria woke at 8 a.m., ate breakfast at 10, and met with her ministers from 11 to 11:30. The poet John Milton was up at 4 a.m. to read and contemplate, so that by 7 a.m. he was ready to be "milked" by his writing.

A routine can be focused on order or arrangement. Confucius insisted that his mat be straight or he would not sit. Jim Schlossnagle, the baseball coach who took over TCU's team after a long run of mediocre play, taught his players to keep their lockers, as well as the dugout, spotless and orderly at all times (the team has never had a losing season since and made it to four straight College World Series). The *ordering* also matters to tennis great Rafael Nadal, who drinks water and a recovery drink in the same order and then sets them in a perfect arrangement.

Routine can be built around a tool or a sound or a scent. Rilke had two pens and two kinds of paper on his desk; one was used for writing, while the other was acceptable for bills, letters, and less important documents. Monks are called to meditation by the chiming of a monastery bell; other monks rub a zuko incense on their hands before ceremonies and meditations.

A routine can also be religious or faith-based. Confucius always gave a sacrificial offering before eating, no matter how inconsequential the meal was. The Greeks consulted the Delphic oracle before any major decision and made sacrifices before battle. The Jews have kept the Sabbath for thousands of years, Abad Ha'am once said, just as the Sabbath has kept the Jews.

Done enough times, done with sincerity and feeling, routine becomes ritual. The regularity of it—the daily cadence—creates deep and meaningful experience. To one person, taking care of a horse is a chore. To Simón Bolívar it was a sacred, essential part of his day. When the body is busy with the familiar, the mind can relax. The monotony becomes muscle memory. To deviate seems dangerous, wrong. As if it's inviting failure in.

Some might sneer at this "superstitious" behavior, but that is the wrong way to think about it. As Rafael Nadal explained, "If it were superstition, why would I keep doing the same thing over and over whether I win or lose? It's a way of placing myself in a match, ordering my surroundings to match the order I seek in my head." Did the Greeks really believe that the oracle of Delphi could tell them what they should do? Or was the consultation process, the journey to Mount Parnassus, the whole point?

Sociologists found that island tribes were more prone to create rituals for activities where luck was a factor than where it wasn't, such as fishing on the open sea compared to on a lagoon. The truth is, luck is always in play for us. Luck is always a factor.

The purpose of ritual isn't to win the gods over to our side (though that can't hurt!). It's to settle our bodies (and our minds) down when Fortune is our opponent on the other side of the net.

Most people wake up to face the day as an endless barrage of bewildering and overwhelming choices, one right after another. *What do I wear? What should I eat? What should I do first? What should I do after that? What sort of work should I do? Should I scramble to address this problem or rush to put out this fire?*

Needless to say, this is exhausting. It is a whirlwind of conflicting impulses, incentives, inclinations, and external interruptions. It is no path to stillness and hardly a way to get the best out of yourself.

The psychologist William James spoke about making habits our ally instead of our enemy. That we can build around us a day and a life that is moral and ordered and still—and in so doing, create a kind of bulwark against the chaos of the world and free up the best of ourselves for the work we do.

> For this, we must make automatic and habitual, as early as possible, as many useful actions as we can, and guard against the growing into ways that are likely to be disadvantageous to us, as we should guard against the plague. The more of the details of our daily life we can hand over to the effortless custody of automatism, the more our higher powers of mind will be set free for their own proper work. There is no more miserable human being than one in whom nothing is habitual but indecision, and for whom the lighting of every cigar, the drinking of every cup, the time of rising and going to bed every day,

and the beginning of every bit of work, are subjects of express volitional deliberation.

When we not only automate and routinize the trivial parts of life, but also make automatic good and virtuous decisions, we free up resources to do important and meaningful exploration. We buy room for peace and stillness, and thus make good work and good thoughts accessible and *inevitable*.

To make that possible, you must go now and get your house in order. Get your day scheduled. Limit the interruptions. Limit the number of choices you need to make.

If you can do this, passion and disturbance will give you less trouble. Because it will find itself boxed out.

For inspiration, take as your model Japanese flower arrangers: Orderly. Quiet. Focused. Clean. Fresh. Deliberate. You will not find them trying to practice in noisy coffee shops or bleary-eyed in a rush at 3 a.m. because they planned poorly. You will not find them picking up their trimmers on a whim, or in their underwear while they talk on the phone to an old friend who has just called. All of that is too random, too chaotic for the true master.

A master is in control. A master has a system. A master turns the ordinary into the sacred.

And so must we.

GET RID OF YOUR STUFF

> For property is poverty and fear; only to have
> possessed something and to have let go of it means
> carefree ownership.
>
> —RAINER MARIA RILKE

Epictetus was born a slave but eventually received his freedom. In time, he came to enjoy the trappings of the good life—or at least the Stoic version of it. He had emperors attend his lectures, trained many students, and made a decent living. With his hard-earned money, he bought a nice iron lamp, which he kept burning in a small shrine in his home.

One evening, he heard a noise in the hallway by his front door. Rushing down, he found that a thief had stolen the prized lamp. Like any person who feels attached to their stuff, he was disappointed and surprised and violated. Someone had come into his home and stolen something that belonged to him.

But then Epictetus caught himself. He remembered his teachings.

"Tomorrow, my friend," he said to himself, "you will find an earthenware lamp; for a man can only lose what he has." For the rest of his life, he kept this cheaper earthen lamp instead. Upon his death, an admirer, entirely missing the point of Epictetus's disdain for material items, purchased it for 3,000 drachmas.

One of Seneca's most powerful metaphors is the slaveowner owned by his slaves, or the wealthy man whose vast estates lord over him rather than the other way around (in modern times, we have our own term for this: being "house poor"). Montaigne was perceptive enough to ask whether it was in fact he who was the pet of his cat. We also find a version of it from the East. Xunzi explained:

> The gentleman makes things his servants. The petty man
> is servant to things.

In short, mental and spiritual independence matter little if the things we own in the physical world end up owning us.

The Cynics took this idea the furthest. Diogenes supposedly lived in a barrel and walked around nearly naked. When he saw a child drinking water from a well with his hands, Diogenes smashed his own cup, realizing that he had been carrying around an extraneous possession.

Today, we might call Diogenes a bum or a loser (or a crazy person), and in some sense he was those things. But on the few occasions when Diogenes met Alexander the Great, then the most powerful man in the world, it was Diogenes who observers came away thinking was the more impressive. Because Alexander, as much as he tried, could neither tempt Diogenes with any favors nor deprive him of anything that he had not already willingly tossed aside.

There was nothing but a shirt between the Stoics and the Cynics, joked the poet Juvenal, meaning the Stoics were sensible enough to wear clothes (and refrain from bodily functions in public), unlike the Cynics. This is a pretty reasonable concession. We don't need to get rid of *all* our possessions, but we should constantly question what we own, why we own it, and whether we could do without.

Have you ever seen a house torn down? A lifetime of earning and savings, countless hours of decorating and accumulating until it was arranged just right, the place of so much living—and in the end it is reduced to a couple dumpsters full of debris. Even the incredibly wealthy, even the heads of state showered with gifts throughout their life, would only fill a few more bins.

Yet how many of us collect and acquire as if the metric tonnage of our possessions is a comment on our worth as individuals? Just as every hoarder becomes trapped by their own garbage, so too are we tied down by what we own. Every piece of expensive jewelry comes with an insurance bill, every mansion with a staff of groundskeepers, every investment with obligations and monthly statements to review, every exotic pet and plant with a set of responsibilities. F. Scott Fitzgerald said that the rich are different than us, and his novels portray them as free and without care.

That's not quite right.

Mo' money, mo' problems, and also mo' stuff, less freedom.

John Boyd, a sort of warrior-monk who revolutionized Western military strategy in the latter half of the twentieth century, refused to take checks from defense contractors and deliberately lived in a small condo even as he advised presidents and generals. "If a man can reduce his needs to zero," he said, "he is truly free: there is nothing that can be taken from him and nothing anyone can do to hurt him." To that we would add, "And he or she can also be still."

No one dogged by creditors is free. Living outside your means—as Churchill could attest—is not glamorous. Behind the appearances, it's *exhausting.*

It's also dangerous. The person who is afraid to lose their stuff, who has their identity wrapped up in their things, gives their enemies an opening. They make themselves extra vulnerable to fate.

The playwright Tennessee Williams spoke of luxury as the "wolf at the door." It wasn't the possessions that were the problem, he said, but the dependency. He called it the catastrophe of success, the way that we become less and less able to do things ourselves, the more and more we cannot be without a certain level of service. Not only is all your stuff a mess, but you need to pay someone to come clean it up.

There is also what we can term "comfort creep." We get so used to a certain level of convenience and luxury that it becomes almost inconceivable that we used to live without it. As wealth grows, so does our sense of "normal." But just a few years ago we were fine without this bounty. We had no problem eating ramen or squeezing into a small apartment. But now that we have more, our mind begins to lie to us. *You need this. Be anxious that you might lose it. Protect it. Don't share.*

It's toxic and scary.

Which is why philosophers have always advocated reducing our needs and limiting our possessions. Monks and priests take vows of poverty because it will mean fewer distractions, and more room (literally) for the spiritual pursuit to which they have committed. No one is saying we have to go that far, but the more we own, the more we oversee, the less room we have to move and, ironically, the less still we become.

Start by walking around your house and filling up trash bags and boxes with everything you don't use. Think of it as clearing more room for your mind and your body. Give yourself space. Give your mind a rest. Want to have less to be mad about? Less to covet or be triggered by? Give more away.

The best car is not the one that turns the most heads, but the one you have to worry about the least. The best clothes are the ones that are the most comfortable, that require you to spend the least amount of time shopping—regardless of what the magazines say. The best house for you is the one that feels the most like *home*. Don't use your money to purchase loneliness, or headaches, or status anxiety.

Your grandmother did not give you that brooch so that you would constantly worry about losing it. The artist who produced the painting on your wall was not working hard so that you might one day fear that a guest would damage it. Nor is the memory of that beautiful summer in Anguilla actually contained in that carved statue or the love you share with your spouse limited to the photograph of the two of you at your wedding. The memory is what's important. The experience itself is what matters. You can access that anytime you want, and no thief can ever deprive you of it.

You will hear people say they don't have room for a relationship in their life ... and they're right. Their stuff is taking up too much space. They're in love with possessions instead of people.

The family who never see each other because the two parents are working late to pay off the extra bedrooms they never use? The fame that keeps someone on the road so much they're a stranger to their kids? The supposed "technology" that is a pain in the ass to figure out, that's always breaking? The fragile, fancy possessions that we're constantly cleaning, buffing, protecting, and trying to find ways to slyly mention in conversation?

This is not a rich life. There is no peace in this.

Take action. Get out from under all your stuff. Get rid of it. Give away what you don't need.

You were born free—free of stuff, free of burden. But since the first time they measured your tiny body for clothes, people have been foisting stuff upon you. And you've been adding links to the pile of chains yourself ever since.

SEEK SOLITUDE

A crowded world thinks that aloneness is always
loneliness and that to seek it is perversion.

—JOHN GRAVES

It was a habit of Leonardo da Vinci's to write little fables to
himself in his notebooks. One tells the story of a good-sized
stone that rested in a pleasant grove, surrounded by flowers,
perched above a busy country road. Despite this peaceful existence, the stone grew restless. "What am I doing among these
herbs?" he asked. "I want to live in the company of my fellow
stones."

Unhappy and alone, the stone contrived to roll itself down
the hill onto the road, where it would be surrounded by countless
other stones. But the change was not quite as wonderful as
expected. Down in the dirt, the stone was trod on by horses,
driven over by wagons, and stepped on by people. It was alternately covered in mud and feces, and chipped at and jostled

and moved—painful moments made all the more painful by the occasional sight the stone was given of its old home, and the solitary peace it had left behind.

Not content to leave the story at that, Leonardo felt the need to put a fine point on it. "This is what happens," he wrote to himself and every one of us, "to those who leave the solitary and contemplative life and choose to live in cities among people full of countless evils."

Of course, Leonardo's biographers were quick to point out that the author didn't always follow the lesson of this fable. He spent most of his life in Florence and Milan and Rome. He painted in a busy studio and attended many spectacles and parties. Even his last years were spent not in secluded retirement but in the bustling court of King Francis I of France.

His occupation required this. As do many of ours.

Which makes cultivating moments of solitude all the more essential. To find solitude, the way Eugen Herrigel said that the Buddhist does, "not in far-off, quiet places; he creates it out of himself, spreads it around him wherever he may be, because he loves it."

While Leonardo was working on *The Last Supper,* he would get up early and arrive at the monastery before any of his assistants or spectators, so he could be alone, in silence, with his thoughts and the mammoth creative challenge in front of him. He was also notorious for leaving his studio and going for long walks by himself, carrying a notebook and simply looking and watching and really seeing what was happening around him. He loved to visit his uncle's farm for inspiration and solitude.

It is difficult to think clearly in rooms filled with other people. It's difficult to understand yourself if you are never by yourself. It's difficult to have much in the way of clarity and insight if your life is a constant party and your home is a construction site.

Sometimes you have to disconnect in order to better connect with yourself and with the people you serve and love.

"If I was to sum up the single biggest problem of senior leadership in the Information Age," four-star Marine Corps general and former secretary of defense James Mattis has said, "it's lack of reflection. Solitude allows you to reflect while others are reacting. We need solitude to refocus on prospective decision-making, rather than just reacting to problems as they arise."

People don't have enough silence in their lives because they don't have enough solitude. And they don't get enough solitude because they don't seek out or cultivate silence. It's a vicious cycle that prevents stillness and reflection, and then stymies good ideas, which are almost always hatched in solitude.

Breakthroughs seem to happen with stunning regularity in the shower or on a long hike. Where don't they happen? Shouting to be heard in a bar. Three hours into a television binge. Nobody realizes just how much they love someone while they're booking back-to back-to-back meetings.

If solitude is the school of genius, as the historian Edward Gibbon put it, then the crowded, busy world is the purgatory of the idiot.

Who isn't stiller in the morning, or when they're up before the house stirs, before the phone rings or the commutes have begun? Who isn't better equipped to notice the meaning of the moment when it's quiet, when your personal space is being respected? In solitude time slows down, and while we might find that speed hard to bear at first, we will ultimately go crazy without this check on the busyness of life and work. And if not driven crazy, we will certainly miss out.

Solitude is not just for hermits, but for healthy, functioning people. Although there is a thing or two we can learn about solitude from the people who turned pro at it.

In 1941, then just twenty-six years old, Thomas Merton reported to the Abbey of Gethsemani in Bardstown, Kentucky, and began his first of many journeys into monkish solitude that would go on, in various forms, for the next twenty-seven years. His solitude was hardly indolent repose. It was instead an active exploration of himself, of religion, of human nature, and later, into solving serious societal problems like inequality, war, and injustice. In his beautiful journals, we find insights into the human experience that would have been impossible if Merton had spent his time in a newspaper bullpen or even on a university campus.

He would come to call solitude his *vocation.* As he wrote:

> To pray and work in the morning and to labor and rest in the afternoon, and to sit still again in meditation in the evening when night falls upon that land and when the silence fills itself with darkness and with stars. This is a true and special vocation. There are few who are willing

to belong completely to such silence, to let it soak into
their bones, to breathe nothing but silence, to feed on silence, and to turn the very substance of their life into a
living and vigilant silence.

In a more emulatable form of Merton's retreat, Microsoft
founder and philanthropist Bill Gates has, twice a year for many
years now, taken what he calls a "think week." He spends seven
days alone in a cabin in the forest. There, physically removing
himself from the daily interruptions of his work, he can really sit
down and think.

He might be alone there, but he is hardly lonely. Gates reads—
sometimes *hundreds* of papers—quietly for hours at a time, sometimes in print, sometimes off computer monitors that look out
over the water. He reads books too, in a library adorned with a
portrait of the author Victor Hugo. He writes long memos to
people across his organization. The only breaks he takes are a
few minutes to play bridge or go for a walk. In those solitary days
in that cabin, Gates is the picture of Thomas à Kempis's line *In
omnibus requiem quaesivi, et nusquam inveni nisi in angulo cum
libro*—"Everywhere I have sought peace and not found it, except
in a corner with a book."

Do not mistake this for some kind of vacation. It is hard
work—long days, some without sleep. It is wrestling with complex topics, contradictory ideas, and identity-challenging concepts. But despite this struggle, Gates emerges recharged and
refocused. He can see further into the distance. He knows what

he wants to prioritize, what to assign his people to work on. He carries the quiet stillness of the woods back to the complicated world he has to navigate as a businessman and philanthropic leader.

Each of us needs to put ourselves, physically, in the position to do that kind of deep work. We need to give our bodies, as Virginia Woolf put it, a room of our own—even if only for a few stolen hours—where we can think and have quiet and solitude. Buddha needed seclusion in his search for enlightenment. He had to step away from the world, go off by himself, and sit.

Don't you think you would benefit from that too?

It's hard to make that time. It's hard (and expensive) to get away. We have responsibilities. But they will be better for our temporary disappearance. We will carry back with us the stillness from our solitude in the form of patience, understanding, gratitude, and insight.

In Leonardo's fable, the stone abandoned the peaceful solitude of the meadow for the road and came to regret it. Merton, for his part, came to occasionally regret his complete solitude. Was there more he could do as a man of the world? Could he have a bigger impact if he abandoned his solitude?

Indeed, very few of us are willing or able to make it the totality of our existence, nor should we. (The dancer Twyla Tharp points out that "solitude *without* purpose" is a killer of creativity.) Even in Merton's case, he was given special privileges from his church superior to communicate with the outside world through letters and writing, and eventually began to travel and speak to large crowds. Because his work was too important and the insights he discovered were too essential to remain locked up in a tiny brick house on the edge of the woods in Kentucky.

Merton eventually came to understand that after so much time by himself in the woods, he now possessed solitude inside himself—and could access it anytime he liked. The wise and busy also learn that solitude and stillness are there in pockets, if we look for them. The few minutes before going onstage for a talk or sitting in your hotel room before a meeting. The morning before the rest of the house wakes up. Or late in the evening after the world has gone to sleep.

Grab these moments. Schedule them. Cultivate them.

BE A HUMAN *BEING*

Work is what horses die of. Everybody should know
that.

—ALEKSANDR SOLZHENITSYN

Compared with most royal couples, Queen Victoria and Prince
Consort Albert of Saxe-Coburg and Gotha were excep-
tional. They actually loved each other and they actually worked
at, and took seriously, their jobs as heads of state. This was all
very good.

But it could also be argued that any positive trait—even hard
work—taken to excess becomes a vice.

In both their cases, as a couple for whom, by the nature of
their profession, even the idea of "work/life balance" was impossible, the virtue of their self-discipline and dedication became a fatal vice.

Albert, a Bavarian prince who married into the British royal
family, was a hard worker from the day he married Victoria. He

brought much-needed order and routine to the life of his queen. He streamlined processes and took up a share of the burdens that had previously fallen on Victoria alone. Indeed, many of the so-called Victorian traits of the era originated with him. He was disciplined, fastidious, ambitious, conservative.

Under his pressing, their schedule became one meeting, dispatch, and social event after another. Albert was almost constantly busy, working so much that he occasionally vomited from stress. Never shirking a responsibility or an opportunity, he took on every bit of the burden of power his wife was willing to share, and in turn, together they seized every formal and informal bit of influence the monarchy had in the British Empire at that time. They were a pair of workaholics and proud of it.

As Albert wrote to an advisor, he spent hours a day reading newspapers in German, French, and English. "One can let nothing pass," he said, "without losing the connection and coming in consequence to wrong conclusions." He was right, the stakes were certainly high. For instance, his expert understanding of geopolitics helped Britain avoid being drawn into the U.S. Civil War.

But the truth was, Albert threw himself equally hard into projects of much less importance. Organizing the Great Exhibition of 1851, a nearly six-month-long carnival that showed off the wonders of the British Empire, consumed years of his life. A few days before it opened, he wrote to his stepmother, "I am more dead than alive from overwork." It was, to be certain, a beautiful and memorable event, but his health never recovered.

He was like Winston Churchill, only he and his wife knew no moderation and had little fun. "I go on working at my treadmill, as life seems to me," Albert said. It's not a bad description of the exhausting and repetitive life he and Victoria led. Starting in 1840, Victoria bore nine children in seventeen years, four of whom were born in consecutive years. In a time when women still regularly died during childbirth (anesthesia—chloroform— became available only for her eighth pregnancy), Victoria, who was a mere five feet tall, was constantly pregnant. Even with the benefits of limitless household help, she bore an enormous physical burden on top of her duties as queen. Upon her death, it was found that she was suffering from a prolapsed uterus and a hernia that must have caused her incredible and constant pain.

There's nothing wrong with having a large family—the throne did need heirs—but it never seemed to have occurred to the couple that they had any say in the matter. "Man is a beast of burden," Albert wrote to his brother, "and he is only happy if he has to drag his burden and if he has little free will. My experience teaches me every day to understand the truth of this more and more." As a result, his and Victoria's existence was hardly one of privilege or relaxation or freedom. It was instead an endless cycle of obligation after obligation, done at a breakneck pace that the two of them inflicted on themselves.

It is a testament to their affection for each other that their marriage survived. Victoria was at least aware of the deleterious effects all this work had on Albert. She wrote of the consequences of his "over-love of business" on their relationship, and she also noticed that his health was flagging. His racing mind kept him awake at night, his stomach cramped, and his skin drooped.

Instead of listening to these warning signs, he soldiered on for years, working harder and harder, forcing his body to comply. And then, suddenly, in 1861, it quit on him. His strength failed. He drifted into incoherency, and at 10:50 p.m. on December 14, Albert took his three final breaths and died. The cause? Crohn's disease, exacerbated by extreme stress. He had literally worked his guts out.

Modern medicine has hardly saved us from these tragedies. In Japan they have a word, *karōshi*, which translates to death from overwork. In Korean it's *gwarosa*.

Is that what you want to be? A workhorse that draws its load until it collapses and dies, still shod and in the harness? Is that what you were put on this planet for?

Remember, the main cause of injury for elite athletes is not tripping and falling. It's not collisions. It's overuse. Pitchers and quarterbacks throw out their arms. Basketball players blow out their knees. Others just get tired of the grinding hours and the pressure. Michael Phelps prematurely ended his swimming career due to burnout—despite all the gold medals, he never wanted to get in a pool again. It's hard to blame him either; he'd put everything, including his own sanity and health, second to shaving seconds off his times.

Meanwhile, Eliud Kipchoge, possibly the greatest distance runner ever to live, actively works to make sure he is not *overworking*. In training, he deliberately does not give his full effort, saving that instead for the few times per year when he races. He prefers instead to train at 80 percent of his capacity—on occasion to 90 percent—to maintain and preserve his longevity (and sanity) as an athlete. When Michael Phelps came back to swimming after his breakdown in 2012, it was possible because he was willing to reimagine his approach to training and to approach it with more balance.

Pacing is something athletes are often forced to come to terms with as they age, while young athletes needlessly burn themselves out because they think they have a bottomless well of energy. Yes, there is purity and meaning in giving your best to whatever you do—but life is much more of a marathon than it is a sprint. In a way, this is the distinction between confidence and ego. Can you trust yourself and your abilities enough to keep something in reserve? Can you protect the stillness and the inner peace necessary to win the longer race of life?

It was a malicious lie that the Nazis hung over the gates of Auschwitz: *Arbeit macht frei*—"Work will set you free."*

No. No. No.

The Russian proverb had it better: Work just makes you bent over.

Man is *not* a beast of burden. Yes, we have important duties—to our country, to our coworkers, to provide for our families.

---

*It is worth noting, with dark irony, that Hitler's descent into delirium toward the end of World War II was in many ways brought on by extreme overwork.

Many of us have talents and gifts that are so extraordinary that we owe it to ourselves and the world to express and fulfill them. But we're not going to be able to do that if we're not taking care of ourselves, or if we have stretched ourselves to the breaking point.

The moral of the American tall tale about the rail worker John Henry is often lost on people. He challenges the steam-powered drilling machine, and through sheer strength and inhuman will, he beats it. It's great. Inspiring. Except he dies at the end! Of exhaustion! "In real life," George Orwell observed, "it is always the anvil that breaks the hammer."

Work will not set you free. It will kill you if you're not careful.

Prince Albert's children would have gladly traded a less exciting Great Exhibition to have Albert for a little longer, and so too would Queen Victoria and the British people.

The email you think you need so desperately to respond to can wait. Your screenplay does not need to be hurried, and you can even take a break between it and the next one. The only person truly requiring you to spend the night at the office is yourself. It's okay to say no. It's okay to opt out of that phone call or that last-minute trip.

Good decisions are not made by those who are running on empty. What kind of interior life can you have, what kind of thinking can you do, when you're utterly and completely over-worked? It's a vicious cycle: We end up having to work more to fix the errors we made when we would have been better off resting, having consciously said no instead of reflexively saying yes. We end up pushing good people away (and losing relationships) because we're wound so tight and have so little patience.

The bull in Robert Earl Keen's "Front Porch Song" whose "work is never done"? Do you want to be the artist who loses their joy for the process, who has strip-mined their soul in such a way that there is nothing left to draw upon? Burn out or fade away—that was the question in Kurt Cobain's suicide note. How is that even a dilemma?

It's human *being,* not human doing, for a reason.

Moderation. Being present. Knowing your limits.

This is the key. The body that each of us has was a gift. Don't work it to death. Don't burn it out.

Protect the gift.

GO TO SLEEP

> There is a time for many words and there is a time for
> sleep.
>
> —HOMER, *THE ODYSSEY*

American Apparel was a billion-dollar company that failed for many reasons. It borrowed too much money. It had a toxic workplace culture. It was besieged by lawsuits. It opened too many stores. This was all written about many times during the company's public disintegration in 2014.

But one cause of its failure—a major reason why more than ten thousand people lost their jobs and a company with $700 million in annual sales simply disappeared—was overlooked by most outside observers.*

When Dov Charney founded American Apparel, he had the notion that he would be a completely accessible boss. As the

---

*It was one I saw firsthand.

company grew from a dorm room operation to a global retailer and one of the largest garment manufacturers in the world, he stuck to that. In fact, his ego swelled at the idea of being at the center of every part of the business.

It was a true open-door policy. Not just open-door but phone and email too. Any employee, at any level of the company, from sleeve sewer to sales associate to photographer, could reach out whenever they had a problem. For good measure, during one of the company's many public relations crises, Charney posted his phone number online for any journalist or customer who had an issue as well.

Early on, this policy had advantages. Charney was constantly in tune with what was happening in the company, and it prevented bureaucracy from establishing itself and bogging people down. But not only did the advantage not scale well, but the costs began to take their toll as well.

You can imagine what happened when the company suddenly had 250 stores in 20 countries. By 2012, Charney was sleeping only a few hours a night. By 2014, he wasn't sleeping at all. How could he? There was always someone with a problem and someone *somewhere in some distant time zone* taking him up on the open-door policy. The human reality of getting older didn't help either.

It was this extreme, cumulative sleep deprivation that was the root of so much of the company's catastrophic failure. How could it not be? Research has shown that as we approach twenty or so hours without sleep, we are as cognitively impaired as a drunk person. Our brains respond more slowly and our judgment is significantly impaired.

In 2014, during a difficult transition between distribution facilities, Charney moved into the shipping and fulfillment warehouse, installing a shower and cot in a small office. To him and some diehard loyalists, this was proof of his heroic dedication to the company. In truth, bad judgment had bungled the transition in the first place, and then his constant presence and micromanaging on site—which became increasingly erratic the longer it went on and the longer he went without sleep—only compounded the difficulties.

Charney descended into madness in front of his employees. Unshaven. Bleary-eyed. At the mercy of his temper, unmoored from even the most basic judgment or propriety. Issuing orders that contradicted orders he had issued just minutes before, he seemed almost hell-bent on destruction. But he was the boss. What could people do?

Eventually, his *mother* was called in to bring him home, to coax him into taking care of himself before it was too late. But he was well past saving. Even back in the normal office, he would call employees late, late into the night and sweetly talk about work until he drifted off, finding that collapsing from exhaustion was the only way he could put himself to bed.

Within a few months of the warehouse episode, Dov Charney was on the verge of losing control of the company. Terms of desperate rounds of financing had made him vulnerable to a takeover, but he agreed to them without thinking through the implications. Sitting before his handpicked board of directors, he mixed package after package of pure Nescafé powder in cold water—essentially mainlining caffeine to stay awake. By the time he left the meeting, he no longer had a job.

Within a few months, his shares of the company were worthless. Investors and debt collectors would find little left to salvage when they sorted through the wreckage. He now owes a hedge fund twenty million dollars and cannot even afford a lawyer.

It was an epic implosion along relatively common lines. The overworked person creates a crisis that they try to solve by working harder. Mistakes are piled upon mistakes by the exhausted, delirious mind. The more they try, the worse it gets and the angrier *they* get that no one appreciates their sacrifice.

People say, "I'll sleep when I'm dead," as they hasten that very death, both literally and figuratively. They trade their health for a few more working hours. They trade the long-term viability of their business or their career before the urgency of some temporal crisis.

If we treat sleep as a luxury, it is the first to go when we get busy. If sleep is what happens only when everything is done, work and others will constantly be impinging on your personal space. You will feel frazzled and put upon, like a machine that people don't take care of and assume will always function.

The philosopher and writer Arthur Schopenhauer used to say that "sleep is the source of all health and energy." He said it better still on a separate occasion: "Sleep is the interest we have to pay on the capital which is called in at death. The higher the interest rate and the more regularly it is paid, the further the date of redemption is postponed."

Arianna Huffington woke up on the floor of her bathroom a few years ago, covered in blood, her head searing with pain. She had passed out from fatigue and broken her cheekbone. Her sister, who was in the apartment at the time, recalls the sickening sound of hearing the body hit the tile. It was a literal wake-up call for both of them. This was no way to live. There was no glamour in working oneself to the bone, trading sleep for an extra conference call or a few minutes on television or a meeting with an important person.

That's not success. It's torture. And no human can endure it for long. Indeed, your mind and soul are incapable of peace when your body is battling for survival, when it is drawing on its reserves for even basic functioning. Happiness? Stillness? Milking the solitude or beauty out of your surroundings? Out of the question for the exhausted, overworked fool.

The bloodshot engineer six Red Bulls deep has no chance of stillness. Nor does the recent grad—or not-so-recent grad—who still parties like she's in college. Nor does the writer who plans poorly and promises himself he'll finish his book in a sleepless three-day sprint. A 2017 study actually found that lack of sleep increases negative repetitive thinking. Abusing the body leads the mind to abuse itself.

Sleep is the other side of the work we're doing—sleep is the recharging of the internal batteries whose energy stores we recruit in order to do our work. It is a meditative practice. It is stillness. It's the time when we turn *off*. It's built into our biology for a reason.

We have only so much energy for our work, for our relationships, for ourselves. A smart person understands this and guards it carefully. The greats—they protect their sleep because it's where the best state of mind comes from. They say no to things. They turn in when they hit their limits. They don't let the creep of sleep deprivation undermine their judgment. They know there are some people who can function without sleep, but they are also smart and self-aware enough to know that *everyone* functions better when well-rested.

Anders Ericsson, of the classic ten-thousand-hours study, found that master violinists slept eight and a half hours a night on average and took a nap most days. (A friend said of Churchill, "He made in Cuba one discovery which was to prove far more important to his future life than any gain in military experience, the life-giving powers of the siesta.") According to Ericsson, great players nap *more* than lesser ones.

How did the Zen master Hakuin prepare for his epic lecture, *The Records of Old Sokko*? He slept. A lot. He slept so much and so soundly that one of his students said that "his snores reverberated through the house like rumblings of thunder." It went on for more than a month, with Hakuin waking only to see the occasional visitor. But every other minute was spent facedown, passed out in blissful, restful slumber.

His attendants, who had not yet learned to appreciate the power of sleep, began to worry. The day the talks would be given was rapidly approaching. Was the master ever going to get serious about it? Or was he just going to waste his days asleep? They begged him to start working while there was still time. He simply rolled over and slept some more. Finally, as the deadline loomed large, but without a hint of urgency, Hakuin got up. Sitting, he called to his attendants, and began with perfect clarity to dictate the talk.

It was all there. It was brilliant.

It was the product of a rested mind that took care of its body. A healthy soul that could sleep soundly. And it has echoed down through the ages.

If you want peace, there is just one thing to do. If you want to be your best, there is just one thing to do.

Go to sleep.

FIND A HOBBY

This is the main question, with what activity one's
leisure is filled.

—ARISTOTLE

William Gladstone, the four-time prime minister of England, in the generation before Winston Churchill, had an
unusual hobby. He loved going out into the woods near his home
and chopping down trees.

Huge trees. By hand.

In January 1876, he spent two full days working on an elm
tree with a girth of some sixteen feet. From Gladstone's diary,
we note that on more than one *thousand* occasions he went to the
forest with his axe, often bringing his family along and making
an outing of it. It was said that he found the process so consum-
ing, he had no time to think of anything but where the next
stroke of his axe would fall.

Many critics, one of whom happened to be Churchill's father, criticized Gladstone's hobby as destructive. It really wasn't. Gladstone planted many trees in his life, pruned hundreds more, and aggressively protected the health of the forests near his home, believing that removing dead or decaying trees was a minor but important service. In response to some critics who questioned why he had taken down a particular oak, he explained that removing the rotten members from the forest allowed more light and air to get to the good trees—just as in politics (a joke for which he was promptly cheered). His daughters also sold slivers of wood from the trees their father had cut down as souvenirs to raise money for charity.

But above all, Gladstone's arboreal activity was a way to rest a mind that was often wearied by politics and the stresses of life. During his final three terms as prime minister, from 1880 to the early 1890s, Gladstone was out in the woods inspecting or chopping more than three hundred times. Nor was an axe the only tool he used to relax or be present. Gladstone was also said to enjoy vigorous hikes, and mountain climbing well into old age, and the only thing that appears in his diary more than tree felling is reading. (He collected and read some *twenty-five thousand* books during his life.) These activities were a relief from the pressures of politics, a challenge for which effort was always rewarded and with which his opponents could not interfere.

Without these release valves, who knows if he could have been as good a leader? Without the lessons he learned in those woods—about persistence, about patience, about doing your best, about the importance of momentum and gravity—could he have fought the long and good fight for the causes he believed in?

Nope.

When most of us hear the word "leisure," we think of lounging around and doing nothing. In fact, this is a perversion of a sacred notion. In Greek, "leisure" is rendered as *scholé*—that is, *school*. Leisure historically meant simply freedom from the work needed to survive, freedom *for* intellectual or creative pursuits. It was learning and study and the pursuit of higher things.

As society advanced and jobs became increasingly less physical, but more exhausting mentally and spiritually, it became common for leisure to include a diverse array of activities, from reading to woodwork. Jesus, for instance, rested out on the water, fishing with his disciples. Seneca wrote about how Socrates loved to play with children, how Cato loved to relax with wine, how Scipio was passionate about music. And we know this because Seneca's own leisure from politics was writing thoughtful, philosophical letters to friends. John Cage picked up the hobby of mushroom hunting. He observed that traipsing through the woods opened up the mind and encouraged ideas to "fly into one's head like birds." Fred Rogers had his swimming. Saint Teresa of Ávila loved to dance, and so did Mae Carol Jemison, the first African American woman in space. Simón Bolívar too found dancing a helpful tool in balancing the affairs of state and the burdens of revolution. The writer David Sedaris likes to walk the back roads of his neighborhood in the English countryside and pick up garbage, often for hours at a time. John Graves poured himself into carving out his ranch from the Texas Hill Country, fixing fences, raising cattle, and cultivating the land. Herbert Hoover loved fishing so much, he wrote a book about it. The title: *Fishing for Fun: And to Wash Your Soul.*

The swordsman Musashi, whose work was aggressively and violently physical, took up painting late in life, and observed that each form of art enriched the other. Indeed, flower arranging, calligraphy, and poetry have long been popular with Japanese generals and warriors, a wonderful pairing of opposites—strength and gentleness, stillness and aggression. Hakuin, the Zen master, excelled at painting and calligraphy, producing thousands of works in his lifetime. NBA champion Chris Bosh taught himself how to code. Einstein had his violin, Pythagoras has his lyre. William Osler, the founder of Johns Hopkins University, told aspiring medical students that when chemistry or anatomy distressed their soul, "seek peace in the great pacifier, Shakespeare."

Reading. Boxing. Collecting stamps. Whatever. Let it relax you and give you peace.

In his essay on leisure, Josef Pieper wrote that "the ability to be 'at leisure' is one of the basic powers of the human soul." But that's what's so interesting about it. It's a physical state—a physical *action*—that somehow replenishes and strengthens the soul. Leisure is not the absence of activity, it *is* activity. What is absent is any external justification—you can't do leisure for pay, you can't do it to impress people.

You have to do it *for you.*

But the good news is that leisure can be anything. It can be cutting down trees, or learning another language. Camping or restoring old cars. Writing poetry or knitting. Running marathons, riding horses, or walking the beach with a metal detector. It can be, as it was for Churchill, painting or bricklaying.

Pieper said that leisure was like saying a prayer before bed. It might help you go to sleep—just as leisure might help you get better at your job—but that can't be the point.

Many people find relief in strenuous exercise. Sure, it might make them stronger at work, but that's not why they do it. It's meditative to put the body in motion and direct our mental efforts at conquering our physical limitations. The repetition of a long swim, the challenge of lifting heavy weights, the breathlessness of a sprint—there is a cleansing experience, even if it is accompanied by suffering. It's a wonderful feeling there, right before the sweat breaks, when we can feel ourselves working the stress up from the deep recesses of our soul and our conscious mind and then out of the body.

"If an action tires your body but puts your heart at ease," Xunzi said, "do it." There is a reason philosophers in the West often trained in wrestling and boxing, while philosophers in the East trained in martial arts. These are not easy activities, and if you're not present while you do them, you'll get your ass kicked.

The point isn't to simply fill the hours or distract the mind. Rather, it's to engage a pursuit that simultaneously challenges and relaxes us. Students observed that in his leisure moments, Confucius was "composed and yet fully at ease." (He was also said to be very skilled at "menial" tasks.) That's the idea. It's an opportunity to practice and embody stillness but in another context.

It's in this leisure, Ovid observed, that "we reveal what kind of people we are."

Assembling a puzzle, struggling with a guitar lesson, sitting on a quiet morning in a hunting blind, steadying a rifle or a bow while we wait for a deer, ladling soup in a homeless shelter. Our bodies are busy, but our minds are open. Our hearts too.

Of course, leisure can easily become an escape, but the second that happens it's not leisure anymore. When we take something relaxing and turn it into a compulsion, it's not leisure, because we're no longer *choosing* it.

There is no stillness in that.

While we don't want our leisure to become work, we do have to *work* to make time for them. "For me," Nixon wrote in his memoir, "it is often harder to be away from the job than to be working at it." On the job, we are busy. We are needed. We have power. We are validated. We have conflict and urgency and an endless stream of distractions. Nixon said that the constant grind was "absolutely necessary for superior performance." But was his performance really that superior? Or was that the whole problem?

At leisure, we are with ourselves. We are present. It's us and the fishing pole and the sound of the line going into the water. It's us and the waiting, giving up control. It's us and the flash cards for the language we are learning. It's the humility of being bad at something because we are a beginner, but having the confidence to trust in the process.

No one is making us do this. We can quit if we're struggling, we can cut corners and cheat (ourselves) without fear of repercussion. No money is on the line to motivate us, no rewards or validation but the experience. To do leisure well—to be present, to be open, to be virtuous, to be connected—is hard. We cannot let it turn into a job, into another thing to dominate and to dominate others through.

We must be disciplined about our discipline and moderate in our moderation.

Life is about balance, not about swinging from one pole to the other. Too many people alternate between working and bingeing, on television, on food, on video games, on lying around wondering why they are bored. The chaos of life leads into the chaos of planning a vacation.

Sitting alone with a canvas? A book club? A whole afternoon for cycling? Chopping down trees? Who has the time?

If Churchill had the time, if Gladstone had the time, you have the time.

Won't my work suffer if I step away from it?

Seneca pointed out how readily we take risks with uncertain payoffs in our career—but we're afraid to risk even one minute of time for leisure.

There's nothing to feel guilty about for being idle. It's not reckless. It's an investment. There is nourishment in pursuits that have no purpose—that *is* their purpose.

Leisure is also a reward for the work we do. When we think about the ideal "Renaissance man," we see someone who is active and busy, yes, but also fulfilled and balanced. Getting to know yourself is the luxury of the success you've had. Finding fulfillment and joy in the pursuit of higher things, you've earned it. It's there for you, take it.

Make the time. Build the discipline.

You deserve it. You need it.

Your stillness depends on it.

BEWARE ESCAPISM

Me miserable! which way shall I fly
Infinite wrath, and infinite despair?
Which way I fly is Hell; myself am Hell.

—JOHN MILTON

After the crushing disappointment of the unexpected failure of his great novel *Ask the Dust,* John Fante needed an escape. He would have loved to hit the road, to flee the town and the state that had broken his heart, but he couldn't. Fante was alternately too poor and then too successful as a screenwriter to afford to leave Hollywood. And soon after that, he was too married and had too many kids to support.

Over the years he found many ways to numb the pain he felt. By playing pinball for hours on end (his addiction was extreme enough to be immortalized as a character in William Saroyan's *The Time of Your Life*). By drinking for hours on end in

Hollywood bars, where he kept company with F. Scott Fitzgerald and William Faulkner. By spending so many hours on the course that he turned his ever-patient wife, Joyce, into a golf widow.

It wasn't restoration that Fante was chasing, nor was it leisure, it was *escape* from real life.

In his own words, Fante pissed away decades golfing, reading, and drinking, and by extension *not* writing novels. Because that felt better than getting rejected again and again. Because it was easier than sitting alone by himself in a room, doing battle with the demons that made his writing so beautiful in the first place.

That's the difference between leisure and escapism. It's the intention. Travel is wonderful, but is there not something sad to the story in Johnny Cash's life, as his first marriage fell apart and his music became more formulaic and less fulfilling? Landing in L.A. at the end of a long tour, instead of heading home to his family, he walked up to the counter and asked to buy a ticket. To where? "Wherever the next plane will take me," he told the attendant.

Despair and restlessness go together.

The problem is that you can't flee despair. You can't escape, with your body, problems that exist in your mind and soul. You can't run away from your choices—you can only fix them with better choices.

There's nothing wrong with a good vacation (particularly if the aim is solitude and quiet) or a round of golf, just as there is nothing wrong with cracking a beer to take the edge off. Certainly

Churchill loved to travel and enjoyed champagne, though he stunk at golf.

But too often, the frenzied or the miserable think that an escape—literal or chemical—is a positive good. Sure, the rush of traveling, the thrill of surfing, or the altered state of a psychedelic can relieve some of the tension that's built up in our lives. Maybe you get some pretty pictures out of it, and some pseudo-profundity that impresses your friends.

But when that wears off? What's left?

Nixon watched nearly *five hundred* movies during his time in the White House. We know the darkness he was running from. There's no question that for Tiger Woods, his addictions were in part driven by a desire to escape the pain left over from his childhood. But each time he hopped on a private plane to Vegas instead of opening up to his wife (or to his father while he was still alive), he was setting himself up for more pain down the road. Each time John Fante hit the golf course instead of the keys of his typewriter, or went out drinking instead of being at home, he might have felt a temporary escape, but it came at a very high cost.

When you defer and delay, interest is accumulating. The bill still comes due . . . and it will be even harder to afford then than it will be right now.

The one thing you can't escape in your life is *yourself.*

Anyone who's traveled long enough knows this. It's eventually clear we carry with us on the road more baggage than just our suitcase and our backpacks.

Emerson, who in his own life traveled to England and Italy and France and Malta and Switzerland (as well as extensively across America), pointed out that the people who built the sights and wonders that tourists liked to see didn't do so while they traveled. You can't make something great flitting around. You have to *stick fast,* like an axis of the earth. Those who think they will find solutions to all their problems by traveling far from home, perhaps as they stare at the Colosseum or some enormous moss-covered statue of Buddha, Emerson said, are bringing *ruins to ruins.* Wherever they go, whatever they do, their sad self comes along.

A plane ticket or a pill or some plant medicine is a treadmill, not a shortcut. What you seek will come only if you sit and do the work, if you probe yourself with real self-awareness and patience.

You have to be still enough to discover what's really going on. You have to let the muddy water settle. That can't happen if you're jetting off from one place to another, if you're packing your schedule with every activity you can think of in order to avoid the possibility of having to spend even a moment alone with your own thoughts.

In the fourth century BC, Mengzi spoke of how the Way is near, but people seek it in what is distant. A few generations after that, Marcus Aurelius pointed out that we don't need to "get away from it all." We just need to *look within.* "Nowhere you can go is more peaceful—more free of interruptions," he said, "than your own soul."

The next time we feel the urge to flee, to hit the road or bury ourselves in work or activity, we need to catch ourselves. Don't book a cross-country flight—go for a walk instead. Don't get high—get some solitude, find some quiet. These are far easier, far more accessible, and ultimately far more sustainable strategies for accessing the stillness we were born with. Travel inside your heart and your mind, and let the body stay put. "A quick visit should be enough to ward off all," Marcus wrote, "and send you back ready to face what awaits you."

Tuning out accomplishes nothing. *Tune in.*

If true peace and clarity are what you seek in this life—and by the way, they are what you deserve—know that you will find them nearby and not far away. Stick fast, as Emerson said. Turn *into* yourself. Stand in place.

Stand in front of the mirror. Get to know your front porch.

You were given one body when you were born—don't try to be someone else, somewhere else. Get to know yourself.

Build a life that you don't need to escape from.

ACT BRAVELY

To see people who will notice a need in the world and
do something about it.... Those are my heroes.

—FRED ROGERS

In Camus's final novel, *The Fall,* his narrator, Clamence, is walking alone on a street in Amsterdam when he hears what sounds like a woman falling into the water. He's not totally certain that's what he heard, but mostly, riding the high of a nice evening with his mistress, he does not want to be bothered, and so he continues on.

A respected lawyer with a reputation as a person of great virtue in his community, Clamence returns to his normal life the following day and attempts to forget the sound he heard. He continues to represent clients and entertain his friends with persuasive political arguments, as he always has.

Yet he begins to feel off.

One day, after a triumphant appearance in court arguing for a blind client, Clamence gets the feeling he is being mocked and laughed at by a group of strangers he can't quite locate. Later, approaching a stalled motorist at an intersection, he is unexpectedly insulted and then assaulted. These encounters are unrelated, but they contribute to a weakening of the illusions he has long held about himself.

It is not with an epiphany or from a blow to the head that the monstrous truth of what he has done becomes clear. It is a slow, creeping realization that comes to Clamence that suddenly and irrevocably changes his self-perception: That night on the canal he shrugged off a chance to save someone from committing suicide.

This realization is Clamence's undoing and the central focus of the book. Forced to see the hollowness of his pretensions and the shame of his failings, he unravels. He had believed he was a good man, but when the moment (indeed moments) called for goodness, he slunk off into the night.

It's a thought that haunts him incessantly. As he walks the streets at night, the cry of that woman—the one he ignored so many years ago—never ceases to torment him. It toys with him too, because his only hope of redemption is that he might hear it again in real life and then seize the opportunity to dive in and save someone from the bottom of the canal.

It's too late. He has failed. He will never be at peace again.

The story is fictional, of course, but a deeply incisive one, written not coincidentally in the aftermath of the incredible moral failings of Europe in the Second World War. Camus's message to the reader pierces us like the scream of the woman in Clamence's memory: High-minded thoughts and inner work are one thing, but all that matters is what you *do*. The health of our spiritual ideals depends on what we do with our bodies in moments of truth.

It is worth comparing the agony and torture of Clamence with a more recent example from another French philosopher, Anne Dufourmantelle, who died in 2017, aged fifty-three, rushing into the surf to save two drowning children who were not her own. In her writing, Anne had spoken often of risk—saying that it was impossible to live life without risk and that in fact, *life is risk*. It is in the presence of danger, she once said in an interview, that we are gifted with the "strong incentive for action, dedication, and surpassing oneself."

And when, on the beach in Saint-Tropez, she was faced with a moment of danger and risk, an opportunity to turn away or to *do good,* she committed the full measure of devotion to her ideals.

What is better? To live as a coward or to die a hero? To fall woefully short of what you know to be right or to fall in the line of duty? And which is more natural? To refuse a call from your fellow humans or to dive in bravely and help them when they need you?

Stillness is not an excuse to withdraw from the affairs of the world. Quite the opposite—it's a tool to let you do more good for more people.

Neither the Buddhists nor the Stoics believed in what has come to be called "original sin"—that we are a fallen and flawed and broken species. On the contrary, they believe we were born good. To them, the phrase "Be natural" was the same as "Do the right thing." For Aristotle, virtue wasn't just something contained in the soul—it was how we lived. It was what we did. He called it *eudaimonia:* human flourishing.

A person who makes selfish choices or acts contrary to their conscience will never be at peace. A person who sits back while others suffer or struggle will never feel good, or feel that they are *enough,* no matter how much they accomplish or how impressive their reputation may be.

A person who *does* good regularly will feel good. A person who contributes to their community will feel like they are a part of one. A person who puts their body to good use—volunteering, protecting, serving, *standing up for*—will not need to treat it like an amusement park to get some thrills.

Virtue is not an abstract notion. We are not clearing our minds and separating the essential from the inessential for the purposes of a parlor trick. Nor are we improving ourselves so that we can get richer or more powerful.

We are doing it to live better and *be* better.

Every person we meet and every situation we find ourselves in is an opportunity to prove that.

It's the old Boy Scout motto: "Do a Good Turn Daily."

Some good turns are big, like saving a life or protecting the environment. But good turns can also be small, Scouts are taught, like a thoughtful gesture, mowing a neighbor's lawn, calling 911 when you see something amiss, holding open a door, making friends with a new kid at school. It's the brave who do these things. It's the people who do these things who make the world worth living in.

Marcus Aurelius spoke of moving from one unselfish action to another—"only there," he said, can we find "delight and stillness." In the Bible, Matthew 5:6 says that those who do right will be made full by God. Too many believers seem to think that *belief* is enough. How many people who claim to be of this religion or that one, if caught and investigated, would be found guilty of *living* the tenets of love and charity and selflessness?

Action is what matters.

Pick up the phone and make the call to tell someone what they mean to you. Share your wealth. Run for office. Pick up the trash you see on the ground. Step in when someone is being bullied. Step in even if you're scared, even if you might get hurt. Tell the truth. Maintain your vows, keep your word. Stretch out a hand to someone who has fallen.

Do the *hard* good deeds. "You must do the thing you cannot do," Eleanor Roosevelt said.

It will be scary. It won't always be easy, but know that what is on the other side of goodness is true stillness.

Think of Dorothy Day, and indeed, many other less famous Catholic nuns, who worked themselves to the bone helping other people. While they may have lacked for physical possessions and wealth, they found great comfort in seeing the shelters they had provided, and the self-respect they'd restored for people whom society had cast aside. Let us compare that to the anxiety of the helicopter parents who think of nothing but which preschool to enroll their toddler in, or the embezzling business partner who is just one audit away from getting caught. Compare that to the nagging insecurity we feel knowing that we are not living the way we should or that we are not doing enough for other people.

If you see fraud, and do not say fraud, the philosopher Nassim Taleb has said, *you are a fraud.* Worse, you will feel like a fraud. And you will never feel proud or happy or confident.

Will we fall short of our own standards? Yes. When this happens, we don't need to whip ourselves, as Clamence did, we must simply let it instruct and teach us, as all injuries do.

That's why twelve-step groups ask their members to be of service as part of their recovery. Not because good deeds can undo the past, but because they help get us out of our heads, and in the process, help us write the script for a better future.

If we want to be good and feel good, we have to *do* good.

There is no escaping this.

Dive in when you hear the cry for help. Reach out when you see the need. Do kindness where you can.

Because you'll have to find a way to live with yourself if you don't.

ON TO THE FINAL ACT

As a well-spent day brings a happy sleep, so a well-employed life brings a happy death.

—LEONARDO DA VINCI

It was AD 161 and the emperor Antoninus Pius knew he was going to die. He was seventy-four years old and he could feel the life leaving his body. A fever had taken hold and his stomach pained him. With his last bit of strength, he called his adopted son Marcus Aurelius into the room and began the process of transferring the state over to him. When this task was complete, Antoninus turned to his royal audience and spoke his final word—a word that would echo down through not just the life of his son but all of history, down even to us today: *aequanimitas.*

A few hundred years before, in roughly 400 BC, Buddha accepted with equal equanimity that he too would soon pass from this earth. He was a little older than Antoninus, but he had not certified a successor, for although he was born a prince, he'd re-nounced his patrimony in the pursuit of enlightenment. Still, he could tell that his students were worried about losing him, about how they would continue their journey without his guidance and love.

"You may be thinking," he said to them, "'The word of the Teacher is now a thing of the past; now we have no more teacher.' But that is not how you should see it. Let the Dhamma and the Discipline that I have taught you be your Teacher when I am gone."

Then, just as Antoninus had done, he prepared for his final words. His last chance for passing on wisdom to the people he loved, to the people he knew would face all the difficulties that life throws at us. "All individual things pass away," he said. "Seek your liberation with diligence."

Then Buddha fell into a deep sleep and never woke again.

It is fitting that between the deaths of these two titans came Epicurus, the philosopher whose unique way of living almost perfectly bridges the Eastern and Western schools. In 270 BC, he also had the self-awareness to know he did not have much more time. "On this happy day, which is the last day of my life," Epicurus began his final letter, "I write the following words to you." Despite the considerable pain he felt, his body racked by blockages in the bladder and bowels, he wrote instead of the joy in his heart, and the fond recollections he had of conversations with his friends. Then he got to the purpose of the letter—a set of instructions for the care of a promising pupil he wanted to make sure was looked after. Within a few hours and without much fanfare, Epicurus would join Buddha and Antoninus in eternity, in death.

Three approaches. Different, but in the end the same.

Clear.

Calm.

Kind.

Still.

Each of the domains we have studied addressed in their own way.

The mind.

The soul.

The body.

The mental. The spiritual. The physical.

Three legs in a stool. Three points along a perfect circle.

None of us are long for this world. Death hangs over us all, whether we notice or not, whether we believe it or not.

Tomorrow, we could discover we have cancer. Two weeks from now, a heavy branch could fall from a tree and take us with it. The prognosis is terminal for each and every person and has been from the moment we were born. Our heart beats without fail for an uncertain amount of time, and then one day, suddenly, it is still.

Memento mori.

This is a fact that, perhaps more than anything else, is

responsible for incredible amounts of anxiety and distress. It's scary to think that we will die. As is the fact that we cannot know for certain what will happen when death comes, whenever that is. Is there such a thing as heaven? Or hell? Is death painful? Is it nothingness, a dark backward abysm of time?

Seneca reminded himself that before we were born we were still and at peace, and so we will be once again after we die. A light loses nothing by being extinguished, he said, it just goes back to how it was before.

The denial of this simple, humbling reality—the denial of death—is why we attempt to build monuments to our own greatness, it's why we worry and argue so much, why we chase pleasure and money and cannot be still while we are alive. It's ironic that we spend so much of our precious time on earth either impotently fighting death or futilely attempting to ignore the thought of it.

It was Cicero who said that to *study philosophy is to learn how to die*.

Most of this book has been about how to live well. But in so doing, it is also about how to die well. Because they are the same thing. Death is where the three domains we have studied in these pages come together.

We must learn to think rationally and clearly about our own fate.

We must find spiritual meaning and goodness while we are alive.

We must treat the vessel we inhabit on this planet well—or we will be forced to abandon it early.

Death brings an end to everything, to our minds, our souls, and our bodies, in a final, permanent stillness.

So we end this book there as well.

AFTERWORD

It's getting to be early evening now, and about time for me to get up from the computer, having made some progress on the pages you just read. Years ago I got myself out of the busy city and set up my family here, on a little spread outside town, with a picture of Oliver Sacks and his "No!" sign hanging above my desk. Now that my writing day is done, I've got work to do on the farm—chickens to feed, some donkeys to sneak carrots to, and fences to inspect. Not unlike the plot of that Zen poem about the taming of the bull, my neighbor's longhorn has gotten onto my property, and I need to go find him.

My young son helps me load some tools into the back of the ATV—"the tractor, the *twahktor*!" he calls it—and then I hug him and head down the levee, through to the middle pasture, and back down by the creek. The fence there has started to weaken, from the elements and the explorations of the wayward bull, and I spend the next hour grabbing and pinching T-post clips. You take the clip and wrap it around the back of the post, grab the end with the pliers, hooking it over the wire and twisting it tight so it can't come loose. Wrap, grab, hook, twist. Wrap, grab, hook, twist.

No thinking, just doing.

The sweat gets going quickly in Texas, and my leather gloves are shades darker almost as soon as I start. But by the end the fence is tight. I tell myself it will hold—or so I hope. Next up is moving the hay, backing the buggy up to the round bale, letting the arm fall over top of it, and then gunning the engine of the ATV. It catches, teeters, flips up, and falls over, two thousand pounds of food now lying flat on the trailer. By the time I've driven to where I need to drop it, the cows have gotten wise to the sound and come running to investigate. I line it up with the hay ring, back up again, and watch it come tumbling off the back. With the knife in my pocket, I cut off the netting and drop the heavy steel hay ring over it to prevent waste. The cows begin to eat, yelling in appreciation, jostling with each other for their place at the bale.

With them properly distracted, it's time for me to go find this bull. I heard him when I was working and suspect he's over in the back corner of the front pasture. I find him there, a ton or more of muscle and horns. I'm a little frustrated. This is not my problem, though my neighbor seems not to mind that this keeps happening. I behold him there, as the poem says, but keep my distance. Not just because I don't want to be gored, but because in rushing this process before, in getting him worked up, I've run the bull right through a barbed-wire fence—a costly reminder of the risks of impatience.

The key is to nudge him in the direction you want to go, to eliminate the other options and then get him moving. It's got to feel like it's his idea. Otherwise, he'll panic and get angry. And the problem goes from bad to worse.

So I just stand there, resting against some cedar, looking up at the first croppings of the Violet Crown—the Texas sunset that settles over Austin—that is coming toward the horizon. In this moment, I am at peace. It doesn't matter how tough things have been lately. It doesn't matter what's going on in the world. My breathing is slowing down. There is no social media here. The outrage factory that has become the news cycle can't reach me. Neither can my clients or business partners—there's no reception in these woods. I am far from this manuscript I have been working on. Far from my research and my notes, from my comfortable office and the craft that I love. And here, far from my work, the story of Shawn Green, which I read months ago, and what he was really teaching us slips from my subconscious into the front of my mind. I get it now. I get what he was after.

Chop wood, carry water. Fix fences, load hay, seize the bull.
My mind is empty. My heart is full. My body is busy.
Attamen tranquillus.

Ryan Holiday
Austin, Texas

WHAT'S NEXT?

Each morning, I write a meditation inspired by Stoic and other ancient philosophy for DailyStoic.com. You can follow along with nearly two hundred thousand other people by signing up at:

DailyStoic.com/email

Or if you'd like some reading recommendations—nourishing, inspiring, challenging books of the sort that wisdom is made from—you can sign up for a monthly list at:

RyanHoliday.net/reading-list

ACKNOWLEDGMENTS

One of the simplest and most accessible entry points into stillness is gratitude. Gratitude for being alive, for the lucky breaks you've gotten, and for all the people in your life who have helped you. Each morning, I try to take some time to think about these very things, but for the most part, such thanks remain private. With this little space allowed to me here, I'd like to thank everyone who helped make this book possible—my wife, Samantha, first and foremost. I am grateful for her guidance and support and natural stillness, which I learn from constantly. My son, Clark, who went on many long walks with me as I worked out the words in this book. My sister, Amy, whose poise and strength as she battles cancer has deeply moved and humbled me. I am grateful to my agent and collaborator, Steve Hanselman, who helped not only with translations but with the shaping of the idea. Nils Parker, who has been a sounding board for my writing ideas for over a decade now, and Brent Underwood for all his help marketing and building my platform. Thank you to Hristo Vassilev for all his important research and fact-checking help.

Niki Papadopoulos, my editor, and the rest of the Portfolio team at Penguin Random House—thank you for all the work on *all* my books. To the *logos* that brought all these people and factors together . . .

I should also thank my donkeys and cows and goats (for their lessons on *being,* not doing), but there are too many to name. I'm also grateful for the chance to workshop many of the ideas in this book on *Thought Catalog, Observer, Medium,* and DailyStoic.com

My final and most serious gratitude goes out to the thinkers and philosophers whose ideas make up this book. It would not have been possible without them, but more important, their insights and writings have made my life better. I'm grateful too to the heroes (and villains) in the stories written here, as their all-too-human successes and failures both inspire and caution anyone in search of happiness, excellence, and stillness. My own search is nowhere near complete, but their example has helped me make a few inches on a journey that—God(s) willing—is only just beginning.

SOURCES AND BIBLIOGRAPHY

My aim for this book is for it to be as lean and portable as possible. Since there is limited room here and no desire to leave any valuable source out, anyone who wants a bibliography for this book can email:

hello@stillnessisthekey.com

For those looking to do more reading on Eastern or Western philosophy, I recommend the following:

Meditations, by Marcus Aurelius (Modern Library)

Readings in Classical Chinese Philosophy, by Philip J. Ivanhoe and Bryan W. Van Norden (Hackett)

Letters of a Stoic by Seneca (Penguin Classics)

The Bhagavad Gita (Penguin Classics)

The Art of Happiness, by Epicurus (Penguin Classics)

The New Testament: A Translation, by David Bentley Hart (Yale University Press)

Buddha, by Karen Armstrong (Penguin Lives Biographies)

Also by Ryan Holiday

Also by Ryan Holiday and Stephen Hanselman

RyanHoliday.net
DailyStoic.com

PORTFOLIO
PENGUIN

"Ryan Holiday is one of his generation's finest thinkers, and this book is his best yet."

—STEVEN PRESSFIELD, author of *The War of Art*

"The comedian Bill Hicks said the world was tainted with fevered egos. In *Ego Is the Enemy*, Ryan Holiday writes us all a prescription: humility. This book is packed with stories and quotes that will help you get out of your own way. Whether you're starting out or starting over, you'll find something to steal here."

—AUSTIN KLEON, author of *Steal Like an Artist*

"This is a book I want every athlete, aspiring leader, entrepreneur, thinker, and doer to read. Ryan Holiday is one of the most promising young writers of his generation."

—GEORGE RAVELING, Hall of Fame Basketball coach and Nike's Director of International Basketball

"I see the toxic vanity of ego at play every day and it never ceases to amaze me how often it wrecks promising creative endeavors. Read this book before it wrecks you or the projects and people you love. Consider it as urgently as you do a proper workout regimen and eating right. Ryan's insights are priceless."

—MARC ECKO, founder of Ecko Unltd and Complex

"I don't have many rules in life, but one I never break is: If Ryan Holiday writes a book, I read it as soon as I can get my hands on it."

—BRIAN KOPPELMAN, screenwriter and director of *Rounders, Ocean's Thirteen,* and *Billions*

"In his new book Ryan Holiday attacks the greatest obstacle to mastery and true success in life—our insatiable ego. In an inspiring yet practical way, he teaches us how to manage and tame this beast within us so that we can focus on what really matters—producing the best work possible."

—ROBERT GREENE, author of *Mastery*

"We're often told that to achieve success, we need confidence. With refreshing candor, Ryan Holiday challenges that assumption, highlighting how we can earn confidence by pursuing something bigger than our own success."

—ADAM GRANT, author of *Originals* and *Give and Take*

"Once again Ryan Holiday has laid down the gauntlet for readers willing to challenge themselves with the tough questions of our time. Every reader will find truths that are pertinent to each of our lives. Ego can be the enemy if we are unarmed with the cautionary insights of history, scripture, and philosophy. As was said to St. Augustine more than a thousand years ago, 'Pick it up and read'; for to not do so is to allow the enemy to bring despair."

—DR. DREW PINSKY, host of HLN's *Dr. Drew On Call* and *Loveline*

"In this day and age where everyone seeks instant gratification, the idea of success is skewed—many believing the road to their goals is a linear path. As a former professional athlete I can tell you that the road is anything but linear. In fact, it is one that consists of twists, turns, and ups and downs—it requires you to put your head down and put in the work. Ryan Holiday hits the nail on the head with this book, reminding us that the real success is in the journey and learning process. I only wish I had had this gem as a reference during my playing days."

—LORI LINDSEY, former U.S. Women's National Team soccer player

"I would like to rip out every page and use them as wallpaper so I could be reminded constantly of the humility and work it takes to truly succeed. In the margins of my copy, I have scrawled the same message over and over—'pre-Gold.' Reading this inspiring book brought me back to the humility and work ethic it took to win the Olympics."

—CHANDRA CRAWFORD, Olympic Gold Medalist

"What a valuable book for those in positions of authority! It has made me a better judge."

—THE HONORABLE FREDERIC BLOCK, U.S. District Judge and author of *Disrobed*

EGO
IS THE
ENEMY

ALSO BY RYAN HOLIDAY

Growth Hacker Marketing: A Primer on the Future of PR, Marketing, and Advertising

Trust Me, I'm Lying: Confessions of a Media Manipulator

The Obstacle Is the Way: The Timeless Art of Turning Trials into Triumph

The Daily Stoic: 366 Meditations on Wisdom, Perseverance, and the Art of Living

Perennial Seller: The Art of Making and Marketing Work that Lasts

Conspiracy: Peter Thiel, Hulk Hogan, Gawker, and the Anatomy of Intrigue

Stillness is the Key

Lives of the Stoic: The Art of Living from Zeno to Marcus Aurelius

Courage is Calling: Fortune Favors the Brave

RYAN HOLIDAY

EGO
IS THE
ENEMY

PORTFOLIO

PENGUIN

PORTFOLIO / PENGUIN
An imprint of Penguin Random House LLC
penguinrandomhouse.com

Copyright © 2016 by Ryan Holiday
Penguin Random House supports copyright. Copyright fuels creativity, encourages
diverse voices, promotes free speech, and creates a vibrant culture. Thank you for
buying an authorized edition of this book and for complying with copyright laws
by not reproducing, scanning, or distributing any part of it in any form without
permission. You are supporting writers and allowing Penguin Random House to
continue to publish books for every reader.

ISBN 9781591847816 (hardcover)
ISBN 9780698192157 (ebook)

Printed in the United States of America
28th Printing

Do not believe that he who seeks to comfort you lives untroubled among the simple and quiet words that sometimes do you good. His life has much difficulty and sadness and remains far behind yours. Were it otherwise he would never have been able to find those words.

—RAINER MARIA RILKE

CONTENTS

PART II. SUCCESS

PART III. FAILURE

THE PAINFUL PROLOGUE

This is not a book about me. But since this is a book about ego, I'm going to address a question that I'd be a hypocrite not to have thought about.

Who the hell am I to write it?

My story is not particularly important for the lessons that follow, but I want to tell it briefly here at the beginning in order to provide some context. For I have experienced ego at each of its stages in my short life: Aspiration. Success. Failure. And back again and back again.

When I was nineteen years old, sensing some astounding and life-changing opportunities, I dropped out of college. Mentors vied for my attention, groomed me as their protégé. Seen as going places, I was *the kid*. Success came quickly.

After I became the youngest executive at a Beverly Hills talent management agency, I helped sign and work with a number of huge rock bands. I advised on books that went on to sell millions of copies and invent their own literary genres. Around the time I turned twenty-one, I came on as a strategist for American Apparel, then one of the hottest fashion brands in the world. Soon, I was the director of marketing.

By twenty-five, I had published my first book—which was an immediate and controversial best seller—with my face prominently on the cover. A studio optioned the rights to create a television show about my life. In the next few years, I accumulated many of the trappings of success—influence, a platform, press, resources, money, even a little notoriety. Later, I built a successful company on the back of those assets, where I worked with well-known, well-paying clients and did the kind of work that got me invited to speak at conferences and fancy events.

With success comes the temptation to tell oneself a story, to round off the edges, to cut out your lucky breaks and add a certain mythology to it all. You know, that arcing narrative of Herculean struggle for greatness against all odds: sleeping on the floor, being disowned by my parents, suffering for my ambition. It's a type of storytelling in which eventually your talent becomes your identity and your accomplishments become your worth.

But a story like this is never honest or helpful. In my retelling to you just now, I left a lot out. Conveniently omitted were the stresses and temptations; the stomach-turning drops and the mistakes—all the mistakes—were left on the cutting-room floor in favor of the highlight reel. They are the times I would rather not discuss: A public evisceration by someone I looked up to, which so crushed me at the time that I was later taken to the emergency room. The day I lost my nerve, walked into my boss's office, and told him I couldn't cut it and was going back to school—and meant it. The ephemeral nature of best-sellerdom, and how short it actually was (a week). The book signing that *one* person showed up at. The company I founded tearing itself to pieces and having to rebuild it. Twice. These are just some of the moments that get nicely edited out.

This fuller picture itself is still only a fraction of a life, but at least it hits more of the important notes—at least the important ones for this book: ambition, achievement, and adversity.

I'm not someone who believes in epiphanies. There is no one moment that changes a person. There are many. During a period of about six months in 2014, it seemed those moments were all happening in succession.

First, American Apparel—where I did much of my best work—teetered on the edge of bankruptcy, hundreds of millions of dollars in debt, a shell of its former self. Its founder, who I had deeply admired since I was a young man, was unceremoniously fired by his own handpicked board of directors, and down to sleeping on a friend's couch. Then the talent agency where I made my bones was in similar shape, sued peremptorily by clients to whom it owed a lot of money. Another mentor of mine seemingly unraveled around the same time, taking our relationship with him.

These were the people I had shaped my life around. The people I looked up to and trained under. Their stability—financially, emotionally, psychologically—was not just something I took for granted, it was central to my existence and self-worth. And yet, there they were, imploding right in front of me, one after another.

The wheels were coming off, or so it felt. To go from wanting to be like someone your whole life to realizing you *never* want to be like him is a kind of whiplash that you can't prepare for.

Nor was I exempt from this dissolution myself. Just when I could least afford it, problems I had neglected in my own life began to emerge.

Despite my successes, I found myself back in the city I started in, stressed and overworked, having handed much of my hard-earned freedom away because I couldn't say no to money and the thrill of a good crisis. I was wound so tight that the slightest disruption sent me into a sputtering, inconsolable rage. My work, which had always come easy, became labored. My faith in myself and other people collapsed. My quality of life did too.

I remember arriving at my house one day, after weeks on the road, and having an intense panic attack because the Wi-Fi wasn't working—*If I don't send these e-mails. If I don't send these e-mails. If I don't send these e-mails. If I don't send these e-mails . . .*

You think you're doing what you're supposed to. Society rewards you for it. But then you watch your future wife walk out the door because you aren't the person you used to be.

How does something like this happen? Can you really go from feeling like you're standing on the shoulders of giants one day, and then the next you're prying yourself out of the rubble of multiple implosions, trying to pick up the pieces from the ruins?

One benefit, however, was that it forced me to come to terms with the fact that I was a workaholic. Not in an "Oh, he just works too much" kind of way, or in the "Just relax and play it off" sense, but more, "If he doesn't start going to meetings and get clean, he will die an early death." I realized that the same drive and compulsion that had made me successful so early came with a price—as it had for so many others. It wasn't so much the amount of work but the outsized role it had taken in my sense of self. I was trapped so terribly inside my own head that I was a prisoner to my own thoughts. The result was a sort of treadmill of pain and frustration, and I needed to figure out why—unless I wanted to break in an equally tragic fashion.

For a long time, as a researcher and writer, I have studied history and business. Like anything that involves people, seen over a long enough timeline universal issues begin to emerge. These are the topics I had long been fascinated with. Foremost among them was ego.

I was not unfamiliar with ego and its effects. In fact, I had been researching this book for nearly a year before the events I have just recounted for you. But my painful experiences in this period brought the notions I was studying into focus in ways that I could never have previously understood.

It allowed me to see the ill effects of ego played out not just in myself, or across the pages of history, but in friends and clients and colleagues, some at the highest levels of many industries. Ego has cost the people I admire hundreds of millions of dollars, and like Sisyphus, rolled them back from their goals just as they've achieved them. I have now at least peeked over that precipice myself.

A few months after my own realization, I had the phrase "EGO IS THE ENEMY" tattooed on my right forearm. Where the words came from I don't know, probably from a book I read long, long ago, but they were immediately a source of great solace and direction. On my left arm, of similarly muddled attribution, it says: "THE OBSTACLE IS

THE WAY." It's these two phrases that I look at now, every single day, and use them to guide the decisions in my life. I can't help but see them when I swim, when I meditate, when I write, when I get out of the shower in the morning, and both prepare me—admonish me—to choose the right course in essentially any situation I might face.

I wrote this book not because I have attained some wisdom I feel qualified to preach, but because it's the book I wish existed at critical turning points in my own life. When I, like everyone else, was called to answer the most critical questions a person can ask themselves in life: Who do I want to be? And: What path will I take? (*Quod vitae sectabor iter.*)

And because I've found these questions to be timeless and universal, except for this note, I have tried to rely on philosophy and historical examples in this book instead of my personal life.

While the history books are filled with tales of obsessive, visionary geniuses who remade the world in their image with sheer, almost irrational force, I've found that if you go looking you'll find that history is also made by individuals who fought their egos at every turn, who eschewed the spotlight, and who put their higher goals above their desire for recognition. Engaging with and retelling these stories has been my method of learning and absorbing them.

Like my other books, this one is deeply influenced by Stoic philosophy and indeed all the great classical thinkers. I borrow heavily from them all in my writing just as I have leaned on them my entire life. If there is anything that helps you in this book, it will be because of them and not me.

The orator Demosthenes once said that virtue begins with understanding and is fulfilled by courage. We must begin by seeing ourselves and the world in a new way for the first time. Then we must fight to be different and fight to stay different—that's the hard part. I'm not saying you should repress or crush every ounce of ego in your life—or that doing so is even possible. These are just reminders, moral stories to encourage our better impulses.

In Aristotle's famous *Ethics*, he uses the analogy of a warped piece of wood to describe human nature. In order to eliminate warping or curvature, a skilled woodworker slowly applies pressure in the opposite direction—essentially, bending it straight. Of course, a couple of thousand years later Kant snorted, "Out of the crooked timber of humanity, nothing can be made straight." We might not ever be straight, but we can strive for *straighter*.

It's always nice to be made to feel special or empowered or inspired. But that's not the aim of this book. Instead, I have tried to arrange these pages so that you might end in the same place I did when I finished writing it: that is, you will think less of yourself. I hope you will be less invested in the story you tell about your own specialness, and as a result, you will be liberated to *accomplish* the world-changing work you've set out to achieve.

EGO
IS THE
ENEMY

INTRODUCTION

The first principle is that you must not fool yourself—
and you are the easiest person to fool.

—RICHARD FEYNMAN

Maybe you're young and brimming with ambition. Maybe you're young and you're struggling. Maybe you've made that first couple million, signed your first deal, been selected to some elite group, or maybe you're already accomplished enough to last a lifetime. Maybe you're stunned to find out how empty it is at the top. Maybe you're charged with leading others through a crisis. Maybe you just got fired. Maybe you just hit rock bottom.

Wherever you are, whatever you're doing, your worst enemy already lives inside you: your ego.

"Not me," you think. "No one would ever call me an egomaniac." Perhaps you've always thought of yourself as a pretty balanced person. But for people with ambitions, talents, drives, and potential to fulfill, ego comes with the territory. Precisely what makes us so promising as thinkers, doers, creatives, and entrepreneurs, what drives us to the top of those fields, makes us vulnerable to this darker side of the psyche.

1

Now this is not a book about ego in the Freudian sense. Freud was fond of explaining the ego by way of analogy—our ego was the rider on a horse, with our unconscious drives representing the animal while the ego tried to direct them. Modern psychologists, on the other hand, use the word "egotist" to refer to someone dangerously focused on themselves and with disregard for anyone else. All these definitions are true enough but of little value outside a clinical setting.

The ego we see most commonly goes by a more casual definition: an unhealthy belief in our own importance. Arrogance. Self-centered ambition. That's the definition this book will use. It's that petulant child inside every person, the one that chooses getting his or her way over anything or anyone else. The need to be *better* than, *more* than, *recognized* for, far past any reasonable utility—that's ego. It's the sense of superiority and certainty that exceeds the bounds of confidence and talent.

It's when the notion of ourselves and the world grows so inflated that it begins to distort the reality that surrounds us. When, as the football coach Bill Walsh explained, "self-confidence becomes arrogance, assertiveness becomes obstinacy, and self-assurance becomes reckless abandon." This is the ego, as the writer Cyril Connolly warned, that "sucks us down like the law of gravity."

In this way, ego is the enemy of what you want and of what you have: Of mastering a craft. Of real creative insight. Of working well with others. Of building loyalty and support. Of longevity. Of repeating and retaining your success. It repulses advantages and opportunities. It's a magnet for enemies and errors. It is Scylla and Charybdis.

Most of us aren't "egomaniacs," but ego is there at the

root of almost every conceivable problem and obstacle, from why we can't win to why we need to win all the time and at the expense of others. From why we don't have what we want to why having what we want doesn't seem to make us feel any better.

We don't usually see it this way. We think something else is to blame for our problems (most often, other people). We are, as the poet Lucretius put it a few thousand years ago, the proverbial "sick man ignorant of the cause of his malady." Especially for successful people who can't see what ego prevents them from doing because all they can see is what they've already done.

With every ambition and goal we have—big or small— ego is there undermining us on the very journey we've put everything into pursuing.

The pioneering CEO Harold Geneen compared egoism to alcoholism: "The egotist does not stumble about, knocking things off his desk. He does not stammer or drool. No, instead, he becomes more and more arrogant, and some people, not knowing what is underneath such an attitude, mistake his arrogance for a sense of power and self-confidence." You could say they start to mistake that about themselves too, not realizing the disease they've contracted or that they're killing themselves with it.

If ego is the voice that tells us we're better than we really are, we can say ego inhibits true success by preventing a direct and honest connection to the world around us. One of the early members of Alcoholics Anonymous defined ego as "a conscious separation *from*." From what? Everything.

The ways this separation manifests itself negatively are

immense: We can't work with other people if we've put up walls. We can't improve the world if we don't understand it or ourselves. We can't take or receive feedback if we are incapable of or uninterested in hearing from outside sources. We can't recognize opportunities—or create them—if instead of seeing what is in front of us, we live inside our own fantasy. Without an *accurate* accounting of our own abilities compared to others, what we have is not confidence but delusion. How are we supposed to reach, motivate, or lead other people if we can't relate to their needs—because we've lost touch with our own?

The performance artist Marina Abramović puts it directly: "If you start believing in your greatness, it is the death of your creativity."

Just one thing keeps ego around—comfort. Pursuing great work—whether it is in sports or art or business—is often terrifying. Ego soothes that fear. It's a salve to that insecurity. Replacing the rational and aware parts of our psyche with bluster and self-absorption, ego tells us what we want to hear, when we want to hear it.

But it is a short-term fix with a long-term consequence.

EGO WAS ALWAYS THERE. NOW IT'S EMBOLDENED.

Now more than ever, our culture fans the flames of ego. It's never been easier to talk, to puff ourselves up. We can brag about our goals to millions of our fans and followers—things only rock stars and cult leaders used to have. We can follow and interact with our idols on Twitter, we can read books and sites and watch TED Talks, drink from a fire hose of inspiration and validation like never before (there's an app for that). We can name ourselves CEO of our exists-only-on-paper company. We can announce big news on social media and let the congratulations roll in. We can publish articles about ourselves in outlets that used to be sources of objective journalism.

Some of us do this more than others. But it's only a matter of degree.

Besides the changes in technology, we're told to believe in our uniqueness above all else. We're told to think big, live big, to be memorable and "dare greatly." We think that success requires a bold vision or some sweeping plan—after all, that's what the founders of this company or that championship team supposedly had. (But did they? Did they really?) We see risk-taking swagger and successful people in the media, and eager for our own successes, try to reverse engineer the right attitude, the right pose.

We intuit a causal relationship that isn't there. We assume the symptoms of success are the same as success itself—and in our naiveté, confuse the by-product with the cause.

Sure, ego has worked for some. Many of history's most famous men and women were notoriously egotistical. But so were many of its greatest failures. Far more of them, in fact. But here we are with a culture that urges us to roll the dice. To make the gamble, ignoring the stakes.

WHEREVER YOU ARE, EGO IS TOO.

At any given time in life, people find themselves at one of three stages. We're aspiring to something—trying to make a dent in the universe. We have achieved success—perhaps a little, perhaps a lot. Or we have failed—recently or continually. Most of us are in these stages in a fluid sense—we're aspiring until we succeed, we succeed until we fail or until we aspire to more, and after we fail we can begin to aspire or succeed again.

Ego is the enemy every step along this way. In a sense, ego is the enemy of building, of maintaining, and of recovering. When things come fast and easy, this might be fine. But in times of change, of difficulty . . .

And therefore, the three parts that this book is organized into: Aspire. Success. Failure.

The aim of that structure is simple: to help you suppress ego early before bad habits take hold, to replace the temptations of ego with humility and discipline when we experience success, and to cultivate strength and fortitude so that when fate turns against you, you're not wrecked by failure. In short, it will help us be:

- Humble in our aspirations
- Gracious in our success
- Resilient in our failures

This is not to say that you're not unique and that you don't have something amazing to contribute in your short time on this planet. This is not to say that there is not room to push past creative boundaries, to invent, to feel inspired, or to aim for truly ambitious change and innovation. On the contrary, in order to properly do these things and take these risks we need balance. As the Quaker William Penn observed, "Buildings that lie so exposed to the weather need a good foundation."

SO, WHAT NOW?

This book you hold in your hands is written around one optimistic assumption: Your ego is not some power you're forced to satiate at every turn. It can be managed. It can be directed.

In this book, we'll look at individuals like William Tecumseh Sherman, Katharine Graham, Jackie Robinson, Eleanor Roosevelt, Bill Walsh, Benjamin Franklin, Belisarius, Angela Merkel, and George C. Marshall. Could they have accomplished what they accomplished—saving faltering companies, advancing the art of war, integrating baseball, revolutionizing football offense, standing up to tyranny, bravely bearing misfortune—if ego had left them ungrounded and self-absorbed? It was their sense of reality and awareness—one that the author and strategist Robert Greene once said we must take to like a spider in its web—that was at the core of their great art, great writing, great design, great business, great marketing, and great leadership.

What we find when we study these individuals is that they were grounded, circumspect, and unflinchingly real. Not that any of them were wholly without ego. But they knew how to suppress it, channel it, subsume it when it counted. They were great yet humble.

Wait, but so-and-so had a huge ego and was successful. But what about Steve Jobs? What about Kanye West?

We can seek to rationalize the worst behavior by pointing to outliers. But no one is truly successful *because* they are delusional, self-absorbed, or disconnected. Even if these traits are correlated or associated with certain well-known individuals, so are a few others: addiction, abuse (of themselves and

7

EGO IS THE ENEMY

others), depression, mania. In fact, what we see when we study these people is that they did their best work in the moments when they fought back against these impulses, disorders, and flaws. Only when free of ego and baggage can anyone perform to their utmost.

For this reason, we're also going to look at individuals like Howard Hughes, the Persian king Xerxes, John De-Lorean, Alexander the Great, and at the many cautionary tales of others who lost their grip on reality and in the process made it clear what a gamble ego can be. We'll look at the costly lessons they learned and the price they paid in misery and self-destruction. We'll look at how often even the most successful people vacillate between humility and ego and the problems this causes.

When we remove ego, we're left with what is real. What replaces ego is humility, yes—but rock-hard humility and confidence. Whereas ego is artificial, this type of confidence can hold weight. Ego is stolen. Confidence is earned. Ego is self-anointed, its swagger is artifice. One is girding yourself, the other gaslighting. It's the difference between potent and poisonous.

As you'll see in the pages that follow, that self-confidence took an unassuming and underestimated general and turned him into America's foremost warrior and strategist during the Civil War. Ego took a different general from the heights of power and influence after that same war and drove him to destitution and ignominy. One took a quiet, sober German scientist and made her not just a new kind of leader but a force for peace. The other took two different but equally brilliant and bold engineering minds of the twentieth century and built them up in a whirlwind of hype and celebrity before dashing their hopes against the rocks of failure, bankruptcy, scandal, and insanity. One guided one of the worst teams in NFL history to the Super Bowl in three seasons, and then on to be one of most dominant dynasties in the game. Meanwhile, countless other coaches, politicians, entrepreneurs, and writers have overcome similar odds—only to succumb to the more inevitable probability of handing the top spot right back to someone else.

Some learn humility. Some choose ego. Some are prepared for the vicissitudes of fate, both positive and negative. Others are not. Which will you choose? Who will you be?

You've picked up this book because you sense that you'll need to answer this question eventually, consciously or not.

Well, here we are. Let's get to it.

PART I

ASPIRE

Here, we are setting out to do something. We have a goal, a calling, a new beginning. Every great journey begins here—yet far too many of us never reach our intended destination. Ego more often than not is the culprit. We build ourselves up with fantastical stories, we pretend we have it all figured out, we let our star burn bright and hot only to fizzle out, and we have no idea why. These are symptoms of ego, for which humility and reality are the cure.

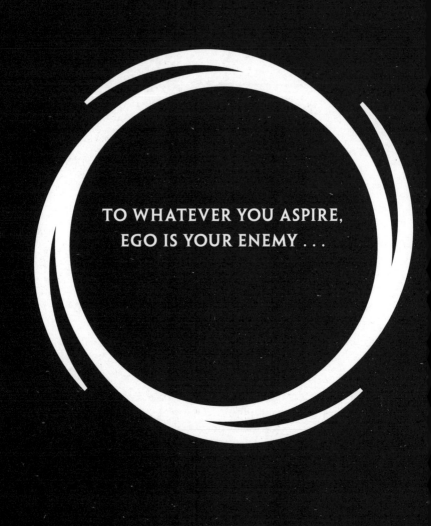

TO WHATEVER YOU ASPIRE,
EGO IS YOUR ENEMY . . .

He is a bold surgeon, they say, whose hand does not tremble when he performs an operation upon his own person; and he is often equally bold who does not hesitate to pull off the mysterious veil of self-delusion, which covers from his view the deformities of his own conduct.

—ADAM SMITH

Sometime around the year 374 B.C., Isocrates, one of the most well-known teachers and rhetoricians in Athens, wrote a letter to a young man named Demonicus. Isocrates had been a friend of the boy's recently deceased father and wanted to pass on to him some advice on how to follow his father's example.

The advice ranged from practical to moral—all communicated in what Isocrates described as "noble maxims." They were, as he put it, "precepts for the years to come."

Like many of us, Demonicus was ambitious, which is why Isocrates wrote him, because the path of ambition can be dangerous. Isocrates began by informing the young man that "no adornment so becomes you as modesty, justice, and self-control; for these are the virtues by which, as all men are agreed, the character of the young is held in restraint."

"Practice self-control," he said, warning Demonicus not to fall under the sway of "temper, pleasure, and pain." And "abhor flatterers as you would deceivers; for both, if trusted, injure those who trust them."

He wanted him to "Be affable in your relations with those who approach you, and never haughty; for the pride of the arrogant even slaves can hardly endure" and "Be slow in deliberation, but be prompt to carry out your resolves" and that the "best thing which we have in ourselves is good judgment." Constantly train your intellect, he told him, "for the greatest thing in the smallest compass is a sound mind in a human body."

Some of this advice might sound familiar. Because it made its way over the next two thousand years to William Shakespeare, who often warned about ego run amok. In fact, in *Hamlet*, using this very letter as his model, Shakespeare puts Isocrates' words in the mouth of his character Polonius in a speech to his son, Laertes. The speech, if you happen to have heard it, wraps up with this little verse.

> *This above all: to thine own self be true,*
> *And it must follow, as the night the day,*
> *Thou canst not then be false to any man.*
> *Farewell. My blessing season this in thee!*

As it happened, Shakespeare's words also made their way to a young United States military officer named William Tecumseh Sherman, who would go on to become perhaps this country's greatest general and strategic thinker. He may never have heard of Isocrates, but he loved the play and often quoted this very speech.

Like Demonicus', Sherman's father died when he was very young. Like Demonicus, he was taken under the wing of a wise, older man, in this case Thomas Ewing, a soon-to-be U.S. senator and friend of Sherman's father, who adopted the young boy and raised him as his own.

What's interesting about Sherman is that despite his connected father, almost no one would have predicted much more than regional accomplishments—least of all that he would one day need to take the unprecedented step of *refusing the presidency of the United States*. Unlike a Napoleon, who bursts upon the scene from nowhere and disappears in failure just as quickly, Sherman's ascent was a slow and gradual one.

He spent his early years at West Point, and then in the army. For his first few years in service, Sherman traversed nearly the entire United States on horseback, slowly learning with each posting. As the rumblings of Civil War broke out, Sherman made his way east to volunteer his services and he was shortly put to use at the Battle of Bull Run, a rather disastrous Union defeat. Benefiting from a dire shortage of leadership, Sherman was promoted to brigadier general and was summoned to meet with President Lincoln and his top military adviser. On several occasions, Sherman freely strategized and planned with the president, but at the end of his trip, he made one strange request; he'd accept his new promotion only with the assurance that he'd *not* have to assume superior command. Would Lincoln give him his word on that? With every other general asking for as much rank and power as possible, Lincoln happily agreed.

At this point in time, Sherman felt more comfortable as a

number two. He felt he had an honest appreciation for his own abilities and that this role best suited him. Imagine that—an ambitious person turning down a chance to advance in responsibilities because he actually wanted to be ready for them. Is that really so crazy?

Not that Sherman was always the perfect model of restraint and order. Early in the war, tasked with defending the state of Kentucky with insufficient troops, his mania and tendency to doubt himself combined in a wicked way. Ranting and raving about being undersupplied, unable to get out of his own head, paranoid about enemy movements, he broke form and spoke injudiciously to several newspaper reporters. In the ensuing controversy, he was temporarily recalled from his command. It took weeks of rest for him to recover. It was one of a few nearly catastrophic moments in his otherwise steadily ascendant career.

It was after this brief stumble—having learned from it—that Sherman truly made his mark. For instance, during the siege at Fort Donelson, Sherman technically held a senior rank to General Ulysses S. Grant. While the rest of Lincoln's generals fought amongst themselves for personal power and recognition, Sherman waived his rank, choosing to cheerfully support and reinforce Grant instead of issuing orders. This is your show, Sherman told him in a note accompanying a shipment of supplies; call upon me for any assistance I can provide. Together, they won one of the Union's first victories in the war.

Building on his successes, Sherman began to advocate for his famous march to the sea—a strategically bold and audacious plan, not born out of some creative genius but rather relying on the exact topography he had scouted and studied as a young officer in what had then seemed like a pointless backwater outpost.

Where Sherman had once been cautious, he was now confident. But unlike so many others who possess great ambition, he *earned* this opinion. As he carved a path from Chattanooga to Atlanta and then Atlanta to the sea, he avoided traditional battle after traditional battle. Any student of military history can see how the exact same invasion, driven by ego instead of a strong sense of purpose, would have had a far different ending.

His realism allowed him to see a path through the South that others thought impossible. His entire theory of maneuver warfare rested on deliberately avoiding frontal assaults or shows of strength in the form of pitched battles, and ignoring criticism designed to bait a reaction. He paid no notice and stuck to his plan.

By the end of the war, Sherman was one of the most famous men in America, and yet he sought no public office, had no taste for politics, and wished simply to do his job and then eventually retire. Dismissing the incessant praise and attention endemic to such success, he wrote as a warning to his friend Grant, "Be natural and yourself and this glittering flattery will be as the passing breeze of the sea on a warm summer day."

One of Sherman's biographers summarized the man and his unique accomplishments in a remarkable passage. It is why he serves as our model in this phase of our ascent.

> Among men who rise to fame and leadership two types are recognizable—those who are born with a belief in themselves and those in whom it is a slow growth dependent on actual achievement. To the

men of the last type their own success is a constant surprise, and its fruits the more delicious, yet to be tested cautiously with a haunting sense of doubt whether it is not all a dream. In that doubt lies true modesty, not the sham of insincere self-depreciation but the modesty of "moderation," in the Greek sense. It is poise, not pose.

One must ask: if your belief in yourself is *not* dependent on actual achievement, then what is it dependent on? The answer, too often when we are just setting out, is *nothing*. Ego. And this is why we so often see precipitous rises followed by calamitous falls.

So which type of person will you be?

Like all of us, Sherman had to balance talent and ambition and intensity, especially when he was young. His victory in this struggle was largely why he was able to manage the life-altering success that eventually came his way.

This probably all sounds strange. Where Isocrates and Shakespeare wished us to be self-contained, self-motivated, and ruled by principle, most of us have been trained to do the opposite. Our cultural values almost try to make us dependent on validation, entitled, and ruled by our emotions. For a generation, parents and teachers have focused on building up everyone's *self-esteem*. From there, the themes of our gurus and public figures have been almost exclusively aimed at inspiring, encouraging, and assuring us that we can do whatever we set our minds to.

In reality, this makes us weak. Yes, you, with all your talent and promise as a boy wonder or a girl-who's-going-places. We take it for granted that you have promise. It's why you've landed in the prestigious university you now attend, why you've secured the funding you have for your business, why you've been hired or promoted, why whatever opportunity you now have has fallen into your lap. As Irving Berlin put it, "Talent is only the starting point." The question is: Will you be able to make the most of it? Or will you be your own worst enemy? Will you snuff out the flame that is just getting going?

What we see in Sherman was a man deeply tied and connected to reality. He was a man who came from nothing and accomplished great things, without ever feeling that he was in someway *entitled* to the honors he received. In fact, he regularly and consistently deferred to others and was more than happy to contribute to a winning team, even if it meant less credit or fame for himself. It's sad to think that generations of young boys learned about Pickett's glorious cavalry charge, a Confederate charge that *failed,* but the model of Sherman as a quiet, unglamorous realist is forgotten, or worse, vilified.

One might say that the ability to evaluate one's own ability is the most important skill of all. Without it, improvement is impossible. And certainly ego makes it difficult every step of the way. It is certainly more pleasurable to focus on our talents and strengths, but where does that get us? Arrogance and self-absorption inhibit growth. So does fantasy and "vision."

In this phase, you must practice seeing yourself with a little distance, cultivating the ability to get out of your own head. Detachment is a sort of natural ego antidote. It's *easy* to be emotionally invested and infatuated with your own work. Any and every narcissist can do that. What is rare is not raw talent, skill, or even confidence, but humility, diligence, and self-awareness.

For your work to have truth in it, it must come from truth. If you want to be more than a flash in the pan, you must be prepared to focus on the long term.

We will learn that though we *think* big, we must act and live small in order to accomplish what we seek. Because we will be *action* and *education* focused, and forgo validation and status, our ambition will not be grandiose but iterative—one foot in front of the other, learning and growing and putting in the time.

With their aggression, intensity, self-absorption, and endless self-promotion, our competitors don't realize how they jeopardize their own efforts (to say nothing of their sanity). We will challenge the myth of the self-assured genius for whom doubt and introspection is foreign, as well as challenge the myth of pained, tortured artist who must sacrifice his health for his work. Where they are both divorced from reality and divorced from other people, we will be deeply connected, aware, and learning from all of it.

Facts are better than dreams, as Churchill put it.

Although we share with many others a *vision* for greatness, we understand that our *path* toward it is very different from theirs. Following Sherman and Isocrates, we understand that ego is our enemy on that journey, so that when we do achieve our success, it will not sink us but make us stronger.

TALK, TALK, TALK

Those who know do not speak.
Those who speak do not know.

—LAO TZU

In his famous 1934 campaign for the governorship of California, the author and activist Upton Sinclair took an unusual step. Before the election, he published a short book titled *I, Governor of California and How I Ended Poverty*, in which he outlined, in the past tense, the brilliant policies he had enacted as governor . . . the office he had not yet won.

It was an untraditional move from an untraditional campaign, intended to leverage Sinclair's best asset—as an author, he knew he could communicate with the public in a way that others couldn't. Now, Sinclair's campaign was always a long shot and hardly in good shape when they published the book. But observers at the time noticed immediately the effect it had—not on the voters, but on Sinclair himself. As Carey McWilliams later wrote about his friend's gubernatorial bid as it went south, "Upton not only realized that he would be defeated but seemed somehow to have lost interest in the campaign. In that vivid imagination of his, he had already acted out the part of 'I, Governor of California,' . . . so why bother to enact it in real life?"

The book was a best seller, the campaign a failure. Sinclair lost by something like a quarter of a million votes (a margin of more than 10 percentage points); he was utterly decimated in what was probably the first modern election. It's clear what happened: his talk got out ahead of his campaign and the will to bridge the gap collapsed. Most politicians don't write books like that, but they get ahead of themselves just the same.

It's a temptation that exists for everyone—for talk and hype to replace action.

The empty text box: "What's on your mind?" Facebook asks. "Compose a new tweet," Twitter beckons. Tumblr. LinkedIn. Our inbox, our iPhones, the comments section on the bottom of the article you just read.

Blank spaces, begging to be filled in with thoughts, with photos, with stories. With what we're *going* to do, with what things *should* or *could* be like, what we hope will happen. Technology, asking you, prodding you, soliciting *talk*.

Almost universally, the kind of performance we give on social media is *positive*. It's more "Let me tell you how well things are going. Look how great I am." It's rarely the truth: "I'm scared. I'm struggling. I don't know."

At the beginning of any path, we're excited and nervous. So we seek to comfort ourselves externally instead of inwardly. There's a weak side to each of us, that—like a trade union—isn't exactly malicious but at the end of the day still wants to get as much public credit and attention as it can for doing the least. That side we call ego.

The writer and former Gawker blogger Emily Gould—a real-life Hannah Horvath if there ever was one—realized this during her two-year struggle to get a novel published. Though she had a six-figure book deal, she was stuck. Why? She was too busy "spending a lot of time on the Internet," that's why.

> In fact, I can't really remember anything else I did in 2010. I tumbld, I tweeted, and I scrolled. This didn't earn me any money but it felt like work. I justified my habits to myself in various ways. I was building my brand. Blogging was a creative act—even "curating" by reblogging someone else's post was a creative act, if you squinted. It was also the only creative thing I was doing.

In other words, she did what a lot of us do when we're scared or overwhelmed by a project: she did everything *but* focus on it. The actual novel she was supposed to be working on stalled completely. For a year.

It was easier to talk about writing, to do the exciting things related to art and creativity and literature, than to commit the act itself. She's not the only one. Someone recently published a book called *Working On My Novel*, filled with social media posts from writers who are clearly *not* working on their novels.

Writing, like so many creative acts, is hard. Sitting there, staring, mad at yourself, mad at the material because it doesn't seem good enough and *you* don't seem good enough.

In fact, many valuable endeavors we undertake are painfully difficult, whether it's coding a new startup or mastering a craft. But talking, talking is always easy.

We seem to think that silence is a sign of weakness. That being ignored is tantamount to death (and for the ego, this is true). So we talk, talk, talk as though our life depends on it.

In actuality, silence is strength—particularly early on in any journey. As the philosopher (and as it happens, a hater of newspapers and their chatter) Kierkegaard warned, "Mere gossip anticipates real talk, and to express what is still in thought weakens action by forestalling it."

And that's what is so insidious about *talk*. Anyone can talk about himself or herself. Even a child knows how to gossip and chatter. Most people are decent at hype and sales. So what is scarce and rare? Silence. The ability to deliberately keep yourself out of the conversation and subsist without its validation. Silence is the respite of the confident and the strong.

Sherman had a good rule he tried to observe. "Never give reasons for what you think or do until you must. Maybe, after a while, a better reason will pop into your head." The baseball and football great Bo Jackson decided he had two things he wanted to accomplish as an athlete at Auburn: he would win the Heisman Trophy and be taken first in the NFL draft. Do you know who he told? Nobody but his girlfriend.

Strategic flexibility is not the only benefit of silence while others chatter. It is also psychology. The poet Hesiod had this in mind when he said, "A man's best treasure is a thrifty tongue."

Talk depletes us. Talking and doing fight for the same

resources. Research shows that while goal visualization is important, after a certain point our mind begins to confuse it with actual progress. The same goes for verbalization. Even talking aloud to ourselves while we work through difficult problems has been shown to significantly decrease insight and breakthroughs. After spending so much time thinking, explaining, and talking about a task, we start to feel that we've gotten closer to achieving it. Or worse, when things get tough, we feel we can toss the whole project aside because we've given it our best try, although of course we haven't.

The more difficult the task, the more uncertain the outcome, the more costly talk will be and the farther we run from actual accountability. It's sapped us of the energy desperately needed to conquer what Steven Pressfield calls the "Resistance"—the hurdle that stands between us and creative expression. Success requires a full 100 percent of our effort, and talk flitters part of that effort away before we can use it.

A lot of us succumb to this temptation—particularly when we feel overwhelmed or stressed or have a lot of work to do. In our building phase, resistance will be a constant source of discomfort. Talking—listening to ourselves talk, performing for an audience—is almost like therapy. *I just spent four hours talking about this. Doesn't that count for something?* The answer is no.

Doing great work is a struggle. It's draining, it's demoralizing, it's frightening—not always, but it can feel that way when we're deep in the middle of it. We talk to fill the void and the uncertainty. "Void," Marlon Brando, a quiet actor if there ever was one, once said, "is terrifying to most people." It is almost as if we are assaulted by silence or confronted by it, particularly if we've allowed our ego to lie to us over the years. Which is so damaging for one reason: the greatest work and art comes from *wrestling* with the void, facing it instead of scrambling to make it go away. The question is, when faced with your particular challenge—whether it is researching in a new field, starting a business, producing a film, securing a mentor, advancing an important cause—do you seek the respite of talk or do you face the struggle head-on?

Think about it: a *voice of a generation* doesn't call itself that. In fact, when you think about it, you realize just how *little* these voices seem to talk. It's a song, it's a speech, it's a book—the volume of work may be light, but what's inside it is concentrated and impactful.

They work quietly in the corner. They turn their inner turmoil into product—and eventually to stillness. They ignore the impulse to seek recognition before they act. They don't talk much. Or mind the feeling that others, out there in public and enjoying the limelight, are somehow getting the better end of the deal. (They are not.) They're too busy working to do anything else. When they do talk—it's *earned*.

The only relationship between work and chatter is that one kills the other.

Let the others slap each other on the back while you're back in the lab or the gym or pounding the pavement. Plug that hole—that one, right in the middle of your face—that can drain you of your vital life force. Watch what happens. Watch how much better you get.

TO BE OR TO DO?

In this formative period, the soul is unsoiled by warfare
with the world. It lies, like a block of pure, uncut Parian
marble, ready to be fashioned into—what?

—ORISON SWETT MARDEN

One of the most influential strategists and practitioners in modern warfare is someone most people have never heard of. His name was John Boyd.

He was a truly great fighter pilot, but an even better teacher and thinker. After flying in Korea, he became the lead instructor at the elite Fighter Weapons School at Nellis Air Force Base. He was known as "Forty-Second Boyd"—meaning that he could defeat any opponent, from any position, in less than forty seconds. A few years later he was quietly summoned to the Pentagon, where his real work began.

In one sense, the fact that the average person might not have heard of John Boyd is not unexpected. He never published any books and he wrote only one academic paper. Only a few videos of him survive and he was rarely, if ever, quoted in the media. Despite nearly thirty years of impeccable service, Boyd wasn't promoted above the rank of colonel.

On the other hand, his theories transformed maneuver warfare in almost every branch of the armed forces, not just in his own lifetime but even more so after. The F-15 and F-16 fighter jets, which reinvented modern military aircraft, were his pet projects. His primary influence was as an adviser; through legendary briefings he taught and instructed nearly every major military thinker in a generation. His input on the war plans for Operation Desert Shield came in a series of direct meetings with the secretary of defense, not through public or official policy input. His primary means of effecting change was through the collection of pupils he mentored, protected, taught, and inspired.

There are no military bases named after him. No battleships. He retired assuming that he'd be forgotten, and without much more than a small apartment and a pension to his name. He almost certainly had more enemies than friends.

This unusual path—What if it were deliberate? What if it made him *more* influential? How crazy would that be?

In fact, Boyd was simply living the exact lesson he tried to teach each promising young acolyte who came under his wing, who he sensed had the potential to be something—to be something different. The rising stars he taught probably have a lot in common with us.

The speech Boyd gave to a protégé in 1973 makes this clear. Sensing what he knew to be a critical inflection point in the life of the young officer, Boyd called him in for a meeting. Like many high achievers, the soldier was insecure and impressionable. He wanted to be promoted, and he wanted to do well. He was a leaf that could be blown in any direction and Boyd knew it. So he heard a speech that day that Boyd would give again and again, until it became a tradition and a rite of passage for a generation of trans-formative military leaders.

"Tiger, one day you will come to a fork in the road," Boyd said to him. "And you're going to have to make a decision about which direction you want to go." Using his hands to illustrate, Boyd marked off these two directions. "If you go that way you can be somebody. You will have to make com-promises and you will have to turn your back on your friends. But you will be a member of the club and you will get pro-moted and you will get good assignments." Then Boyd paused, to make the alternative clear. "Or," he said, "you can go that way and you can do something—something for your country and for your Air Force and for yourself. If you decide you want to do something, you may not get promoted and you may not get the good assignments and you certainly will not be a favorite of your superiors. But you won't have to compromise yourself. You will be true to your friends and to yourself. And your work might make a difference. To be somebody or to do something. In life there is often a roll call. That's when you will have to make a decision."

And then Boyd concluded with words that would guide that young man and many of his peers for the rest of their lives. "To be or to do? Which way will you go?"

Whatever we seek to do in life, reality soon intrudes on our youthful idealism. This reality comes in many names and forms: incentives, commitments, recognition, and poli-tics. In every case, they can quickly redirect us from *doing* to *being*. From *earning* to *pretending*. Ego aids in that deception every step of the way. It's why Boyd wanted young people to see that if we are not careful, we can very easily find ourselves corrupted by the very occupation we wish to serve.

How do you prevent derailment? Well, often we fall in love with an *image* of what success looks like. In Boyd's world, the number of stars on your shoulder or the nature of your appointment or its location could easily be confused as a proxy for real accomplishment. For other people, it's their job title, the business school they went to, the number of assistants they have, the location of their parking space, the grants they earn, their access to the CEO, the size of their paycheck, or the number of fans they have.

Appearances are deceiving. *Having* authority is not the same as *being* an authority. *Having* the right and *being* right are not the same either. Being promoted doesn't necessarily mean you're doing good work and it doesn't mean you are worthy of promotion (they call it failing upward in such bureaucracies). *Impressing people is utterly different from being truly impressive.*

So who are you with? Which side will you choose? This is the roll call that life puts before us.

Boyd had another exercise. Visiting with or speaking to groups of Air Force officers, he'd write on the chalkboard in big letters the words: DUTY, HONOR, COUNTRY. Then he would cross those words out and replace them with three others: PRIDE, POWER, GREED. His point was that many of the systems and structures in the military—the ones that soldiers navigate in order to get ahead—can corrupt the very values they set out to serve. There's a quip from the historian Will Durant, that a nation is born stoic and dies epicurean. That's the sad truth Boyd was illustrating, how positive virtues turn sour.

How many times have we seen this played out in our own short lives—in sports, in relationships, or projects or people that we care deeply about? This is what the ego does. It crosses out what matters and replaces it with what doesn't.

A lot of people want to change the world, and it's good that they do. You want to be the best at what you do. Nobody *wants* to just be an empty suit. But in practical terms, which of the three words Boyd wrote on the chalkboard are going to get you there? Which are you practicing now? What's fueling you?

The choice that Boyd puts in front of us comes down to purpose. *What is your purpose? What are you here to do?* Because purpose helps you answer the question "To be or to do?" quite easily. If what matters is *you*—your reputation, your inclusion, your personal ease of life—your path is clear: Tell people what they want to hear. Seek attention over the quiet but important work. Say yes to promotions and generally follow the track that talented people take in the industry or field you've chosen. Pay your dues, check the boxes, put in your time, and leave things essentially as they are. Chase your fame, your salary, your title, and enjoy them as they come.

"A man is worked upon by what he works on," Frederick Douglass once said. He would know. He'd been a slave, and he saw what it did to everyone involved, including the *slaveholders* themselves. Once a free man, he saw that the choices people made, about their careers and their lives, had the same effect. What you choose to do with your time and what you choose to do for money works on you. The egocentric path requires, as Boyd knew, many compromises.

If your purpose is something larger than you—to accomplish something, to prove something to yourself—then suddenly everything becomes both easier and more difficult.

Easier in the sense that you know now what it is you need to do and what is important to you. The other "choices" wash away, as they aren't really choices at all. They're distractions. It's about the *doing*, not the recognition. Easier in the sense that you don't need to compromise. Harder because each opportunity—no matter how gratifying or rewarding—must be evaluated along strict guidelines: Does this help me do what I have set out to do? Does this *allow* me to do what I need to do? Am I being selfish or self*less*?

In this course, it is not "Who do I want to be in life?" but "What is it that I want to accomplish in life?" Setting aside selfish interest, it asks: What calling does it serve? What principles govern my choices? Do I want to be like everyone else or do I want to do something different?

In other words, it's harder because *everything* can seem like a compromise.

Although it's never too late, the earlier you ask yourself these questions the better.

Boyd undeniably changed and improved his field in a way that almost no other theorist has since Sun Tzu or von Clausewitz. He was known as Genghis John for the way he never let obstacles or opponents stop him from what he needed to do. His choices were not without their costs. He was also known as the ghetto colonel because of his frugal lifestyle. He died with a drawerful of thousands of dollars in uncashed expense checks from private contractors, which he equated with bribes. That he never advanced above colonel was not his doing; he was repeatedly held back for promotions. He was forgotten by history as a punishment for the work he did.

Think about this the next time you start to feel entitled,

the next time you conflate fame and the American Dream. Think about how you might measure up to a great man like that.

Think about this the next time you face that choice: Do I *need* this? Or is it really about ego? Are you ready to make the right decision? Or do the prizes still glitter off in the distance?

To be or to do—life is a constant roll call.

BECOME A STUDENT

Let No Man's Ghost Come Back to Say My Training Let
Me Down.

—SIGN IN THE NEW YORK FIRE DEPARTMENT
TRAINING ACADEMY

I n April in the early 1980s, a single day became one guitarist's nightmare and became another's dream, and
dream job. Without notice, members of the underground metal band Metallica assembled before a planned
recording session in a decrepit warehouse in New York and
informed their guitarist Dave Mustaine he was being thrown
out of the group. With few words, they handed him a bus
ticket back to San Francisco.

That same day, a decent young guitarist, Kirk Hammett,
barely in his twenties and member of a band called Exodus,
was given the job. Thrown right into a new life, he performed
his first show with the band a few days later.

One would assume that this was the moment Hammett
had been waiting for his whole life. Indeed it was. Though
only known in small circles at the time, Metallica was a band
that seemed destined to go places. Their music had already

begun to push the boundaries of the genre of thrash metal, and cult stardom had already begun. Within a few short years, it would be one of the biggest bands in the world, eventually selling more than 100 million albums.

It was around this time that Kirk came to what must have been a humbling realization—that despite his years of playing and being invited to join Metallica, he wasn't as good as he'd like to be. At his home in San Francisco, he looked for a guitar teacher. In other words, despite joining his dream group and quite literally turning professional, Kirk insisted that he needed more instruction—that he was still a student. The teacher he sought out had a reputation for being a teacher's teacher, and for working with musical prodigies like Steve Vai.

Joe Satriani, the man Hammett chose as his instructor, would himself go on to become known as one of the best guitar players of all time and sell more than 10 million records of his unique, virtuosic music. Teaching out of a small music shop in Berkeley, Satriani's playing style made him an unusual choice for Hammett. That was the point—Kirk wanted to learn what he didn't know, to firm up his understanding of the fundamentals so that he might continue exploring this new genre of music he now had a chance to pursue.

Satriani makes it clear where Hammett was lacking—it wasn't talent, certainly. "The main thing with Kirk . . . was he was a really good guitar player when he walked in the door. He was already playing lead guitar . . . he was already shredding. He had a great right hand, he knew most of his chords, he just didn't learn how to play in an environment where he learned all the names and how to connect everything together."

That didn't mean that their sessions were some sort of fun study group. In fact, Satriani explained that what separated Hammett from the others was his willingness to endure the type of instruction they wouldn't. "He was a good student. Many of his friends and contemporaries would storm out complaining thinking I was too harsh a teacher."

Satriani's system was clear: that there would be weekly lessons, that these lessons must be learned, and if they weren't, that Hammett was wasting everyone's time and needn't bother to come back. So for the next two years Kirk did as Satriani required, returning every week for objective feedback, judgment, and drilling in technique and musical theory for the instrument he would soon be playing in front of thousands, then tens of thousands, and then literally hundreds of thousands of people. Even after that two-year study period, he would bring to Satriani licks and riffs he'd been working on with the band, and learned to pare down the instinct for *more*, and hone his ability to do more with fewer notes, and to focus on *feeling* those notes and expressing them accordingly. Each time, he improved as a player and as an artist.

The power of being a student is not just that it is an extended period of instruction, it also places the ego and ambition in someone else's hands. There is a sort of ego ceiling imposed—one knows that he is not better than the "master" he apprentices under. Not even close. You defer to them, you subsume yourself. You cannot fake or bullshit them. An education can't be "hacked"; there are no short-cuts besides *hacking it* every single day. If you don't, they drop you.

We don't like thinking that someone is better than us. Or

that we have a lot left to learn. We want to be done. We want to be ready. We're busy and overburdened. For this reason, updating your appraisal of your talents in a downward direction is one of the most difficult things to do in life—but it is almost always a component of mastery. The pretense of knowledge is our most dangerous vice, because it prevents us from getting any better. Studious self-assessment is the antidote.

The result, no matter what your musical tastes happen to be, was that Hammett became one of the great metal guitarists in the world, taking thrash metal from an underground movement into a thriving global musical genre. Not only that, but from those lessons, Satriani honed his own technique and became much better himself. Both the student and the teacher would go on to fill stadiums and remake the musical landscape.

The mixed martial arts pioneer and multi-title champion Frank Shamrock has a system he trains fighters in that he calls plus, minus, and equal. Each fighter, to become great, he said, needs to have someone better that they can learn from, someone lesser who they can teach, and someone equal that they can challenge themselves against.

The purpose of Shamrock's formula is simple: to get real and continuous feedback about what they know and what they don't know from every angle. It purges out the ego that puffs us up, the fear that makes us doubt ourselves, and any laziness that might make us want to coast. As Shamrock observed, "False ideas about yourself destroy you. For me, I always stay a student. That's what martial arts are about, and you have to use that humility as a tool. You put yourself beneath someone you trust." This begins by accepting that others know more than you and that you can benefit from their knowledge, and then seeking them out and knocking down the illusions you have about yourself.

The need for a student mind-set doesn't stop with fighting or music. A scientist must know the core principles of science and the discoveries occurring on the cutting edge. A philosopher must know deeply, and also know how little they know, as Socrates did. A writer must be versed in the canon—and read and be challenged by her contemporaries too. A historian must know ancient and modern history, as well as their specialty. Professional athletes have teams of coaches, and even powerful politicians have advisers and mentors.

Why? To become great and to stay great, they must all know what came before, what is going on now, and what comes next. They must internalize the fundamentals of their domain and what surrounds them, without ossifying or becoming stuck in time. They must be always learning. We must all become our own teachers, tutors, and critics.

Think about what Hammett could have done—what we might have done in his position were we to suddenly find ourselves a rock star, or a soon-to-be-rock star in our chosen field. The temptation is to think: I've made it. I've arrived. They tossed the other guy because he's not as good as I am. They chose me *because I have what it takes*. Had he done that, we'd probably have never heard of him or the band. There are, after all, plenty of forgotten metal groups from the 1980s.

A true student is like a sponge. Absorbing what goes on around him, filtering it, latching on to what he can hold. A student is self-critical and self-motivated, always trying to improve his understanding so that he can move on to the next topic, the next challenge. A real student is also his own teacher and his own critic. There is no room for ego there.

Take fighting as an example again, where self-awareness is particularly crucial because opponents are constantly looking to match strength against weakness. If a fighter is not capable of learning and practicing every day, if he is not relentlessly looking for areas of improvement, examining his own shortcomings, and finding new techniques to borrow from peers and opponents, he will be broken down and destroyed.

It is not all that different for the rest of us. Are we not fighting for or against something? Do you think you are the only one who hopes to achieve your goal? You can't possibly believe you're the only one reaching for that brass ring.

It tends to surprise people how humble aspiring greats seem to have been. *What do you mean they weren't aggressive, entitled, aware of their own greatness or their destiny?* The reality is that, though they were confident, the act of being an eternal student kept these men and women humble.

"It is impossible to learn that which one thinks one already knows," Epictetus says. *You can't learn if you think you already know.* You will not find the answers if you're too conceited and self-assured to ask the questions. You cannot get better if you're convinced you are the best.

The art of taking feedback is such a crucial skill in life, particularly harsh and critical feedback. We not only need to take this harsh feedback, but actively solicit it, labor to seek out the negative precisely when our friends and family and brain are telling us that we're doing great. The ego avoids such feedback at all costs, however. Who wants to remand themselves to remedial training? It thinks it already knows how and who we are—that is, it thinks we are spectacular, perfect, genius, truly innovative. It dislikes reality and prefers its own assessment.

Ego doesn't allow for proper incubation either. To become what we ultimately hope to become often takes long periods of obscurity, of sitting and wrestling with some topic or paradox. Humility is what keeps us there, concerned that we don't know enough and that we must continue to study. Ego rushes to the end, rationalizes that patience is for losers (wrongly seeing it as a weakness), and assumes that we're good enough to give our talents a go in the world.

As we sit down to proof our work, as we make our first elevator pitch, prepare to open our first shop, as we stare out into the dress rehearsal audience, ego is the enemy—giving us wicked feedback, disconnected from reality. It's defensive, precisely when we cannot afford to be defensive. It blocks us from improving by telling us that we don't need to improve. Then we wonder why we don't get the results we want, why others are better and why their success is more lasting.

Today, books are cheaper than ever. Courses are free. Access to teachers is no longer a barrier—technology has done away with that. There is no excuse for not getting your education, and because the information we have before us is so vast, there is no excuse for ever ending that process either.

Our teachers in life are not only those we pay, as Hammett paid Satriani. Nor are they necessarily part of some training dojo, like it is for Shamrock. Many of the best teachers are free. They volunteer because, like you, they once were young and had the same goals you do. Many don't even know they are teaching—they are simply exemplars, or even historical figures whose lessons survive in books and essays. But ego makes us so hardheaded and hostile to feedback that it drives them away or puts them beyond our reach.

It's why the old proverb says, "When student is ready, the teacher appears."

DON'T BE PASSIONATE

> You seem to want that *vivida vis animi* which spurs and
> excites most young men to please, to shine, to excel.
> Without the desire and the pains necessary to be consid-
> erable, depend upon it, you never can be so.
>
> —LORD CHESTERFIELD

Passion—it's all about passion. Find your passion. Live
passionately. Inspire the world with your passion.

People go to Burning Man to find passion, to be
around passion, to rekindle their passion. Same goes for
TED and the now enormous SXSW and a thousand other
events, retreats, and summits, all fueled by what they claim
to be life's most important force.

Here's what those same people haven't told you: your
passion may be the very thing holding you back from power
or influence or accomplishment. Because just as often, we
fail with—no, *because of*—passion.

Early on in her ascendant political career, a visitor once
spoke of Eleanor Roosevelt's "passionate interest" in a piece
of social legislation. The person had meant it as a compliment. But Eleanor's response is illustrative. "Yes," she did

support the cause, she said. "But I hardly think the word 'passionate' applies to me."

As a genteel, accomplished, and patient woman born while the embers of the quiet Victorian virtues were still warm, Roosevelt was above passion. She had purpose. She had direction. She wasn't driven by passion, but by *reason*.

George W. Bush, Dick Cheney, and Donald Rumsfeld, on the other hand, were passionate about Iraq. Christopher McCandless was bursting with passion as he headed "into the wild." So was Robert Falcon Scott as he set out to explore the arctic, bitten as he was with "the Pole mania" (as were many climbers of the tragic 1996 Everest climb, momentarily struck with what psychologists now call "goalodicy"). The inventor and investors of the Segway believed they had a world-changing innovation on their hands and put everything into evangelizing it. That all of these talented, smart individuals were fervent believers in what they sought to do is without dispute. It's also clear that they were also unprepared and incapable of grasping the objections and real concerns of everyone else around them.

The same is true for countless entrepreneurs, authors, chefs, business owners, politicians, and designers that you've never heard of—and never will hear of, because they sunk their own ships before they'd hardly left the harbor. Like every other dilettante, they had passion and lacked something else.

To be clear, I'm not talking about *caring*. I'm talking about passion of a different sort—unbridled enthusiasm, our willingness to pounce on what's in front of us with the full measure of our zeal, the "bundle of energy" that our teachers and gurus have assured us is our most important asset. It is that burning, unquenchable desire to start or to achieve some vague, ambitious, and distant goal. This seemingly innocuous motivation is so far from the right track it hurts.

Remember, "zealot" is just a nice way to say "crazy person."

A young basketball player named Lewis Alcindor Jr., who won three national championships with John Wooden at UCLA, used one word to describe the style of his famous coach: "*dispassionate*." As in *not* passionate. Wooden wasn't about rah-rah speeches or inspiration. He saw those extra emotions as a burden. Instead, his philosophy was about being in control and doing your job and never being "passion's slave." The player who learned that lesson from Wooden would later change his name to one you remember better: Kareem Abdul-Jabbar.

No one would describe Eleanor Roosevelt or John Wooden or his notoriously quiet player Kareem as apathetic. They wouldn't have said they were frenetic or zealous either. Roosevelt, one of the most powerful and influential female activists in history and certainly America's most important First Lady, was known primarily for her grace, her poise, and her sense of direction. Wooden won ten titles in twelve years, including seven in a row, because he developed a system for winning and worked with his players to follow it. Neither of them were driven by excitement, nor were they bodies in constant motion. Instead, it took them years to become the person they became known as. It was a process of accumulation.

In our endeavors, we will face complex problems, often in situations we've never faced before. Opportunities are not usually deep, virgin pools that require courage and boldness to dive into, but instead are obscured, dusted over, blocked by various forms of resistance. What is really called for in these circumstances is clarity, deliberateness, and methodological determination.

But too often, we proceed like this . . .

A flash of inspiration: I want to do the best and biggest _____ ever. Be the youngest _____. The only one to _____. The "firstest with the mostest."

The advice: Okay, well, here's what you'll need to do step-by-step to accomplish it.

The reality: We hear what we want to hear. We do what we feel like doing, and despite being incredibly busy and working very hard, we accomplish very little. Or worse, find ourselves in a mess we never anticipated.

Because we only seem to hear about the passion of successful people, we forget that failures shared the same trait. We don't conceive of the consequences until we look at their trajectory. With the Segway, the inventor and investors wrongly assumed a demand much greater than ever existed. With the run-up to the war in Iraq, its proponents ignored objections and negative feedback because they conflicted with what they so deeply needed to believe. The tragic end to the *Into the Wild* story is the result of youthful naiveté and a lack of preparation. With Robert Falcon Scott, it was overconfidence and zeal without consideration of the real dangers. We imagine Napoleon was brimming with passion as he contemplated the invasion of Russia and only finally became free of it as he limped home with a fraction of the men he'd so confidently left with. In many more examples we see the same mistakes: overinvesting, underinvesting, acting before someone is really ready, breaking things that required delicacy—not so much malice as the drunkenness of passion.

Passion typically masks a weakness. Its breathlessness and impetuousness and franticness are poor substitutes for discipline, for mastery, for strength and purpose and perseverance. You need to be able to spot this in others and in yourself, because while the origins of passion may be earnest and good, its effects are comical and then monstrous.

Passion is seen in those who can tell you in great detail who they intend to become and what their success will be like—they might even be able to tell you specifically when they intend to achieve it or describe to you legitimate and sincere worries they have about the burdens of such accomplishments. They can tell you all the things they're going to do, or have even begun, but they cannot show you their progress. Because there rarely is any.

How can someone be busy and not accomplish anything? Well, that's the passion paradox.

If the definition of insanity is trying the same thing over and over and expecting different results, then passion is a form of mental retardation—deliberately blunting our most critical cognitive functions. The waste is often appalling in retrospect; the best years of our life burned out like a pair of spinning tires against the asphalt.

Dogs, god bless them, are passionate. As numerous squirrels, birds, boxes, blankets, and toys can tell you, they do not accomplish most of what they set out to do. A dog has an advantage in all this: a graciously short short-term memory that keeps at bay the creeping sense of futility and impotence. Reality for us humans, on the other hand, has no reason to be sensitive to the illusions we operate under. Eventually it will intrude.

What humans require in our ascent is purpose and realism. Purpose, you could say, is like passion with boundaries. Realism is detachment and perspective.

When we are young, or when our cause is young, we feel so intensely—passion like our hormones runs strongest in youth—that it seems wrong to take it slow. This is just our impatience. This is our inability to see that burning ourselves out or blowing ourselves up isn't going to hurry the journey along.

Passion is *about*. (I am so passionate about _____.) Purpose is *to* and *for*. (I must do _____. I was put here to accomplish _____. I am willing to endure _____ for the sake of this.) Actually, purpose deemphasizes the *I*. Purpose is about pursuing something outside yourself as opposed to pleasuring yourself.

More than purpose, we also need realism. Where do we start? What do we do first? What do we do right now? How are we sure that what we're doing is moving us forward? What are we benchmarking ourselves against?

"Great passions are maladies without hope," as Goethe once said. Which is why a deliberate, purposeful person operates on a different level, beyond the sway or the sickness. They hire professionals and *use* them. They ask questions, they ask what could go wrong, they ask for examples. They plan for contingencies. Then they are off to the races. Usually they get started with small steps, complete them, and look for feedback on how the next set can be better. They lock in gains, and then get better as they go, often leveraging those gains to grow exponentially rather than arithmetically.

Is an iterative approach less exciting than manifestos, epiphanies, flying across the country to surprise someone, or sending four-thousand-word stream-of-consciousness e-mails in the middle of the night? Of course. Is it less glamorous and bold than going all in and maxing out your credit cards because you believe in yourself? Absolutely. Same goes for the spreadsheets, the meetings, the trips, the phone calls, software, tools, and internal systems—and every how-to article ever written about them and the routines of famous people. Passion is form over function. Purpose is function, function, function.

The critical work that you want to do will require your deliberation and consideration. Not passion. Not naïveté.

It'd be far better if you were intimidated by what lies ahead—humbled by its magnitude and determined to see it through regardless. Leave passion for the amateurs. Make it about what you feel you *must* do and say, not what you care about and wish to be. Remember Talleyrand's epigram for diplomats, "Surtout, pas trop de zèle" ("Above all, not too much zeal"). Then you will do great things. Then you will stop being your old, good-intentioned, but ineffective self.

FOLLOW THE CANVAS STRATEGY

Great men have almost always shown themselves as ready
to obey as they afterwards proved able to command.

—LORD MAHON

In the Roman system of art and science, there existed a
concept for which we have only a partial analog. Successful businessmen, politicians, or rich playboys would sub-
sidize a number of writers, thinkers, artists, and performers.
More than just being paid to produce works of art, these
artists performed a number of tasks in exchange for protec-
tion, food, and gifts. One of the roles was that of an
anteambulo—literally meaning "one who clears the path." An
anteambulo proceeded in front of his patron anywhere they
traveled in Rome, making way, communicating messages,
and generally making the patron's life easier.

The famous epigrammist Martial fulfilled this role for
many years, serving for a time under the patron Mela, a
wealthy businessman and brother of the Stoic philosopher
and political adviser Seneca. Born without a rich family,
Martial also served under another businessman named

Petilius. As a young writer, he spent most of his day traveling from the home of one rich patron to another, providing services, paying his respects, and receiving small token payments and favors in return.

Here's the problem: like most of us with our internships and entry-level positions (or later on, publishers or bosses or clients), Martial absolutely hated every minute of it. He seemed to believe that this system somehow made him a slave. Aspiring to live like some country squire, like the patrons he serviced, Martial wanted money and an estate that was all his own. There, he dreamed, he could finally produce his works in peace and independence. As a result, his writing often drags with a hatred and bitterness about Rome's upper crust, from which he believed he was cruelly shunted aside.

For all his impotent rage, what Martial couldn't see was that it was his unique position as an outsider to society that gave him such fascinating insight into Roman culture that it survives to this day. Instead of being pained by such a system, what if he'd been able to come to terms with it? What if—gasp—he could have appreciated the opportunities it offered? Nope. It seemed to eat him up inside instead.

It's a common attitude that transcends generations and societies. The angry, unappreciated genius is forced to do stuff she doesn't like, for people she doesn't respect, as she makes her way in the world. *How dare they force me to grovel like this! The injustice! The waste!*

We see it in recent lawsuits in which interns sue their employers for pay. We see kids more willing to live at home with their parents than to submit to something they're "overqualified" to work for. We see it in an inability to meet anyone else on their terms, an unwillingness to take a step back in order to potentially take several steps forward. *I will not let them get one over on me. I'd rather we both have nothing instead.*

It's worth taking a look at the supposed indignities of "serving" someone else. Because in reality, not only is the apprentice model responsible for some of the greatest art in the history of the world—everyone from Michelangelo to Leonardo da Vinci to Benjamin Franklin has been forced to navigate such a system—but if you're going to be the big deal you think you are going to be, isn't this a rather trivial temporary imposition?

When someone gets his first job or joins a new organization, he's often given this advice: Make other people look good and you will do well. Keep your head down, they say, and serve your boss. Naturally, this is not what the kid who was chosen over all the other kids for the position wants to hear. It's not what a Harvard grad expects—after all, they got that degree precisely to avoid this supposed indignity.

Let's flip it around so it doesn't seem so demeaning: It's not about kissing ass. It's not about making someone *look* good. It's about providing the support so that others can *be* good. The better wording for the advice is this: Find canvases for other people to paint on. Be an *anteambulo*. Clear the path for the people above you and you will eventually create a path for yourself.

When you are just starting out, we can be sure of a few fundamental realities: 1) You're not nearly as good or as important as you think you are; 2) You have an attitude that needs to be readjusted; 3) Most of what you think you know or most of what you learned in books or in school is out of date or wrong.

There's one fabulous way to work all that out of your system: attach yourself to people and organizations who are already successful and subsume your identity into theirs and move both forward simultaneously. It's certainly more glamorous to pursue your own glory—though hardly as effective. Obeisance is the way forward.

That's the other effect of this attitude: it reduces your ego at a critical time in your career, letting you absorb everything you can without the obstructions that block others' vision and progress.

No one is endorsing sycophancy. Instead, it's about seeing what goes on from the inside, and looking for opportunities for someone *other than yourself.* Remember that *anteambulo* means clearing the path—finding the direction someone already intended to head and helping them pack, freeing them up to focus on their strengths. In fact, making things better rather than simply looking as if you are.

Many people know of Benjamin Franklin's famous pseudonymous letters written under names like Silence Dogood. What a clever young prodigy, they think, and miss the most impressive part entirely: Franklin wrote those letters, submitted them by sliding them under the print-shop door, and received absolutely no credit for them until much later in his life. In fact, it was his brother, the owner, who profited from their immense popularity, regularly running them on the front page of his newspaper. Franklin was playing the long game, though—learning how public opinion worked, generating awareness of what he believed in, crafting his style and tone and wit. It was a strategy he used time and again over his career—once even publishing in his competitor's paper in order to undermine a third competitor—for

Franklin saw the constant benefit in making *other people* look good and letting them take credit for your ideas.

Bill Belichick, the four-time Super Bowl–winning head coach of the New England Patriots, made his way up the ranks of the NFL by loving and mastering the one part of the job that coaches disliked at the time: analyzing film. His first job in professional football, for the Baltimore Colts, was one he volunteered to take without pay—and his insights, which provided ammunition and critical strategies for the game, were attributed exclusively to the more senior coaches. He thrived on what was considered grunt work, asked for it and strove to become the best at precisely what others thought they were too good for. "He was like a sponge, taking it all in, listening to everything," one coach said. "You gave him an assignment and he disappeared into a room and you didn't see him again until it was done, and then he wanted to do more," said another. As you can guess, Belichick started getting paid very soon.

Before that, as a young high school player, he was so knowledgeable about the game that he functioned as a sort of assistant coach even while playing the game. Belichick's father, himself an assistant football coach for Navy, taught him a critical lesson in football politics: that if he wanted to give his coach feedback or question a decision, he needed to do it in private and self-effacingly so as not to offend his superior. He learned how to be a rising star without threatening or alienating anyone. In other words, he had mastered the canvas strategy.

You can see how easily entitlement and a sense of superiority (the trappings of ego) would have made the accomplishments of either of these men impossible. Franklin would never have been published if he'd prioritized credit over creative expression—indeed, when his brother found out, he literally beat him out of jealousy and anger. Belichick would have pissed off his coach and then probably been benched if he had one-upped him in public. He certainly wouldn't have taken his first job for free, and he wouldn't have sat through thousands of hours of film if he cared about status. Greatness comes from humble beginnings; it comes from grunt work. It means you're the least important person in the room—until you change that with results.

There is an old saying, "Say little, do much." What we really ought to do is update and apply a version of that to our early approach. Be *lesser*, do *more*. Imagine if for every person you met, you thought of some way to help them, something you could do for them? And you looked at it in a way that entirely benefited them and not you. The cumulative effect this would have over time would be profound: You'd learn a great deal by solving diverse problems. You'd develop a reputation for being indispensable. You'd have countless new relationships. You'd have an enormous bank of favors to call upon down the road.

That's what the canvas strategy is about—helping yourself by helping others. Making a concerted effort to trade your short-term gratification for a longer-term payoff. Whereas everyone else wants to get credit and be "respected," you can forget credit. You can forget it so hard that you're *glad* when others get it instead of you—that was your aim, after all. Let the others take their credit on credit, while you defer and earn interest on the principal.

The *strategy* part of it is the hardest. It's easy to be bitter, like Martial. To hate even the thought of subservience. To despise those who have more means, more experience, or more status than you. To tell yourself that every second not spent doing your work, or working on yourself, is a waste of your gift. To insist, *I will not be demeaned like this.*

Once we fight this emotional and egotistical impulse, the canvas strategy is easy. The iterations are endless.

- Maybe it's coming up with ideas to hand over to your boss.
- Find people, thinkers, up-and-comers to introduce them to each other. Cross wires to create new sparks.
- Find what nobody else wants to do and do it.
- Find inefficiencies and waste and redundancies. Identify leaks and patches to free up resources for new areas.
- Produce more than everyone else and give your ideas away

In other words, discover opportunities to promote their creativity, find outlets and people for collaboration, and eliminate distractions that hinder their progress and focus. It is a rewarding and infinitely scalable power strategy. Consider each one an investment in relationships and in your own development.

The canvas strategy is there for you at any time. There is no expiration date on it either. It's one of the few that age does not limit—on either side, young or old. You can start at any time—before you have a job, before you're hired and while you're doing something else, or if you're starting something new or find yourself inside an organization without strong allies or support. You may even find that there's no reason to ever stop doing it, even once you've graduated to heading your own projects. Let it become natural and permanent; let others apply it to you while you're too busy applying it to those above you.

Because if you pick up this mantle once, you'll see what most people's egos prevent them from appreciating: the person who clears the path ultimately controls its direction, just as the canvas shapes the painting.

RESTRAIN YOURSELF

I have observed that those who have accomplished the greatest results are those who "keep under the body"; are those who never grow excited or lose self-control, but are always calm, self-possessed, patient, and polite.

—BOOKER T. WASHINGTON

People who knew Jackie Robinson as a young man probably wouldn't have predicted that they'd one day see him become the first black player in Major League Baseball. Not that he wasn't talented, or that the idea of eventually integrating white baseball was inconceivable, it's that he wasn't exactly known for his restraint and poise.

As a teenager, Robinson ran with a small gang of friends who regularly found themselves in trouble with local police. He challenged a fellow student to a fight at a junior college picnic for using a slur. In a basketball game, he surreptitiously struck a hard-fouling white opponent with the ball so forcefully that the kid bled everywhere. He was arrested more than once for arguing with and challenging police, who he felt treated him unfairly.

Before he started at UCLA, he spent the night in jail (and had a gun drawn on him by an officer) for nearly fighting a white man who'd insulted his friends. And in addition to rumors of inciting protests against racism, Jackie Robinson effectively ended his career as a military officer at Camp Hood in 1944 when a bus driver attempted to force him to sit in the back in spite of laws that forbade segregation on base buses. By arguing and cursing at the driver and then directly challenging his commanding officer after the fracas, Jackie set in motion a series of events that led to a court-martial. Despite being acquitted, he was discharged shortly afterward.

It's not just understandable and human that he did this; it was probably the right thing to do. Why should he let anyone else treat him that way? No one should have to stand for that.

Except sometimes they do. Are there not goals so important that we'd put up with anything to achieve them?

When Branch Rickey, the manager and owner of the Brooklyn Dodgers, scouted Jackie to potentially become the first black player in baseball, he had one question: Do you have the guts? "I'm looking," Rickey told him, "for a ball player with the guts *not* to fight back." In fact, in their famous meeting, Rickey playacted the abuse that Robinson was likely to experience if he accepted Rickey's challenge: a hotel clerk refusing him a room, a rude waiter in a restaurant, an opponent shouting slurs. This, Robinson assured him, he was ready to handle.

There were plenty of players Rickey could have gone with. But he needed one who wouldn't let his ego block him from seeing the bigger picture.

As he started in baseball's farm system, then in the pros, Robinson faced more than just slights from service staff or reticent players. There was an aggressive, coordinated campaign to libel, boo, provoke, freeze out, attack, maim, or even kill. In his career, he was hit by more than seventy-two pitches, nearly had his Achilles tendon taken out by players who aimed their spikes at him, and that says nothing of the calls he was cheated out of and the breaks of the game that didn't go his way. Yet Jackie Robinson held to his unwritten pact with Rickey, never giving into explosive anger— however deserved. In fact, in nine years in the league, he never hit another player with his fist.

Athletes seem spoiled and hotheaded to us today, but we have no concept of what the leagues were like then. In 1956, Ted Williams, one of the most revered and respected players in the history of the game, was once caught *spitting* at his fans. As a white player he could not only get away with this, he later told reporters, "I'm not a bit sorry for what I did. I was right and I'd spit again at the same people who booed me today . . . Nobody's going to stop me from spitting." For a black player, this sort of behavior would have been not only unthinkable but shortsighted beyond comprehension. Robinson had no such freedom—it would have ended not only his career, but set back his grand experiment for a generation.

Jackie's path called for him to put aside both his ego and in some respects his basic sense of fairness and rights as a human being. Early in his career, the manager of the Philadelphia Phillies, Ben Chapman, was particularly brutal in his taunting during a game. "They're waiting for you in the jungles, black boy!" he yelled over and over. "We don't want you here, nigger." Not only did Jackie *not* respond—despite, as he later wrote, wanting to "grab one of those white sons of bitches and smash his teeth in with my despised black fist"—a month later he agreed to take a friendly photo with Chapman to help save the man's job.

The thought of touching, posing with such an asshole, even sixty years removed, almost turns the stomach. Robinson called it one of the most difficult things he ever did, but he was willing to because it was part of a larger plan. He understood that certain forces were trying to bait him, to ruin him. Knowing what he wanted and needed to do in baseball, it was clear what he would have to tolerate in order to do it. He shouldn't have had to, but he did.

Our own path, whatever we aspire to, will in some ways be defined by the amount of nonsense we are willing to deal with. Our humiliations will pale in comparison to Robinson's, but it will still be hard. It will still be tough to keep our self-control.

The fighter Bas Rutten sometimes writes the letter *R* on both his hands before fights—for the word *rustig*, which means "relax" in Dutch. Getting angry, getting emotional, losing restraint is a recipe for failure in the ring. You cannot, as John Steinbeck once wrote to his editor, "[lose] temper as a refuge from despair." Your ego will do you no favors here, whether you're struggling with a publisher, with critics, with enemies, or a capricious boss. It doesn't matter that they don't understand or that you know better. It's too early for that. It's too soon.

Oh, you went to *college*? That doesn't mean the world is yours by right. But it was *the Ivy League*? Well, people are still going to treat you poorly, and they will still yell at you. You have a million dollars or a wall full of awards? That doesn't mean anything in the new field you're trying to tackle.

It doesn't matter how talented you are, how great your connections are, how much money you have. When you want to do something—something big and important and meaningful—you will be subjected to treatment ranging from indifference to outright sabotage. Count on it.

In this scenario, ego is the absolute opposite of what is needed. Who can afford to be jerked around by impulses, or believe that you're god's gift to humanity, or too important to put up with anything you don't like?

Those who have subdued their ego understand that it doesn't degrade *you* when others treat you poorly; it degrades them.

Up ahead there will be: Slights. Dismissals. Little fuck yous. One-sided compromises. You'll get yelled at. You'll have to work behind the scenes to salvage what should have been easy. All this will make you angry. This will make you want to fight back. This will make you want to say: *I am better than this. I deserve more.*

Of course, you'll want to throw that in other people's faces. Worse, you'll want to get in other people's faces, people who don't *deserve* the respect, recognition, or rewards they are getting. In fact, those people will often get perks *instead* of you. When someone doesn't reckon you with the seriousness that you'd like, the impulse is to correct them. (As we all wish to say: *Do you know who I am?!*) You want to remind them of what they've forgotten; your ego screams for you to indulge it.

Instead, you must do nothing. Take it. Eat it until you're sick. Endure it. Quietly brush it off and work harder. Play the game. Ignore the noise; for the love of God, do not let it distract you. Restraint is a difficult skill but a critical one. You will often be tempted, you will probably even be overcome. No one is perfect with it, but try we must.

It is a timeless fact of life that the up-and-coming must endure the abuses of the entrenched. Robinson was *twenty-eight* when he started with the Dodgers, and he'd already paid plenty of dues in life as both a black man and a soldier. Still, he was forced to do it again. It's a sad fact of life that new talents are regularly missed, and even when recognized, often unappreciated. The reasons always vary, but it's a part of the journey.

But you're not able to change the system until *after* you've made it. In the meantime, you'll have to find some way to make it suit your purposes—even if those purposes are just extra time to develop properly, to learn from others on their dime, to build your base and establish yourself.

As Robinson succeeded, after he had proved himself as the Rookie of the Year and as an MVP, and as his spot on the Dodgers was certain, he began to more clearly assert himself and his boundaries as a player and as a man. Having carved out his space, he felt that he could argue with umpires, he could throw his shoulder if he needed to make a player back off or to send a message.

No matter how confident and famous Robinson became, he never spit on fans. He never did anything that undermined his legacy. A class act from opening day until the end, Jackie

Robinson was not without passion. He had a temper and frustrations like all of us do. But he learned early that the tightrope he walked would tolerate only restraint and had no forgiveness for ego.

Honestly, not many paths do.

GET OUT OF YOUR OWN HEAD

A person who thinks all the time has nothing to think
about except thoughts, so he loses touch with reality and
lives in a world of illusions.

—ALAN WATTS

I t is Holden Caulfield, the self-absorbed boy walking the
streets of Manhattan, struggling to adjust to the world.
It is a young Arturo Bandini in Los Angeles, alienating
every person he meets as he tries to become a famous
writer. It is the blue blood Binx Bolling in 1950s uptown
New Orleans, trying to escape the "everydayness" of life.

These fictional characters all had something in common:
they couldn't get out of their own heads.

In J. D. Salinger's *The Catcher in the Rye*, Holden can't stay
in school, is petrified of growing up, and wants desperately
to get away from it all. In John Fante's *Ask the Dust* (part of
a series known as *The Bandini Quartet*), this young writer
doesn't *experience* the life he is living, he sees it all "across a
page in a typewriter," wondering if nearly every second of
his life is a poem, a play, a story, a news article with him as
its main character. In Walker Percy's *The Moviegoer*, his

protagonist, Binx, is addicted to watching movies, preferring an idealized version of life on the screen to his own uncomfortable ennui.

It's always dangerous to psychologize a writer based on his work, but these are famously autobiographical novels. When we look at the writers' lives, the facts are clear: J. D. Salinger really did suffer from a sort of self-obsession and immaturity that made the world too much for him to bear, driving him from human contact and paralyzing his genius. John Fante struggled to reconcile his enormous ego and insecurity with relative obscurity for most of his career, eventually abandoning his novels for the golf course and Hollywood bars. Only near death, blind with diabetes, was he finally able to get serious again. *The Moviegoer,* Walker Percy's first book, came only after he'd conquered his almost teenage indolence and existential crisis, which lasted alarmingly into his forties.

How much better could these writers have been had they managed to get through these troubles earlier? How much easier would their lives have been? It's an urgent question they pushed onto their readers with their cautionary characters.

Because sadly, this trait, the inability to get out of one's head, is not restricted to fiction. Twenty-four hundred years ago, Plato spoke of the type of people who are guilty of "feasting on their own thoughts." It was apparently common enough even then to find people who "instead of finding out how something they desire might actually come about, [they] pass that over, so as to avoid tiring deliberations about what's possible. They assume that what they desire is available and proceed to arrange the rest, taking pleasure in thinking through everything they'll do when they have what they want, thereby making their lazy souls even lazier." Real people preferring to live in passionate fiction than in actual reality.

The Civil War general George McClellan is the perfect example of this archetype. He was chosen to command the Union forces because he checked all the boxes of what a great general should be: West Point grad, proven in battle, a student of history, of regal bearing, loved by his men.

Why did he turn out to be quite possibly the worst Union general, even in a crowded field of incompetent and self-absorbed leaders? Because he could never get out of his own head. He was in love with his vision of himself as the head of a grand army. He could prepare an army for battle like a professional, but when it came to *lead* one into battle, when the rubber needed to meet the road, troubles arose.

He became laughably convinced that the enemy was growing larger and larger (it wasn't—at one point he actually had a three-times *advantage*). He was convinced of constant threats and intrigues from his political allies (there weren't any). He was convinced that the only way to win the war was with the perfect plan and a single decisive campaign (he was wrong). He was so convinced of all of it that he froze and basically did nothing . . . for months at a time.

McClellan was constantly thinking *about himself* and how wonderful he was doing—congratulating himself for victories not yet won, and more often, horrible defeats he had saved the cause from. When anyone—including his superiors—questioned this comforting fiction, he reacted like a petulant, delusional, vainglorious, and selfish ass. By itself that's insuf-

GET OUT OF YOUR OWN HEAD

ferable, but it meant another thing: his personality made it impossible to do what he needed to do most—win battles.

A historian who fought under McClellan at Antietam later summed it up: "His egotism is simply colossal—there is no other word for it." We tend to think that ego equals confidence, which is what we need to *be in charge*. In fact, it can have the opposite effect. In McClellan's case it deprived him of the ability to lead. It robbed him of the ability to think that he even needed to act.

The repeated opportunities he missed would be laughable were it not for the thousands and thousands of lives they cost. The situation was made worse by the fact that two pious, quiet Southerners—Lee and Stonewall Jackson— with a penchant for taking the initiative were able to embarrass him with inferior numbers and inferior resources. Which is what happens when leaders get stuck in their own heads. It can happen to us too.

The novelist Anne Lamott describes that ego story well. "If you are not careful," she warns young writers, "station KFKD (K-Fucked) will play in your head twenty-four hours a day, nonstop, in stereo."

> Out of the right speaker in your inner ear will come the endless stream of self-aggrandizement, the recitation of one's specialness, of how much more open and gifted and brilliant and knowing and misunderstood and humble one is. Out of the left speaker will be the rap songs of self-loathing, the lists of all the things one doesn't do well, of all the mistakes one has made today and over an entire lifetime, the doubt, the assertion that everything that one touches turns to

69

shit, that one doesn't do relationships well, that one is in every way a fraud, incapable of selfless love, that one had no talent or insight, and on and on and on.

Anyone—particularly the ambitious—can fall prey to this narration, good and bad. It is natural for any young, ambitious person (or simply someone whose ambition is young) to get excited and swept up by their thoughts and feelings. Especially in a world that tells us to keep and promote a "personal brand." We're required to tell stories in order to sell our work and our talents, and after enough time, forget where the line is that separates our fictions from reality.

Ultimately this disability will paralyze us. Or it will become a wall between us and the information we need to do our jobs—which is largely why McClellan continually fell for flawed intelligence reports he ought to have known were wrong. The idea that his task was relatively straightforward, that he just needed to get started, was almost too easy and too obvious to someone who had thought so much about it all.

He's not that different from the rest of us. We're all full of anxieties, doubts, impotence, pains, and sometimes a little tinge of crazy. We're like teenagers in this regard.

As the psychologist David Elkind has famously researched, adolescence is marked by a phenomenon known now as the "imaginary audience." Consider a thirteen-year-old so embarrassed that he misses a week of class, positive that the entire school is thinking and murmuring about some tiny incident that in truth hardly anyone noticed. Or a teenage girl who spends three hours in front of the mirror each morning, as if she's about to go on stage. They do this because they're convinced that their every move is being watched with rapt attention by the rest of the world.

Even as adults, we're susceptible to this fantasy during a harmless walk down the street. We plug in some headphones and all of a sudden there's a soundtrack. We flip up our jacket collar and consider briefly how cool we must look. We replay the successful meeting we're heading *toward* in our head. The crowds part as we pass. We're fearless warriors, on our way to the top.

It's the opening credits montage. It's a scene in a novel. It feels good—so much better than those feelings of doubt and fear and normalness—and so we stay stuck inside our heads instead of participating in the world around us.

That's ego, baby.

What successful people do is curb such flights of fancy. They ignore the temptations that might make them feel important or skew their perspective. General George C. Marshall—essentially the opposite of McClellan even though they briefly held the same position a few generations apart—refused to keep a diary during World War II despite the requests of historians and friends. He worried that it would turn his quiet, reflective time into a sort of performance and self-deception. That he might second-guess difficult decisions out of concern for his reputation and future readers and warp his thinking based on how they would look.

All of us are susceptible to these obsessions of the mind—whether we run a technology startup or are working our way up the ranks of the corporate hierarchy or have fallen madly in love. The more creative we are, the easier it is to lose the thread that guides us.

Our imagination—in many senses an asset—is dangerous

when it runs wild. We have to rein our perceptions in. Otherwise, lost in the excitement, how can we accurately predict the future or interpret events? How can we stay hungry and aware? How can we appreciate the present moment? How can we be creative within the realm of practicality?

Living clearly and presently takes courage. Don't live in the haze of the abstract, live with the tangible and real, even if—especially if—it's uncomfortable. Be part of what's going on around you. Feast on it, adjust for it.

There's no one to perform for. There is just work to be done and lessons to be learned, in all that is around us.

THE DANGER OF EARLY PRIDE

A proud man is always looking down on things and people; and, of course, as long as you are looking down, you cannot see something that is above you.

—C. S. LEWIS

At eighteen, a rather triumphant Benjamin Franklin returned to visit Boston, the city he'd run away from seven months before. Full of pride and self-satisfaction, he had a new suit, a watch, and a pocketful of coins that he spread out and showed to everyone he ran into—including his older brother, whom he particularly hoped to impress. All posturing by a boy who was not much more than an employee in a print shop in Philadelphia.

In a meeting with Cotton Mather, one of the town's most respected figures, and a former adversary, Franklin quickly illustrated just how ridiculously inflated his young ego had become. Chatting with Mather as they walked down a hallway, Mather suddenly admonished him, "Stoop! Stoop!" Too caught up in his performance, Franklin walked right into a low ceiling beam. Mather's response was perfect: "Let this be a caution to you not always to hold your head so high," he said wryly. "Stoop, young man, stoop—as you go through this world—and you'll miss many hard thumps."

Christians believe that pride is a sin because it is a lie—it convinces people that they are better than they are, that they are better than God made them. Pride leads to arrogance and then away from humility and connection with their fellow man.

You don't have to be Christian to see the wisdom in this. You need only to care about your career to understand that pride—even in real accomplishments—is a distraction and a deluder.

"Whom the gods wish to destroy," Cyril Connolly famously said, "they first call promising." Twenty-five hundred years before that, the elegiac poet Theognis wrote to his friend, "The first thing, Kurnos, which gods bestow on one they would annihilate, is pride." Yet we pick up this mantle on purpose!

Pride blunts the very instrument we need to own in order to succeed: our mind. Our ability to learn, to adapt, to be flexible, to build relationships, all of this is dulled by pride. Most dangerously, this tends to happen either early in life or in the process—when we're flushed with beginner's conceit. Only later do you realize that that bump on the head was the least of what was risked.

Pride takes a minor accomplishment and makes it feel like a major one. It smiles at our cleverness and genius, as though what we've exhibited was merely a hint of what ought to come. From the start, it drives a wedge between the possessor and reality, subtly and not so subtly changing her perceptions of what something is and what it isn't. It is these strong opinions, only loosely secured by fact or accomplishment, that send us careering toward delusion or worse.

Pride and ego say:

- I am an *entrepreneur* because I struck out on my own.
- I am going to *win* because I am currently in the lead.
- I am a *writer* because I published something.
- I am *rich* because I made some money.
- I am *special* because I was chosen.
- I am *important* because I think I should be.

At one time or another, we all indulge this sort of gratifying label making. Yet every culture seems to produce words of caution against it. Don't count your chickens before they hatch. Don't cook the sauce before catching the fish. The way to cook a rabbit is first to catch a rabbit. Game slaughtered by words cannot be skinned. Punching above your weight is how you get injured. Pride goeth before the fall.

Let's call that attitude what it is: fraud. If you're doing the work and putting in the time, you won't need to cheat, you won't need to overcompensate.

Pride is a masterful encroacher. John D. Rockefeller, as a young man, practiced a nightly conversation with himself. "Because you have got a start," he'd say aloud or write in his diary, "you think you are quite a merchant; look out or you will lose your head—go steady."

Early in his career, he'd had some success. He'd gotten a

good job. He was saving money. He had a few investments. Considering his father had been a swindler, this was no small feat. Rockefeller was on the right track. Understandably, a sort of self-satisfaction with his accomplishments—and the trajectory he was heading in—began to seep in. In a moment of frustration, he once shouted at a bank officer who refused to lend him money, "Some day I'll be the richest man in the world!"

Let's count Rockefeller as maybe the only man in the world to say that and then go on to *become* the richest man in the world. But for every one of him, there are a dozen more delusional assholes who said the exact same thing and genuinely believed it, and then came nowhere close—in part because their pride worked against them, and made other people hate them too.

All of this was why Rockefeller knew he needed to rein himself in and to privately manage his ego. Night after night he asked himself, "Are you going to be a fool? Are you going to let this money puff you up?" (However small it was.) "Keep your eyes open," he admonished himself. "Don't lose your balance."

As he later reflected, "I had a horror of the danger of arrogance. What a pitiful thing it is when a man lets a little temporary success spoil him, warp his judgment, and he forgets what he is!" It creates a sort of myopic, onanistic obsession that warps perspective, reality, truth, and the world around us. The childlike little prince in Saint-Exupéry's famous story makes the same observation, lamenting that "vain men never hear anything but praise." That's exactly why we can't afford to have it as a translator.

Receive feedback, maintain hunger, and chart a proper course in life. Pride dulls these senses. Or in other cases, it tunes up other negative parts of ourselves: sensitivity, a persecution complex, the ability to make everything about *us*.

As the famous conqueror and warrior Genghis Khan groomed his sons and generals to succeed him later in life, he repeatedly warned them, "If you can't swallow your pride, you can't lead." He told them that pride would be harder to subdue than a wild lion. He liked the analogy of a mountain. He would say, "Even the tallest mountains have animals that, when they stand on it, are higher than the mountain."

We tend to be on guard against negativity, against the people who are discouraging us from pursuing our callings or doubting the visions we have for ourselves. This is certainly an obstacle to beware of, though dealing with it is rather simple. What we cultivate less is how to protect ourselves against the validation and gratification that will quickly come our way if we show promise. What we don't protect ourselves against are people and things that make us feel good—or rather, *too* good. We must prepare for pride and kill it early—or it will kill what we aspire to. We must be on guard against that wild self-confidence and self-obsession. "The first product of self-knowledge is humility," Flannery O'Connor once said. This is how we fight the ego, by really knowing ourselves.

The question to ask, when you feel pride, then, is this: What am I missing right now that a more humble person might see? What am I avoiding, or running from, with my bluster, franticness, and embellishments? It is far better to ask and answer these questions now, with the stakes still low, than it will be later.

It's worth saying: just because you are quiet doesn't mean that you are without pride. Privately thinking you're better than others is still pride. It's still dangerous. "That on which you so pride yourself will be your ruin," Montaigne had inscribed on the beam of his ceiling. It's a quote from the playwright Menander, and it ends with "you who think yourself to be someone."

We are still striving, and it is the strivers who should be our peers—not the proud and the accomplished. Without this understanding, pride takes our self-conception and puts it at odds with the reality of our station, which is that we still have so far to go, that there is still so much to be done.

After hitting his head and hearing from Mather, Franklin spent a lifetime battling against his pride, because he wanted to do much and understood that pride would made it much harder. Which is why, despite what would be dizzying accomplishments in any era—wealth, fame, power—Franklin never had to experience most of the "misfortunes brought upon people by their carrying their heads too high."

At the end, this isn't about deferring pride because you don't deserve it yet. It isn't "Don't boast about what hasn't happened yet." It is more directly "Don't boast." There's nothing in it for you.

WORK, WORK, WORK

The best plan is only good intentions unless it *degenerates into work.*

—PETER DRUCKER

The painter Edgar Degas, though best known for his beautiful Impressionist paintings of dancers, toyed briefly with poetry. As a brilliant and creative mind, the potential for great poems was all there—he could see beauty, he could find inspiration. Yet there are no great Degas poems. There is one famous conversation that might explain why. One day, Degas complained to his friend, the poet Stéphane Mallarmé, about his trouble writing. "I can't manage to say what I want, and yet I'm full of ideas." Mallarmé's response cuts to the bone. "It's not with ideas, my dear Degas, that one makes verse. It's with words."

Or rather, with *work*.

The distinction between a professional and a dilettante occurs right there—when you accept that having an idea is not enough; that you must work until you are able to recreate your experience effectively in words on the page. As the philosopher and writer Paul Valéry explained in 1938, "A poet's function . . . is not to experience the poetic state: that is a private affair. His function is to create it in others." That is, his job is to produce work.

To be both a craftsman and an artist. To cultivate a product of labor and industry instead of just a product of the mind. It's here where abstraction meets the road and the real, where we trade thinking and talking for working.

"You can't build a reputation on what you're *going* to do," was how Henry Ford put it. The sculptor Nina Holton hit the same note in psychologist Mihaly Csikszentmihalyi's landmark study on creativity. "That germ of an idea," she told him, "does not make a sculpture which stands up. It just sits there. So the next stage, of course, is the hard work." The investor and serial entrepreneur Ben Horowitz put it more bluntly: "The hard thing isn't setting a big, hairy, audacious goal. The hard thing is laying people off when you miss the big goal. . . . The hard thing isn't dreaming big. The hard thing is waking up in the middle of the night in a cold sweat when the dream turns into a nightmare."

Sure, you get it. You know that all things require work and that work might be quite difficult. But do you *really* understand? Do you have any idea just how much work there is going to be? Not work until you get your big break, not work until you make a name for yourself, but work, work, work, forever and ever.

Is it ten thousand hours or twenty thousand hours to mastery? The answer is that it doesn't matter. There is no end zone. To think of a number is to live in a conditional future. We're simply talking about a lot of hours—that to get where we want to go isn't about brilliance, but continual effort. While that's not a terribly sexy idea, it should be an encouraging one. Because it means it's all within reach—for all of us, provided we have the constitution and humbleness to be patient and the fortitude to put in the work.

By this point, you probably understand why the ego would bristle at this idea. *Within reach?!* it complains. *That means you're saying I don't have it now.* Exactly right. You don't. No one does.

Our ego wants the ideas and the fact that we aspire to do something about them to be enough. Wants the hours we spend *planning* and attending conferences or chatting with impressed friends to count toward the tally that success seems to require. It wants to be paid well for its time and it wants to do the fun stuff—the stuff that gets attention, credit, or glory.

That's the reality. Where we decide to put our energy decides what we'll ultimately accomplish.

As a young man, Bill Clinton began a collection of note cards upon which he would write names and phone numbers of friends and acquaintances who might be of service when he eventually entered politics. Each night, before he ever had a reason to, he would flip through the box, make phone calls, write letters, or add notations about their interactions. Over the years, this collection grew—to ten thousand cards (before it was eventually digitized). It's what put him in the Oval Office and continues to return dividends.

Or think of Darwin, working for decades on his theory of evolution, refraining from publishing it because it wasn't yet perfect. Hardly anyone knew what he was working on. No one said, *Hey Charles, it's okay that you're taking so long, because what you're working on is just so important.* They didn't know. *He* couldn't have known. He just knew that it wasn't done yet, that it could be better, and that that was enough to keep him going.

So: Do we sit down, alone, and struggle with our work? Work that may or may not go anywhere, that may be discouraging or painful? Do we *love* work, making a living to do work, not the other way around? Do we *love* practice, the way great athletes do? Or do we chase short-term attention and validation—whether that's indulging in the endless search for *ideas* or simply the distraction of talk and chatter?

Fac, si facis. (Do it if you're going to do it.)

There is another apt Latin expression: *Materiam superabat opus.* (The workmanship was better than the material.) The material we've been given genetically, emotionally, financially, that's where we begin. We don't control that. We do control what we make of that material, and whether we squander it.

As a young basketball player, Bill Bradley would remind himself, "When you are not practicing, remember, someone somewhere is practicing, and when you meet him he will win." The Bible says something similar in its own way: "Blessed are those servants whom the master finds awake when he comes." You can lie to yourself, saying that you put in the time, or pretend that you're working, but eventually someone will show up. You'll be tested. And quite possibly, found out.

Since Bradley went on to be an All-American, a Rhodes Scholar, then a two-time champion with the New York Knicks and a U.S. senator, you get the sense that this sort of dedication will take you places.

So we must have it. Because there is no triumph without toil.

Wouldn't it be great if work was as simple as opening a vein and letting the genius pour out? Or if you could walk into that meeting and spit brilliance off the top of your head? You walk up to the canvas, hurl your paint at it, and modern art emerges, right? That is the fantasy—rather, that is the lie.

Back to another popular old trope: Fake it 'til you make it. It's no surprise that such an idea has found increasing relevance in our noxiously bullshit, Nerf world. When it is difficult to tell a real producer from an adept self-promoter, of course some people will roll the dice and manage to play the confidence game. Make it so you don't have to fake it— that's the key. Can you imagine a doctor trying to get by with anything less? Or a quarterback, or a bull rider? More to the point, would you want them to? So why would you try otherwise?

Every time you sit down to work, remind yourself: I am delaying gratification by doing this. I am passing the marshmallow test. I am earning what my ambition burns for. I am making an investment in myself instead of in my ego. Give yourself a little credit for this choice, but not so much, because you've got to get back to the task at hand: practicing, working, improving.

Work is finding yourself alone at the track when the weather kept everyone else indoors. Work is pushing through the pain and crappy first drafts and prototypes. It is ignoring whatever plaudits others are getting, and more importantly, ignoring whatever plaudits *you* may be getting. Because there is work to be done. Work doesn't *want* to be good. It is made so, despite the headwind.

There is another old expression: You know a workman by the chips they leave. It's true. To judge your progress properly, just take a look at the floor.

FOR EVERYTHING THAT COMES
NEXT, EGO IS THE ENEMY . . .

'Tis a common proof,
That lowliness is young ambition's ladder.

—SHAKESPEARE

We know where we want to end up: success. We want to matter. Wealth and recognition and reputation are nice too. We want it all.

The problem is that we're not sure that humility can get us there. We are petrified, as the Reverend Dr. Sam Wells put it, that if we are humble, we will end up "subjugated, trodden on, embarrassed and irrelevant."

Midway through his career, if you'd asked our model Sherman how he felt, he probably would have described himself in almost exactly those terms. He had not made much money. He had won no great battles. He had not seen his name in lights or headlines. He might have, at that moment, before the Civil War, begun to question the path he'd chosen, and whether those who follow it finished last.

This is the thinking that creates the Faustian bargain that turns most clean ambition into shameless addiction. In the early stages, ego can be temporarily adaptive. Craziness

EGO IS THE ENEMY

can pass for audaciousness. Delusions can pass for confidence, ignorance for courage. But it's just kicking the costs down the road.

Because no one ever said, reflecting on the whole of someone's life, "Man, that monstrous ego sure was worth it."

The internal debate about confidence calls to mind a well-known concept from the radio pioneer Ira Glass, which could be called the Taste/Talent Gap.

All of us who do creative work . . . we get into it because we have good taste. But it's like there's a gap, that for the first couple years that you're making stuff, what you're making isn't so good . . . It's really not that great. It's *trying* to be good, it has ambition to be good, but it's not quite that good. But your taste—the thing that got you into the game—your taste is still killer, and your taste is good enough that you can tell that what you're making is kind of a disappointment to you.

It is in precisely this gap that ego can seem comforting. Who wants to look at themselves and their work and find that it does not measure up? And so here we might bluster our way through. Cover up hard truths with sheer force of personality and drive and passion. *Or,* we can face our shortcomings honestly and put the time in. We can let this humble us, see clearly where we are talented and where we need to improve, and then put in the work to bridge that gap. And we can set upon positive habits that will last a lifetime.

If ego was tempting in Sherman's time, in this era, we

are like Lance Armstrong training for the 1999 Tour de France. We are Barry Bonds debating whether to walk into the BALCO clinic. We flirt with arrogance and deceit, and in the process grossly overstate the importance of winning at all costs. Everyone is juicing, the ego says to us, you should too. *There's no way to beat them without it,* we think.

Of course, what is truly ambitious is to face life and proceed with quiet confidence in spite of the distractions. Let others grasp at crutches. It will be a lonely fight to be real, to say "I'm not going to take the edge off." To say, "I am going to be myself, the best version of that self. I am in this for the long game, no matter how brutal it might be." To *do,* not *be.*

For Sherman, it was precisely his choice that prepared him for the time his country and history most needed him—and allowed him to navigate the massive responsibilities that shortly came his way. In this quiet crucible, he'd forged a personality that was ambitious but patient, innovative without being brash, brave without being dangerous. He was a *real* leader.

You have a chance to do this yourself. To play a different game, to be *utterly* audacious in your aims. Because what comes next is going to test you in ways that you cannot begin to understand. For ego is a wicked sister of success.

And you're about to experience what that means.

PART II

SUCCESS

Here we are at the top of a mountain we worked hard to climb—or at least the summit is in sight. Now we face new temptations and problems. We breathe thinner air in an unforgiving environment. Why is success so ephemeral? Ego shortens it. Whether a collapse is dramatic or a slow erosion, it's always possible and often unnecessary. We stop learning, we stop listening, and we lose our grasp on what matters. We become victims of ourselves and the competition. Sobriety, open-mindedness, organization, and purpose—these are the great stabilizers. They balance out the ego and pride that comes with achievement and recognition.

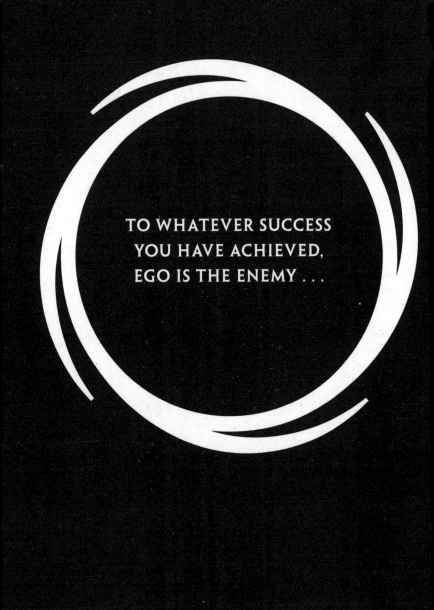

TO WHATEVER SUCCESS
YOU HAVE ACHIEVED,
EGO IS THE ENEMY . . .

Two different characters are presented to our emulation; the one, of proud ambition and ostentatious avidity. The other, of humble modesty and equitable justice. Two different models, two different pictures, are held out to us, according to which we may fashion our own character and behaviour; the one more gaudy and glittering in its colouring; the other more correct and more exquisitely beautiful in its outline.

—ADAM SMITH

At a business meeting in January 1924, Howard Hughes Sr., the successful inventor and tool magnate, stood up, convulsed, and died from a sudden heart attack at the age of fifty-four. His son, a quiet, reserved, and sheltered boy of just eighteen, inherited three fourths of the private company, which held patents and leases critical to oil drilling, worth nearly $1 million. Various family members were bequeathed the remaining shares.

In a move of almost incomprehensible foresight, the young Hughes, whom many saw as a spoiled little boy, made the decision to buy out his relatives and control the entire company himself. Against their objections and still legally considered a minor, Hughes leveraged his personal assets and nearly all the company's funds to purchase the stock, and in doing so, consolidated ownership of a business that would create billions of dollars of cash profit over the next century.

It was a bold move for a young man with essentially zero experience in business. And it was with similar boldness that over his career he would create one of the most embarrassing, wasteful, and dishonest business track records in history. In retrospect, his years at the helm of the Hughes empire resemble a deranged crime spree more than a capitalistic enterprise.

One cannot argue whether Hughes was gifted, visionary, and brilliant. He just was. Literally a mechanical genius, he was also one of the best and bravest pilots in the pioneer days of aviation. And as a businessman and filmmaker he had the ability to predict wide, sweeping changes that came to transform not just the industries he was involved in, but America itself.

Yet, after filtering out his acumen from the legend, glamour, and self-promotion at which he was so adept, only one image remains: an egomaniac who evaporated *hundreds of millions* of dollars of his own wealth and met a miserable, pathetic end. Not by accident, not because he was beset by unforeseen circumstances or competition, but almost exclusively due to his own actions.

A quick rundown of his feats—if you can call them that—provides a stark perspective:

After purchasing control of his father's tool company from his family, Hughes abandoned it almost immediately except to repeatedly siphon off its cash. He left Houston and never stepped foot in the company's headquarters again. He moved to Los Angeles, where he decided to become a film producer and celebrity. Trading stocks from his bedside, he lost more than $8 million in the market leading up to the Depression. His most well-known movie, *Hell's Angels*, took three years to make, lost $1.5 million on a budget of $4.2 million, and nearly bankrupted the tool company in the process. Then, not having learned a lesson the first time, Hughes lost another $4 million on Chrysler stock in early 1930.

He then put all this aside to enter the aviation business, creating a defense contractor called the Hughes Aircraft Company. Despite some astounding personal achievements as an inventor, Hughes's company was a failure. His two contracts during World War II, worth $40 million, were massive failures at the expense of the American taxpayer and himself. The most notable, the *Spruce Goose*—which Hughes called the *Hercules* and which was one of the biggest planes ever made—took more than five years to develop, cost roughly $20 million, and flew just a single time for barely a mile, only 70 feet above the water. At his insistence and expense, it then sat in an air-conditioned hangar in Long Beach for decades at the cost of $1 million a year. Deciding to double down on the film business, Hughes purchased the movie studio RKO and produced losses of over $22 million (and went from two thousand employees to fewer than five hundred as he ran it into the ground over several years). Tiring of these businesses as he had of the tool company, he forsook defense contracting and handed it off to executives to run, where it slowly began to thrive . . . because of his absence.

It would make sense to stop here to avoid belaboring the

issue—but that would risk skipping Hughes's egregious tax fraud; the plane crashes and fatal car accidents; the millions he wasted on private investigators, lawyers, contracts for starlets he refused to let act, property he never lived in; the fact that the only thing that got him to behave responsibly was the threat of public exposure; the paranoia, racism, and bullying; the failed marriages; the drug addiction; and dozens of other ventures and businesses he mismanaged.

"That we have made a hero out of Howard Hughes," a young Joan Didion wrote, "tells us something interesting about ourselves." She's absolutely right. For Howard Hughes, despite his reputation, was quite possibly one of the worst businessmen of the twentieth century. Usually a bad businessman fails and ceases to be in business anymore, making it hard to see what truly caused his failures. But thanks to the steady chain of profits from his father's company, which he found too boring to interfere with, Hughes was able to stay afloat, allowing us to see the damage that his ego repeatedly wrought—to himself as a person, to the people around him, to what he wanted to accomplish.

There is a scene from Howard's slow descent into madness that bears illustrating. His biographers have him sitting naked in his favorite white chair, unwashed, unkempt, working around the clock to battle lawyers, investigations, investors, in an attempt to save his empire and to hide his shameful secrets. One minute he would dictate some irrational multipage memo about Kleenex, food preparation, or how employees should not speak to him directly, and then he would turn around and seize upon a genuinely brilliant strategy to outrun his creditors and enemies. It was as if, they observed, his mind and business were split in two parts. It was as if, they wrote, "IBM had deliberately established a pair of subsidiaries, one to produce computers and profits, another to manufacture Edsels and losses." If someone was looking for a flesh-and-blood metaphor for ego and destruction, it would be hard to do better than this image of a man working furiously with one hand toward a goal and with the other working equally hard to undermine it.

Howard Hughes, like all of us, was not completely crazy or completely sane. His ego, fueled and exacerbated by physical injuries (mostly from plane and car crashes for which he was at fault) and various addictions, led him into a darkness that we can scarcely comprehend. There were brief moments of lucidity when the sharp mind of Hughes broke through—times when he made some of his best moves—but as he progressed through life, these moments became increasingly rare. Eventually, ego killed Howard Hughes as much as the mania and trauma did—if they were ever separate to begin with.

You can only see this if you want to see it. It's more attractive and exciting to see the rebel billionaire, the eccentric, the world renown, and the fame, and think: *Oh, how I want that.* You do not. Howard Hughes, like so many wealthy people, died in an asylum of his own making. He felt little joy. He enjoyed almost nothing of what he had. Most importantly, he *wasted.* He wasted so much talent, so much bravery, and so much energy.

Without virtue and training, Aristotle observed, "it is hard to bear the results of good fortune suitably." We can learn from Hughes because he was so publicly and visibly unable to bear his birthright properly. His endless taste for the spotlight, no matter how unflattering, gives us an opportunity to see our own tendencies, our own struggles with success and luck, refracted back through his tumultuous life. His enormous ego and its destructive path through Hollywood, through the defense industry, through Wall Street, through the aviation industry give us a look inside someone who was repeatedly felled by impulses we all have.

Of course, he's far from the only person in history to follow such an arc. Will you follow his trajectory?

Sometimes ego is suppressed on the ascent. Sometimes an idea is so powerful or timing is so perfect (or one is born into wealth or power) that it can temporarily support or even compensate for a massive ego. As success arrives, like it does for a team that has just won a championship, ego begins to toy with our minds and weaken the will that made us win in the first place. We know that empires always fall, so we must think about why—and why they seem to always collapse from within.

Harold Geneen was the CEO who more or less invented the concept of the modern international conglomerate. Through a series of acquisitions, mergers, and takeovers (more than 350 in all), he took a small company called ITT from $1 million in revenues in 1959 to nearly $17 *billion* in 1977, the year he retired. Some claimed that Geneen himself was an egotist—in any case, he spoke candidly about the effects that ego had in his industry and warned executives against it.

"The worst disease which can afflict business executives

in their work is not, as popularly supposed, alcoholism; it's egotism," Geneen famously said. In the *Mad Men* era of corporate America, there was a major drinking problem, but ego has the same roots—insecurity, fear, a dislike for brutal objectivity. "Whether in middle management or top management, unbridled personal egotism blinds a man to the realities around him; more and more he comes to live in a world of his own imagination; and because he sincerely believes he can do no wrong, he becomes a menace to the men and women who have to work under his direction," he wrote in his memoirs.

Here we are having accomplished something. After we give ourselves proper credit, ego wants us to think, *I'm special. I'm better. The rules don't apply to me.*

"Man is pushed by drives," Viktor Frankl observed. "But he is pulled by values." Ruled by or *ruling*? Which are you? Without the right values, success is brief. If we wish to do more than flash, if we wish to last, then it is time to understand how to battle this new form of ego and what values and principles are required in order to beat it.

Success is intoxicating, yet to sustain it requires sobriety. We can't keep learning if we think we already know everything. We cannot buy into myths we make ourselves, or the noise and chatter of the outside world. We must understand that we are a small part of an interconnected universe. On top of all this, we have to build an organization and a system around what we do—one that is about the *work* and not about *us*.

The verdict on Hughes is in. Ego wrecked him. A similar judgment awaits us all at some point. Over the course of your own career, you will face the choices that he did—that all people do. Whether you built your empire from nothing or inherited it, whether your wealth is financial or merely a cultivated talent, entropy is seeking to destroy it as you read this.

Can you handle success? Or will it be the worst thing that ever happened to you?

ALWAYS STAY A STUDENT

Every man I meet is my master in some point, and in that I learn of him.

—RALPH WALDO EMERSON

The legend of Genghis Khan has echoed through history: A barbarian conqueror, fueled by bloodlust, terrorizing the civilized world. We have him and his Mongol horde traveling across Asia and Europe, insatiable, stopping at nothing to plunder, rape, and kill not just the people who stood in their way, but the cultures they had built. Then, not unlike his nomadic band of warriors, this terrible cloud simply disappeared from history, because the Mongols built nothing that could last.

Like all reactionary, emotional assessments, this could not be more wrong. For not only was Genghis Khan one of the greatest military minds who ever lived, he was a perpetual student, whose stunning victories were often the result of his ability to absorb the best technologies, practices, and innovations of each new culture his empire touched.

In fact, if there is one theme in his reign and in the several *centuries* of dynastic rule that followed, it's this: appropriation.

Under Genghis Khan's direction, the Mongols were as ruthless about stealing and absorbing the best of each culture they encountered as they were about conquest itself. Though there were essentially no technological inventions, no beautiful buildings or even great Mongol art, with each battle and enemy, their culture learned and absorbed something new. Genghis Khan was not born a genius. Instead, as one biographer put it, his was "a persistent cycle of pragmatic learning, experimental adaptation, and constant revision driven by his uniquely disciplined and focused will."

He was the greatest conqueror the world ever knew because he was more open to learning than any other conqueror has ever been.

Khan's first powerful victories came from the reorganization of his military units, splitting his soldiers into groups of ten. This he stole from neighboring Turkic tribes, and unknowingly converted the Mongols to the decimal system. Soon enough, their expanding empire brought them into contact with another "technology" they'd never experienced before: walled cities. In the Tangut raids, Khan first learned the ins and outs of war against fortified cities and the strategies critical to laying siege, and quickly became an expert. Later, with help from Chinese engineers, he taught his soldiers how to build siege machines that could knock down city walls. In his campaigns against the Jurched, Khan learned the importance of winning hearts and minds. By working with the scholars and royal family of the lands he conquered, Khan was able to hold on to and manage these territories in ways that most empires could not. Afterward, in every country or city he held, Khan would call for the smartest astrologers, scribes, doctors, thinkers, and advisers—anyone who could aid his troops and their efforts. His troops traveled with interrogators and translators for precisely this purpose.

It was a habit that would survive his death. While the Mongols themselves seemed dedicated almost solely to the art of war, they put to good use every craftsman, merchant, scholar, entertainer, cook, and skilled worker they came in contact with. The Mongol Empire was remarkable for its religious freedoms, and most of all, for its love of ideas and convergence of cultures. It brought lemons to China for the first time, and Chinese noodles to the West. It spread Persian carpets, German mining technology, French metalworking, and Islam. The cannon, which revolutionized warfare, was said to be the resulting fusion of Chinese gunpowder, Muslim flamethrowers, and European metalwork. It was Mongol openness to learning and new ideas that brought them together.

As we first succeed, we will find ourselves in new situations, facing new problems. The freshly promoted soldier must learn the art of politics. The salesman, how to manage. The founder, how to delegate. The writer, how to edit others. The comedian, how to act. The chef turned restaurateur, how to run the other side of the house.

This is not a harmless conceit. The physicist John Wheeler, who helped develop the hydrogen bomb, once observed that "as our island of knowledge grows, so does the shore of our ignorance." In other words, each victory and advancement that made Khan smarter also bumped him against new situations he'd never encountered before. It takes a special kind of humility to grasp that you know less, even as you know and grasp more and more. It's remembering Socrates' wisdom lay in the fact that he knew that he knew next to nothing.

With accomplishment comes a growing pressure to pretend that we know more than we do. To pretend we already know everything. *Scientia infla* (knowledge puffs up). That's the worry and the risk—thinking that we're set and secure, when in reality understanding and mastery is a fluid, continual process.

The nine-time Grammy– and Pulitzer Prize–winning jazz musician Wynton Marsalis once advised a promising young musician on the mind-set required in the lifelong study of music: "Humility engenders learning because it beats back the arrogance that puts blinders on. It leaves you open for truths to reveal themselves. You don't stand in your own way. . . . Do you know how you can tell when someone is truly humble? I believe there's one simple test: because they consistently observe and listen, the humble improve. They don't assume, 'I know the way.'"

No matter what you've done up to this point, you better still be a student. If you're not still learning, you're already dying.

It is not enough only to be a student at the beginning. It is a position that one has to assume for life. Learn from *everyone* and *everything*. From the people you beat, and the people who beat you, from the people you dislike, even from your supposed enemies. At every step and every juncture in life, there is the opportunity to learn—and even if the lesson is purely remedial, we must not let ego block us from hearing it again.

Too often, convinced of our own intelligence, we stay in a comfort zone that ensures that we never feel stupid (and are never challenged to learn or reconsider what we know). It obscures from view various weaknesses in our understanding, until eventually it's too late to change course. This is where the silent toll is taken.

Each of us faces a threat as we pursue our craft. Like sirens on the rocks, ego sings a soothing, validating song—which can lead to a wreck. The second we let the ego tell us we have *graduated*, learning grinds to a halt. That's why Frank Shamrock said, "Always *stay* a student." As in, it never ends.

The solution is as straightforward as it is initially uncomfortable: Pick up a book on a topic you know next to nothing about. Put yourself in rooms where you're the least knowledgeable person. That uncomfortable feeling, that defensiveness that you feel when your most deeply held assumptions are challenged—what about subjecting yourself to it *deliberately*? Change your mind. Change your surroundings.

An amateur is defensive. The professional finds learning (and even, occasionally, being shown up) to be enjoyable; they like being challenged and humbled, and engage in education as an ongoing and endless process.

Most military cultures—and people in general—seek to impose values and control over what they encounter. What made the Mongols different was their ability to weigh each situation objectively, and if need be, swap out previous practices for new ones. All great businesses start this way, but then something happens. Take the theory of disruption, which posits that at some point in time, every industry will be disrupted by some trend or innovation that, despite all the resources in the world, the incumbent interests will be incapable of responding to. Why is this? Why can't businesses change and adapt?

A large part of it is because they lost the ability to learn. They stopped being students. The second this happens to you, your knowledge becomes fragile.

The great manager and business thinker Peter Drucker says that it's not enough simply to want to learn. As people progress, they must also understand *how* they learn and then set up processes to facilitate this continual education. Otherwise, we are dooming ourselves to a sort of self-imposed ignorance.

DON'T TELL YOURSELF A STORY

Myth becomes myth not in the living but in the retelling.
—DAVID MARANISS

Starting in 1979, football coach and general manager Bill Walsh took the 49ers from being the worst team in football, and perhaps professional sports, to a Super Bowl victory, in just three years. It would have been tempting, as he hoisted the Lombardi Trophy over his head, to tell himself that the quickest turnaround in NFL history had been his plan all along. It would have been tempting decades later, when he assembled his memoirs, to assume that narrative as well.

It's a sexy story. That his takeover, his turnaround, and the transformation were assiduously scheduled. That it all happened exactly as he wanted—because he was just that good and that talented. No one would have faulted him if he said that.

Yet he refused to indulge in those fantasies. When people asked Walsh whether he had a timetable for winning the Super Bowl, do you know what his answer was? The answer was always *no*. Because when you take over a team that bad, such ambitions would have been utterly delusional.

The year before he arrived, the 49ers were 2 and 14. The organization was demoralized, broken, without draft picks, and fully ensconced in a culture of losing. His first season, they lost another fourteen games. He nearly resigned midway through his second year, because he wasn't sure he could do it. Yet, twenty-four months from taking over (and a little over a year from having almost quit), there he was, the Super Bowl champion "genius."

How did it happen? How was that not part of the "plan"?

The answer is that when Bill Walsh took control, he wasn't focused on winning per se. Instead, he implemented what he called his "Standard of Performance." That is: *What* should be done. *When. How.* At the most basic level and throughout the organization, Walsh had only one timetable, and it was all about instilling these standards.

He focused on seemingly trivial details: Players could not sit down on the practice field. Coaches had to wear a tie and tuck their shirts in. Everyone had to give maximum effort and commitment. Sportsmanship was essential. The locker room must be neat and clean. There would be no smoking, no fighting, no profanity. Quarterbacks were told where and how to hold the ball. Linemen were drilled on thirty separate critical drills. Passing routes were monitored and graded down to the *inch*. Practices were scheduled to the minute.

It would be a mistake to think this was about control. The Standard of Performance was about instilling excellence. These seemingly simple but exacting standards mattered more than some grand vision or power trip. In his eyes, if the players take care of the details, "the score takes care of itself." The winning would happen.

Walsh was strong and confident enough to know that these standards would eventually contribute to victory. He was also humble enough to know that *when* victory would happen was not something he could predict. That it happened faster than for any coach in history? Well, that was a fortuitous break of the game. It was not because of his grand vision. In fact, in his second season, a coach complained to the owner that Walsh was too caught up in minutiae and had no goals to win. Walsh fired that coach for tattling.

We want so desperately to believe that those who have great empires *set out* to build one. Why? So we can indulge in the pleasurable planning of ours. So we can take full credit for the good that happens and the riches and respect that come our way. Narrative is when you look back at an improbable or unlikely path to your success and say: I knew it all along. Instead of: I hoped. I worked. I got some good breaks. Or even: I thought this *could* happen. Of course you didn't really know all along—or if you did, it was more faith than knowledge. But who wants to remember all the times you doubted yourself?

Crafting stories out of past events is a very human impulse. It's also dangerous and untrue. Writing our own narrative leads to arrogance. It turns our life into a story—and turns us into caricatures—while we still have to live it. As the author Tobias Wolff writes in his novel *Old School*, these explanations and stories get "cobbled together later, more or less sincerely, and after the stories have been repeated they put on the badge of memory and block all other routes of exploration."

Bill Walsh understood that it was really the Standard of Performance—the deceptively small things—that was responsible for the team's transformation and victory. But that's too boring for newspaper headlines. It's why he ignored it when they called him "the Genius."

To accept the title and the story wouldn't be a harmless personal gratification. These narratives don't change the past, but they do have the power to negatively impact our future.

His players shortly proved the risks inherent in letting a story go to their heads. Like most of us, they wanted to believe that their unlikely victory occurred because they were special. In the two seasons after their first Super Bowl, the team failed terribly—partly due to the dangerous confidence that accompanies these kinds of victories—losing 12 of 22 games. This is what happens when you prematurely credit yourself with powers you don't yet have control of. This is what happens when you start to think about what your rapid achievements *say about you* and begin to slacken the effort and standards that initially fueled them.

Only when the team returned wholeheartedly to the Standard of Performance did they win again (three more Super Bowls and nine conference or division championships in a decade). Only when they stopped with the stories and focused on the task at hand did they begin to win like they had before.

Here's the other part: once you win, everyone is gunning for you. It's during your moment at the top that you can afford ego the least—because the stakes are so much higher, the margins for error are so much smaller. If anything, your ability to listen, to hear feedback, to improve and grow matter more now than ever before.

Facts are better than stories and image. The twentieth-century financier Bernard Baruch had a great line: "Don't try to buy at the bottom and sell at the top. This can't be done—except by liars." That is, people's claims about what they're doing in the market are rarely to be trusted. Jeff Bezos, the founder of Amazon, has talked about this temptation. He reminds himself that there was "no aha moment" for his billion-dollar behemoth, no matter what he might read in his own press clippings. The founding of a company, making money in the market, or the formation of an idea is messy. Reducing it to a narrative retroactively creates a clarity that never was and never will be there.

When we are aspiring we must resist the impulse to reverse engineer success from other people's stories. When we achieve our own, we must resist the desire to pretend that everything unfolded exactly as we'd planned. There was no grand narrative. You should remember—you were there when it happened.

A few years ago, one of the founders of Google gave a talk in which he said that the way he judges prospective companies and entrepreneurs is by asking them "if they're going to change the world." Which is fine, except that's not how Google started. (Larry Page and Sergey Brin were two Stanford PhDs working on their dissertations.) It's not how You-Tube started. (Its founders weren't trying to reinvent TV; they were trying to share funny video clips.) It's not how most true wealth was created, in fact.

Investor Paul Graham (who invested in Airbnb, reddit, Dropbox, and others), working in the same city as Walsh a few decades later, explicitly warns startups against having bold, sweeping visions early on. Of course, as a capitalist, he wants to fund companies that massively disrupt industries and change the world—that's where the money is. He wants them to have "frighteningly ambitious" ideas, but explains, "The way to do really big things seems to be to start with deceptively small things." He's saying you don't make a frontal attack out of ego; instead, you start with a small bet and iteratively scale your ambitions as you go. His other famous piece of advice, "Keep your identity small," fits well here. Make it about the work and the principles behind it—not about a glorious vision that makes a good headline.

Napoleon had the words "To Destiny!" engraved on the wedding ring he gave his wife. Destiny was what he'd always believed in, it was how he justified his boldest, most ambitious ideas. It was also why he overreached time and time again, until his real destiny was divorce, exile, defeat, and infamy. A great destiny, Seneca reminds us, is great slavery.

There is a real danger in believing it when people use the word "genius"—and it's even more dangerous when we let hubris tell ourselves we are one. The same goes for any label that comes along with a career: are we suddenly a "filmmaker," "writer," "investor," "entrepreneur," or "executive" because we've accomplished one thing? These labels put you at odds not just with reality, but with the real strategy that made you successful in the first place. From that place, we might think that success in the future is just the natural next part of the story—when really it's rooted in work, creativity, persistence, and luck.

Certainly Google's alienation from its own roots (confusing vision and potential with *scientific and technological prowess*) will cause it to stumble soon enough. In fact, the public failures of projects like Google Glass and Google Plus might be evidence of it already. They're not alone. Too often, artists who think it was "inspiration" or "pain" that fueled their art and create an image around that—instead of hard work and sincere hustle—will eventually find themselves at the bottom of a bottle or on the wrong end of a needle.

The same goes for us, whatever we do. Instead of pretending that we are living some great story, we must remain focused on the execution—and on executing with excellence. We must shun the false crown and continue working on what got us here.

Because that's the only thing that will keep us here.

WHAT'S IMPORTANT TO YOU?

To know what you like is the beginning of wisdom and of old age.

—ROBERT LOUIS STEVENSON

At the end of the Civil War, Ulysses S. Grant and his friend William Tecumseh Sherman were two of the most respected and important men in America. Essentially the dual architects of the Union's victory, a grateful country, with a snap of its fingers, said: Whatever you like, as long as you live, is yours.

With this freedom at their disposal, Sherman and Grant took different paths. Sherman, whose track we followed earlier, abhorred politics and repeatedly declined entreaties to run for office. "I have all the rank I want," he told them. Having seemingly mastered his ego, he would later retire to New York City, where he lived in what was, by all appearances, happiness and contentment.

Grant, who had expressed almost no prior interest in politics, and, in fact, had succeeded as a general precisely because he didn't know how to play politics, chose instead to pursue the highest office in the land: the presidency. Elected by a landslide, he then presided over one of the most corrupt, contentious, and least effective administrations in American history. A genuinely good and loyal individual, he was not cut out for the dirty world of Washington, and it made quick work of him. He left office a maligned and controversial figure after two exhausting terms, almost surprised by how poorly it had gone.

After the presidency, Grant invested almost every penny he had to create a financial brokerage house with a controversial investor named Ferdinand Ward. Ward, a Bernie Madoff of his day, turned it into a Ponzi scheme, and publicly bankrupted Grant. As Sherman wrote with sympathy and understanding of his friend, Grant had "aimed to rival the millionaires, who would have given their all to have won any of his battles." Grant had accomplished so much, but to him, it wasn't enough. He couldn't decide what was important—what actually mattered—to him.

That's how it seems to go: we're never happy with what *we* have, we want what others have too. We want to have *more* than everyone else. We start out knowing what is important to us, but once we've achieved it, we lose sight of our priorities. Ego sways us, and can ruin us.

Compelled by his sense of honor to cover the debts of the firm, Grant took out a loan using his priceless war mementos as collateral. Broken in mind, spirit, and body, the last years of his life found him battling painful throat cancer, and racing to finish his memoirs so that he might leave his family with something to live on. He made it, just barely.

One shudders to think of the vital forces drained from this hero, who died at just sixty-three in agony and defeat, this straightforward, honest man who just couldn't help himself, who couldn't manage to focus, and ended up far outside the bounds of his ample genius. What could he have done with those years instead? How might have America looked otherwise? How much more could he have done and accomplished?

Not that he is unique in this regard. All of us regularly say yes unthinkingly, or out of vague attraction, or out of greed or vanity. Because we can't say no—because we might miss out on something if we did. We think "yes" will let us accomplish more, when in reality it prevents exactly what we seek. All of us waste precious life doing things we don't like, to prove ourselves to people we don't respect, and to get things we don't want.

Why do we do this? Well, it should be obvious by now.

Ego leads to envy and it rots the bones of people big and small. Ego undermines greatness by deluding its holder.

Most of us begin with a clear idea of what we want in life. We know what's important to us. The success we achieve, especially if it comes early or in abundance, puts us in an unusual place. Because now, all of a sudden, we're in a new place and have trouble keeping our bearings.

The farther you travel down that path of accomplishment, whatever it may be, the more often you meet other successful people who make you feel insignificant. It doesn't matter how well you're doing; your ego and their accomplishments make you feel like *nothing*—just as others make them feel the same way. It's a cycle that goes on ad infinitum . . . while our brief time on earth—or the small window of opportunity we have here—does not.

So we unconsciously pick up the pace to keep up with

others. But what if different people are running for different reasons? What if there is more than one race going on?

That's what Sherman was saying about Grant. There is a certain "Gift of the Magi" irony in how badly we chase what will not be truly pleasurable. At the very least, it won't last. If only we could all stop for a second.

Let's be clear: competitiveness is an important force in life. It's what drives the market and is behind some of mankind's most impressive accomplishments. On an individual level, however, it's absolutely critical that you know *who* you're competing with and *why*, that you have a clear sense of the space you're in.

Only you know the race you're running. That is, unless your ego decides the only way you have value is if you're *better* than, *have more* than, *everyone everywhere*. More urgently, each one of us has a unique potential and purpose; that means that we're the only ones who can evaluate and set the terms of our lives. Far too often, we look at other people and make their approval the standard we feel compelled to meet, and as a result, squander our very potential and purpose.

According to Seneca, the Greek word *euthymia* is one we should think of often: it is the sense of our own path and how to stay on it without getting distracted by all the others that intersect it. In other words, it's not about beating the other guy. It's not about having more than the others. It's about being what you are, and being as good as possible at it, without succumbing to all the things that draw you away from it. It's about going where you set out to go. About accomplishing the most that you're capable of in what you choose. That's it. No more and no less. (By the way, *euthymia* means "tranquillity" in English.)

It's time to sit down and think about what's truly important to you and then take steps to forsake the rest. Without this, success will not be pleasurable, or nearly as complete as it could be. Or worse, it won't last.

This is especially true with money. If you don't know how much you need, the default easily becomes: more. And so without thinking, critical energy is diverted from a person's calling and toward filling a bank account. When "you combine insecurity and ambition," the plagiarist and disgraced journalist Jonah Lehrer said when reflecting back on his fall, "you get an inability to say no to things."

Ego rejects trade-offs. Why compromise? Ego wants it *all*.

Ego tells you to cheat, though you love your spouse. Because you want what you have *and* what you don't have. Ego says that sure, even though you're just starting to get the hang of one thing, why not jump right in the middle of another? Eventually, you say yes to too much, to something too far beyond the pale. We're like Captain Ahab, chasing Moby Dick, for reasons we don't even understand anymore.

Maybe your priority actually is money. Or maybe it's family. Maybe it's influence or change. Maybe it's building an organization that lasts, or serves a purpose. All of these are perfectly fine motivations. But you do need to know. You need to know what you don't want and what your choices preclude. Because strategies are often mutually exclusive. One cannot be an opera singer *and* a teen pop idol at the same time. Life requires those trade-offs, but ego can't allow it.

So why do you do what you do? That's the question you need to answer. Stare at it until you can. Only then will you understand what matters and what doesn't. Only then can you say no, can you opt out of stupid races that don't matter, or even exist. Only then is it easy to ignore "successful" people, because most of the time they aren't—at least relative to you, and often even to themselves. Only then can you develop that quiet confidence Seneca talked about.

The more you have and do, the harder maintaining fidelity to your purpose will be, but the more critically you will need to. Everyone buys into the myth that *if only they had that*—usually what someone else has—they would be happy. It may take getting burned a few times to realize the emptiness of this illusion. We all occasionally find ourselves in the middle of some project or obligation and can't understand why we're there. It will take courage and faith to stop yourself.

Find out why you're after what you're after. Ignore those who mess with your pace. Let them covet what you have, not the other way around. Because that's independence.

ENTITLEMENT, CONTROL, AND PARANOIA

One of the symptoms of approaching nervous breakdown is the belief that one's work is terribly important.

—BERTRAND RUSSELL

When Xerxes, the Persian emperor, crossed the Hellespont during his invasion of Greece, the waters surged up and destroyed the bridges his engineers had spent days building. And so he threw chains into the river, ordered it be given three hundred lashes, and branded it with hot irons. As his men delivered his punishment, they were ordered to harangue it: "You salt and bitter stream, your master lays this punishment upon you for injuring him, who never injured you." Oh, and he cut off the heads of the men who had built the bridges.

Herodotus, the great historian, called the display "presumptuous," which is probably an understatement. Surely "preposterous" and "delusional" are more appropriate. Then again, it was part of his personality. Shortly before this, Xerxes had written a letter to a nearby mountain in which he needed to cut a canal. You may be tall and proud, he wrote, but don't you dare cause me any trouble. Otherwise, I'll topple you into the sea.

How hilarious is that? More important, how pathetic?

Xerxes' delusional threats are unfortunately not a historical anomaly. With success, particularly power, come some of the greatest and most dangerous delusions: entitlement, control, and paranoia.

Hopefully you won't find yourself so crazed that you start anthropomorphizing, and inflicting retribution on inanimate objects. That's pure, recognizable crazy, and thankfully rare. What's more likely, and more common, is we begin to overestimate our own power. Then we lose perspective. Eventually, we can end like Xerxes, a monstrous joke.

"The Strongest Poison ever known," the poet William Blake wrote, "came from Caesar's Laurel Crown." Success casts a spell over us.

The problem lies in the path that got us to success in the first place. What we've accomplished often required feats of raw power and force of will. Both entrepreneurship and art required the creation of something where nothing existed before. Wealth means beating the market and the odds. Athletic champions have proved their physical superiority over opponents.

Achieving success involved ignoring the doubts and reservations of the people around us. It meant rejecting rejection. It required taking certain risks. We could have given up at any time, but we're here precisely because we didn't. Persistence and courage in the face of ridiculous odds are partially irrational traits—in some cases *really* irrational. When it works, those tendencies can feel like they've been vindicated.

And why shouldn't they? It's human to think that since it's been done once—that the world was changed in some big or small way—that there is now a magical power in our possession. We're here because we're bigger, stronger, smarter. That we *make* the reality we inhabit.

Right before he destroyed his own billion-dollar company, Ty Warner, creator of Beanie Babies, overrode the cautious objections of one of his employees and bragged, "I could put the Ty heart on manure and they'd buy it!" He was wrong. And the company not only catastrophically failed, he later narrowly missed going to jail.

It doesn't matter if you're a billionaire, a millionaire, or just a kid who snagged a good job early. The complete and utter sense of certainty that got you here can become a liability if you're not careful. The demands and dream you had for a better life? The ambition that fueled your effort? These begin as earnest drives but left unchecked become hubris and entitlement. The same goes for the instinct to take charge; now you're addicted to control. Driven to prove the doubters wrong? Welcome to the seeds of paranoia.

Yes, there are legitimate stresses and anguish that come with the responsibilities of your new life. All the things you're managing, the frustrating mistakes of people who should know better, the endless creep of obligations—no one prepares us for that, which makes the feelings all the harder to deal with. The promised land was supposed to be nice, not aggravating. But you can't let the walls close in on you. You've got to get yourself—and your perceptions—under control.

When Arthur Lee was sent to France and England to serve as one of America's diplomats during the Revolutionary War, instead of relishing the opportunity to work with his fellow diplomat Silas Deane and elder statesman Benjamin Franklin, he raged and resented them and suspected them of disliking him. Finally, Franklin wrote him a letter (one that we've probably all deserved to get at one point or another): "If you do not cure yourself of this temper," Franklin advised, "it will end in insanity, of which it is the symptomatic forerunner." Probably because he was in such command of his own temper, Franklin decided that writing the letter was cathartic enough. He never sent it.

If you've ever listened to the Oval Office tapes of Richard Nixon, you can hear the same sickness, and you wish someone could have sent him such a letter. It's a harrowing insight into a man who has lost his grip not just on what he is legally allowed to do, on what his job was (to *serve* the people), but on reality itself. He vacillates wildly from supreme confidence to dread and fear. He talks over his subordinates and rejects information and feedback that challenges what he wants to believe. He lives in a bubble in which no one can say no—not even his conscience.

There's a letter from General Winfield Scott to Jefferson Davis, then the secretary of war for the United States. Davis belligerently pestered Scott repeatedly about some trivial matter. Scott ignored it until, finally, forced to address it, he wrote that he pitied Davis. "Compassion is always due," he said to him, "to an enraged imbecile, who lays about him in blows which hurt only himself."

Ego is its own worst enemy. It hurts the ones we love too. Our families and friends suffer for it. So do our customers, fans, and clients. A critic of Napoleon nailed it when remarking: "He despises the nation whose applause he seeks."

EGO IS THE ENEMY

He couldn't help but see the French people as pieces to be manipulated, people he had to be better than, people who, unless they were totally, unconditionally supportive of him, were against him.

A smart man or woman must regularly remind themselves of the limits of their power and reach.

Entitlement assumes: This is mine. I've earned it. At the same time, entitlement nickels and dimes *other* people because it can't conceive of valuing another person's time as highly as its own. It delivers tirades and pronouncements that exhaust the people who work for and with us, who have no choice other than to go along. It overstates our abilities to ourselves, it renders generous judgment of our prospects, and it creates ridiculous expectations.

Control says, It all must be done *my* way—even little things, even inconsequential things. It can become paralyzing perfectionism, or a million pointless battles fought merely for the sake of exerting its say. It too exhausts people whose help we need, particularly quiet people who don't object until we've pushed them to their breaking point. We fight with the clerk at the airport, the customer service representative on the telephone, the agent who examines our claim. To what end? In reality, we don't control the weather, we don't control the market, we don't control other people, and our efforts and energies in spite of this are pure waste.

Paranoia thinks, I can't trust anyone. I'm in this totally by myself and for myself. It says, I'm surrounded by fools. It says, focusing on my work, my obligations, myself is not enough. I also have to be orchestrating various machinations behind the scenes—to get them before they get me; to get them back for the slights I perceive.

ENTITLEMENT, CONTROL, AND PARANOIA

Everyone has had a boss, a partner, a parent like this. All that strife, anger, chaos, and conflict. How did it go for them? How did it end?

"He who indulges empty fears earns himself real fears," wrote Seneca, who as a political adviser witnessed destructive paranoia at the highest levels.

The sad feedback loop is that the relentless "looking out for number one" can encourage other people to undermine and fight us. They see that behavior for what it really is: a mask for weakness, insecurity, and instability. In its frenzy to protect itself, paranoia creates the persecution it seeks to avoid, making the owner a prisoner of its own delusions and chaos.

Is this the freedom you envisioned when you dreamed of your success? Likely not.

So stop.

MANAGING YOURSELF

> It is not enough to have great qualities; we should also
> have the management of them.
>
> —LA ROCHEFOUCAULD

In 1953, Dwight D. Eisenhower returned from his inaugural parade and entered the White House for the first time as president late in the evening. As he walked into the Executive Mansion, his chief usher handed Eisenhower two letters marked "Confidential and Secret" that had been sent to him earlier in the day. Eisenhower's reaction was swift: "Never bring me a sealed envelope," he said firmly. "That's what I have a staff for."

How snobbish, right? Had the office really gone to his head already?

Not at all. Eisenhower recognized the seemingly insignificant event for what it was: a symptom of a disorganized, dysfunctional organization. Not everything needed to run through him. Who was to say that the envelope was even important? Why hadn't anyone screened it?

As president, his first priority in office was organizing the executive branch into a smooth, functioning, and order-driven unit, just like his military units had been—not because he didn't want to work himself, but because everyone had a job and he trusted and empowered them to do it. As his chief of staff later put it, "The president does the most important things. I do the *next* most important things."

The public image of Eisenhower is of the man playing golf. In reality, he was not someone who ever slacked off, but the leisure time he did have was available because he ran a tight ship. He knew that urgent and important were not synonyms. His job was to set the priorities, to think big picture, and then trust the people beneath him to do the jobs they were hired for.

Most of us are not *the* president, or even president of a *company*, but in moving up the ladder in life, the system and work habits that got us where we are won't necessarily keep us there. When we're aspiring or small time, we can be idiosyncratic, we can compensate for disorganization with hard work and a little luck. That's not going to cut it in the majors. In fact, it'll sink you if you can't grow up and *organize*.

We can contrast Eisenhower's system in the White House with the infamous car company created by John DeLorean, when he walked away from GM to produce his brand of futuristic cars. A few decades removed from the company's spectacular implosion, we can be forgiven for thinking the man was just ahead of his time. In fact, his rise and fall is as timeless a story as there is: Power-hungry narcissist undermines his own vision, and loses millions of dollars of other people's money in the process.

DeLorean was convinced that the culture of order and discipline at GM had held brilliant creatives like himself down.

When he set out to found his company, he deliberately did everything differently, flouting conventional wisdom and business practices. The result was not the freewheeling, creative sanctuary that DeLorean naively envisioned. It was, instead, an overbearingly political, dysfunctional, and even corrupt organization that collapsed under its own weight, eventually resorting to criminality and fraud, and losses of some $250 million.

The DeLorean failed both as a car and as a company because it was mismanaged from top to bottom—with an emphasis on the mismanagement at the top, by the top. That is: DeLorean himself was the problem. Compared to Eisenhower, he worked constantly, with very different results.

As one executive put it, DeLorean "had the ability to recognize a good opportunity but he didn't know how to make it happen." Another executive described his management style as "chasing colored balloons"—he was constantly distracted and abandoning one project for another. He was a genius. Sadly, that's rarely enough.

Though probably not on purpose, DeLorean created a culture in which ego ran free. Convinced that continued success was simply his by right, he seemed to bristle at concepts like discipline, organization, or strategic planning. Employees were not given enough direction, and then at other times, overwhelmed with trivial instructions. DeLorean couldn't delegate—except to lackeys whose blind loyalty was prized over competence or skill. On top of all this, he was often late or preoccupied.

Executives were allowed to work on extracurricular activities on the company dime, encouraged specifically to chase side projects that benefited their boss at the expense of the company. As CEO, DeLorean often bent the truth to investors, fellow officers, and suppliers, and this habit was contagious throughout the company.

Like many people driven by a demon, DeLorean's decisions were motivated by everything *but* what would have been efficient, manageable, or responsible. Instead of improving or fixing GM's system, it's as if he threw out order altogether. What ensued was chaos in which no one followed the rules, no one was accountable, and very little got done. The only reason it didn't collapse immediately was that DeLorean was a master of public relations—a skill that held the whole story together until the first faulty cars came off the assembly line.

Not surprisingly, the cars were *terrible*. They didn't work. Cost per unit was massively over budget. They hadn't secured enough dealers. They couldn't deliver cars to the ones they had. The launch was a disaster. DeLorean Motor Company never recovered.

It turns out that becoming a great leader is difficult. *Who knew?!*

DeLorean couldn't manage himself, and so he had trouble managing others. And so he managed to fail, both himself and the dream.

Management? That's the reward for all your creativity and new ideas? Becoming the Man? Yes—in the end, we all face becoming the adult supervision we originally rebelled against. Yet often we react petulantly and prefer to think: *Now that I'm in charge, things are going to be different!*

Think about Eisenhower. He was the damn president—the most powerful man in the world. He could have kicked back and done things how he liked. If he was disorganized, people would have just had to deal with it (there have been plenty of those presidents before). Yet he wasn't. He understood that order and responsibility were what the country needed. And that this far outweighed his own concerns.

What was so sad about DeLorean is that, like a lot of talented people, his ideas were on point. His car was an exciting innovation. His model could have worked. He had all the assets and the talent. It was his ego and the disorganization that resulted from it that prevented the ingredients from coming together—just as they do for so many of us.

As you become successful in your own field, your responsibilities may begin to change. Days become less and less about *doing* and more and more about making decisions. Such is the nature of leadership. This transition requires reevaluating and updating your identity. It requires a certain humility to put aside some of the more enjoyable or satisfying parts of your previous job. It means accepting that others might be more qualified or specialized in areas in which you considered yourself competent—or at least their time is better spent on them than yours.

Yes, it would be more fun to be constantly involved in every tiny matter, and might make us feel important to be the person called to put out fires. The little things are endlessly engaging and often flattering, while the big picture can be hard to discern. It's not always fun, but it is the job. If you don't think big picture—because you're too busy playing "boss man"—who will?

Of course, there is no "right" system. Sometimes systems are better decentralized. Sometimes they are better in a strict hierarchy. Every project and goal deserves an approach fitted perfectly to what needs to be done. Maybe a creative, relaxed environment makes the most sense for what you're doing. Maybe you can run your business remotely, or maybe it's better for everyone to see each other face-to-face.

What matters is that you learn how to manage yourself and others, before your industry eats you alive. Micromanagers are egotists who can't manage others and they quickly get overloaded. So do the charismatic visionaries who lose interest when it's time to execute. Worse yet are those who surround themselves with yes-men or sycophants who clean up their messes and create a bubble in which they can't even see how disconnected from reality they are.

Responsibility requires a readjustment and then *increased* clarity and purpose. First, setting the top-level goals and priorities of the organization and your life. Then enforcing and observing them. To produce results and only results.

A fish stinks from the head, is the saying. Well, you're the head now.

BEWARE THE DISEASE OF ME

If I am not for myself who will be for me? If I am only for myself, who am I?

—HILLEL

There were great Allied generals of World War II—Patton, Bradley, Montgomery, Eisenhower, MacArthur, Zhukov—and then there was George Catlett Marshall Jr. Although all of them served their countries and fought and led bravely, one stands apart.

Today, we see World War II as a clear fight in which good aligned selflessly against evil. The problem is that victory and the passage of time have obscured the all-too-humanness of the people who were on the right side of that fight. That is: we forget the politics, the backstabbing, the spotlight coveting, the posturing, the greed, and the ass-covering among the Allies. While the other generals protected their turf, fought with each other, and eagerly aspired to their place in history, that behavior was virtually absent in one man: General George Marshall.

More impressively, Marshall quietly outpaced all of them

with the magnitude of his accomplishments. What was his secret?

Pat Riley, the famous coach and manager who led the Los Angeles Lakers and Miami Heat to multiple championships, says that great teams tend to follow a trajectory. When they start—before they have won—a team is innocent. If the conditions are right, they come together, they watch out for each other and work together toward their collective goal. This stage, he calls the "Innocent Climb."

After a team starts to win and media attention begins, the simple bonds that joined the individuals together begin to fray. Players calculate their own importance. Chests swell. Frustrations emerge. Egos appear. The Innocent Climb, Pat Riley says, is almost always followed by the "Disease of Me." It can "strike any winning team in any year and at any moment," and does with alarming regularity.

It's Shaq and Kobe, unable to play together. It's Jordan punching Steve Kerr, Jud Buechler, *and* Will Perdue—his own team members. He punched people on his own team! It's Enron employees plunging California into darkness for personal profit. It's leaks to the media from a disgruntled executive hoping to scuttle a project he dislikes. It's negging and every other intimidation tactic.

For us, it's beginning to think that we're better, that we're special, that our problems and experiences are so incredibly different from everyone else's that no one could possibly understand. It's an attitude that has sunk far better people, teams, and causes than ours.

With General Marshall, who began his term as chief of staff of the U.S. Army on the day Germany invaded Poland in 1939 and served through the entire war, we see one of history's few exceptions to this trend. Marshall somehow never caught the Disease of Me, and in many ways, often shamed it out of the people who did.

It begins with his balanced relationship to rank, an obsession for most people in his line of work.

He was not a man who abstained from *every* public show of rank or status. He insisted that the president call him General Marshall, not George, for example. (He earned it, right?) But while other generals regularly lobbied for promotions— General MacArthur advanced over other officers in the prewar years largely due to the aggressive efforts of *his mother*—Marshall actively discouraged it. When others began to push for Marshall to be chief of staff, he asked them to stop, because "[it] makes me conspicuous in the army. Too conspicuous in fact." Later, he discouraged an effort by the House to pass a bill awarding him the rank of field marshal—not only because he thought the name Field Marshal *Marshall* would sound ridiculous, but because he didn't want to outrank or hurt his mentor, General Pershing, who was near death and a constant source of advice and guidance.

Can you imagine? In all these cases, his sense of honor meant turning down honors, and often letting them go to other people. Like any normal human being, he wanted them, only the right way. More important, he knew that, however nice they would have been to have, he could do without them while perhaps others could not. Ego needs honors in order to be validated. Confidence, on the other hand, is able to wait and focus on the task at hand regardless of external recognition.

Early on in our careers, we may be able to make these

sacrifices more easily. We can drop out of a prestigious college to start our own company. Or we can tolerate being looked over once in a while. Once we've "made it," the tendency is to switch to the mind-set of "getting what's mine." Now, all of a sudden awards and recognition matter—even though they weren't what got us here. We *need* that money, that title, that media attention—not for the team or the cause, but for ourselves. Because we've *earned* it.

Let's make one thing clear: we never earn the right to be greedy or to pursue our interests at the expense of everyone else. To think otherwise is not only egotistical, it's counterproductive.

Marshall was tested on this to the extreme. A job he'd trained his whole life for was up for grabs: command of the troops on D-Day, essentially the largest coordinated invasion the world had ever seen. Roosevelt let it be known that it was Marshall's if he wanted it. A general's place in history is assured by his feats in battle, so even though Marshall was needed in Washington, Roosevelt wanted to give him the opportunity to take command. Marshall would have none of it. "The decision is yours, Mr. President; my wishes have nothing to do with the matter." The role and the glory went to Eisenhower.

It came to be that Eisenhower was, in fact, the best man for that job. He performed superbly and helped win the war. Would anything else have been worth the trade-off?

Yet this is what we regularly refuse to do; our ego precludes serving any larger mission we're a part of.

What are we going to do? Let someone get one over on us?

The writer Cheryl Strayed once told a young reader, "You're becoming who you are going to be and so you might as well not be an asshole." This is one of the most dangerous ironies of success—it can make us someone we never wanted to be in the first place. The Disease of Me can corrupt the most innocent climb.

There was a general who treated Marshall poorly— essentially banishing him to some obscure postings in the middle of his career. Later, Marshall surpassed him and had his chance for revenge. Except—he didn't take it. Because whatever the man's flaws, Marshall saw that he was still of use and that the country would be worse off without him. What were the thanks for this quiet suppression of ego? Just another job well done—and not much more.

The word for that is one we don't use much anymore: magnanimous. It was good strategy too, of course, but mostly Marshall was gracious, forgiving, and magnanimous because it was right. According to observers as high up as President Truman, what separated Marshall from nearly everyone else in the military and politics is that "never did General Marshall think about himself."

There is another story of Marshall sitting for one of the many official portraits that was required of him. After appearing many times and patiently honoring the requests, Marshall was finally informed by the painter that he was finished and free to go. Marshall stood up and began to leave. "Don't you want to see the painting?" the artist asked. "No, thank you," Marshall said respectfully and left.

Is that to say that managing your image isn't important? Of course not. Early in your career, you'll notice that you jump on every opportunity to do so. As you become more accomplished, you'll realize that so much of it is a distraction from your work—time spent with reporters, with awards, and with marketing are time away from what you really care about.

Who has time to look at a picture of himself? What's the point?

As his wife later observed, the people who saw George Marshall as simply modest or quiet missed what was special about the man. He had the same traits that everyone has—ego, self-interest, pride, dignity, ambition—but they were "tempered by a sense of humility and selflessness."

It doesn't make you a bad person to want to be remembered. To want to make it to the top. To provide for yourself and your family. After all, that's all part of the allure.

There is a balance. Soccer coach Tony Adams expresses it well. Play for the name on the front of the jersey, he says, and they'll remember the name on the back.

When it comes to Marshall, the old idea that selflessness and integrity could be weaknesses or hold someone back are laughably disproven. Sure, some people might have trouble telling you much about him—but each and every one of them lives in a world he was largely responsible for shaping.

The credit? Who cares.

MEDITATE ON THE IMMENSITY

> A monk is a man who is separated from all and who is in harmony with all.
>
> —EVAGRIUS PONTICUS

In 1879, the preservationist and explorer John Muir took his first trip to Alaska. As he explored the fjords and rocky landscapes of Alaska's now famous Glacier Bay, a powerful feeling struck him all at once. He'd always been in love with nature, and here in the unique summer climate of the far north, in this single moment, it was as if the entire world was in sync. As if he could see the entire ecosystem and circle of life before him. His pulse began to pick up, and he and the group were "warmed and quickened into sympathy with everything, taken back into the heart of nature" from which we all came. Thankfully, Muir noticed and recorded in his journal the beautiful cohesion of the world around him, which few have ever matched since.

> We feel the life and motion about us, and the universal beauty: the tides marching back and forth with weariless industry, laving the beautiful shores, and

swaying the purple dulse of the broad meadows of the sea where the fishes are fed, the wild streams in rows white with waterfalls, ever in bloom and ever in song, spreading their branches over a thousand mountains; the vast forests feeding on the drenching sunbeams, every cell in a whirl of enjoyment; misty flocks of insects stirring all the air, the wild sheep and goats on the grassy ridges above the woods, bears in the berry-tangles, mink and beaver and otter far back on many a river and lake; Indians and adventurers pursuing their lonely ways; birds tending to their young—everywhere, everywhere, beauty and life, and glad, rejoicing action.

In this moment, he was experiencing what the Stoics would call *sympatheia*—a connectedness with the cosmos. The French philosopher Pierre Hadot has referred to it as the "oceanic feeling." A sense of belonging to something larger, of realizing that "human things are an infinitesimal point in the immensity." It is in these moments that we're not only free but drawn toward important questions: *Who am I? What am I doing? What is my role in this world?*

Nothing draws us away from those questions like material success—when we are always busy, stressed, put upon, distracted, reported to, relied on, apart from. When we're wealthy and told that we're important or powerful. Ego tells us that meaning comes from activity, that being the center of attention is the only way to matter.

When we lack a connection to anything larger or bigger than us, it's like a piece of our soul is gone. Like we've detached ourselves from the traditions we hail from, whatever that happens to be (a craft, a sport, a brotherhood or sister-hood, a family). Ego blocks us from the beauty and history in the world. It stands in the way.

No wonder we find success empty. No wonder we're exhausted. No wonder it feels like we're on a treadmill. No wonder we lose touch with the energy that once fueled us.

Here's an exercise: walk onto ancient battlefield or a place of historical significance. Look at the statues and you can't help but see how similar the people look, how little has changed since then—since before, and how it will be forever after. Here a great man once stood. Here another brave woman died. Here a cruel rich man lived, in this palatial home . . . It's the sense that others have been here before you, generations of them, in fact.

In those moments, we have a sense of the immensity of the world. Ego is impossible, because we realize, if only fleet-ingly, what Emerson meant when he said that "Every man is a quotation from all his ancestors." They are part of us, we are part of a tradition. Embrace the power of this position and learn from it. It is an exhilarating feeling to grasp this, like the one that Muir felt in Alaska. Yes, we are small. We are also a piece of this great universe and a process.

The astrophysicist Neil deGrasse Tyson has described this duality well—it's possible to bask in both your relevance and irrelevance to the cosmos. As he says, "When I look up in the universe, I know I'm small, but I'm also big. I'm big because I'm connected to the universe and the universe is connected to me." We just can't forget which is bigger and which has been here longer.

Why do you think that great leaders and thinkers throughout history have "gone out into the wilderness" and come back with inspiration, with a plan, with an experience that puts them on a course that changes the world? It's because in doing so they found perspective, they understood the larger picture in a way that wasn't possible in the bustle of everyday life. Silencing the noise around them, they could finally hear the quiet voice they needed to listen to.

Creativity is a matter of receptiveness and recognition. This cannot happen if you're convinced the world revolves around you.

By removing the ego—even temporarily—we can access what's left standing in relief. By widening our perspective, more comes into view.

It's sad how disconnected from the past and the future most of us really are. We forget that woolly mammoths walked the earth while the pyramids were being built. We don't realize that Cleopatra lived closer to our time than she did to the construction of those famous pyramids that marked her kingdom. When British workers excavated the land in Trafalgar Square to build Nelson's Column and its famous stone lions, in the ground they found the bones of *actual* lions, who'd roamed that exact spot just a few thousand years before. Someone recently calculated that it takes but a chain of six individuals who shook hands with one another across the centuries to connect Barack Obama to George Washington. There's a video you can watch on YouTube of a man on a CBS game show, "I've Got a Secret," in 1956, in an episode that also happened to feature a famous actress named Lucille Ball. His secret? He was in Ford's Theatre when Lincoln was assassinated. England's government only recently paid off debts it incurred as far back as 1720 from events like the South Sea Bubble, the Napoleonic wars, the empire's abolition of slavery, and the Irish potato famine—meaning that in the twenty-first century there was still a direct and daily connection to the eighteenth and nineteenth centuries.

As our power or talents grow, we like to think that makes us special—that we live in blessed, unprecedented times. This is compounded by the fact that so many of the photos we see from even fifty years ago are still in black and white, and we seem to assume that the *world* was in black and white. Obviously, it wasn't—their sky was the same color as ours (in some places brighter than ours), they bled the same way we did, and their cheeks got flushed just like ours do. We are just like them, and always will be.

"It's hard to be humble when you're as great as I am," Muhammad Ali once said. Yeah, okay. That's why great people have to work even harder to fight against this headwind. It's hard to be self-absorbed and convinced of your own greatness inside the solitude and quiet of a sensory deprivation tank. It's hard to be anything *but* humble walking alone along a beach late at night with an endless black ocean crashing loudly against the ground next to you.

We have to actively seek out this cosmic sympathy. There's the famous Blake poem that opens with "To see a World in a Grain of Sand / And a Heaven in a Wild Flower / Hold Infinity in the palm of your hand / And Eternity in an hour." That's what we're after here. That's the transcendental experience that makes our petty ego impossible.

Feel unprotected against the elements or forces or surroundings. Remind yourself how pointless it is to rage and fight and try to one-up those around you. Go and put yourself in touch with the infinite, and end your conscious separation from the world. Reconcile yourself a bit better with the realities of life. Realize how much came before you, and how only wisps of it remain.

Let the feeling carry you as long as you can. Then when you start to feel better or bigger than, go and do it again.

MAINTAIN YOUR SOBRIETY

The height of cultivation runs to simplicity.

—BRUCE LEE

Angela Merkel is the antithesis of nearly every assumption we make about a head of state—especially a German one. She is plain. She is modest. She cares little for presentation or flash. She gives no fiery speeches. She has no interest in expansion or domination. Mostly, she is quiet and reserved.

Chancellor Angela Merkel is *sober*, when far too many leaders are intoxicated—with ego, with power, with position. This sobriety is precisely what has made her a wildly popular three-term leader and, paradoxically, a powerful, sweeping force for freedom and peace in modern Europe.

There is a story about Merkel as a young girl, at a swimming lesson. She walked out on the diving board and stood there, thinking about whether she should jump. Minutes ticked by. More minutes. Finally, just as the bell marking the end of the lesson began to ring, she jumped. Was she afraid or just cautious? Many years later, she would remind Europe's leaders during a major crisis that "Fear is a bad advisor." As a kid on that diving board, she wanted to use every allotted second to make the *right* decision, not driven by recklessness or fear.

In most cases, we think that people become successful through sheer energy and enthusiasm. We almost excuse ego because we think it's part and parcel of the personality required to "make it big." Maybe a bit of that overpowering-ness is what got you where you are. But let's ask: Is it really sustainable for the next several decades? Can you really out-work and outrun everyone *forever*?

The answer is no. The ego tells us we're invincible, that we have unlimited force that will never dissipate. But that can't be what greatness requires—energy without end?

Merkel is the embodiment of Aesop's fable about the tor-toise. She is slow and steady. The historic night the Berlin Wall fell, she was thirty-five. She had one beer, went to bed, and showed up early for work the next day. A few years later, she had worked to become a respected but obscure physicist. Only then did she enter politics. In her fifties, she became chancel-lor. It was a diligent, plodding path.

Yet the rest of us want to get to the top as fast as humanly possible. We have no patience for waiting. We're high on getting high up the ranks. Once we've made it, we tend to think that ego and energy is the only way to stay there. It's not.

When Russian president Vladimir Putin once attempted to intimidate Merkel by letting his large hunting dog barge into a meeting (she is reportedly not a dog lover), she didn't flinch and later joked about it. As a result, he was the one who looked foolish and insecure. During her rise and especially during her time in power, she has consistently maintained her equilibrium and clearheadedness, regardless of the immediate stressors or stimuli.

In a similar position, we might have sprung into "bold" action; we might have gotten angry or drawn a line in the sand. We have to stand up for ourselves, right? But do we? So often, this is just ego, escalating tension more than dealing with it. Merkel is firm, clear, and patient. She's willing to compromise on everything except the principle at stake—which far too many people lose sight of.

That is sobriety. That is command of oneself.

She did not become the most powerful woman in the Western world by accident. More importantly, she's maintained her perch for three terms with the same formula.

The great philosopher king Marcus Aurelius knew this very well. Called to politics almost against his will, he served the Roman people in continually higher offices from his teens until his death. There was always pressing business—appeals to hear, wars to fight, laws to pass, favors to grant. He strove to escape what he called "imperialization"—the stain of absolute power that had wrecked previous emperors. To do that, he wrote *to himself,* he must "fight to be the person philosophy tried to make you."

This is why the Zen philosopher Zuigan is supposed to have called out to himself everyday:

"MASTER—"
"YES, SIR?"

Then he would add:

"BECOME SOBER."
"YES, SIR."

He would conclude by saying:

"DO NOT BE DECEIVED BY OTHERS."
"YES SIR, YES SIR."

Today, we might add to that:

"DON'T BE DECEIVED BY RECOGNITION YOU HAVE
GOTTEN OR THE AMOUNT OF MONEY IN YOUR BANK
ACCOUNT."

We have to fight to stay sober, despite the many different forces swirling around our ego.

The historian Shelby Foote observed that "power doesn't so much corrupt; that's too simple. It fragments, closes options, mesmerizes." That's what ego does. It clouds the mind precisely when it needs to be clear. Sobriety is a counterbalance, a hangover cure—or better, a prevention method.

Other politicians are bold and charismatic. But as Merkel supposedly said, "You can't solve . . . tasks with charisma." She is rational. She analyzes. She makes it about the situation, not about herself, as people in power often do. Her background in science is helpful here, surely. Politicians are often vain, obsessing about their image. Merkel is too objective for that. She cares about results and little else. A German writer observed in a tribute on her fiftieth birthday that *unpretentiousness* is Merkel's main weapon.

David Halberstam, writing about the Patriots' coach Bill

Belichick, observed that the man was "not only in the steak business, he had contempt for sizzle." You could say the same about Merkel. Leaders like Belichick and Merkel know that steak is what wins games and moves nations forward. Sizzle, on the other hand, makes it harder to make the *right* decisions—how to interact with others, who to promote, which plays to run, what feedback to listen to, where to come down on an issue.

Churchill's Europe required one type of leader. Today's interconnected world requires its own. Because there is so much information to be sorted through, so much competition, so much change, without a clear head . . . all is lost.

We're not talking about abstinence from drugs or alcohol obviously, but there certainly is an element of restraint to egoless sobriety—an elimination of the unnecessary and the destructive. No more obsessing about your image; treating people beneath you or above you with contempt; needing first-class trappings and the star treatment; raging, fighting, preening, performing, lording over, condescending, and marveling at your own awesomeness or self-anointed importance.

Sobriety is the counterweight that must balance out success. Especially if things keep getting better and better.

As James Basford remarked, "It requires a strong constitution to withstand repeated attacks of prosperity." Well, that's where we are now.

There's an old line about how if you want to live happy, live hidden. It's true. The problem is, that means the rest of us are deprived of really good examples. We're lucky to see someone like Merkel in the public eye, because she is the representative of a very large, silent majority.

As hard as it might be to believe from what we see in the

media, there actually are some successful people with modest apartments. Like Merkel, they have normal private lives with their spouses (her husband skipped her first inauguration). They lack artifice, they wear normal clothes. Most successful people are people you've never heard of. They want it that way.

It keeps them sober. It helps them do their jobs.

FOR WHAT OFTEN COMES NEXT, EGO IS THE ENEMY . . .

The evidence is in, and you are the verdict.

—ANNE LAMOTT

Here you are at the pinnacle. What have you found? Just how tough and tricky it is to manage. You thought it would get easier when you arrived; instead, it's even harder—a different animal entirely. What you found is that you must manage yourself in order to maintain your success.

The philosopher Aristotle was not unfamiliar with the worlds of ego and power and empire. His most famous pupil was Alexander the Great, and partially through Aristotle's teachings, the young man conquered the entire known world. Alexander was brave and brilliant and often generous and wise. Still, it's clear that he ignored Aristotle's most important lesson—and that's partially why he died at age thirty-two, far from home, likely killed by his own men, who had finally said, "Enough."

It's not that he was wrong to have great ambitions. Alexander just never grasped Aristotle's "golden mean"—that is, the middle ground. Repeatedly, Aristotle speaks of virtue and excellence as points along a spectrum. Courage, for instance, lies between cowardice on one end and reckless-ness on the other. Generosity, which we all admire, must stop short of either profligacy and parsimony in order to be of any use. Where the line—this golden mean—is can be dif-ficult to tell, but without finding it, we risk dangerous extremes. This is why it is so hard to be excellent, Aristotle wrote. "In each case, it is hard work to find the intermediate; for instance, not everyone, but only one who knows, finds the midpoint in a circle."

We can use the golden mean to navigate our ego and our desire to achieve.

Endless ambition is easy; anyone can put their foot down hard on the gas. Complacency is easy too; it's just a matter of taking that foot *off* the gas. We must avoid what the busi-ness strategist Jim Collins terms the "undisciplined pursuit of more," as well as the complacency that comes with plau-dits. To borrow from Aristotle again, what's difficult is to apply the right amount of pressure, at the right time, in the right way, for the right period of time, in the right car, going in the right direction.

If we don't do this, the consequences can be dire.

There is a line from Napoleon, who, like Alexander, died miserably. He said, "Men of great ambition have sought hap-piness . . . and have found fame." What he means is that behind every goal is the drive to be happy and fulfilled—but when egotism takes hold, we lose track of our goal and end up somewhere we never intended. Emerson, in his famous essay on Napoleon, takes pains to point out that just a few years after his death, Europe was essentially exactly as it was before Napoleon began his precipitous rise. All that death, that effort, that greed, and those honors—for what? For basically nothing. Napoleon, he wrote, quickly faded away, just like the smoke from his artillery.

Howard Hughes—despite his current reputation as some kind of bold maverick—was not a happy man, no matter how awesome his life may seem from history or movies. When he was near death, one of his aides sought to reassure a suffering Hughes. "What an incredible life you have led," the aide said. Hughes shook his head and replied with the sad, emphatic honesty of someone whose time has clearly come, "If you had ever swapped places in life with me, I would be willing to bet that you would have demanded to swap back before the passage of the first week."

We do not have to follow in those footsteps. We know what decisions we must make to avoid that ignominious, even pathetic end: protecting our sobriety, eschewing greed and paranoia, staying humble, retaining our sense of purpose, connecting to the larger world around us.

Because even if we manage ourselves well, prosperity holds no guarantees. The world conspires against us in many ways, and the laws of nature say that everything regresses toward the mean. In sports, the schedule gets harder after a winning season, the bad teams get better draft picks, and the salary cap makes it tough to keep a team together. In life, taxes go up the more you make, and the more obligations society foists on you. The media is harder on those it has covered before. Rumors and gossip are the cost of renown: He's a drunk. She's gay. He's a hypocrite. She's a bitch. The crowd roots for the underdog, and roots *against* the winners.

These are just facts of life. Who can afford to add denial to all that?

Instead of letting power make us delusional and instead of taking what we have for granted, we'd be better to spend our time preparing for the shifts of fate that inevitably occur in life. That is, adversity, difficulty, failure.

Who knows—maybe a downturn is exactly what's coming next. Worse, maybe you caused it. Just because you did something once, doesn't mean you'll be able to do it successfully forever.

Reversals and regressions are as much a part of the cycle of life as anything else.

But we can manage that too.

PART III

FAILURE

Here we are experiencing the trials endemic to any journey. Perhaps we've failed, perhaps our goal turned out to be harder to achieve than anticipated. No one is permanently successful, and not everyone finds success on the first attempt. We all deal with setbacks along the way. Ego not only leaves us unprepared for these circumstances, it often contributed to their occurrence in the first place. The way through, the way to rise again, requires a reorientation and increased self-awareness. We don't need pity—our own or anyone else's—we need purpose, poise, and patience.

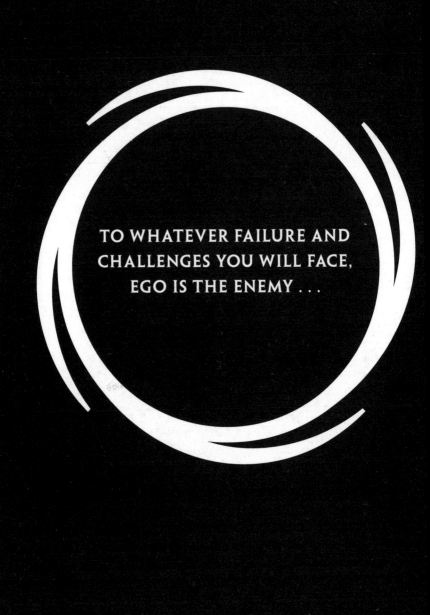

TO WHATEVER FAILURE AND
CHALLENGES YOU WILL FACE,
EGO IS THE ENEMY . . .

⸺⸺⸺⸺⸺⸺⸺⸺ ❧ ⸺⸺⸺⸺⸺⸺⸺⸺

It is because mankind are disposed to sympathize more entirely with our joy than with our sorrow, that we make parade of our riches, and conceal our poverty. Nothing is so mortifying as to be obliged to expose our distress to the view of the public, and to feel, that though our situation is open to the eyes of all mankind, no mortal conceives for us the half of what we suffer.

—ADAM SMITH

For the first half of her life, Katharine Graham saw pretty much everything go right.

Her father, Eugene Meyer, was a financial genius who made a fortune in the stock market. Her mother was a beautiful as well as brilliant socialite. As a child, Katharine had the best of everything: the best schools, the best teachers, big houses, and servants to wait on her.

In 1933, her father bought the *Washington Post*, then a struggling but important newspaper, which he began to turn around. The only child to express any serious interest in it, Katharine inherited the paper when she was older and handed over the management to her equally impressive husband, Philip Graham.

She was not another Howard Hughes, who squandered

her family's fortune. She was not another rich kid who took the easy road in life because she could. But it was a cushy life, no question about it. She had been, in her words, content to be the tail to her husband's (and parent's) kite.

Then life took a turn. Phil Graham's behavior became increasingly erratic. He drank heavily. He made reckless business decisions and bought things they couldn't afford. He began having affairs. He publicly humiliated his wife in front of nearly everyone they knew. Rich people problems, right? It turns out that he had suffered a severe mental breakdown, and as Katharine attempted to nurse him back to health, he killed himself with a hunting rifle while she napped in the next room.

In 1963, at forty-six years old, Katharine Graham, a mother of three with no work experience, found herself in charge of the Washington Post Company, a vast corporation with thousands of employees. She was unprepared, timid, and naive.

Though tragic, these events were not exactly a cataclysmic failure. Graham was still rich, still white, still privileged. Still, it was not what she thought life had planned for her. That's the point. Failure and adversity are relative and unique to each of us. Almost without exception, this is what life does: it takes our plans and dashes them to pieces. Sometimes once, sometimes lots of times.

As the financial philosopher and economist George Goodman once observed, it is as if "we are at a wonderful ball where the champagne sparkles in every glass and soft laughter falls upon the summer air. We know at some moment the black horsemen will come shattering through the terrace doors wreaking vengeance and scattering the

FAILURE

survivors. Those who leave early are saved, but the ball is so splendid no one wants to leave while there is still time. So everybody keeps asking—what time is it? But none of the clocks have hands."

He was speaking of economic crises, although he may as well have been talking about where all of us find ourselves, not just once in our lifetimes, but often. Things are going well. Perhaps we're aspiring to some big goal. Perhaps we're finally enjoying the fruits of our labors. At any point, fate can intervene.

If success is ego intoxication, then failure can be a devastating ego blow—turning slips into falls and little troubles into great unravelings. If ego is often just a nasty side effect of great success, it can be fatal during failure.

We have many names for these problems: Sabotage. Unfairness. Adversity. Trials. Tragedy. No matter the label, it's a trial. We don't like it, and some of us are sunk by it. Others seem to be built to make it through. In either case, it's a trial each person must endure.

This fate is as much written for us as it was written five thousand years ago for the young king in *Gilgamesh*:

He will face a battle he knows not,
he will ride a road he knows not.

That's what came to Katharine Graham. It turned out that taking over the paper was the first in a series of trying and wrenching events that lasted for nearly two decades.

Thomas Paine, remarking about George Washington, once wrote that there is a "natural firmness in some minds which cannot be unlocked by trifles, but which, when unlocked, discovers a cabinet of fortitude." Graham seems to have possessed a similar cabinet.

As she settled into her leadership position, Graham found that the paper's conservative board was a constant obstacle. They were patronizing and risk averse and had held the company back. To succeed, she would have to develop her own compass and not defer to others the way she always had. It eventually became clear that she needed a new executive editor. Against the board's advice, she replaced the well-liked good old boy with an unknown young upstart. Simple enough.

The next turn of the screw wasn't. Just as the company was filing to go public, the *Post* received a collection of stolen government documents that editors asked Graham if they could run, despite a court order preventing their publication. She consulted the company's lawyers. She consulted the board. All advised against it—fearing it could sink the IPO or tie the company up in lawsuits for years. Torn, she decided to proceed and publish them—a decision with essentially no precedent. Shortly thereafter, the paper's investigation of a burglary at the Democratic National Committee's headquarters—relying on an anonymous source—threatened to put the company permanently at odds with the White House and Washington's powerful elite (as well as jeopardizing the government licenses they needed for the TV stations the *Post* owned). At one point, Nixon loyalist and the *attorney general of the United States* John Mitchell threatened that Graham had so overreached that her "tit" was going to be "caught in a big fat wringer." Another aide bragged that the White House was now thinking about how to screw the paper over. Put yourself in her shoes: the most powerful office in the world explicitly strategizing, "How can we hurt the *Post* the most?"

On top of that, the *Post*'s stock price was less than stellar. The market was poor. In 1974, an investor began aggressively buying up shares in the company. The board was terrified. It could mean a hostile takeover. Graham was dispatched to deal with him. The following year, the paper's printers' union began a vicious, protracted strike. At one point, union members wore shirts that said, "Phil Shot the Wrong Graham." Despite—or perhaps because of—these tactics, she decided to fight the strike. They fought back. At four o'clock one morning came a frantic call: the union had sabotaged company machinery, beaten up an innocent staffer, and then set one of the printing presses on fire. Typically, during printing strikes competitors will help fellow papers out with their printing but Graham's competitors refused, costing the *Post* $300,000 a day in advertising revenue.

Then, a suite of major investors began to sell their stock positions in the Washington Post Company, ostensibly having lost their faith in its prospects. Graham, pushed by the activist investor she'd met with earlier, decided her best option was to spend an enormous amount of the company's money to buy back its own shares on the public markets—a dangerous move that almost no one was doing at the time.

That's a list of problems exhausting to read about let alone live through. Yet because of Graham's perseverance, it shook out better than anyone could have possibly predicted.

The leaked documents Katharine Graham published

became known as the Pentagon Papers and were one of the most important stories in the history of journalism. The paper's Watergate reporting, which so incensed the Nixon White House, changed American history and took down an entire administration. It also won the paper a Pulitzer Prize. The investor others had feared turned out to be a young Warren Buffett, who became her business mentor and an enormous advocate and steward of the company. (His small investments in her family's company would one day be worth hundreds of millions.) She prevailed in negotiations with the union and the strike eventually ended. Her main competitor in Washington, the one that had refused to come to her aid, the *Star,* suddenly folded and was acquired by the *Post.* Her stock buybacks—made contrary not only to business wisdom, but the judgment of the market—made the company *billions* of dollars.

It turns out that the long hard slog she endured, the mistakes she made, the repeated failures, crises, and attacks were all leading somewhere. If you'd invested $1 in the *Post*'s IPO in 1971, it would be worth $89 by the time Graham stepped down in 1993—compared to $14 for her industry and $5 for the S&P 500. It makes her not just one of the most successful female CEOs of her generation and the first to run a Fortune 500 company, but one of the best CEOs ever, period.

For someone born with a silver spoon in her mouth, the first decade and a half was what you'd call a baptism of fire. Graham faced difficulty after difficulty, difficulties that she wasn't really equipped to handle, or so it seemed. There were times when it probably felt like she should have just sold the damn thing and enjoyed her massive wealth.

Graham didn't cause her husband's suicide, but it was left to her to carry on without him. She didn't ask for Watergate and the Pentagon Papers, but it fell on her to navigate their incendiary nature. While others went on buying and merger sprees in the eighties, she didn't. She doubled down on herself and her own company, despite the fact that it was treated as a weakling by Wall Street. She could have taken the easy way a hundred times, but did not.

At any given moment, there is the chance of failure or setbacks. Bill Walsh says, "Almost always, your road to victory goes through a place called 'failure.'" In order to taste success again, we've got to understand what led to this moment (or these years) of difficulty, what went wrong and why. We must deal with the situation in order to move past it. We'll need to accept it *and* to push through it.

Graham was alone in most of this. She was blindly feeling her way through the dark, trying to figure out a tough situation she never expected to be in. She's an example of how you can do most everything right and still find yourself in deep shit.

We think that failure only comes to egomaniacs who were begging for it. Nixon deserved to fail; did Graham? The reality is that while yes, often people set themselves up to crash, good people fail (or other people fail them) all the time too. People who have already been through a lot find themselves stuck with more. Life isn't fair.

Ego loves this notion, the idea that something is "fair" or not. Psychologists call it narcissistic injury when we take personally totally indifferent and objective events. We do that when our sense of self is fragile and dependent on life going our way all the time. Whether what you're going through is your fault or your problem doesn't matter, because it's yours to deal with right now. Graham's ego didn't cause her to fail, but if she'd had one, it certainly would have prevented her from succeeding ever again. You could say that failure always arrives uninvited, but through our ego, far too many of us allow it to stick around.

What did Graham need through all this? Not swagger. Not bluster. She needed to be strong. She needed confidence and a willingness to endure. A sense of right and wrong. *Purpose.* It wasn't about *her.* It was about preserving her family's legacy. Protecting the paper. Doing her job.

What about you? Will your ego betray you when things get difficult? Or can you proceed without it?

When we face difficulty, particularly public difficulty (doubters, scandals, losses), our friend the ego will show its true colors.

Absorbing the negative feedback, ego says: I knew you couldn't do it. *Why did you ever try?* It claims: This isn't worth it. This isn't fair. This is somebody else's problem. *Why don't you come up with a good excuse and wash your hands of this?* It tells us we shouldn't have to put up with this. It tells us that we're not the problem.

That is, it adds self-injury to every injury you experience.

To paraphrase Epicurus, the narcissistically inclined live in an "unwalled city." A fragile sense of self is constantly under threat. Illusions and accomplishments are not defenses, not when you've got the special sensitive antennae trained to receive (and create) the signals that challenge your precarious balancing act.

It is a miserable way to live.

The year before Walsh took over the 49ers, they went 2 and 14. His first year as head coach and general manager, they went . . . 2 and 14. Can you imagine the disappointment? All the changes, all the work that went into that first year, and to end up in the exact same spot as the incompetent coach who preceded you? That's how most of us would think. And then we'd probably start blaming other people.

Walsh realized he "had to look for evidence elsewhere" that it was turning around. For him, it was in how the games were being played, the good decisions and the changes that were being made inside the organization. Two seasons later, they won the Super Bowl and then several more after that. At rock bottom those victories must have felt like a long way off, which is why you have to be able to see past and through.

As Goethe once observed, the great failing is "to see yourself as more than you are and to value yourself at less than your true worth." A good metaphor might be the kind of stock buybacks that Katharine Graham made in the late seventies and eighties. Stock buybacks are controversial—they usually come from a company that is stalled or whose growth is decelerating. With buybacks, a CEO is making a rather incredible statement. She's saying: The market is wrong. It's valuing our company so incorrectly, and clearly has so little idea where we are heading, that we're going to spend the company's precious cash on a bet that they're wrong.

Too often, dishonest or egotistical CEOs buy back company stock because they're delusional. Or because they want to artificially inflate the stock price. Conversely, timid or weak CEOs wouldn't even consider betting on themselves. In

Graham's case, she made a value judgment; with Buffett's help she could see objectively that the market didn't appreciate the true worth of the company's assets. She knew that the reputational hits, the learning curve, had all contributed to a suppressed stock price, which aside from reducing her personal wealth, created a massive opportunity for the company. Over a short period, she would buy nearly 40 percent of the company's shares at a fraction of what they'd later be worth. The stock that Katharine Graham bought for approximately $20 a share would less than a decade later be worth more than $300.

What both Graham and Walsh were doing was adhering to a set of internal metrics that allowed them to evaluate and gauge their progress while everyone on the outside was too distracted by supposed signs of failure or weakness.

This is what guides us through difficulty.

You might not get into your first choice college. You might not get picked for the project or you might get passed over for the promotion. Someone might outbid you for the job, for your dream house, for the opportunity you feel everything depends on. This might happen tomorrow, it might happen twenty-five years from now. It could last for two minutes or ten years. We know that everyone experiences failure and adversity, that we're all subject to the rules of gravity and averages. What does that mean? It means we'll face them too.

As Plutarch finely expressed, "The future bears down upon each one of us with all the hazards of the unknown." The only way out is through.

Humble and strong people don't have the same trouble with these troubles that egotists do. There are fewer complaints and far less self-immolation. Instead, there's stoic—even cheerful—resilience. Pity isn't necessary. Their identity isn't threatened. They can get by without constant validation.

This is what we're aspiring to—much more than mere success. What matters is that we can respond to what life throws at us.

And how we make it through.

ALIVE TIME OR DEAD TIME?

Vivre sans temps mort. (Live without wasted time.)
—PARISIAN POLITICAL SLOGAN

Malcolm X was a criminal. He wasn't Malcolm X at the time—they called him Detroit Red and he was a criminal opportunist who did a little bit of everything. He ran numbers. He sold drugs. He worked as a pimp. Then he moved up to armed robbery. He had his own burglary gang, which he ruled over with a combination of intimidation and boldness—exploiting the fact that he did not seem afraid to kill or die.

Then, finally, he was arrested trying to fence an expensive watch he'd stolen. He was carrying a gun at the time, though to his credit he made no move to fight the officers who had trapped him. In his apartment, they found jewelry, furs, an arsenal of guns, and all his burglary tools.

He got ten years. It was February 1946. He was barely twenty-one years old.

Even accounting for the shameful American racism and whatever systematic legal injustices existed at the time, Malcolm X was guilty. He deserved to go to jail. Who knows who

ALIVE TIME OR DEAD TIME?

else he would have hurt or killed had he continued his escalating life of crime?

When your actions land you a lengthy prison sentence—
rightly tried and convicted—something has gone wrong.
You've failed not only yourself, but the basic standards of
society and morality. That was the case with Malcolm.

So there he was in prison. A number. A body with roughly
a decade to sit in a cage.

He faced what Robert Greene—a man who sixty years later
would find his wildly popular books banned in many federal
prisons—calls an "Alive Time or Dead Time" scenario. How
would the seven years ultimately play out? What would Malcolm do with this time?

According to Greene, there are two types of time in our
lives: dead time, when people are passive and waiting, and
alive time, when people are learning and acting and utiliz-
ing every second. Every moment of failure, every moment
or situation that we did not deliberately choose or control,
presents this choice: Alive time. Dead time.

Which will it be?

Malcolm chose *alive time*. He began to learn. He explored
religion. He taught himself to be a reader by checking out
a pencil and the dictionary from the prison library and not
only consumed it from start to finish, but *copied it down long-
hand* from cover to cover. All these words he'd never known
existed before were transferred to his brain.

As he said later, "From then until I left that prison, in
every free moment I had, if I was not reading in the library,
I was reading in my bunk." He read history, he read sociol-
ogy, he read about religion, he read the classics, he read
philosophers like Kant and Spinoza. Later, a reporter asked

Malcolm, "What's your alma mater?" His one word answer: "Books." Prison was his college. He transcended confinement through the pages he absorbed. He reflected that months passed without his even thinking about being detained against his will. He had "never been so truly free in his life."

Most people know what Malcolm X did after he got out of prison, but they don't realize or understand how prison made that possible. How a mix of acceptance, humility, and strength powered the transformation. They also aren't aware of how common this is in history, how many figures took seemingly terrible situations—a prison sentence, an exile, a bear market or depression, military conscription, even being sent to a concentration camp—and through their attitude and approach, turned those circumstances into fuel for their unique greatness.

Francis Scott Key wrote the poem that became the national anthem of the United States while trapped on a ship during a prisoner exchange in the War of 1812. Viktor Frankl refined his psychologies of meaning and suffering during his ordeal in *three* Nazi concentration camps.

Not that these opportunities always come in such serious situations. The author Ian Fleming was on bed rest and, per doctors' orders, forbidden from using a typewriter. They were worried he'd exert himself by writing another Bond novel. So he created Chitty Chitty Bang Bang by hand instead. Walt Disney made his decision to become a cartoonist while laid up after stepping on a rusty nail.

Yes, it would feel much better in the moment to be angry, to be aggrieved, to be depressed or heartbroken. When injustice or the capriciousness of fate are inflicted on someone, the normal reaction is to yell, to fight back, to resist. You know the feeling: *I don't want this. I want _____. I want it my way.* This is shortsighted.

Think of what you have been putting off. Issues you declined to deal with. Systemic problems that felt too overwhelming to address. Dead time is revived when we use it as an opportunity to do what we've long needed to do.

As they say, this moment is not your life. But it is a moment *in* your life. How will you use it?

Malcolm could have doubled down on the life that brought him to prison. Dead time isn't only dead because of sloth or complacency. He could have spent those years becoming a better criminal, strengthening his contacts, or planning his next score, but it still would have been dead time. He might have *felt* alive doing it, even as he was slowly killing himself.

"Many a serious thinker has been produced in prisons," as Robert Greene put it, "where we have nothing to do but think." Yet sadly, prisons—in their literal and figurative forms—have produced far more degenerates, losers, and ne'er-do-wells. Inmates might have had nothing to do but think; it's just that what they chose to think about made them worse and not better.

That's what so many of us do when we fail or get ourselves into trouble. Lacking the ability to examine ourselves, we reinvest our energy into exactly the patterns of behavior that caused our problems to begin with.

It comes in many forms. Idly dreaming about the future. Plotting our revenge. Finding refuge in distraction. Refusing to consider that our choices are a reflection of our character. We'd rather do basically anything else.

But what if we said: This is an opportunity for me. I am using it for my purposes. I will not let this be dead time for me.

The dead time was when we were controlled by ego. Now—now we can live.

Who knows what you're currently doing. Hopefully it's not a prison term, even if it might feel like it. Maybe you're sitting in a remedial high school class, maybe you're on hold, maybe it's a trial separation, maybe you're making smoothies while you save up money, maybe you're stuck waiting out a contract or a tour of duty. Maybe this situation is one totally of your own making, or perhaps it's just bad luck.

In life, we all get stuck with dead time. Its occurrence isn't in our control. Its use, on the other hand, is.

As Booker T. Washington most famously put it, "Cast down your bucket where you are." Make use of what's around you. Don't let stubbornness make a bad situation worse.

THE EFFORT IS ENOUGH

> What matters to an active man is to do the right thing;
> whether the right thing comes to pass should not
> bother him.
>
> —GOETHE

Belisarius is one of the greatest yet unknown military generals in all of history. His name has been so obscured and forgotten by history that he makes the underappreciated General Marshall seem positively famous. At least they named the Marshall Plan after George.

As Rome's highest-ranking commander under the Byzantine emperor Justinian, Belisarius saved Western civilization on at least three occasions. As Rome collapsed and the seat of the empire moved to Constantinople, Belisarius was the only bright light in a dark time for Christianity.

He won brilliant victories at Dara, Carthage, Naples, Sicily, and Constantinople. With just a handful of bodyguards against a crowd of tens of thousands, Belisarius saved the throne when an uprising had grown so riotous that the emperor made plans to abdicate. He reclaimed far-flung territories that had been lost for years despite being undermanned and deprived of resources. He recaptured and defended Rome for the first time since the barbarians had sacked and taken it. All of this before he was forty.

His thanks? He was not given public triumphs. Instead, he was repeatedly placed under suspicion by the paranoid emperor he served, Justinian. His victories and sacrifices were undone with foolish treaties and bad faith. His personal historian, Procopius, was corrupted by Justinian to tarnish the man's image and legacy. Later, he was relieved of command. His only remaining title was the deliberately humiliating "Commander of the Royal Stable." Oh, and at the end of his illustrious career, Belisarius was stripped of his wealth, and according to the legend, *blinded*, and forced to beg in the streets to survive.

Historians, scholars, and artists have lamented and argued about this treatment for centuries. Like all fair-minded people, they're outraged at the stupidity, the ungratefulness, and injustice that this great and unusual man was subjected to.

The one person we don't hear complaining about any of this? Not at the time, not at the end of his life, not even in private letters: Belisarius himself.

Ironically, he probably could have taken the throne on numerous occasions, though it appears he was never even tempted. While the Emperor Justinian fell prey to all the vices of absolute power—control, paranoia, selfishness, greed—we see hardly a trace of them in Belisarius.

In his eyes, he was just doing his job—one he believed was his sacred duty. He knew that he did it well. He knew he had done what was right. That was enough.

In life, there will be times when we do everything right,

perhaps even perfectly. Yet the results will somehow be negative: failure, disrespect, jealousy, or even a resounding yawn from the world.

Depending on what motivates us, this response can be crushing. If ego holds sway, we'll accept nothing less than full appreciation.

A dangerous attitude because when someone works on a project—whether it's a book or a business or otherwise—at a certain point, that thing leaves their hands and enters the realm of the world. It is judged, received, and acted on *by other people*. It stops being something he controls and it depends on them.

Belisarius could win his battles. He could lead his men. He could determine his personal ethics. He could not control whether his work was appreciated or whether it aroused suspicion. He had no ability to control whether a powerful dictator would treat him well.

This reality rings essentially true for everyone in every kind of life. What was so special about Belisarius was that he accepted the bargain. Doing the right thing was enough. Serving his country, his God, and doing his duty faithfully was all that mattered. Any adversity could be endured and any rewards were considered extra.

Which is good, because not only was he often not rewarded for the good he did, he was *punished* for it. That seems galling at first. Indignation is the reaction we'd have if it happened to us or someone we know. What was his alternative? Should he have done the wrong thing instead?

We are all faced with this same challenge in the pursuit of our own goals: Will we work hard for something that can be taken away from us? Will we invest time and energy even if an outcome is not guaranteed? With the right motives we're willing to proceed. With ego, we're not.

We have only minimal control over the rewards for our work and effort—other people's validation, recognition, rewards. So what are we going to do? Not be kind, not work hard, not produce, because there is a chance it wouldn't be reciprocated? C'mon.

Think of all the activists who will find that they can only advance their cause so far. The leaders who are assassinated before their work is done. The inventors whose ideas languish "ahead of their time." According to society's main metrics, these people were not rewarded for their work. *Should they have not done it?*

Yet in ego, every one of us has considered doing precisely that.

If that is your attitude, how do you intend to endure tough times? What if you're ahead of the times? What if the market favors some bogus trend? What if your boss or your clients don't understand?

It's far better when doing good work is sufficient. In other words, the less attached we are to *outcomes* the better. When fulfilling our *own* standards is what fills us with pride and self-respect. When the effort—not the results, good or bad—is enough.

With ego, this is not nearly sufficient. No, we need to be recognized. We need to be compensated. Especially problematic is the fact that, often, we get that. We are praised, we are paid, and we start to assume that the two things always go together. The "expectation hangover" inevitably ensues.

There was an unusual encounter between Alexander the Great and the famous Cynic philosopher Diogenes. Allegedly, Alexander approached Diogenes, who was lying down, enjoying the summer air, and stood over him and asked what he, the most powerful man in the world, might be able to do for this notoriously poor man. Diogenes could have asked for anything. What he requested was epic: "Stop blocking my sun." Even two thousand years later we can feel exactly where in the solar plexus that must have hit Alexander, a man who always wanted to prove how important he was. As the author Robert Louis Stevenson later observed about this meeting, "It is a sore thing to have labored along and scaled arduous hilltops, and when all is done, find humanity indifferent to your achievement."

Well, get ready for it. It will happen. Maybe your parents will never be impressed. Maybe your girlfriend won't care. Maybe the investor won't see the numbers. Maybe the audience won't clap. But we have to be able to push through. We can't let *that* be what motivates us.

Belisarius had one last run. He was found innocent of the charges and his honors were restored—just in time to save the empire as a white-haired old man.

Except no, life is not a fairy tale. He was again wrongly suspected of plotting against the emperor. In the famous Longfellow poem about our poor general, at the end of his life he is impoverished and disabled. Yet he concludes with great strength:

This, too, can bear;—I still
Am Belisarius!

You will be unappreciated. You will be sabotaged. You will experience surprising failures. Your expectations will not be met. You will lose. You will fail.

How do you carry on then? How do you take pride in yourself and your work? John Wooden's advice to his players says it: Change the definition of success. "Success is peace of mind, which is a direct result of self-satisfaction in knowing you made the *effort* to do your best to become the best that you are capable of becoming." "Ambition," Marcus Aurelius reminded himself, "means tying your well-being to what other people say or do . . . Sanity means tying it to your own actions."

Do your work. Do it well. Then "let go and let God." That's all there needs to be.

Recognition and rewards—those are just extra. Rejection, that's on them, not on us.

John Kennedy Toole's great book *A Confederacy of Dunces* was universally turned down by publishers, news that so broke his heart that he later committed suicide in his car on an empty road in Biloxi, Mississippi. After his death, his mother discovered the book, advocated on its behalf until it was published, and it eventually won the Pulitzer Prize.

Think about that for a second. What changed between those submissions? Nothing. The book was the same. It was equally great when Toole had it in manuscript form and had fought with editors about it as it was when the book was published, sold copies, and won awards. If only he could have realized this, it would have saved him so much heartbreak. He couldn't, but from his painful example we can at least see how arbitrary many of the breaks in life are.

This is why we can't let externals determine whether something was worth it or not. It's on us.

The world is, after all, indifferent to what we humans "want." If we persist in wanting, in *needing,* we are simply setting ourselves up for resentment or worse.

Doing the work is enough.

FIGHT CLUB MOMENTS

If you shut up truth and bury it under the ground, it will but grow, and gather to itself such explosive power that the day it bursts through it will blow up everything in its way.

—EMILE ZOLA

There is hardly the space to list all the successful people who have hit rock bottom.

The notion everyone experiences jarring, perspective-altering moments is almost a cliché. That doesn't mean it isn't true.

J. K. Rowling finds herself seven years after college with a failed marriage, no job, single parent, kids she can barely feed, and approaching homelessness. A teenage Charlie Parker thinks he is tearing it up on stage, right in the pocket with the rest of the crew, until Jo Jones throws a cymbal at him and chases him away in humiliation. A young Lyndon Johnson is beaten to a pulp by a Hill Country farm boy over a girl, finally shattering his picture of himself as "cock of the walk."

There are many ways to hit bottom. Almost everyone does in their own way, at some point.

In the novel *Fight Club*, the character Jack's apartment is blown up. All of his possessions—"every stick of furniture," which he pathetically loved—were lost. Later it turns out that Jack blew it up himself. He had multiple personalities, and "Tyler Durden" orchestrated the explosion to shock Jack from the sad stupor he was afraid to do anything about. The result was a journey into an entirely different and rather dark part of his life.

In Greek mythology, characters often experience *katabasis*—or "a going down." They're forced to retreat, they experience a depression, or in some cases literally descend into the underworld. When they emerge, it's with heightened knowledge and understanding.

Today, we'd call that hell—and on occasion we all spend some time there.

We surround ourselves with bullshit. With distractions. With lies about what makes us happy and what's important. We become people we shouldn't become and engage in destructive, awful behaviors. This unhealthy and ego-derived state hardens and becomes almost permanent. Until *katabasis* forces us to face it.

Duris dura franguntur. Hard things are broken by hard things.

The bigger the ego the harder the fall.

It would be nice if it didn't have to be that way. If we could nicely be nudged to correct our ways, if a quiet admonishment was what it took to shoo away illusions, if we could manage to circumvent ego on our own. But it is just not so. The Reverend William A. Sutton observed some 120 years ago that "we cannot be humble except by enduring humiliations." How much better it would be to spare ourselves these experiences, but sometimes it's the only way the blind can be made to see.

In fact, many significant life changes come from moments in which we are thoroughly demolished, in which everything we thought we knew about the world is rendered false. We might call these "Fight Club moments." Sometimes they are self-inflicted, sometimes inflicted on us, but whatever the cause they can be catalysts for changes we were petrified to make.

Pick a time in your life (or perhaps it's a moment you're experiencing now). A boss's eviscerating critique of you in front of the entire staff. That sit-down with the person you loved. The Google Alert that delivered the article you'd hoped would never be written. The call from the creditor. The news that threw you back in your chair, speechless and dumbfounded.

It was in those moments—when the break exposes something unseen before—that you were forced to make eye contact with a thing called Truth. No longer could you hide or pretend.

Such a moment raises many questions: *How do I make sense of this? How do I move onward and upward? Is this the bottom, or is there more to come? Someone told me my problems, so how do I fix them? How did I let this happen? How can it never happen again?*

A look at history finds that these events seem to be defined by three traits:

1. They almost always came at the hands of some outside force or person.

2. They often involved things we already knew about ourselves, but were too scared to admit.
3. From the ruin came the opportunity for great progress and improvement.

Does everyone take advantage of that opportunity? Of course not. Ego often causes the crash and then blocks us from improving.

Was the 2008 financial crisis not a moment in which everything was laid bare for many people? The lack of accountability, the overleveraged lifestyles, the greed, the dishonesty, the trends that could not possibly continue. For some, this was a wake-up call. Others, just a few years later, are back exactly where they were. For them, it will be worse next time.

Hemingway had his own rock-bottom realizations as a young man. The understanding he took from them is expressed timelessly in his book *A Farewell to Arms*. He wrote, "The world breaks every one and afterward many are strong at the broken places. But those that will not break it kills."

The world can show you the truth, but no one can force you to accept it.

In 12-step groups, almost all the steps are about suppressing the ego and clearing out the entitlements and baggage and wreckage that has been accumulated—so that you might see what's left when all of that is stripped away and the real you is left.

It's always so tempting to turn to that old friend denial (which is your ego refusing to believe that what you don't like could be true).

Psychologists often say that threatened egotism is one of the most dangerous forces on earth. The gang member whose "honor" is impugned. The narcissist who is rejected. The bully who is made to feel shame. The impostor who is exposed. The plagiarist or the embellisher whose story stops adding up.

These are not people you want to be near when they are cornered. Nor is it a corner you would want to back yourself into. That's where you get: *How can these people talk to me this way? Who do they think they are? I'll make them all pay.*

Sometimes because we can't face what's been said or what's been done, we do the unthinkable in response to the unbearable: we escalate. This is ego in its purest and most toxic form.

Look at Lance Armstrong. He cheated, but so did a lot of people. It was when this cheating was made public and he was forced to see—if only for a second—that *he was a cheater* that things got really bad. He insisted on denying it despite all the evidence. He insisted on ruining other people's lives. We're so afraid to lose our own esteem or, God forbid, the esteem of others, that we contemplate doing terrible things.

"Everyone who does wicked things hates the light and does not come to the light, lest his works should be exposed," reads John 3:20. Big and small, this is what we do. Getting hit with that spotlight doesn't feel good—whether we're talking the exposure of ordinary self-deception or true evil—but turning away only delays the reckoning. For how long, no one can say.

Face the symptoms. Cure the disease. Ego makes it so

hard—it's easier to delay, to double down, to deliberately avoid seeing the changes we need to make in our lives.

But change begins by hearing the criticism and the words of the people around you. Even if those words are mean spirited, angry, or hurtful. It means weighing them, discarding the ones that don't matter, and reflecting on the ones that do.

In *Fight Club*, the character has to firebomb his own apartment to finally break through. Our expectations and exaggerations and lack of restraint made such moments inevitable, ensuring that it would be painful. Now it's here, what will you make of it? You can change, or you can deny.

Vince Lombardi said this once: "A team, like men, must be brought to its knees before it can rise again." So yes, hitting bottom is as brutal as it sounds.

But the feeling after—it is one of the most powerful perspectives in the world. President Obama described it as he neared the end of his tumultuous, trying terms. "I've been in the barrel tumbling down Niagara Falls and I emerged, and I lived, and that's such a liberating feeling."

If we could help it, it would be better if we never suffered illusions at all. It'd be better if we never had to kneel or go over the edge. That's what we've spent so much time talking about so far in this book. If that fight is lost, we end up here.

In the end, the only way you can appreciate your progress is to stand on the edge of the hole you dug for yourself, look down inside it, and smile fondly at the bloody claw prints that marked your journey up the walls.

DRAW THE LINE

It can ruin your life only if it ruins your character.

—MARCUS AURELIUS

John DeLorean ran his car company into the ground with a mix of outsized ambition, negligence, narcissism, greed, and mismanagement. As the bad news began to pile up and the picture was made clear and public, how do you think he responded?

Was it with resigned acceptance? Did he acknowledge the errors his disgruntled employees were speaking out about for the first time? Was he able to reflect, even slightly, on the mistakes and decisions that had brought him, his investors, and his employees so much trouble?

Of course not. Instead he put in motion a series of events that would end in a $60 million drug deal and his subsequent arrest. That's right, after his company began to fail—failure almost exclusively tied to his unprofessional management style—he figured the best way to save it all would be to secure financing through an illegal shipment of 220 pounds of cocaine.

Sure, after his publicized and very embarrassing arrest,

DeLorean was eventually acquitted on the charges on the rather implausible argument of "entrapment." Except he is on video, holding up a baggie of cocaine, saying with giddy excitement, "This stuff is as good as gold."

There's no question about who caused John DeLorean's disintegration. There's also no question about who made it so much worse. The answer is: HIM. He found himself in a hole and kept digging until he made it all the way to hell.

If only he'd stopped. If at any point he'd said: Is this the person I want to be?

People make mistakes all the time. They start companies they think they can manage. They have grand and bold visions that were a little too grandiose. This is all perfectly fine; it's what being an entrepreneur or a creative or even a business executive is about.

We take risks. We mess up.

The problem is that when we get our identity tied up in our work, we worry that any kind of failure will then say something bad about us *as a person*. It's a fear of taking responsibility, of admitting that we might have messed up. It's the sunk cost fallacy. And so we throw good money and good life after bad and end up making everything so much worse.

Let's say the walls feel like they're closing in. It might feel as if you've been betrayed or your life's work is being stolen. These are not rational, good emotions that will lead to rational, good actions.

Ego asks: *Why is this happening to me? How do I save this and prove to everyone I'm as great as they think?* It's the animal fear of even the slightest sign of weakness.

You've seen this. You've done this. Fighting desperately for something we're only making worse.

It is not a path to great things.

Take Steve Jobs. He was 100 percent responsible for his firing from Apple. Due to his later success, Apple's decision to fire him seems like an example of poor leadership, but he was, at the time, unmanageable. His ego was unequivocally out of control. If you were John Sculley and CEO of Apple, you'd have fired that version of Steve Jobs too—and been right to do so.

Now Steve Jobs's response to his firing was understandable. He cried. He fought. When he lost, he sold all but a single share of his stock in Apple and swore never to think of the place again. But then he started a new company and threw his whole life into it. He tried to learn as best he could from the management mistakes at the root of his first failure. He started another company after that too, called Pixar. Steve Jobs, the famous egomaniac who parked in handicap parking spaces just because he could, responded in this critical moment in a surprising way. Humble for CEOs convinced of their own genius, anyway. He worked until he'd not only proven himself again, but significantly resolved the flaws that had caused his downfall to begin with.

It's not often that successful or powerful people are able to do this. Not when they experience heartrending failure.

American Apparel's founder Dov Charney is an example. After losses of some $300 million and numerous scandals, the company offered him a choice: step aside as CEO and guide the company as a creative consultant (for a large salary), or be fired. He rejected both options and picked something much worse.

After filing a lawsuit in protest, he gambled his entire ownership in the company to initiate a hostile takeover with a hedge fund and insisted that his conduct be investigated and judged. It was, and he was not vindicated. His personal life was splashed across the headlines and embarrassing details revealed. The lawyer he chose to represent him in his lawsuits happened to be the same one who'd already sued Charney close to half a dozen times for sexual harassment and financial irregularities. In the past, Charney had accused this man of shaking him down and making bogus legal claims. Now they were working together.

American Apparel spent more than $10 million it didn't have to fight him off. A judge issued a restraining order. Sales slumped. Finally, the company began laying off factory workers and longtime employees—the exact people he claimed to be fighting for—just to stay afloat. A year later, they were bankrupt and he was out of money too.*

It's like the disgraced statesman and general Alcibiades. In the Peloponnesian War, he first fought for his home country and greatest love, Athens. Then driven out for a drunken crime he may or may not have committed, he defected to Sparta, Athens' sworn enemy. Then running afoul of the Spartans, he defected to Persia—the sworn enemy of both. Finally, he was recalled to Athens, where his ambitious plans to invade Sicily drove the Athenians to their ultimate ruin.

Ego kills what we love. Sometimes, it comes close to killing us too.

It is interesting that Alexander Hamilton, who of all the

---

*I was there and saw all of it. It broke my heart.

Founding Fathers met the most tragic and unnecessary end, would have wise words on this topic. But indeed he does (if only he could have remembered his own advice before fighting his fatal duel). "Act with *fortitude* and *honor*," he wrote to a distraught friend in serious financial and legal trouble of the man's own making. "If you cannot reasonably hope for a favorable extrication, do not plunge deeper. Have the courage to make a full stop."

A *full stop*. It's not that these folks should have quit everything. It's that a fighter who can't tap out or a boxer who can't recognize when it's time to retire gets hurt. Seriously so. You have to be able to see the bigger picture.

But when ego is in control, who can?

Let's say you've failed and let's even say it was your fault. Shit happens and, as they say, sometimes shit happens *in public*. It's not fun. The questions remain: Are you going to make it worse? Or are you going to emerge from this with your dignity and character intact? Are you going to live to fight another day?

When a team looks like they're going to lose a game, the coach doesn't call them all over and lie to them. Instead, he or she reminds them who they are and what they're capable of, and urges them to go back out there and embody that. With winning or miracles off their minds, a good team does its best to complete the game at the highest standard possible (and share the playing time with other players who don't regularly play). And sometimes, they even come back and win.

Most trouble is temporary . . . unless you make that not so. Recovery is not grand, it's one step in front of the other. Unless your cure is more of the disease.

Only ego thinks embarrassment or failure are more than

what they are. History is full of people who suffered abject humiliations yet recovered to have long and impressive careers. Politicians who lost elections or lost offices due to indiscretions—but came back to lead after time had passed. Actors whose movies bombed, authors who got writer's block, celebrities who made gaffes, parents who made mistakes, entrepreneurs with faltering companies, executives who got fired, athletes who were cut, people who lived too well at the top of the market. All these folks felt the hard edge of failure, just like we have. When we lose, we have a choice: Are we going to make this a lose-lose situation for ourselves and everyone involved? Or will it be a lose . . . and then win?

Because you will lose in life. It's a fact. A doctor has to call time of death at some point. They just do.

Ego says we're the immovable object, the unstoppable force. This delusion causes the problems. It meets failure and adversity with rule breaking—betting everything on some crazy scheme; doubling down on behind-the-scenes machinations or unlikely Hail Marys—even though that's what got you to this pain point in the first place.

At any given time in the circle of life, we may be aspiring, succeeding, or failing—though right now we're failing. With wisdom, we understand that these positions are transitory, not statements about your value as a human being. When success begins to slip from your fingers—for whatever reason—the response isn't to grip and claw so hard that you shatter it to pieces. It's to understand that you must work yourself back to the aspirational phase. You must get back to first principles and best practices.

"He who fears death will never do anything worthy of a

living man," Seneca once said. Alter that: He who will do anything to avoid failure will almost certainly do something *worthy of a failure.*

The only real failure is abandoning your principles. Killing what you love because you can't bear to part from it is selfish and stupid. If your reputation can't absorb a few blows, it wasn't worth anything in the first place.

MAINTAIN YOUR OWN SCORECARD

I never look back, except to find out about mistakes . . .
I only see danger in thinking back about things you are
proud of.

—ELISABETH NOELLE-NEUMANN

On April 16, 2000, the New England Patriots drafted an extra quarterback out of the University of Michigan. They'd scouted him thoroughly and had their eye on him for some time. Seeing that he was still available, they took him. It was the 6th round and the 199th pick of the draft.

The young quarterback's name was Tom Brady.

He was fourth string at the beginning of his rookie season. By his second season, he was a starter. New England won the Super Bowl that year. Brady was named MVP.

In terms of return on investment, it's probably the single greatest draft pick in the history of football: four Super Bowl rings (out of 6 appearances), 14 starting seasons, 172 wins, 428 touchdowns, 3 Super Bowl MVPs, 58,000 yards, 10 Pro Bowls, and more division titles than any quarterback in history. It's not even finished paying dividends. Brady may still have many more seasons left in him.

So you'd think that the Patriots' front office would be ecstatic with how it turned out, and indeed, they were. They were also disappointed—deeply so—in themselves. Brady's surprising abilities meant that the Patriots' scouting reports were way off. For all their evaluations of players, they'd somehow missed or miscalculated all of his intangible attributes. They'd let this gem wait until the *sixth round*. Someone else could have drafted him. More than that, they didn't even know they were right about Brady until injuries knocked out Drew Bledsoe, their prized starter, and forced them to realize his potential.

So, even though their bet paid off, the Patriots honed in on the specific intelligence failure that could have prevented the pick from happening in the first place. Not that they were nit-picking. Or indulging in perfectionism. They had higher standards of performance to adhere to.

For years, Scott Pioli, director of personnel for the Patriots, kept a photo on his desk of Dave Stachelski, a player the team had drafted in the 5th round, but who never made it through training camp. It was a reminder: You're not as good as you think. You don't have it all figured out. Stay focused. Do better.

Coach John Wooden was very clear about this too. The scoreboard was not the judge of whether he or the team had achieved success—that wasn't what constituted "winning." Bo Jackson wouldn't get impressed when he hit a home run or ran for a touchdown because he knew "he hadn't done it *perfect*." (In fact, he didn't ask for the ball after his first hit in major-league baseball for that reason—to him it was "just a ground ball up the middle.")

This is characteristic of how great people think. It's not

that they find failure in every success. They just hold themselves to a standard that exceeds what society might consider to be objective success. Because of that, they don't much care what other people think; they care whether they meet their own standards. And these standards are much, much higher than everyone else's.

The Patriots saw the Brady pick as being more lucky than smart. And though some people are fine giving themselves credit for luck, they weren't. No one would say the Patriots—or any team in the NFL—are without ego. But in this instance, instead of celebrating or congratulating themselves, they put their heads back down and focused on how to get *even better*. That's what makes humility such a powerful force—organizationally, personally, professionally.

This isn't necessarily fun, by the way. It can feel like self-inflicted torture sometimes. But it does force you to always keep going, and always improve.

Ego can't see both sides of the issue. It can't get better because it only sees the validation. Remember, "Vain men never hear anything but praise." It can only see what's going well, not what isn't. It's why you might see egomaniacs with temporary leads, but rarely lasting runs of it.

For us, the scoreboard can't be the only scoreboard. Warren Buffett has said the same thing, making a distinction between the inner scorecard and the external one. Your potential, the absolute best you're capable of—that's the metric to measure yourself against. Your standards are. Winning is not enough. People can get lucky and win. People can be assholes and win. Anyone can win. But not everyone is the best possible version of themselves.

Harsh, yes. The flip side is that it means being honestly

able to be proud and strong during the occasional defeat as well. When you take ego out of the equation, other people's opinions and external markers won't matter as much. That's more difficult, but ultimately a formula for resilience.

The economist (and philosopher) Adam Smith had a theory for how wise and good people evaluate their actions:

> There are two different occasions upon which we examine our own conduct, and endeavour to view it in the light in which the impartial spectator would view it: first, when we are about to act; and secondly, after we have acted. Our views are apt to be very partial in both cases; but they are apt to be most partial when it is of most importance that they should be otherwise. When we are about to act, the eagerness of passion will seldom allow us to consider what we are doing, with the candour of an indifferent person. . . . When the action is over, indeed, and the passions which prompted it have subsided, we can enter more coolly into the sentiments of the indifferent spectator.

This "indifferent spectator" is a sort of guide with which we can judge our behavior, as opposed to the groundless applause that society so often gives out. Not that it's just about validation, though.

Think of all the people who excuse their behavior—politicians, powerful CEOs, and the like—as "not technically illegal." Think of the times that you've excused your own with "no one will know." This is the moral gray area that our ego loves to exploit. Holding your ego against a standard (inner or indifferent or whatever you want to call it) makes it less and less likely that excess or wrongdoing is going to be tolerated by you. Because it's not about what you can get away with, it's about what you should or shouldn't do.

It's a harder road at first, but one that ultimately makes us less selfish and self-absorbed. A person who judges himself based on his own standards doesn't crave the spotlight the same way as someone who lets applause dictate success. A person who can think long term doesn't pity herself during short-term setbacks. A person who values the team can share credit and subsume his own interests in a way that most others can't.

Reflecting on what went well or how amazing we are doesn't get us anywhere, except maybe to where we are right now. But we want to go further, we want more, we want to continue to improve.

Ego blocks that, so we subsume it and smash it with continually higher standards. Not that we are endlessly pursuing more, as if we're racked with greed, but instead, we're inching our way toward real improvement, with discipline rather than disposition.

ALWAYS LOVE

And why should we feel anger at the world?
As if the world would notice!

—EURIPIDES

In 1939, a young prodigy named Orson Welles was given one of the most unheard-of deals in Hollywood history. He could write, act, and direct in two films of his choosing for RKO, a major movie studio. For his first picture, he decided to tell the story of a mysterious newspaper baron who became a prisoner of his enormous empire and lifestyle.

William Randolph Hearst, the infamous media magnate, decided that this movie was based on his life and, more important, that it did so offensively. He then began, and initially succeeded in, an all-consuming campaign to destroy one of the greatest films of all time.

Here's what's so interesting about this. First, Hearst most likely never even saw the movie so he had no idea what was actually in it. Second, it wasn't intended to be about him—or at least solely about him. (As far as we know, the character Charles Foster Kane was an amalgam of several historical figures including Samuel Insull and Robert McCormick; the movie was inspired by two similar portraits of power by Charlie Chaplin and Aldous Huxley; and it wasn't supposed to vilify, but to humanize.) Third, Hearst was one of the richest men in the world at the time, and at seventy-eight, near the end of his life. Why would he spend so much time on something as inconsequential as a fictional movie by a first-time director? Fourth, it was his campaign to stop it that secured the movie's place in popular lore and made it clear the extent to which his drive to control and manipulate would go. Ironically, he cemented his own legacy as a reviled American figure more than any critic ever could have.

Thus, the paradox of hate and bitterness. It accomplishes almost exactly the opposite of what we hope it does. In the Internet age, we call this the Streisand effect (named after a similar attempt by the singer and actress Barbra Streisand, who tried to legally remove a photo of her home from the Web. Her actions backfired and far more people saw it than would have had she left the issue alone.) Attempting to destroy something out of hate or ego often ensures that it will be preserved and disseminated forever.

The lengths that Hearst went to were absurd. He sent his most influential and powerful gossip columnist, Louella Parsons, to the studio to demand a screening. Based on her feedback, he decided he would do everything in his power to block it from being made public. He issued a directive that none of his newspapers were to make any mention of any RKO film—the company producing *Citizen Kane*—*period*. (More than a decade later, this ban still applied to Welles for all Hearst papers.) Hearst's papers began exploring negative stories about Welles and his private life. His gossip columnist threatened to do the same to each of the

RKO board members. Hearst also made threats to the movie industry as a whole, as a way of turning other studio heads against the picture. An $800,000 offer was made for the rights to the film so that it might be burned or destroyed. Most theater chains were pressured into refusing to show it, and no ads for it were allowed in any Hearst-owned properties. Hearst sympathizers began reporting rumors about Welles to various authorities, and in 1941, J. Edgar Hoover's FBI opened a file on him.

The result was that the movie failed commercially. It took years for it to find its place in the culture. Only at great expense and with great exertion, was Hearst able to hold it back.

We all have stuff that pisses us off. The more successful or powerful we are, the more there will be that we think we need to protect in terms of our legacy, image, and influence. If we're not careful, however, we can end up wasting an incredible amount of time trying to keep the world from displeasing or disrespecting us.

It is a sobering thought to consider for a moment all the needless death and needless waste inflicted over the eons by angry men or aggrieved women on other people, on society, and on themselves. Over what? Reasons that can hardly be remembered.

You know what is a better response to an attack or a slight or something you don't like? Love. That's right, *love*. For the neighbor who won't turn down the music. For the parent that let you down. For the bureaucrat who lost your paperwork. For the group that rejects you. For the critic who attacks you. The former partner who stole your business idea. The bitch or the bastard who cheated on you. Love.

Because, as the song lyrics go, "hate will get you every time."

Okay, maybe love is too much to ask for whatever it is that you've had done to you. You could at the very least try to let it go. You could try to shake your head and laugh about it.

Otherwise the world will witness another example of a timeless and sad pattern: Rich, powerful person becomes so isolated and delusional that when something happens contrary to his wishes, he becomes consumed by it. The same drive that made him great is suddenly a great weakness. He turns a minor inconvenience into a massive sore. The wound festers, becomes infected, and can even kill him.

This is what propelled Nixon forward and then, sadly, downward. Reflecting on his own exile, he later acknowledged that his lifelong image of himself as a scrappy fighter battling a hostile world was his undoing. He'd surrounded himself with other such "tough guys." People forget Nixon was reelected *by a landslide* after Watergate broke. He just couldn't help himself—he kept fighting, he persecuted reporters, and he lashed out at everyone he felt had slighted or doubted him. It's what continued to feed the story and ultimately sank him. Like many such people, he ended up doing more damage to himself than anyone else could. The root of it was his hatefulness and his anger, and even being the most powerful leader in the free world couldn't change it.

It doesn't need to be like that. Booker T. Washington tells an anecdote told to him by Frederick Douglass, about a time he was traveling and was asked to move and ride in the baggage car because of his race. A white supporter rushed up to apologize for this horrible offense. "I am sorry, Mr. Douglass, that you have been degraded in this manner," the person said.

Douglass would have none of that. He wasn't angry. He wasn't hurt. He replied with great fervor: "They cannot degrade Frederick Douglass. The soul that is within me no man can degrade. I am not the one that is being degraded on account of this treatment, but those who are inflicting it upon me."

Certainly, this is an incredibly difficult attitude to maintain. It's far easier to hate. It's natural to lash out.

Yet we find that what defines great leaders like Douglass is that instead of hating their enemies, they feel a sort of pity and empathy for them. Think of Barbara Jordan at the 1992 Democratic National Convention proposing an agenda of " . . . love. Love. Love. Love." Think of Martin Luther King Jr., over and over again, preaching that hate was a burden and love was freedom. Love was transformational, hate was debilitating. In one of his most famous sermons, he took it further: "We begin to love our enemies and love those persons that hate us whether in collective life or individual life by looking at ourselves." We must strip ourselves of the ego that protects and suffocates us, because, as he said, "Hate at any point is a cancer that gnaws away at the very vital center of your life and your existence. It is like eroding acid that eats away the best and the objective center of your life."

Take inventory for a second. What do you dislike? Whose name fills you with revulsion and rage? Now ask: Have these strong feelings really helped you accomplish *anything*?

Take an even wider inventory. Where has hatred and rage ever really gotten *anyone*?

Especially because almost universally, the traits or behaviors that have pissed us off in other people—their dishonesty, their selfishness, their laziness—are hardly going to work out well for them in the end. Their ego and shortsightedness contains its own punishment.

The question we must ask for ourselves is: Are we going to be miserable just because other people are?

Consider how Orson Welles responded to the multidecade campaign by Hearst. According to his own account, he bumped into Hearst in an elevator on the night of the movie's premiere—the very one that Hearst had deployed massive resources to prevent and destroy. Do you know what he did? He invited Hearst to come. When Hearst declined, Welles joked that Charles Foster Kane surely would have accepted.

It took a very long time for Welles's genius in that movie to finally be acknowledged by the rest of the world. No matter, Welles soldiered on, making other movies and producing other fantastic art. By all accounts, he lived a fulfilling and happy life. Eventually, *Citizen Kane* secured its place in the forefront of cinematic history. Seventy years after the movie's debut, it was finally played at Hearst Castle at San Simeon, which is now a state park.

The events he endured weren't exactly fair, but at least he didn't let it ruin his life. As Welles's girlfriend of twenty-plus years said in his eulogy, referring not just to Hearst, but to every slight he ever received in his long career in a notoriously ruthless industry, "I promise you it didn't make him bitter." In other words, he never became like Hearst.

Not everyone is capable of responding that way. At various

points in our lives, we seem to have different capacities for forgiveness and understanding. And even when some people are able to carry on, they carry with them a needless load of resentment. Remember Kirk Hammett, who suddenly became the guitarist in Metallica? The man they kicked out to make room for him, Dave Mustaine, went on to form another band, Megadeth. Even amidst his own unbelievable success, he was eaten up with rage and hatred over the way he'd been treated those many years before. It drove him to addiction and could have killed him. It was eighteen years until he was able to even begin to process it, and said it still felt like yesterday that he'd been hurt and rejected. When you hear him tell it, as he did once on camera to his former bandmates, it sounds like he ended up living under a bridge. In reality, the man sold millions of records, produced great music, and lived the life of a rock star.

We have all felt this pain—and to quote his lyrics, "smile[d] its blacktooth grin." This obsession with the past, with something that someone did or how things should have been, as much as it hurts, is ego embodied. Everyone else has moved on, but you can't, because you can't see anything but your own way. You can't conceive of accepting that someone could hurt you, deliberately or otherwise. So you hate.

In failure or adversity, it's so easy to hate. Hate defers blame. It makes someone else responsible. It's a distraction too; we don't do much else when we're busy getting revenge or investigating the wrongs that have supposedly been done to us.

Does this get us any closer to where we want to be? No. It just keeps us where we are—or worse, arrests our development entirely. If we are already successful, as Hearst was, it tarnishes our legacy and turns sour what should be our golden years.

Meanwhile, love is right there. Egoless, open, positive, vulnerable, peaceful, and productive.

FOR EVERYTHING THAT COMES NEXT, EGO IS THE ENEMY...

> I don't like work—no man does—but I like what is in the work—the chance to find yourself.
>
> —JOSEPH CONRAD

In William Manchester's epic biography of the life of Winston Churchill, the middle volume—a third of the set—is titled *Alone*. For a full eight years, Churchill stood more or less by himself against his shortsighted peers, against the rising threat of fascism, even among the West.

But eventually, he triumphed again. And faced adversity again. And was vindicated again.

Katharine Graham stood alone as she took over her family's newspaper empire. Her son, Donald Graham, must have felt similar pressure as he sought to preserve the company during the dramatic declines of the industry in the mid-2000s. Both made it through. So can you.

There is no way around it: We will experience difficulty. We will feel the touch of failure. As Benjamin Franklin observed, those who "drink to the bottom of the cup must expect to meet with some of the dregs."

But what if those dregs weren't so bad? As Harold Geneen put it, "People learn from their failures. Seldom do they learn anything from success." It's why the old Celtic saying tells us, "See much, study much, suffer much, that is the path to wisdom."

What you face right now could, should, and can be such a path.

Wisdom or ignorance? Ego is the swing vote.

Aspiration leads to success (and adversity). Success creates its own adversity (and, hopefully, new ambitions). And adversity leads to aspiration and more success. It's an endless loop.

All of us exist on this continuum. We occupy different places on it at various points in our lives. But when we do fail, it sucks. No question.

Whatever is next for us, we can be sure of one thing we'll want to avoid. Ego. It makes all the steps hard, but failure is the one it will make permanent. Unless we learn, right here and right now, from our mistakes. Unless we use this moment as an opportunity to understand ourselves and our own mind better, ego will seek out failure like true north.

All great men and women went through difficulties to get to where they are, all of them made mistakes. They found within those experiences some benefit—even if it was simply the realization that they were not infallible and that things would not always go their way. They found that self-awareness was the way out and through—if they hadn't, they wouldn't have gotten better and they wouldn't have been able to rise again.

Which is why we have their mantra to guide us, so that

we can survive and thrive in every phase of our journey. It is simple (though, as always, never easy).

> *Not to aspire or seek out of ego.*
> *To have success without ego.*
> *To push through failure with strength, not ego.*

EPILOGUE

There is something of a civil war going on within all of
our lives. There is a recalcitrant South of our soul revolt-
ing against the North of our soul. And there is this continual struggle within the very structure of every
individual life.

—MARTIN LUTHER KING JR.

I f you're reading this right now, then you've made it
through this book. I was afraid some people might not.
To be perfectly honest, I wasn't sure I'd ever get here
myself.

How do you feel? Tired? Confused? Free?

It is no easy task to go head-to-head with one's ego. To
accept first that ego may be there. Then to subject it to scru-
tiny and criticism. Most of us can't handle uncomfortable
self-examination. It's easier to do just about anything else—
in fact, some of the world's most unbelievable accomplishments are undoubtedly a result of a desire to avoid facing
the darkness of ego.

In any case, just by making it to this point you've struck a serious blow against it. It's not all you'll need to do, but it is a start.

My friend the philosopher and martial artist Daniele Bolelli once gave me a helpful metaphor. He explained that training was like sweeping the floor. Just because we've done it once, doesn't mean the floor is clean forever. Every day the dust comes back. Every day we must sweep.

The same is true for ego. You would be stunned at what kind of damage dust and dirt can do over time. And how quickly it accumulates and becomes utterly unmanageable.

A few days after being fired by the American Apparel board of directors, Dov Charney called me at 3 A.M. He was alternately despondent and angry—genuinely believing himself to be totally blameless for his situation. I asked him, "Dov, what are you going to do? Are you going to pull a Steve Jobs and start a new company? Are you going to make a comeback?" He got quiet and said to me with an earnestness I could feel through the phone and in my bones, "Ryan, Steve Jobs *died*." To him, in this addled state, this failure, this blow was somehow the same as death. That was one of the last times we ever spoke. I watched with horror in the months that followed as he wreaked havoc on the company he had put everything into building.

It was a sad moment and one that has stayed with me.

But for the grace of God go I. But for the grace of God, that could be any of us.

We all experience success and failure in our own way. Struggling to write this book, I went through four hard-fought but rejected drafts of the proposal and dozens of drafts of the manuscript. On my earlier projects, I'm sure the strain would have broken me. Maybe I would have quit or tried to work with someone else. Maybe I would have dug in my heels to get my way and irreparably damaged the book.

At some point during the process, I came up with a therapeutic device. After each draft, I would tear up the pages and feed the paper to a worm compost I keep in my garage. A few months later, those painful pages were dirt that nourished my yard, which I could walk with bare feet. It was a real and tangible connection to that larger immensity. I liked to remind myself that the same process is going to happen to me when I'm done, when I die and nature tears me up.

One of the most freeing realizations came to me while I was writing and thinking about the ideas in the pages you've just read. It occurred to me what a damaging delusion this notion that our lives are "grand monuments" set to last for all time really is. Any ambitious person knows that feeling—that you must do great things, that you must get your way, and that if you don't that you're a worthless failure and the world is conspiring against you. There is so much pressure that eventually we all break under it or are broken by it.

Of course, that is not true. Yes, we all have potential within us. We all have goals and accomplishments that we know we can achieve—whether it's starting a company, finishing a creative work, making a run at a championship, or getting to the top of your respective field. These are worthy aims. A broken person will not get there.

The problem is when ego intrudes on these pursuits, corrupting them and undermining us as we set out to achieve and accomplish. Whispering lies as we embark on that journey and whispering lies as we succeed in it, and worse, whispering painful lies when we stumble along the way. Ego, like any drug, might be indulged at first in a misguided attempt to get an edge or to take one off. The problem is how quickly it becomes an end unto itself. Which is how one finds oneself in surreal moments like the one I experienced on the phone with Dov, or in any of the cautionary tales in this book.

In the course of my work and my life, I've found that most of the consequences of ego are not quite so calamitous. Many of the people in your life—and in our world—who have given over to their ego will not "get what they deserve" in the sense of karmic justice that we were taught to believe in as kids. I wish it were so simple.

Instead, the consequences are closer to the ending of one of my favorite books, *What Makes Sammy Run?* by Budd Schulberg, a novel whose famous character is based on the real lives of entertainment entrepreneurs like Samuel Goldwyn and David O. Selznick. In the book, the narrator is called to the palatial mansion of a calculating, ruthless, egotistical Hollywood mogul whose precipitous rise he has followed with a mix of admiration and confusion and eventually disgust.

In this moment of vulnerability, the narrator catches a true glimpse into the man's life—his lonely, empty marriage, his fear, his insecurity, his inability to be still even for a second. He realizes that the vengeance—the bad karma—he'd hoped for, for all the rules the man had broken, all the cheating ways he had gotten ahead, wasn't coming. Because it was already there. As he writes,

I had expected something conclusive and fatal and now I realized that *what was coming to him* was not a sudden pay-off but a process, a disease he had caught in the epidemic that swept over his birthplace like a plague; a cancer that was slowly eating him away, the symptoms developing and intensifying: success, lone-liness, fear. Fear of all the bright young men, the newer, fresher Sammy Glicks that would spring up to harass him, to threaten him and finally overtake him.

That's how ego manifests itself. And isn't that what we're desperately afraid of becoming?

I'll reveal one last thing I hope will make this come full circle. I first read that passage when I was nineteen years old. It was reading assigned by a seasoned mentor who had found, as I would, early success in the entertainment busi-ness. The book was influential and informative for me, just as he'd known it would be.

Yet over the next few years, I worked myself into a nearly identical situation as the characters in the book. Not just summoned to the palatial home to watch the expected and unavoidable dissolution of a person I admired. But to find myself dangerously close to my own shortly thereafter.

I know the passage struck me because when I went to type it up for this epilogue, I found in my original copy pages covered in my own handwriting, written years before, detailing my reaction, right before I had set out into the world. Clearly I had understood Schulberg's words intellectually, even emotionally—but I had made the wrong choices anyway. I had swept once and thought it was enough.

Ten years after first reading it and writing down my thoughts, I was ready once more. Those lessons came home to me in exactly the way I needed them to.

There's a quote from Bismarck that says, in effect, any fool can learn from experience. The trick is to learn from *other people's* experience. This book started around the latter idea and to my surprise ended up with a painful amount of the former as well. I set out to study ego and came crashing into my own—and to those of the people I had long since looked up to.

It may be that you'll need to experience some of that on your own too. Perhaps it is like Plutarch's reflection that we don't "so much gain the knowledge of things by the words, as words by the experience [we have] of things."

In any case, I want to conclude this book with the idea that has underpinned all of what you've just read. That it's admirable to want to be better businessmen or business-women, better athletes, better conquerors. We should want to be better informed, better off financially . . . We should want, as I've said a few times in this book, to do great things. I know that I do.

But no less impressive an accomplishment: being better people, being happier people, being balanced people, being content people, being humble and selfless people. Or better yet, all of these traits together. And what is most obvious but most ignored is that perfecting the personal regularly leads to success as a professional, but rarely the other way around. Working to refine our habitual thoughts, working to clamp down on destructive impulses, these are not simply the moral requirements of any decent person. They will make us more successful; they will help us navigate the treacherous waters that ambition will require us to travel. And they are also their own reward.

So here you are, at the end of this book about ego, having seen as much as one can be shown about the problems of ego from other people's experiences and my own.

What is left?

Your choices. What will you *do* with this information? Not just now, but going forward?

Every day for the rest of your life you will find yourself at one of three phases: aspiration, success, failure. You will battle the ego in each of them. You will make mistakes in each of them.

You must sweep the floor every minute of every day. And then sweep again.

WHAT SHOULD YOU READ NEXT?

For most people, bibliographies are boring. For those of us who love to read, they can be the best part of an entire book. As one of those people, I have prepared for you—my book-loving reader—a full guide to every single book and source I used in this study of ego. I wanted to show you not just which books deserved citation but what I got out of them, and which ones I strongly recommend you read next. In doing this, I got so carried away that my publisher informed me what I had prepared was too big to fit in the book. So I'd like to send it to you directly—in fully clickable and searchable form.

If you'd like these recommendations, all you have to do is e-mail books@egoistheenemy.com or visit www.EgoIs TheEnemy.com/books. I'll also send you a collection of my favorite quotes and observations about ego—many of which I couldn't fit in this book.

CAN I GET EVEN MORE BOOK RECOMMENDATIONS?

You can also sign up for my monthly book recommenda-tion e-mail. The list of recipients has grown to more than fifty thousand rabid, curious readers like yourself. You'll get one e-mail per month, with recommendations from me based on my own personal reading. It kicks off with ten of my favorite books of all time. Just sign up at ryanholiday .net/reading-newsletter.

SELECTED BIBLIOGRAPHY

Aristotle. trans. Terence Irwin. *Nicomachean Ethics.* Indianapolis, IN: Hackett Publishing, 1999.

Barlett, Donald L., and James B. Steele. *Howard Hughes: His Life and Madness.* London: Andre Deutsch, 2003.

Bly, Robert. *Iron John: A Book About Men.* Cambridge, MA: Da Capo, 2004.

Bolelli, Daniele. *On the Warrior's Path: Fighting, Philosophy, and Martial Arts Mythology.* Berkeley, CA: Frog, 2003.

Brady, Frank. *Citizen Welles: A Biography of Orson Welles.* New York: Scribner, 1988.

Brown, Peter H., and Pat H. Broeske. *Howard Hughes: The Untold Story.* Da Capo, 2004.

C., Chuck. *A New Pair of Glasses.* Irvine, CA: New-Look Publishing, 1984.

Chernow, Ron. *Titan: The Life of John D. Rockefeller, Sr.* New York: Vintage, 2004.

Cook, Blanche Wiesen. *Eleanor Roosevelt: The Defining Years.* New York: Penguin, 2000.

Coram, Robert. *Boyd: The Fighter Pilot Who Changed the Art of War.* Boston: Little, Brown, 2002.

Cray, Ed. *General of the Army: George C. Marshall, Soldier and Statesman*. New York: Cooper Square, 2000.

Csikszentmihalyi, Mihaly. *Creativity: Flow and the Psychology of Discovery and Invention*. New York: Harper Collins, 1996.

Emerson, Ralph Waldo. *Representative Men: Seven Lectures*. Cambridge, MA: Belknap Press of Harvard University Press, 1987.

Geneen, Harold. *Managing*. Garden City, NY: Doubleday, 1984.

Graham, Katharine. *Personal History*. New York: Knopf, 1997.

Grant, Ulysses S. *Personal Memoirs of U.S. Grant, Selected Letters 1839–1865*. New York: Library of America, 1990.

Halberstam, David. *The Education of a Coach*. New York: Hachette, 2006.

Henry, Philip, and J. C. Coulston. *The Life of Belisarius: The Last Great General of Rome*. Yardley, Penn.: Westholme, 2006.

Herodotus, trans. Aubrey De Sélincourt, rev. John Marincola. *The Histories*. London: Penguin, 2003.

Hesiod, *Theogony* and *Works and Days* and Theognis, *Elegies*. Trans, Dorothea Wender. Harmondsworth, U.K.: Penguin, 1973.

Isaacson, Walter. *Benjamin Franklin: An American Life*. New York: Simon & Schuster, 2003.

Lamott, Anne. *Bird by Bird: Some Instructions on Writing and Life*. New York: Anchor, 1995.

Levin, Hillel. *Grand Delusions: The Cosmic Career of John DeLorean*. New York: Viking, 1983.

Liddell Hart, B. H. *Sherman: Soldier, Realist, American*. New York: Da Capo, 1993.

Malcolm X, and Alex Haley. *The Autobiography of Malcolm X*. New York: Ballantine, 1992.

Marcus Aurelius, trans. Gregory Hays. *Meditations*. New York: Modern Library, 2002.

Martial, trans. Craig A. Williams. *Epigrams*. Oxford: Oxford University Press, 2004.

McPhee, John. *A Sense of Where You Are: A Profile of Bill Bradley at Princeton*. New York: Farrar, Straus and Giroux, 1999.

McWilliams, Carey. *The Education of Carey McWilliams*. New York: Simon & Schuster, 1979.

Mosley, Leonard. *Marshall: Hero for Our Times*. New York: Hearst, 1982.

Muir, John. *Wilderness Essays*. Salt Lake City: Peregrine Smith, 1980.

Nixon by Nixon: In His Own Words. Directed by Peter W. Kunhardt. HBO documentary, 2014.

Orth, Maureen. "Angela's Assets." *Vanity Fair,* January 2015.

Packer, George. "The Quiet German." *New Yorker,* December 1, 2014.

Palahniuk, Chuck. *Fight Club*. New York: W. W. Norton, 1996.

Plutarch, trans. Ian Scott-Kilvert. *The Rise and Fall of Athens: Nine Greek Lives*. Harmondsworth, U.K: Penguin, 1960.

Pressfield, Steven. *Tides of War: A Novel of Alcibiades and the Peloponnesian War*. New York: Bantam, 2001.

Rampersad, Arnold. *Jackie Robinson: A Biography*. New York: Knopf, 1997.

Riley, Pat. *The Winner Within: A Life Plan for Team Players.* New York: Putnam, 1993.

Roberts, Russ. *How Adam Smith Can Change Your Life.* New York: Portfolio / Penguin, 2015.

Schulberg, Budd. *What Makes Sammy Run?* New York: Vintage, 1993.

Sears, Stephen W. *George B. McClellan: The Young Napoleon.* New York: Ticknor & Fields, 1988.

Seneca, Lucius Annaeus, trans. C.D.N. Costa. *On the Shortness of Life.* New York: Penguin, 2005.

Shamrock, Frank. *Uncaged: My Life as a Champion MMA Fighter.* Chicago: Chicago Review Press, 2012.

Sheridan, Sam. *The Fighter's Mind: Inside the Mental Game.* New York: Atlantic Monthly, 2010.

Sherman, William T. *Memoirs of General W. T. Sherman.* New York: Literary Classics of the United States, 1990.

Smith, Adam. *The Theory of Moral Sentiments.* New York: Penguin, 2009.

Smith, Jean Edward. *Eisenhower: In War and Peace.* New York: Random House, 2012.

Stevenson, Robert Louis. *An Apology for Idlers.* London: Penguin, 2009.

Walsh, Bill. *The Score Takes Care of Itself: My Philosophy of Leadership.* New York: Portfolio / Penguin, 2009.

Washington, Booker T. *Up from Slavery.* New York: Dover, 1995.

Weatherford, J. *Genghis Khan and the Making of the Modern World.* New York: Three Rivers, 2005.

Wooden, John. *Coach Wooden's Leadership Game Plan for Success: 12 Lessons for Extraordinary Performance and Personal Excellence.* New York: McGraw-Hill Education, 2009.

ACKNOWLEDGMENTS

In my previous books, I've tried to make a point of thanking not only the people and mentors who have helped with the book, but also to make it clear how indebted I am to the many authors and thinkers I have relied on over the years. This book would not only not be possible without them, but I also feel incredibly guilty that readers might credit me for insights that originated with other, wiser writers. Anything valuable in this book came from them and not me.

This book would not be what it is without the editing and valuable advice of my editors Nils Parker and Niki Papadopoulos. Steven Pressfield, Tom Bilyeu, and Joey Roth provided critical notes early on that I am very grateful for.

I want to thank my wife, who not only helped me personally during the writing of this book, but was my most dedicated reader. I want to thank my agent, Steve Hanselman, who has represented me from day one. Thanks to Michael Tunney for his help with the proposal, Kevin Currie for his help, and Hristo Vassilev for his excellent research work and assistance. Thanks to Mike Lombardi at the Patriots for his support and insight. Also I owe a debt of gratitude to Tim Ferriss, whose support of my last book made this one possible, and the same goes to Robert Greene, who helped make me a writer, and Dr. Drew, who introduced me to philosophy. I want to thank John Luttrell and Tobias Keller for their guidance and conversations with me during the chaos at American Apparel. I'm not sure if I would have made it, period, were it not for Workaholics Anonymous, both their meeting in Los Angeles and weekly calls.

In terms of places, the University of Texas at Austin Library, the University of California Riverside Library, various running trails (and my shoes), and my home away from home, the Los Angeles Athletic Club, facilitated the actual writing in this book.

Finally, would it be wrong to thank my pet goats too? If not, thanks to Biscuit, Bucket, and Watermelon for keeping things entertaining.

Also by Ryan Holiday

Also by Ryan Holiday and Stephen Hanselman

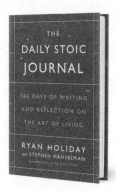

RyanHoliday.net
DailyStoic.com

PORTFOLIO
PENGUIN

THE
OBSTACLE
IS THE
WAY

THE
OBSTACLE
IS THE
WAY

EXPANDED 10TH ANNIVERSARY EDITION

THE TIMELESS ART OF
TURNING TRIALS INTO TRIUMPH

Ryan Holiday

PORTFOLIO / PENGUIN

Portfolio / Penguin
An imprint of Penguin Random House LLC
penguinrandomhouse.com

First published in hardcover as *The Obstacle Is the Way*
by Portfolio / Penguin in 2014
This updated and expanded edition with new material
published by Portfolio / Penguin in 2024

Copyright © 2014, 2024 by Ryan Holiday
Penguin Random House values and supports copyright. Copyright fuels
creativity, encourages diverse voices, promotes free speech, and creates a
vibrant culture. Thank you for buying an authorized edition of this book
and for complying with copyright laws by not reproducing, scanning, or
distributing any part of it in any form without permission. You are
supporting writers and allowing Penguin Random House to continue to
publish books for every reader. Please note that no part of this book may
be used or reproduced in any manner for the purpose of training artificial
intelligence technologies or systems.

Most Portfolio books are available at a discount when purchased in quantity
for sales promotions or corporate use. Special editions, which include
personalized covers, excerpts, and corporate imprints, can be created when
purchased in large quantities. For more information, please call (212) 572-
2232 or email specialmarkets@penguinrandomhouse.com. Your local
bookstore can also assist with discounted bulk purchases using the Penguin
Random House corporate Business-to-Business program. For assistance in
locating a participating retailer, email B2B@penguinrandomhouse.com.

ISBN 9780593719916 (hardcover)
ISBN 9780593719923 (ebook)

Printed in the United States of America
1st Printing

Book design by E. J. Strongin, Neuwirth Associates, Inc.

CONTENTS

PART II: ACTION

PART III: WILL

REFLECTIONS, TEN YEARS LATER

It's not that the last decade—ten years and counting since the publication of this book—was hard for me.

It'd probably be bad form to admit that in a book about overcoming obstacles.

But I think I'm safe to say it was a *lot*.

There were natural disasters, floods and fires, a freeze that broke the power grid and most of our pipes. There was a long drought that was murder on our livestock and land. There was a devastating, tragic pandemic that stretched on for years, dashing so many plans to dust (nearly killing the independent bookstore we opened in the teeth of that virus). There were disputes with business partners, an employee caught embezzling. There were funerals and late-night phone calls with news you never want to get. The company where I made my bones went bankrupt, taking with it not just much of my résumé but what was supposed to be several years' salary worth of stock options.

May you live in interesting times . . . goes the ancient curse.

Well, it's been interesting.

There was a global logistics and supply chain crisis. A paper and printer shortage in publishing. There was a falling out with family. Hundreds of thousands of miles on the road. There was getting skunked on the bestseller lists, creative differences, daily battles with procrastination. There was the steady drift toward fascism, unrest in the streets, the failure of institutions.

It was a lot in a much more welcome direction, too. Ten years of marriage. Having kids. Running businesses. Sunsets and sunrises, beautiful sights and new discoveries. Friendships rekindled, breakthroughs in therapy. Word that this book had made its way into the locker rooms of professional sports teams and the offices of heads of state. Signs that it and my other books had started to sell, like, *really* sell. There was the flood of attention and offers, the financial rewards, the fame, the platform, the expectations that followed . . .

Listening back to the audiobook now (which I've had to re-record for this edition), I hardly recognize the voice of that younger person, that person who had been through so much less, who knew so much less.

Because what's happened in those intervening years is life. Modern life, yes, but also life as it's always been, life not altogether unrecognizable from someone on Zeno's *stoa* back in the third century BCE or nearly five hundred years later in the Rome of Marcus Aurelius.

The simplest idea at the center of this book is that there are hidden advantages in every situation, that businesses and teams and people can take seemingly impossible situations and find ways to triumph over them. "Hard times can be softened," Seneca writes in one of his essays, "tight squeezes widened, and heavy loads made lighter for those who can apply the right pressure."

While this is true and more essential than ever in difficult times, in experiencing life and all its interestingness in the intervening years, I have come to more fully understand what the Stoics were getting at. The suffering and struggle of centuries of existence taught them something more profound than the fact that every downside has an upside.

How glib it is to talk of silver linings to someone with a cancer diagnosis, someone who has buried a child, someone in the grips of a crippling addiction, someone who has been bombed, someone who has lost their livelihood?

What I understand today is that when the Stoics said that there was an opportunity in every obstacle, what they meant was *the opportunity to practice virtue*. To be a good person despite the bad things that have happened. To do good in the world despite the bad that has befallen you. They were speaking of the idea of *arete*. Excellence—in all forms.

Finding professional advantage? Possibly, but this was not their primary concern. What they meant when they said that the obstacle is the way is that the hardest, most heartbreaking moments of life can be transformed by endurance, by selflessness, by courage, by kindness, by decency.

And they also had more in mind than just adversity. Success, too, is an opportunity to practice virtue. Indeed, it demands it. Because with success comes temptations, comes distractions, comes stress, comes responsibility and obligations and obstacles. How great it is, then, in the face of abundance to be humble, to be disciplined, to be decent, to be generous, to hold true to your values.

Great, but challenging.

One of the great gifts of my life was discovering Stoicism, which I came to at the end of my teens, purely by chance. I desperately needed guidance, some sort of compass for life. Around the same time, I began to hear the first soft sounds of my calling to be a writer and, eventually, I was able to combine these two loves into my career.

When I first approached what is now Penguin Random House with the idea for *The Obstacle is the Way* in the summer of 2012, I can't say they were exactly ecstatic. I was slightly offended, but in retrospect, it was an act of extreme open-mindedness and trust that they were interested in a book about an obscure school of ancient philosophy at all (let alone from a twenty-five-year-old college dropout!). This open-mindedness had its limits, naturally, and their offer was less than half of what I had received for my first book, which was then on the bestseller lists and generating headlines.

My editor, long after the book had found its audience, would tell me that her hope was that I'd get this philosophy stuff out of my system and go back to marketing and business books. She was probably right—the idea was crazy, and I am grateful they let me try. Someone else that I thought was a friend and patron was privately telling people that the book would sell no more than five thousand copies.

Being underestimated is usually an advantage—however frustrating it can feel in the moment. The expectations from everyone were low. The concept was so absurd as a business book that it effectively worked as counterprogramming and generated a bit of attention. *The Obstacle is the Way* did okay its first week, and then sales quickly tapered off . . . but they never went to zero. Amazon discounted the ebook as some kind of loss leader and the algorithm blessed me. A year and a half or so later, after news that the New England Patriots had read the book on the way to Super Bowl XLIX (and the Seahawks read it after their gut-wrenching loss), suddenly the publisher couldn't keep it in stock. Here we are, a decade later, and *The Obstacle is the Way* has been published in forty languages and has sold over two million copies in English alone.

Sales are great, but what's far more exciting to me is that the "obscure" school of ancient philosophy is no longer quite so obscure. In 2012 there were a few thousand people interested in Epictetus, Seneca, or Marcus Aurelius spread out across the internet. Today, the *Daily Stoic*, which I started in 2016, reaches a million people before nine a.m. each morning. There are more Stoics walking the earth today than ever before in history!

You'll notice that in the text of this book and in the *Daily Stoic* emails, I do not talk about myself. The word "I" appeared in the body text of the first edition of *Obstacle* only once or twice and even then only by accident (it's been corrected in the version you're about to read). But that doesn't mean that my own experiences have not informed my writing and understanding of Stoicism. Of course they have.

In fact, that is itself yet another confirmation of how the obstacle can always be the way.

"A writer—and, I believe, generally all persons—must think that whatever happens to him or her is a resource," the great Jorge Luis Borges once explained. "All things have been given to us for a purpose, and an artist must feel this more intensely. All that happens to us, including our humiliations, our misfortunes, our embarrassments, all is given to us as raw material, as clay, so that we may shape our art."

Our experiences become the fuel for what we create; the crucible of experience informs and instructs. It doesn't matter how awful, how unfair, how expensive an experience is, I've come to understand that I have the greatest job in the world in that I can take what happens to me, even heartbreak, and turn it into material. In this way, nothing is ever truly a waste; nothing is totally, irredeemably bad. There is always some cold comfort in every experience, some way to move forward from it and use it productively.

I am not alone in this. The same is true for leaders, for comedians, for athletes, for military officers and for parents alike. It doesn't matter what happens to us; it can be for the best if we use it to be better for ourselves and others.

So the pages before you, rooted as they are in history and philosophy, are also the product of my own history—successes and failures, high points and low ones, failures and breakthroughs.

Would I write the book differently if I was starting over? Of course. (Certainly there are changes and corrections I have made in this new anniversary edition). If I were updating it again ten years from now, I would hope I would make changes still, that I would be wiser and understand philosophy more deeply.

But everything in here was something that I needed to hear when I wrote it, a lesson I myself needed to learn most of all. That they have been of value to readers around the world is, as Marcus Aurelius would say, a bit of "nature's inadvertence," a pleasing by-product of a timeless process.

For that's what Stoicism is—a great conversation that

stretches back thousands of years. Men and women talking to themselves, talking themselves through obstacles and opportunities, big moments and small ones, reminding themselves to be excellent, to follow virtue, to do what is demanded of them.

It's my honor to invite you to join it.

The Painted Porch
Bastrop, TX
2024

PREFACE

In the year 170, at night in his tent on the front lines of the war in Germania, Marcus Aurelius, the emperor of Rome, sat down to write. Or perhaps it was before dawn at the palace on the Palatine. Or he stole a few seconds to himself during the games, ignoring the carnage on the floor of the Colosseum below. The exact location is not important. What matters is that this man, known today as the last of the Five Good Emperors, sat down to write.

Not to an audience or for publication but to himself, *for* himself. And what he wrote is undoubtedly one of history's most effective formulas for overcoming every negative situation we may encounter in life. A formula for thriving not just in spite of whatever happens but *because of it*.

At that moment, he wrote only a paragraph. Only a little of it was original. Almost every thought could, in some form or another, be found in the writings of his mentors and idols. But in a scant eighty-five words Marcus Aurelius so clearly defined and articulated a timeless idea that he eclipses the great names of those who came before him: Chrysippus,

Zeno, Cleanthes, Aristo, Junius Rusticus, Epictetus, Seneca, Musonius Rufus.

It is more than enough for us.

> *Our actions may be impeded . . . but there can be no impeding our intentions or dispositions. Because we can accommodate and adapt. The mind adapts and converts to its own purposes the obstacle to our acting.*

And then he concluded with powerful words destined for maxim.

> *The impediment to action advances action.*
> *What stands in the way becomes the way.*

In Marcus's words is the secret to an art known as *turning obstacles upside down*. To act with "a reverse clause" so there is always a way out or another route to get to where you need to go. So that setbacks or problems are always expected and never permanent. Making certain that what impedes us can empower us.

Coming from this particular man, these were not idle words. In his own reign of some nineteen years, he would experience nearly constant war, a horrific plague, possible infidelity, an attempt at the throne by one of his closest allies, repeated and arduous travel across the empire—from Asia Minor to Syria, Egypt, Greece, and Austria—a rapidly depleting treasury, an incompetent and greedy stepbrother as co-emperor, and on and on and on.

And from what we know, he truly saw each and every one of these obstacles as an opportunity to practice some virtue:

patience, courage, humility, resourcefulness, reason, justice, and creativity. The power he held never seemed to go to his head—neither did the stress or burden. He rarely rose to excess or anger, and never to hatred or bitterness. As Matthew Arnold, the essayist, remarked in 1863, in Marcus we find a man who held the highest and most powerful station in the world—and the universal verdict of the people around him was that he proved himself worthy of it.

It turns out that the wisdom of that short passage from Marcus Aurelius can be found in others as well, men and women who followed it like he did. In fact, it is a remarkable constant down through the ages.

One can trace the thread from those days in the decline and fall of the Roman Empire to the creative outpouring of the Renaissance to the breakthroughs of the Enlightenment. It's seen starkly in the pioneer spirit of the American West, the perseverance of the Union cause during the Civil War, and in the bustle of the Industrial Revolution. It appeared again in the bravery of the leaders of the civil rights movement and stood tall in the prison camps of Vietnam. And today it has made its way into the locker rooms of Super Bowl–winning teams, and into the hands of Olympic gold medalists who rely on it just as much as the leaders of cutting-edge businesses, hospitals, and world-changing organizations. It's a tool kit for Special Forces operators and activists alike.

This philosophic approach is the driving force of self-made men and women and the succor to those in positions with great responsibility or great trouble. On the battlefield or in the boardroom, across oceans and many centuries, members of every group, gender, class, cause, and business have had to confront obstacles and struggle to overcome them—learning to turn those obstacles upside down.

That struggle is the one constant in all of their lives. Knowingly or not, each individual was a part of an ancient tradition, employing it to navigate the timeless terrain of opportunities and difficulties, trial and triumph.

We are the rightful heirs to this tradition. It's our birthright. Whatever we face, we have a choice: Will we be blocked by obstacles, or will we advance through and over them?

We might not be emperors, but the world is still constantly testing us. It asks: Are you worthy? Can you get past the things that inevitably fall in your way? Will you stand up and show us what you're made of?

Plenty of people have answered this question in the affirmative. And a rarer breed still has shown that they not only have what it takes, but they thrive and rally at every such challenge. That the challenge makes them better than if they'd never faced the adversity at all.

Now it's your turn to see if you're one of them, if you'll join their company.

This book will show you the way.

THE
OBSTACLE
IS THE
WAY

INTRODUCTION

This thing in front of you. This issue. This obstacle—this frustrating, unfortunate, problematic, unexpected problem preventing you from doing what you want to do. That thing you dread or secretly hope will never happen. What if it wasn't so bad?

What if embedded inside it or inherent in it were certain benefits—benefits only for you? What would you do? What do you think most people would do?

Probably what they've always done, and what you are doing right now: nothing.

Let's be honest: Most of us are paralyzed. Whatever our individual goals, most of us sit frozen before the many obstacles that lie ahead of us.

We wish it weren't true, but it is.

What blocks us is clear. Systemic: decaying institutions, rising unemployment, skyrocketing costs of education, and technological disruption. Individual: too short, too old, too scared, too poor, too stressed, no access, no backers, no confidence. How skilled we are at cataloging what holds us back!

Every obstacle is unique to each of us. But the responses they elicit are the same: Fear. Frustration. Anxiety. Confusion. Resentment. Depression. Anger. Despair.

You know what you want to do but it feels like some invisible enemy has you boxed in, holding you down, holding you back. You try to get somewhere, but something invariably blocks the path, following and thwarting each move you make. You have just enough freedom to feel like you can move, just enough to feel like it's your fault when you can't seem to follow through or build momentum.

We're dissatisfied with our jobs, our relationships, our place in the world. We're trying to get somewhere, but something stands in the way.

So we do nothing.

We blame our bosses, the economy, our politicians, other people, or we write ourselves off as failures or our goals as impossible. When really only one thing is at fault: our attitude and approach.

There have been countless lessons (and books) about achieving success, but no one ever taught us how to overcome failure, how to think about obstacles, how to treat and triumph over them, and so we are stuck. Beset on all sides, many of us are disoriented, reactive, and torn. We have no idea what to do.

On the other hand, not everyone is paralyzed. We watch in awe as some seem to turn those very obstacles, which stymie us, into launching pads for themselves. How do they do that? What's the secret?

Even more perplexing, earlier generations faced worse problems with fewer safety nets and fewer tools. They dealt with the same obstacles we have today *plus* the ones they worked so hard to try to eliminate for their children and others. And yet . . . we're still stuck.

What do these figures have that we lack? What are we missing? It's simple: a method and a framework for understanding, appreciating, and acting upon the obstacles life throws at us.

John D. Rockefeller had it—for him it was coolheadedness and self-discipline. Demosthenes, the great Athenian orator, had it—for him it was a relentless drive to improve himself through action and practice. Abraham Lincoln had it—for him it was humility, endurance, and compassionate will.

There are other names you'll see again and again in this book: Ulysses S. Grant. Thomas Edison. Queen Elizabeth II. Samuel Zemurray. Amelia Earhart. Dwight D. Eisenhower. Richard Wright. Jack Johnson. Theodore Roosevelt. Steve Jobs. James Stockdale. Laura Ingalls Wilder.

Some of these men and women faced unimaginable horrors, from imprisonment to debilitating illnesses, in addition to day-to-day frustrations that were no different from ours. They dealt with the same rivalries, political headwinds, drama, resistance, conservatism, breakups, stresses, and economic calamities. Or worse.

Subjected to those pressures, these individuals were transformed. They were transformed along the lines that Andy Grove, former CEO of Intel, outlined when he described what happens to businesses in tumultuous times: "Bad companies are destroyed by crisis. Good companies survive them. Great companies are improved by them."

Great individuals, like great companies, find a way to transform weakness into strength. It's a rather amazing and even touching feat. They took what should have held them back—what in fact might be holding you back right this very second—and used it to move forward.

As it turns out, this is one thing all great men and women of history have in common. Like oxygen to a fire, obstacles became fuel for the blaze that was their ambition. Nothing could stop them, and they were (and continue to be) impossible to discourage or contain. Every impediment only served to make the inferno within them burn with greater ferocity.

These were people who flipped their obstacles upside down. Who lived the words of Marcus Aurelius and followed a group that Cicero called the only "real philosophers"—the ancient Stoics—even if they'd never read them. They had the ability to see obstacles for what they were, the ingenuity to tackle them, and the will to endure a world mostly beyond their comprehension and control.

Let's be honest. Most of the time we don't find ourselves in horrible situations we must simply endure. Rather, we face some minor disadvantage or get stuck with some less-than-favorable conditions. Or we're trying to do something really hard and find ourselves outmatched, overstretched, or out of ideas. Well, the same logic applies. Turn it around. Find some benefit. Use it as fuel.

It's simple. Simple but, of course, not easy.

This is not a book of gushing, hazy optimism. This is not a book that tells you to deny when stuff sucks or to turn the other cheek when you've been completely screwed over. There will be no folksy sayings or cute but utterly ineffectual proverbs.

This is also not an academic study or history of Stoicism.

There is plenty written about Stoicism out there, much of it by some of the wisest and greatest thinkers who ever lived. There is no need to rewrite what they have written—go read the originals. No philosophic writing is more accessible. It feels like it was written last year, not last millennium.

But here we will take their collective wisdom—as it was passed down in books, diaries, songs, poems, and stories, refined in the crucible of human experience over thousands of years—and help you apply it to the very specific and increasingly urgent goal we all share: overcoming obstacles. Mental obstacles. Physical obstacles. Emotional obstacles. Perceived obstacles.

We face them every day. Getting a little better at facing and dismantling such stumbling blocks is an important first step. But here's a bigger promise: What if you could turn every obstacle into an *advantage*? *What if you could use each one to become who you were meant to become in that moment?*

So this will be a book of ruthless pragmatism and stories from history that illustrate the arts of relentless persistence and indefatigable ingenuity. It teaches you how to get unstuck, unfucked, and unleashed. How to turn the many negative situations we encounter in our lives into positive ones—or at least to snatch whatever benefit we can from them. To steal good fortune from misfortune.

It's not just: *How can I think this is not so bad?* No, it is how to will yourself to see that this must be good—an opportunity to gain a new foothold, move forward, or go in a better direction. Not "be positive" but learn to be ceaselessly creative and opportunistic.

Not: *This is not so bad.*

But: *I can make this good.*

Because it can be done. In fact, it has and *is* being done. Every day. That's the power we will unlock in this book.

The Obstacles That Lie Before Us

There is an old Zen story about a king whose people had grown soft and entitled. Dissatisfied with this state of affairs, he hoped to teach them a lesson. His plan was simple: He would place a large boulder in the middle of the main road, completely blocking entry into the city. He would then hide nearby and observe their reactions.

How would they respond? Would they band together to remove it? Or would they get discouraged, quit, and return home?

With growing disappointment, the king watched as subject after subject came to this impediment and turned away. Or, at best, tried halfheartedly before giving up. Many openly complained or cursed the king or fortune or bemoaned the inconvenience, but none managed to do anything about it.

After several days, a lone peasant came along on his way into town. He did not turn away. Instead he strained and strained, trying to push it out of the way. Then an idea came to him: He scrambled into the nearby woods to find something he could use for leverage. Finally, he returned with a large branch he had crafted into a lever and deployed it to dislodge the massive rock from the road.

Beneath the rock were a purse of gold coins and a note from the king, which said:

The obstacle in the path becomes the path. Never forget, within every obstacle is an opportunity to improve our condition.

What holds you back?

The Physical? Size. Race. Distance. Disability. Money.

The Mental? Fear. Uncertainty. Inexperience. Prejudice.

Perhaps people don't take you seriously. Or you think you're too old. Or you lack support or enough resources. Maybe laws or regulations restrict your options. Or your obligations do. Or false goals and self-doubt.

Whatever it is, here you are. Here we all are.

And . . .

These are obstacles. I get it. No one is denying that.

But run down the list of those who came before you. Athletes who were too small. Pilots whose eyesight wasn't good enough. Dreamers ahead of their time. Members of this race or that. Dropouts and dyslexics. Bastards, immigrants, nouveaux riches, sticklers, believers, and weirdos. Or those who came from nothing or worse, from places where their very existence was threatened on a daily basis. What happened to them?

Well, far too many gave up. But a few didn't. They took "twice as good" as a challenge. They practiced harder. Looked for shortcuts and weak spots. Discerned allies among strange faces. Got kicked around a bit. *Everything* was an obstacle they had to flip.

And so?

Within those obstacles was an opportunity. They seized it. They did something special because of it. We can learn from them.

Whether we're having trouble getting a job, fighting

against discrimination, running low on funds, stuck in a bad relationship, locking horns with some aggressive opponent, have an employee or student we just can't seem to reach, or are in the middle of a creative block, we need to know that there is a way. When we meet with adversity, we can turn it to advantage, based on their example.

All great victories, be they in politics, business, art, or seduction, involved resolving vexing problems with a potent cocktail of creativity, focus, and daring. When you have a goal, obstacles are actually teaching you how to get where you want to go—carving you a path. "The Things which hurt," Benjamin Franklin wrote, "*instruct*."

Today, most of our obstacles are internal, not external. Since World War II we have lived in some of the most prosperous times in history. There are fewer armies to face, fewer fatal diseases, and far more safety nets. But the world still rarely does exactly what we want.

Instead of opposing enemies, we have internal tension. We have professional frustration. We have unmet expectations. We have learned helplessness. And we still have the same overwhelming emotions humans have always had: grief, pain, loss.

Many of our problems come from having too much: rapid technological disruption, junk food, traditions that tell us the way we're supposed to live our lives. We're soft, entitled, and scared of conflict. Great times are great softeners. Abundance can be its own obstacle, as many people can attest.

Our generation needs an approach for overcoming obstacles and thriving amid chaos more than ever. One that will help turn our problems on their heads, using them as canvases on which to paint masterworks. This flexible approach is fit for an entrepreneur or an artist, a conqueror or a coach, whether you're a struggling writer or a sage or a hardworking soccer mom.

The Way Through Them

Objective judgment, now at this very moment.
Unselfish action, now at this very moment.
Willing acceptance—now at this very moment—of all external events.
That's all you need.

—MARCUS AURELIUS

Overcoming obstacles is a discipline of three critical steps.

It begins with how we look at our specific problems, our attitude or approach; then the energy and creativity with which we actively break them down and turn them into opportunities; finally, the cultivation and maintenance of an inner will that allows us to handle defeat and difficulty.

It's three interdependent, interconnected, and fluidly contingent disciplines: *Perception*, *Action*, and the *Will*.

It's a simple process (but again, never easy).

We will trace the use of this process by its practitioners throughout history, business, and literature. As we look at specific examples of each step from every angle, we'll learn to inculcate this attitude and capture its ingenuity—and by doing so discover how to create new openings wherever a door is shut.

From the stories of the practitioners we'll learn how to handle common obstacles—whether we're locked out or hemmed in, the kind of obstacles that have impeded people for all time—and how to apply their general approach to our lives. Because obstacles are not only to be expected but embraced.

Embraced?

Yes, because these obstacles are actually opportunities to test ourselves, to try new things, and, ultimately, to triumph.

The Obstacle is the Way.

PART I

Perception

WHAT IS PERCEPTION? It's how we see and understand what occurs around us—and what we decide those events will mean. Our perceptions can be a source of strength or of great weakness. If we are emotional, subjective, and short-sighted, we only add to our troubles. To prevent becoming overwhelmed by the world around us, we must, as the ancients practiced, learn how to limit our passions and their control over our lives. It takes skill and discipline to bat away the pests of bad perceptions, to separate reliable signals from deceptive ones, to filter out prejudice, expectation, and fear. But it's worth it, for what's left is *truth*. While others are excited or afraid, we will remain calm and imperturbable. We will see things simply and straightforwardly, as they truly are—neither good nor bad. This will be an incredible advantage for us in the fight against obstacles.

THE DISCIPLINE OF PERCEPTION

Before he was an oilman, John D. Rockefeller was a bookkeeper and an aspiring investor—a small-time financier in Cleveland, Ohio. The son of a criminal who'd abandoned his family, the young Rockefeller took his first job in 1855 at the age of sixteen (a day he celebrated as "Job Day" for the rest of his life). All was well enough at fifty cents a day.

Then the panic struck. Specifically, the Panic of 1857, a massive national financial crisis that originated in Ohio and hit Cleveland particularly hard. As businesses failed and the price of grain plummeted across the country, westward expansion quickly came to a halt. The result was a crippling depression that lasted for several years.

Rockefeller could have gotten scared. Here was the greatest market depression in history and it hit him just as he was finally getting the hang of things. He could have pulled out and run like his father. He could have quit finance altogether for a different career with less risk. But even as a young man, Rockefeller had sangfroid: unflappable coolness under pressure. He could keep his head while he was losing his shirt. Better yet, he kept his head while everyone else lost theirs.

And so instead of bemoaning this economic upheaval, Rockefeller eagerly observed the momentous events. Almost perversely, he chose to look at it all as an opportunity to learn, a baptism in the market. He quietly saved his money and watched what others did wrong. He saw the weaknesses in the economy that many took for granted and how this left them all unprepared for change or shocks.

He internalized an important lesson that would stay with him forever: The market was inherently unpredictable and often vicious—only the rational and disciplined mind could hope to profit from it. Speculation led to disaster, he realized, and he needed to always ignore the "mad crowd" and its inclinations.

Rockefeller immediately put those insights to use. At twenty-five, a group of investors offered to put approximately $500,000 at his disposal if he could find the right oil wells in which to deploy the money. Grateful for the opportunity, Rockefeller set out to tour the nearby oil fields. A few days later, he shocked his backers by returning to Cleveland empty-handed, not having spent or invested a dollar of the funds. The opportunity didn't feel right to him at the time, no matter how excited the rest of the market was—so he refunded the money and stayed away from drilling.

It was this intense self-discipline and objectivity that allowed Rockefeller to seize advantage from obstacle after obstacle in his life, during the Civil War, and the panics of 1873, 1907, and 1929. As he once put it: He was inclined to see the opportunity in every disaster. To that we could add: He had the strength to resist temptation or excitement, no matter how seductive, no matter the situation.

Within twenty years of that first crisis, Rockefeller alone would control 90 percent of the oil market. His greedy competitors had perished. His nervous colleagues had sold their shares and left the business. His weakhearted doubters had missed out.

For the rest of his life, the greater the chaos, the calmer Rockefeller would become, particularly when others around him were either panicked or mad with greed. He would make much of his fortune during these market fluctuations—because he could see while others could not. This insight lives on today in Warren Buffett's famous adage to "be fearful when others are greedy and greedy when others are fearful." Rockefeller, like all great investors, could resist impulse in favor of cold, hard common sense.

One activist described the Standard Oil trust as a "mythical protean creature" capable of metamorphosing with every attempt by competitors or the government to dismantle it. They meant it as a criticism (and they had a point), but even this critique, and his clearly illegal monopoly, tell us something of Rockefeller's personality. He was resilient, adaptable, calm, always growing, hard to pin down. He could not be rattled—not by economic crisis, not by a glittery mirage of false opportunities, not by aggressive, bullying enemies, not even by federal prosecutors (for whom he was a notoriously difficult witness to cross-examine, never rising to take the bait or defend himself or get upset). This is what great investors cultivate, a rational self-command that allows them to see what others can't, to size up situations and anticipate what's coming next . . . and then to take advantage of it.

Was Rockefeller born this way? No. This was learned behavior. And Rockefeller got this lesson in discipline somewhere. It began in that crisis of 1857 in what he called "the school of adversity and stress."

"Oh, how blessed young men are who have to struggle for a foundation and beginning in life," he once said. "I shall never cease to be grateful for the three and a half years of apprenticeship and the difficulties to be overcome, all along the way."

Of course, many people experienced the same perilous times as Rockefeller—they all attended the same school of bad times. But few reacted as he did. Not many had trained themselves to see opportunity inside this obstacle, that what befell them was not unsalvageable misfortune but the gift of education—a chance to *learn* from a rare moment in economic history.

You will come across obstacles in life—fair and unfair. And you will discover, time and time again, that what matters most is not what these obstacles are but how we see them, how we react to them, and whether we keep our composure. You will learn that this reaction determines how successful we will be in overcoming—or possibly thriving because of—them.

Where one person sees a crisis, another can see opportunity. Where one is blinded by success, another sees reality with ruthless objectivity. Where one loses control of emotions, another can remain calm. Desperation, despair, fear, powerlessness—these reactions are functions of our perceptions. You must realize: Nothing *makes* us feel this way; we *choose* to give in to such feelings. Or, like Rockefeller, choose *not* to.

And it is precisely at this divergence—between how Rockefeller perceived his environment and how the rest of the world typically does—that his nearly incomprehensible success was born. His careful, cautious self-confidence was an incredible form of power. To perceive what others see as negative, as something to be approached rationally, clearly, and, most important, as an opportunity—not as something to fear or bemoan.

Rockefeller is more than just an analogy.

We live in our own Gilded Age. In a few short decades, we've experienced major economic bubbles, a devastating global pandemic, civil unrest, and technological disruption. Entire industries are crumbling, people feel unmoored. What feels like unfairness abounds. Adversity is everywhere. It's frustrating. It's unfair. It's all awful.

Not necessarily.

Outward appearances are deceptive. What's contained within a circumstance, what we can turn it into, is what matters.

We can learn to perceive things differently, to cut through the illusions that others believe or fear. We can stop seeing the "problems" in front of us as problems. We can learn to focus on what things really are.

Too often we react emotionally, get despondent, and lose our perspective. All that does is turn bad things into really bad things. Unhelpful perceptions can invade our minds—that sacred place of reason, action, and will—and throw off our compass.

Our brains evolved for an environment very different from the one we currently inhabit. As a result, we carry all kinds of biological baggage. Humans are still primed to detect threats and dangers that no longer exist—think of the cold sweat when you're stressed about money, or the fight-or-flight response that kicks in when your boss yells at you. Our safety is not truly at risk here—there is little danger that we will starve or that violence will break out—though it certainly feels that way sometimes.

We have a choice about how we respond to this situation (or any situation, for that matter). We can be blindly led by these primal feelings or we can understand them and learn to filter them. Discipline in perception lets you clearly see the advantage and the proper course of action in every situation—without the pestilence of panic or fear.

Rockefeller understood this well and threw off the fetters of bad, destructive perceptions. He honed the ability to control and channel and understand these signals. It was like a superpower; because most people can't access this part of themselves, they are slaves to impulses and instincts they have never questioned.

Was Rockefeller perfect? No. He was a rapacious tycoon who amassed more money than any person could use in their lifetime. It's good that he gave a lot of it away, that his fortune still has an impact long after his death. But the damage he left in his wake as he destroyed every competitor (and the environment) lingers on as well. We don't have to hold him up as the perfect model of the perfect life—we can simply learn from his ability to perceive and feel his way through panics and bubbles, challenges and crises.

And yes, Rockefeller became obscenely wealthy but that's not the kind of wealth the Stoics were after. "The greatest empire," Seneca—an adviser to emperors and a wealthy man himself—would say, "is command of yourself." Rockefeller ruled over an enormous business empire, but first and foremost, at least when it comes to the art of the market, he ruled over himself.

Each of us has this power. We can learn to see all things

rationally. Or better, like Rockefeller, we can see *opportunity* everywhere, including in disaster, and transform negative situations into an education, a skill set, or a fortune. Seen properly, everything that happens—be it an economic crash or a personal tragedy—is a chance to move forward. Even if it is on a bearing that we did not anticipate.

There are a few things to keep in mind when faced with a seemingly insurmountable obstacle. We must try:

To be objective
To control emotions and keep an even keel
To choose to see the good in a situation
To steady our nerves
To ignore what disturbs or limits others
To place things in perspective
To revert to the present moment
To focus on what can be controlled

This is how you see the opportunity within the obstacle. It does not happen on its own. It is a process—one that results from self-discipline and logic.

And that logic is available to you. You just need to deploy it.

RECOGNIZE YOUR POWER

A podium and a prison is each a place, one high and the
other low, but in either place your freedom of choice
can be maintained if you so wish.

—EPICTETUS

Rubin "Hurricane" Carter, a top contender for the mid-
dleweight title at the height of his boxing career in the
mid-1960s, was wrongly accused of a horrific crime he did
not commit: triple homicide. He went on trial, and a biased,
bogus verdict followed: three life sentences.

It was a dizzying fall from the heights of success and fame.
Carter reported to prison in an expensive, tailored suit, wearing a $5,000 diamond ring and a gold watch. And so, waiting
in line to be entered into the general inmate population, he
asked to speak to someone in charge.

Looking the warden in the eye, Carter proceeded to in-
form him and the guards that he was not giving up the last
thing he controlled: himself. He knew that the guards had
nothing to do with the injustice that brought him to the jail,
and he accepted that he would have to remain there for
some time. He was clear from the beginning: he would not
be treated like a prisoner—because he was not *powerless*.

Instead of breaking down—as many would have done in such a bleak situation—Carter declined to surrender the freedoms that were innately his: his attitude, his beliefs, his choices. Whether they threw him in prison or threw him in solitary confinement for weeks on end, Carter maintained that he still had choices, choices that could not be taken from him even though his physical freedom had been.

Was he angry about what happened? Of course. He was furious. But understanding that anger was not constructive, he refused to rage. He refused to break or grovel or despair. He would not wear a uniform, eat prison food, accept visitors, attend parole hearings, or work in the commissary to reduce his sentence. And he wouldn't be touched. No one could lay a hand on him, unless they wanted a fight.

All of this had a purpose: Every second of his energy was to be spent on his legal case. Every waking minute was spent reading—law books, philosophy, history. They hadn't ruined his life—they'd just put him somewhere he didn't deserve to be and he did not intend to stay there. He would learn and read and make the most of the time he had on his hands. He would leave prison not only a free and innocent man, but a better and improved one.

It took nineteen years and two trials to overturn that verdict, but when Carter walked out of prison, he simply resumed his life. No civil suit to recover damages, Carter did not even request an apology from the court. Because to him, that would imply that they'd taken something of his, that Carter was owed something. That had never been his view, even in the dark depths of solitary confinement. He had made his choice: This can't harm me—I might not have wanted it to happen, but I decide how it will affect me. *No one else has the right.*

We, too, decide what we will make of each and every situation. We decide whether we'll break or whether we'll resist. We decide whether we'll assent or reject. No one can force us to give up or to believe something that is untrue (such as, that a situation is absolutely hopeless or impossible to improve). Our perceptions are the thing that we're in complete control of.

They can throw us in jail, label us, deprive us of our possessions, but they'll never control our thoughts, our beliefs, our *reactions*.

Which is to say, we are never completely powerless.

Even in prison, deprived of nearly everything, some freedoms remain. Your mind remains your own (if you're lucky, you have books) and you have time—lots of time. Carter did not have much power, but he understood that that was not the same thing as being *powerless*. Many great figures, from Nelson Mandela to James Stockdale to Malcolm X, have come to understand this fundamental distinction. It's how they turned prison into the workshop where they transformed themselves and the schoolhouse where they began to transform others.

If an unjust prison sentence can be not only salvaged but transformative and beneficial, then for our purposes, nothing we'll experience is likely without potential benefit. In fact, if we have our wits fully about us, we can step back and remember that situations, by themselves, cannot be good or bad. This is something—a judgment—that we, as human beings, bring to them with our perceptions.

To one person a situation may be negative. To another, that same situation may be positive.

"There is nothing either good or bad, but thinking makes it so," as Shakespeare put it.

Laura Ingalls Wilder, author of the classic series Little

House on the Prairie, lived that idea, facing some of the toughest and most unwelcoming elements on the planet: harsh and unyielding soil, Indian territory, Kansas prairies, and the humid backwoods of Florida. Not afraid, not jaded—because she saw it all as an adventure. Everywhere was a chance to do something new, to persevere with cheery pioneer spirit, whatever fate befell her and her husband.

That isn't to say she saw the world through delusional rose-colored glasses. Instead, she simply chose to see each situation for what it could be—accompanied by hard work and a little upbeat spirit. Others make the opposite choice. As for us, we face things that are not nearly as intimidating, and then we promptly decide we're screwed.

This is how obstacles become obstacles.

In other words, through our perception of events, we are complicit in the creation—as well as the destruction—of every one of our obstacles.

There is no good or bad without us, there is only perception. There is the event itself and the story we tell ourselves about what it means.

That's a thought that changes everything, doesn't it?

An employee in your company makes a careless mistake that costs you business. This can be exactly what you spend so much time and effort trying to avoid. *Or*, with a shift in perception, it can be exactly what you were looking for—the chance to pierce through defenses and teach a lesson that can be learned only by experience. A *mistake* becomes *training*.

Again, the event is the same: Someone messed up. But the evaluation and the outcome are different. With one approach you took advantage; with the other you succumbed to anger or fear.

Just because your mind tells you that something is awful or evil or unplanned or otherwise negative doesn't mean you have to agree. Just because other people say that something is hopeless or crazy or broken to pieces doesn't mean it is. We decide what story to tell ourselves. Or whether we will tell one at all.

Welcome to the power of perception. Applicable in each and every situation, impossible to obstruct. It can only be *relinquished.*

And that is your decision.

STEADY YOUR NERVES

What such a man needs is not courage but nerve control, cool headedness. This he can get only by practice.

—THEODORE ROOSEVELT

Ulysses S. Grant once sat for a photo shoot with the famous Civil War photographer Mathew Brady. The studio was too dark, so Brady sent an assistant up to the roof to uncover a skylight. The assistant slipped and shattered the window. With horror, the spectators watched as shards of glass two inches long fell from the ceiling like daggers, crashing around Grant—each one of them plenty lethal.

As the last pieces hit the ground, Brady looked over and saw that Grant hadn't moved. He was unhurt. Grant glanced up at the hole in the ceiling, then back at the camera as though nothing had happened at all.

During the Overland Campaign, Grant was surveying the scene through field glasses when an enemy shell exploded, killing the horse immediately next to him. Grant's eyes stayed fixed on the front, never leaving the glasses. There's another story about Grant at City Point, Union headquarters, near Richmond. Troops were unloading a steamboat and it suddenly exploded. Everyone hit the dirt except Grant, who was seen running toward the scene of the explosion as debris and shells and even bodies rained down.

He didn't just become this way. It was trained into him. Grant's father had deliberately exposed his son to loud noises to steel his nerves. In fact, as a boy, Grant came to enjoy the challenge of it, once showing a neighbor that he wouldn't cry if a pistol was fired near him. "Fick it again," an unflinching Grant cheered. "Fick it again!"

That's a person no one is going to be able to intimidate or scare.

But back in our lives . . .

We are a pile of raw nerves.

Competitors surround our business. Unexpected problems suddenly rear their heads. Our best worker suddenly quits. The computer system can't handle the load we're putting on it. We're out of our comfort zone. The boss is making us do all the work. Everything is falling and crashing down around us, exactly when we feel like we can't handle any more.

Do we stare it down? Ignore it? Blink once or twice and redouble our concentration? Or do we get shaken up? Do we try to medicate these "bad" feelings away?

And that's just the stuff that happens unintentionally. Don't forget, there are always people out there looking to get you. They want to intimidate you. Rattle you. Pressure you into making a decision before you've gotten all the facts. They want you thinking and acting on their terms, not yours.

So the question is, Are you going to let them?

When we aim high, pressure and stress obligingly come along for the ride. Stuff is going to happen that catches us off guard, threatens or scares us. Surprises (unpleasant ones, mostly) are almost guaranteed. The risk of being over-whelmed is always there.

In these situations, talent is not the most sought-after characteristic. Grace and poise are, because these two attri-butes precede the opportunity to deploy any other skill. We must possess, as Voltaire once explained about the secret to the great military success of the first Duke of Marlborough, that "tranquil courage in the midst of tumult and serenity of soul in danger, which the English call a cool head."

Regardless of how much actual danger we're in, stress puts us at the potential whim of our baser—fearful—instinctual reactions.

Don't think for a second that grace and poise and seren-ity are the soft attributes of some aristocrat. Ultimately, nerve is a matter of defiance and control.

Like: *I* refuse *to acknowledge that. I don't* agree *to be intimi-dated. I* resist *the temptation to declare this a failure.*

But nerve is also a matter of acceptance: *Well, I guess it's on me then. I don't have the luxury of being shaken up about this or replaying close calls in my head. I'm too busy and too many people are counting on me.*

Defiance and acceptance come together well in the fol-lowing principle: There is always a countermove, always an escape or a way through, so there is no reason to get worked up. No one said it would be easy and, of course, the stakes are high, but the path is there for those ready to take it.

This is what we've got to do. And we know that it's going to be tough, maybe even scary.

But we're ready for that. We're collected and serious and aren't going to be frightened off.

This means preparing for the realities of our situation,

steadying our nerves so we can throw our best at it. Steeling ourselves. Shaking off the bad stuff as it happens and soldiering on—staring straight ahead as though nothing has happened.

Because, as you now realize, it's true. If your nerve holds, then nothing really did "happen"—our perception made sure it was nothing of consequence.

CONTROL YOUR EMOTIONS

Would you have a great empire? Rule over yourself.

—PUBLILIUS SYRUS

When America raced to send the first men into space, they trained the astronauts in one skill more than in any other: the art of *not* panicking.

When people panic, they make mistakes. They override systems. They disregard procedures, ignore rules. They deviate from the plan. They become unresponsive and stop thinking clearly. They just react—not to what they need to react to, but to the survival hormones that are coursing through their veins.

Welcome to the source of most of our problems down here on earth. Everything is planned down to the letter, then something goes wrong and the first thing we do is trade in our plan for a good ol' emotional freak-out. Some of us almost crave sounding the alarm, because it's easier than dealing with whatever is staring us in the face.

At 150 miles above earth in a spaceship smaller than a VW, this is death. Panic is suicide.

So panic has to be trained out. And it does not go easily.

Before the first launch, NASA re-created the fateful day for the astronauts over and over, step by step, hundreds of times—from what they'd have for breakfast to the ride to the airfield. Slowly, in a graded series of "exposures," the astronauts were introduced to every sight and sound of the experience of their firing into space. They did it so many times that it became as natural and familiar as breathing. They'd practice all the way through, holding nothing back but the liftoff itself, making sure to solve for every variable and remove all uncertainty.

Uncertainty and fear are relieved by authority. Training is authority. It's a release valve. With enough exposure, you can adapt out those perfectly ordinary, even innate, fears that are bred mostly from unfamiliarity. Fortunately, unfamiliarity is simple to fix (again, not easy), which makes it possible to increase our tolerance for stress and uncertainty.

John Glenn, the first American astronaut to orbit the earth, spent nearly a day in space still keeping his heart rate under a hundred beats per minute. That's a man not simply sitting *at* the controls but *in control* of his emotions. A man who had properly cultivated what Tom Wolfe later called "the right stuff."

But you . . . confront a client or a stranger on the street and your heart is liable to burst out of your chest, or you are called on to address a crowd and your stomach crashes through the floor.

It's time to realize that this is a luxury, an indulgence of our lesser self. In space, the difference between life and death lies in emotional regulation.

Hitting the wrong button, reading the instrument panels incorrectly, engaging a sequence too early—none of these could have been afforded on a successful Apollo mission—the consequences were too great.

Thus, the question for astronauts was not *How skilled a pilot are you?*, but *Can you keep an even strain?* Can you fight the urge to panic and instead focus only on what you can change? On the task at hand?

Life is really no different. Obstacles make us emotional, but the only way we'll survive or overcome them is by keeping those emotions in check—if we can keep steady no matter what happens, no matter how much external events may fluctuate.

The Greeks had a few words for this—*Apatheia. Ataraxia.* We might call it *stillness.*

It's the kind of equanimity and self-command that comes with the absence of irrational or extreme emotions. Not the loss of feeling altogether, just the loss of the harmful, unhelpful kind. Don't let the negativity in, don't let those emotions even get started. Just say: *No, thank you. I can't afford to panic.*

This is the skill that must be cultivated—freedom from disturbance and perturbation—so you can focus your energy exclusively on solving problems, rather than reacting to them.

A boss's urgent email. An asshole at a bar. A call from the bank—your financing has been pulled. A knock at the door—there's been an accident.

As Gavin de Becker writes in *The Gift of Fear,* "When you worry, ask yourself, 'What am I choosing to not see right now?' What important things are you missing because you chose worry over introspection, alertness or wisdom?" The Canadian astronaut Chris Hadfield, who once had both his eyes freeze shut on a solo walk in space, explained that there are always things we can think and do that will make a situation better. But it's worth remembering, he said, "There's no problem so bad that you cannot make it worse also."

Or, another way of putting it: Does getting upset provide you with more options?

Sometimes it does. But in *this* instance?

No, I suppose not.

Well, then.

If an emotion can't change the condition or the situation you're dealing with, it is likely an unhelpful emotion. Or, quite possibly, a destructive one.

But it's what I feel.

Right, no one said anything about not feeling it. No one said you can't ever cry. Forget "manliness." If you need to take a moment, by all means, go ahead. Real strength lies in the *control* or, as Nassim Nicholas Taleb put it, the *domestication* of one's emotions, not in pretending they don't exist.

So go ahead, feel it. Just don't lie to yourself by conflating emoting about a problem and dealing with it. Because they are as different as sleeping and waking.

You can always remind yourself: *I am in control, not my emotions. I see what's really going on here. I'm not going to get excited or upset.*

We defeat emotions with logic, or at least that's the idea. Logic is questions and statements. With enough of them, we get to root causes (which are always easier to deal with).

We lost money.

But aren't losses a pretty common part of business?

Yes.

Are these losses catastrophic?

Not necessarily.

So this is not totally unexpected, is it? How could that be so bad? Why are you all worked up over something that is at least occasionally supposed to happen?

Well . . . uhh . . . I . . .

And not only that, but you've dealt with worse situations than this. Wouldn't you be better off applying some of that resourcefulness rather than getting angry?

Try having that conversation with yourself and see how those extreme emotions hold up. They won't last long, trust that.

After all, you're probably not going to *die* from any of this.

It might help to say it over and over again whenever you feel the anxiety begin to come on: *I am not going to die from this. I am not going to die from this. I am not going to die from this.*

Or try Marcus's question:

Does what happened keep you from acting with justice, generosity, self-control, sanity, prudence, honesty, humility, straightforward-ness?

Nope.

Then get back to work!

We should be constantly asking ourselves this question: *Do I need to freak out about this?*

And the answer—like it is for astronauts, for soldiers, for doctors, and for so many other professionals—must be: *No, because I practiced for this situation and I can control myself.* Or, *No, because I caught myself and I'm able to realize that that doesn't add anything constructive.*

PRACTICE OBJECTIVITY

> Don't let the force of an impression when it first hits you
> knock you off your feet; just say to it: Hold on a moment;
> let me see who you are and what you represent. Let me
> put you to the test.
>
> —EPICTETUS

The phrase "This happened and it is bad" is actually two impressions. The first—"This happened"—is objective. The second—"it is bad"—is subjective.

The seventeenth-century samurai swordsman Miyamoto Musashi won countless fights against feared opponents, even multiple opponents at the same time, in which he was swordless. In *The Book of Five Rings*, he notes the difference between observing and perceiving. The perceiving eye is weak, he wrote; the observing eye is strong.

Musashi understood that the observing eye sees simply what is there. The perceiving eye sees more than what is there.

The observing eye sees events, clear of distractions, exaggerations, and misperceptions. The perceiving eye sees "insurmountable obstacles" or "major setbacks" or even just "issues." It brings its own issues to the fight. The former is helpful, the latter is not.

To paraphrase Nietzsche, sometimes being superficial—taking things only at first glance—is the most profound approach.

In our own lives, how many problems seem to come from applying judgments to things we don't control, as though there were a way they were *supposed* to be? How often do we see what we think is there or should be there, instead of what actually is there?

The Stoics knew that it was not events or things that upset us; *it was our opinion about those things* that caused the problem.

Perceptions often give us "information" that we don't need, exactly at the moment when it would be far better to focus on what is immediately in front of us: the thrust of a sword, a crucial business negotiation, an opportunity, a flash of insight, or anything else, for that matter.

Everything about our animalistic brains tries to compress the space between impression and perception. Think, perceive, act—with milliseconds between them.

A deer's brain tells it to run because things are bad. It runs. Sometimes . . . right into traffic. Our mind tells us we've been insulted, that all is lost, that we're screwed. We can question that impulse. We can disagree with it. We can override the switch, examine the threat before we act. Having steadied ourselves and held back our emotions, we can see things as they really are. We can do that using our observing eye.

But this takes strength. It's a muscle that must be developed. And muscles are developed by tension, by lifting and holding.

This is why Musashi and most martial arts practitioners focus on mental training as much as on physical training.

Both are equally important—and require equally vigorous exercise and practice.

In the writings of the Stoics we see an exercise that might well be described as Contemptuous Expressions. The Stoics use contempt as an agent to lay things bare and "*to strip away the legend that encrusts them.*"

Epictetus told his students, when they'd quote some great thinker, to picture themselves observing the person having sex. It's funny—you should try it the next time someone intimidates you or makes you feel insecure. See them in your mind, grunting, groaning, and awkward in their private life—just like the rest of us.

Marcus Aurelius had a version of this exercise where he'd describe glamorous or expensive things without their euphemisms—roasted meat is a dead animal and vintage wine is old, fermented grapes. The aim was to see these things as they really are, without any of the ornamentation.

We can do this for anyone or to anything that stands in our way. That promotion that means so much, what is it really? Our critics and naysayers who make us feel small, let's put them in their proper place. It's so much better to see things as they truly, actually are, not as we've made them in our minds.

Objectivity means removing "you"—the subjective part—from the equation. Just think, what happens when we give others advice? Their problems are crystal clear to us, the solutions obvious. Something that's present when we deal with our own obstacles is always missing when we hear other people's problems: the baggage. With other people we can be objective.

We take the situation at face value and immediately set

about helping our friend to solve it. Selfishly—and stupidly—we save the pity and the sense of persecution and the complaints for our own lives.

Take your situation and pretend it is not happening to you. Pretend it is not important, that it doesn't matter. How much easier would it be for you to know what to do? How much more quickly and dispassionately could you size up the scenario and its options? You could write it off, greet it calmly.

Think of all the ways that someone could solve a specific problem. No, *really* think. Give yourself clarity, not sympathy—there'll be plenty of time for that later. It's an exercise, which means it takes repetition. The more you try it, the better you get at it. The more skilled you become at seeing things for what they are, the more perception will work for you rather than against you.

ALTER YOUR PERSPECTIVE

Man does not simply exist but always decides what his
existence will be, what he will become the next moment.
By the same token, every human being has the freedom
to change at any instant.

—VIKTOR FRANKL

Once, as the Athenian general Pericles cast off on a naval
mission in the Peloponnesian War, the sun was eclipsed
and his fleet of 150 ships was cast into darkness.

Surprised by this unexpected and confusing event, his
men were thrown into a state of panic. Unlike the crew, Pericles was undaunted. He walked up to a lead steersman, removed the cloak he was wearing, and held it up around the
man's face. He asked the man if he was scared of what he saw.

No, of course not.

So what does it matter, Pericles replied, when the cause of
the darkness differs?

The Greeks were clever. But beneath this particular quip
is the fundamental notion that girds not just Stoic philosophy but cognitive psychology: *Perspective is everything.*

That is, when you can break apart something, or look at it
from some new angle, it loses its power over you.

Fear is debilitating, distracting, tiring, and often irrational. Pericles understood this completely, and he was able to use the power of perspective to defeat it.

The Greeks understood that we often choose the ominous explanation over the simple one, to our detriment. That we are scared of obstacles because our perspective is wrong—that a simple shift in perspective can change our reaction entirely. The task, as Pericles showed, is not to ignore fear but to explain it away. Take what you're afraid of—when fear strikes you—and break it apart.

Remember: We choose how we'll look at things. We retain the ability to inject perspective into a situation. We can't change the obstacles themselves—that part of the equation is set—but the power of perspective can change how the obstacles appear. How we approach, view, and contextualize an obstacle, and what we tell ourselves it means, determines how daunting and trying it will be to overcome.

It's your choice whether you want to put *I* in front of something (I *hate public speaking.* I *screwed up.* I *am harmed by this*). These add an extra element: you in relation to that obstacle, rather than just the obstacle itself. And with the wrong perspective, we become consumed and overwhelmed with something actually quite small. So why subject ourselves to that?

The right perspective has a strange way of cutting obstacles—and adversity—down to size.

But for whatever reason, we tend to look at things in isolation. We kick ourselves for blowing a deal or having to miss a meeting. Individually, that does suck—we just missed 100 percent of that opportunity.

What we're forgetting in that instance, as billionaire

serial entrepreneur Richard Branson likes to say, is that "business opportunities are like buses; there's always another coming around." One meeting is nothing in a lifetime of meetings, one deal is just one deal. In fact, we may have actually dodged a bullet. The next opportunity might be better.

The way we look out at the world changes how we see these things. Is our perspective truly giving us perspective or is it what's actually causing the problem? That's the question.

What we can do is limit and expand our perspective to whatever will keep us calmest and most ready for the task at hand. Think of it as selective editing—not to deceive others, but to properly orient ourselves.

And it *works*. Small tweaks can change what once felt like impossible tasks. Suddenly, where we felt weak, we realize we are strong. With perspective, we discover leverage we didn't know we had.

Perspective has two definitions:

1. Context: a sense of the larger picture of the world, not just what is immediately in front of us
2. Framing: an individual's unique way of looking at the world, a way that interprets its events

Both matter, both can be effectively injected to change a situation that previously seemed intimidating or impossible.

George Clooney spent his first years in Hollywood getting rejected at auditions. He wanted the producers and directors to like him, but they didn't and it hurt and he blamed the system for not seeing how good he was.

This perspective should sound familiar. It's the dominant viewpoint for the rest of us on job interviews or when we pitch clients or try to connect with an attractive stranger in a coffee shop. We think we need them when really it's just as true the other way around.

Everything changed for Clooney when he tried a new perspective. He realized that casting is an obstacle for producers, too—they *need* to find somebody, and they're all hoping that the next person to walk in the room is the *right* somebody. Auditions were a chance to solve their problem, not his.

From Clooney's new perspective, he was that solution. He wasn't going to be someone groveling for a shot. He was someone with something special to offer. He was the answer to their prayers, not the other way around. That was what he began projecting in his auditions—not exclusively his acting skills but that he was the man for the job. That he understood what the casting director and producers were looking for in a specific role and that he would deliver it in each and every situation, in preproduction, on camera, and during promotion.

The difference between the right and the wrong perspective is everything.

How we interpret the events in our lives, our perspective, is the framework for our forthcoming response—whether there will even be one or whether we'll just lie there and take it.

Where the head goes, the body follows. Perception precedes action. Right action follows the right perspective.

IS IT UP TO YOU?

In life our first job is this, to divide and distinguish things
into two categories: externals I cannot control, but the choices
I make with regard to them I do control. Where will I find good
and bad? In me, in my choices.

—EPICTETUS

Tommy John, one of baseball's most savvy and durable
pitchers, played twenty-six seasons in the majors. *Twenty-
six* seasons! His rookie year, Kennedy was president. His final year, it was George H. W. Bush. He pitched to Mickey
Mantle *and* Mark McGwire.

It's an almost superhuman accomplishment. But he was
able to do it because he got really good at asking himself
and others, in various forms, one question over and over
again: *Is there a chance? Do I have a shot? Is there something I
can do?*

All he ever looked for was a yes, no matter how slight or
tentative or provisional the chance. If there was a chance,
he was ready to take it and make good use of it—ready to
give every ounce of effort and energy he had to make it happen. If effort would affect the outcome, he would die on the
field before he let that chance go to waste.

The first time came during the middle of the 1974 season when Tommy John blew out his arm, permanently damaging the ulnar collateral ligament in his pitching elbow. Up until this point in baseball and sports medicine, when a pitcher blew out his arm, that was it. They called it a "dead arm" injury. Game over.

John wouldn't accept that. Was there *anything* that could give him a shot to get back on the mound? It turns out there was. The doctors suggested an experimental surgery in which they would try to replace the ligament in his pitching elbow with a tendon from his other arm. *What are the chances of me coming back after this surgery?* One in one hundred. And without it? *No chance*, they said.

He could have retired. But there was a one in one hundred chance. With rehab and training, the opportunity was *partially* in his control. He took it. And won 164 more games over the next thirteen seasons. That procedure is now famously known as Tommy John surgery.

Less than ten years later, John mustered the same spirit and effort he marshaled for his elbow surgery when his young son fell horrifyingly from a third-story window, swallowed his tongue, and nearly died. Even in the chaos of the emergency room, with doctors convinced that the boy probably wouldn't survive, John reminded his family that whether it took one year or ten years, they wouldn't give up until there was absolutely nothing left that they could do.

His son made a full recovery.

For John, his baseball career seemed to finally come to an end in 1988, when, at the age of forty-five, he was cut by the Yankees at the end of the season. Still, he would not accept it. He called the coach and demanded: If he showed up

THE OBSTACLE IS THE WAY

at spring training as a walk-on the next spring, would he get a fair look? They replied that he shouldn't be playing baseball at his age. He repeated the question: *Be straight with me, if I come down there, would I have a chance?* The baseball officials answered, *Fine, yes, you'll get one look.*

So Tommy John was the first to report to camp. He trained many hours a day, brought every lesson he'd learned playing the sport for a quarter century, and made the team—as the oldest player in the game. He started the season opener—and won, giving up a scant two runs over seven innings on the road at Minnesota.

The things that Tommy John could change—when he had a chance—got a full 100 percent of the effort he could muster. He used to tell coaches that he would die on the field before he quit. He understood that as a professional athlete his job was to parse the difference between the unlikely and the impossible. Seeing that minuscule distinction was what made him who he was.

To harness the same power, recovering addicts learn the Serenity Prayer.

> *God, grant me the serenity to accept the things I cannot*
> *change*
> *The courage to change the things I can,*
> *And the wisdom to know the difference.*

This is how they focus their efforts. It's a lot easier to fight addiction when you aren't also fighting the fact that you were born, that your parents were monsters, or that you lost everything. That stuff is done. Delivered. Zero in one hundred chances that you can change it.

So what if you focused on what you *can* change? That's where you can make a difference.

Behind the Serenity Prayer is a two-thousand-year-old Stoic phrase: "*ta eph'hemin, ta ouk eph'hemin.*" What is up to us, what is not up to us.

And what is up to us?

Our emotions
Our judgments
Our creativity
Our attitude
Our perspective
Our desires
Our decisions
Our determination

This is our playing field, so to speak. Everything there is fair game.

What is not up to us?

Well, you know, everything else. The weather, the economy, circumstances, other people's emotions or judgments, trends, disasters, et cetera.

If what's up to us is the playing field, then what is not up to us are the rules and conditions of the game. Factors that winning athletes make the best of and don't spend time arguing against (because there is no point).

To argue, to complain, or worse, to just give up, these are choices. Choices that more often than not do *nothing* to get us across the finish line.

When it comes to perception, this is the crucial distinction to make: the difference between the things that are in our power and the things that aren't. That's the difference between the people who can accomplish great things and the people who find it impossible to stay sober—to avoid not just drugs or alcohol but *all* addictions.

In its own way, the most harmful dragon we chase is the one that makes us think we can change things that are simply not ours to change. That someone decided not to fund your company, this isn't up to you. But the decision to refine and improve your pitch? That is. That someone stole your idea or got to it first? No. To pivot, improve it, or fight for what's yours? Yes.

Focusing exclusively on what is in our power magnifies and enhances our power. But every ounce of energy directed at things we can't actually influence is wasted—self-indulgent and self-destructive. So much power—ours and other people's—is frittered away in this manner.

To see an obstacle as a challenge, to make the best of it anyway, that is also a choice—a choice that is *up to us.*

Will I have a chance, Coach?

Ta eph'hemin?

Is this up to me?

LIVE IN THE PRESENT MOMENT

The trick to forgetting the big picture is to look
at everything close-up.

—CHUCK PALAHNIUK

Do yourself a favor and run down the list of businesses
started during depressions or economic crises.

Fortune magazine (ninety days after the market crash
of 1929)

FedEx (oil crisis of 1973)

UPS (Panic of 1907)

Walt Disney Company (After eleven months of
smooth operation, the twelfth was the market
crash of 1929.)

Hewlett-Packard (Great Depression, 1935)

Charles Schwab (market crash of 1974–75)

Standard Oil (Rockefeller bought out his partners in
what became Standard Oil and took over in
February 1865, the final year of the Civil War)

Coors (Depression of 1873)

Costco (recession in the late 1970s)

Revlon (Great Depression, 1932)

General Motors (Panic of 1907)
Procter & Gamble (Panic of 1837)
United Airlines (Crash of 1929)
Microsoft (recession in 1973–75)
LinkedIn (2002, post-dot-com bubble)

For the most part, these businesses had little awareness they were in some historically significant depression. Why? Because the founders were too busy existing in the present—actually dealing with the situation at hand. They didn't know whether it would get better or worse, they just knew what *was*. They had a job they wanted to do, a great idea they believed in or a product they thought they could sell. They knew they had payroll to meet.

Yet in our own lives, we aren't content to deal with things as they happen. We have to dive endlessly into what everything "means," whether something is "fair" or not, what's "behind" this or that, and what everyone else is doing. Then we wonder why we don't have the energy to actually deal with our problems. Or we get ourselves so worked up and intimidated because of the overthinking that if we'd just gotten to work we'd probably be done already.

Our understanding of the world of business is all mixed up with storytelling and mythology. Which is funny because we're missing the real story by focusing on individuals. In fact, half the companies in the Fortune 500 were started during a bear market or recession. *Half.*

The point is that *most people* start from disadvantage (often with no idea they are doing so) and do just fine. It's not unfair, it's universal. Those who survive it survive because they took things day by day—that's the real secret.

Focus on the moment, not the monsters that may or may not be up ahead.

A business must take the operating constraints of the world around it as a given and work for whatever gains are possible. Those people with an entrepreneurial spirit are like animals, blessed to have no time and no ability to think about the ways things should be, or how they'd prefer them to be.

For all species other than us humans, things just are what they are. Our problem is that we're always trying to figure out what things *mean*—why things are the way they are. As though the why matters. Emerson put it best: "We cannot spend the day in explanation." Don't waste time on false constructs.

It doesn't matter whether this is the worst time to be alive or the best, whether you're in a good job market or a bad one, or that the obstacle you face is intimidating or burdensome. What matters is that right now is right now.

The implications of our obstacle are theoretical—they exist in the past and the future. We live *in the moment.* And the more we embrace that, the easier the obstacle will be to face and move.

You can take the trouble you're dealing with and use it as an opportunity to focus on the present moment. To ignore the totality of your situation and learn to be content with what happens, as it happens. To have no "way" that the future needs to be to confirm your predictions, because you didn't make any. To let each new moment be a refresh wiping clear what came before and what others were hoping would come next.

You'll find the method that works best for you, but there are many things that can pull you into the present moment:

Strenuous exercise. Unplugging. A walk in the park. Meditation. Getting a dog—they're a constant reminder of how pleasant the present is.

One thing is certain. It's not simply a matter of saying: *Oh, I'll live in the present.* You have to *work* at it. Catch your mind when it wanders—don't let it get away from you. Discard distracting thoughts. Leave things well enough alone—no matter how much you feel like doing otherwise.

But it's easier when the choice to limit your scope feels like editing rather than acting. Remember that this moment is not your life, it's just a moment *in* your life. Focus on what is in front of you, right now. Ignore what it "represents" or it "means" or "why it happened to you."

There is plenty else going on right here to care about any of that.

THINK DIFFERENTLY

Genius is the ability to put into effect what is in your mind.
There's no other definition of it.

—F. SCOTT FITZGERALD

Steve Jobs was famous for what observers called his "reality distortion field." Part motivational tactic, part sheer drive and ambition, this field made him notoriously dismissive of phrases such as "It can't be done" or "We need more time."

Having learned early in life that reality was falsely hemmed in by rules and compromises that people had been taught as children, Jobs had a much more aggressive idea of what was or wasn't possible. To him, when you factored in vision and work ethic, much of life was malleable. Assumptions were not law, they needed to be questioned.

For instance, in the design stages for a new mouse for an early Apple product, Jobs had high expectations. He wanted it to move fluidly in any direction—a new development for any mouse at that time—but a lead engineer was told by one of his designers that this would be commercially impossible. What Jobs wanted wasn't realistic and wouldn't work. The next day, the lead engineer arrived at work to find that Steve

Jobs had fired the employee who'd said that. When the replacement came in, his first words were: "I can build the mouse."

This was Jobs's view of reality at work. Confident, adamant, convinced of a person's agency to change it. He wasn't delusional—he had decades of experience behind him, teaching him that limits could be pushed and the "impossible" achieved. He knew that to aim low meant to accept mediocre accomplishment. But a high aim could, if things went right, create something extraordinary. He was Napoleon shouting to his soldiers: "There shall be no Alps!"

For most of us, this does not come easy. It's understandable. So many people in our lives have preached the need to be realistic or conservative or worse—to not rock the boat. This is an enormous disadvantage when it comes to trying big things. Because though our doubts (and self-doubts) feel real, they have very little bearing on what is and isn't possible.

Our perceptions determine, to an incredibly large degree, what we are and are not capable of. In many ways, they determine reality itself. When we believe in the obstacle more than in the goal, which will inevitably triumph?

Isn't that the history of art, the history of new visions and styles? Isn't that the history of science, the history of discoveries and breakthroughs? The old definition of what "worked" is blown apart, and now a new world emerges.

This is why we shouldn't listen too closely to what other people say (or to what the voice in our head says, either). We'll find ourselves erring on the side of accomplishing nothing.

Be open. Question.

Though of course we don't *control* reality, our perceptions do influence it.

One week before the first Macintosh computer was supposed to ship, the engineers told Jobs they couldn't make the deadline. On a hastily assembled conference call, the engineers explained that they needed just two additional weeks' work before it was ready. Jobs responded calmly, explaining to the engineers that if they could make it in two weeks, they could surely make it one—there was no real difference in such a short period of time. And, more important, since they'd come this far and done so much good work, there was no way they would *not* ship on January 16, the original ship date. The engineers rallied and made their deadline. His insistence pushed them, once again, past what they ever thought possible.

Now, how do we usually deal with an impossible deadline handed down from someone above us? We complain. We get angry. We criticize. *How could they? What's the point? Who do they think I am?* We look for a way out and feel sorry for ourselves.

Of course, none of these things affect the objective reality of that deadline. Not in the way that pushing forward can. Jobs refused to tolerate people who didn't believe in their own abilities to succeed. Even if his demands were unfair, uncomfortable, or ambitious.

The genius and wonder of his products—which often felt impossibly intuitive and futuristic—embody that trait. He had pushed through what others thought were hard limitations and, as a result, he created something totally new. No one believed Apple could make the products it made. And look, sometimes they couldn't: Jobs was pushed out in 1985, in part because he was way behind schedule and his products weren't working. (Ironically, some board members believed Apple's expansion into consumer products was a "lunatic plan.") But Jobs learned from this and honed his skill in a new domain—forming Pixar, which redefined what was possible in movies.

Jobs learned to reject the first judgments and the objections that spring out of them because those objections are so often rooted in fear. When he ordered a special kind of glass for the first iPhone, the manufacturer was aghast at the aggressive deadline. "We don't have capacity," they said. "Don't be afraid," Jobs replied. "You can do it. Get your mind around it. You can do it." Nearly overnight, manufacturers transformed their facilities into glassmaking behemoths, and within six months they'd made enough for the whole first run of the phone.

This is radically different from how we've been taught to act. *Be realistic*, we're told. *Listen to feedback. Play well with others. Compromise.* Well, what if the "other" party is wrong? What if conventional wisdom is too conservative? It's this all-too-common impulse to *complain, defer, and then give up* that holds us back.

An entrepreneur is someone with faith in their ability to make something where there was nothing before. To them, the idea that no one has ever done this or that is a good thing. When given an unfair task, some rightly see it as a chance to test what they're made of—to give it all they've got, knowing full well how difficult it will be to win. They see it as an opportunity because it is often in that desperate nothing-to-lose state that we are our most creative.

Our best ideas come from there, where obstacles illuminate new options.

FINDING THE OPPORTUNITY

A good person dyes events with his own color . . . and turns
whatever happens to his own benefit.

—SENECA

One of the most intimidating and shocking develop-
ments in modern warfare was the German Blitzkrieg
(lightning war). In World War II the Germans wanted to
avoid the drawn-out trench fighting of previous wars. So they
concentrated mobile divisions into rapid, narrow offensive
forces that caught their enemies completely unprepared.

Like the tip of a spear, columns of panzer tanks rushed
into Poland, the Netherlands, Belgium, and France with
devastating results and little opposition. In most cases, the
opposing commanders simply surrendered rather than face
what felt like an invincible, indefatigable monster bearing
down on them. The Blitzkrieg strategy was designed to exploit the flinch of the enemy—that they would collapse at
the sight of what appears to be overwhelming force. Its success depends completely on this response. This military strategy works because the set-upon troops see the offensive force
as an enormous obstacle bearing down on them.

This is how the Allied opposition regarded the Blitzkrieg for most of the war. They could see only its power, and their own vulnerability to it. In the weeks and months after the successful invasion of Normandy by Allied forces, they faced it again: a set of massive German counteroffensives. How could they stop it? Would it throw them back to the very beaches they just purchased at such high cost?

A great leader answered that question. Striding into the conference room at headquarters in France, General Dwight D. Eisenhower made an announcement: He'd have no more of this quivering timidity from his deflated generals. "The present situation is to be regarded as opportunity for us and not disaster," he commanded. "There will be only cheerful faces at this conference table."

In the surging counteroffensive, Eisenhower was able to see the tactical solution that had been in front of them the entire time: The Nazi strategy carried its own destruction within itself.

Only then were the Allies able to see the opportunity *inside* the obstacle rather than simply the obstacle that threatened them. Properly seen, as long as the Allies could bend and not break, this attack would send more than fifty thousand Germans rushing headfirst into a net—or a "meat grinder," as Patton eloquently put it.

"By rushing out from his fixed defense the enemy may give us the chance to turn his greatest gamble into his worst defeat," Eisenhower explained. "So I call upon every man of all the Allies to rise to new heights of courage, of resolution, and of effort."

That's what they did and that's what Eisenhower was able to make happen. He didn't get rattled. He *redoubled*. The

Battle of the Bulge, and before that the Battle of the Falaise Pocket, looked like major setbacks at first but became the Allies' greatest triumphs. By allowing a forward wedge of the German army through and then attacking from the sides, the Allies encircled the enemy completely from the rear. The invincible, penetrating thrust of the German panzers wasn't just impotent but suicidal—a textbook example of why you never leave your flanks exposed.

Our judgment and experience are able to look a situation in the eye, and say to it, as Marcus Aurelius wrote: "This is what you really are, regardless of what you may look like." That's step one. Not being overwhelmed and rattled and discouraged, as the Blitzkrieg and so many problems in life want you to be. This is something that few are able to do. But after you have controlled your emotions, the next step is for our adaptability to come in, Marcus Aurelius wrote, and to add, *You're just what I was looking for.*

And that's what we have to do. Look for it. Laura Ingalls Wilder said that "there is good in everything, if only we look for it." Yet we are so bad at looking. We close our eyes to the gift. It's easy to see the defeat, right? The problem is obvious. But the opportunity, that requires a little squinting, it demands we put our glasses on or pull out our microscope.

It's our preconceptions that are so often at the root of the problem. They tell us that things should or need to be a certain way, so when they're not, we naturally assume that we are at a disadvantage or that we'd be wasting our time to pursue an alternate course. When really, it's all fair game, and every situation is an opportunity for us to act.

Let's take a circumstance we've all been in: having a bad

boss. All we see is the hell. All we see is that thing bearing down on us. We flinch.

But what if you regarded it as an opportunity instead of a disaster?

If you mean it when you say you're at the end of your rope and would rather quit, you actually have a unique chance to grow and improve yourself. A unique opportunity to experiment with different solutions, to try different tactics, or to take on new projects to add to your skill set. You can study this bad boss and learn from them—while you fill out your résumé and hit up contacts for a better job elsewhere. You can prepare yourself for that job by trying new styles of communication or standing up for yourself, all with a perfect safety net for yourself: quitting and getting out of there.

With this new attitude and fearlessness, who knows, you might be able to extract concessions and find that you like the job again. One day, the boss will make a mistake, and then you'll make your move and outmaneuver them. It will feel so much better than the alternative—whining, badmouthing, duplicity, spinelessness.

Or take that longtime rival at work (or that rival company), the one who causes endless headaches? Note the fact that they also:

> keep you alert
> raise the stakes
> motivate you to prove them wrong
> harden you
> help you to appreciate true friends
> provide an instructive antipode—an example of whom
>   you don't want to become

Or that computer glitch that erased all your work? It's a chance to start fresh. By doing it a second time, even if it comes out exactly the same, you will now be twice as good.

Blessings and burdens are not mutually exclusive. It's a lot more complicated. Socrates supposedly had a rather mean and argumentative wife; he always said that being married to her was good practice for philosophy.

When people are:

—rude or disrespectful:

They underestimate us. A huge advantage.

—conniving:

We won't have to apologize when we make an example out of them.

—critical or question our abilities:

Lower expectations are easier to exceed.

—lazy:

They cede more control (and credit) to us.

Of course if we had a choice, we'd choose things to be easy and nice and not overwhelming. But what if you were able to remember, in the moment, the second act that seems to come with the unfortunate situations we try so hard to avoid?

Sports psychologists once did a study of elite athletes who were struck with some adversity or serious injury. Initially, each reported feeling isolation, emotional disruption, and doubts about their athletic ability. Yet afterward, each reported gaining a desire to help others, additional perspective, and realization of their own strengths. In other words, every fear and doubt they felt during the injury turned into greater abilities in those exact areas.

It's a beautiful idea. Psychologists call it adversarial growth and post-traumatic growth. "That which doesn't kill me makes me stronger" is not a cliché but fact.

The struggle against an obstacle inevitably propels the fighter to a new level of functioning. It presents new opportunities, new operations. The extent of the struggle determines the extent of the growth. The obstacle is an advantage, not adversity. The enemy is any perception that prevents us from seeing this.

Or we can fight and deny and run away. The result is the same. But the obstacle still exists. The benefit is still there below the surface. Which will you choose?

The package may be poorly wrapped. It may be repulsive. But what do we care? Because what we need is beneath the packaging. The gift—the opportunity—is what happens after you tear all that off, when you find what you were looking for within.

PREPARE TO ACT

Then imitate the action of the tiger;
stiffen the sinews, summon up the blood.

—SHAKESPEARE

Problems are rarely as bad as we think—or rather, they are *precisely* as bad as we *think*.

It's a huge step forward to realize that the worst thing to happen is never the event, but the event *and* losing your head. It's the telling yourself that it's the worst thing that ever happened. Because then you'll have two problems (one of them unnecessary and post hoc).

The demand on you is this: Once you see the world as it is, for what it is, you must act. The proper perception—objective, rational, ambitious, clean—isolates the obstacle and exposes it for what it is.

A clearer head makes for steadier hands.

And then those hands must be put to work. *Good* use.

We all have to make assumptions in life, we have to weigh the costs and benefits. No one is asking you to look at the world through rose-colored glasses. No one is asking for noble failure or martyrdom.

But *boldness* is acting anyway, even though you understand the negative and the reality of your obstacle. Decide to tackle what stands in your way—not because you're a gambler defying the odds but because you've calculated them and boldly embraced the risk.

After all, now that you've managed perceptions properly, what's next is to act.

Are you ready?

PART II

Action

WHAT IS ACTION? Action is commonplace, right action is not. As a discipline, it's not any kind of action that will do, but directed action. Everything must be done in the service of the whole. Step by step, action by action, we'll dismantle the obstacles in front of us. With persistence and flexibility, we'll act in the best interest of our goals. Action requires courage, not brashness—creative application and not brute force. Our movements and decisions define us: We must be sure to act with deliberation, boldness, and persistence. Those are the attributes of right and effective action. Nothing else—not thinking or evasion or aid from others. Action is the solution and the cure to our predicaments.

THE DISCIPLINE OF ACTION

There was little evidence that Demosthenes was destined to become the greatest orator of Athens, let alone all of history. He was born sickly and frail with a nearly debilitating speech impediment. At seven years old, he lost his father. And then things got worse.

The large inheritance left to him—intended to pay for tutors and the best schools—was stolen by the guardians entrusted to protect him. They refused to pay his tutors, depriving him of the education he was entitled to. Still weak and sick, Demosthenes was also unable to distinguish himself in the other critical sphere of Greek life: the floor of the gymnasia.

Here was this fatherless, effeminate, awkward child who no one understood, who everyone laughed at. Not exactly the boy you'd expect would soon hold the power to mobilize a nation to war by his voice alone.

Disadvantaged by nature, abandoned by the people he depended on, nearly every wrong that can be inflicted on a child befell Demosthenes. None of it was fair, none of it was right. Most of us, were we in his position, would have given up right then and there. But Demosthenes did not.

Stuck in his young mind was the image of a great orator, a man he'd once witnessed speaking at the court at Athens.

This lone individual, so skilled and powerful, had held the admiration of the crowd, who hung on his every word for hours—subduing all opposition with no more than the sound of his voice and the strength of his ideas. It inspired and challenged Demosthenes, weak, beaten on, powerless, and ignored; for in many ways, this strong, confident speaker was the opposite of him.

So he did something about it.

To conquer his speech impediment, he devised his own strange exercises. He would fill his mouth with pebbles and practice speaking. He rehearsed full speeches into the wind or while running up steep inclines. He learned to give entire speeches with a single breath. And soon, his quiet, weak voice erupted with booming, powerful clarity.

Demosthenes locked himself away underground—literally—in a dugout he had built in which to study and educate himself. To ensure he wouldn't indulge in outside distractions, he shaved half his head so he'd be too embarrassed to go outside. And from that point forward, he dutifully descended each day into his study to work with his voice, his facial expressions, and his arguments.

When he did venture out, it was to learn even more. Every moment, every conversation, every transaction was an opportunity for him to improve his art. All of it aimed at one goal: to face his enemies in court and win back what had been taken from him. Which he did.

When he came of age, he finally filed suits against the negligent guardians who had wronged him. They evaded his efforts and hired their own lawyers, but he refused to be stopped. Flexible and creative, he matched them suit for suit and delivered countless speeches. Confident in his new strengths, driven on by his own toil, they were no match. Demosthenes eventually won.

Only a fraction of the original inheritance remained, but the money had become secondary. Demosthenes's reputation as an orator, ability to command a crowd, and his peerless knowledge of the intricacies of the law were worth more than whatever remained of a once-great fortune.

Every speech he delivered made him stronger, every day that he stuck with it made him more determined. He could see through bullies and stare down fear. In struggling with his unfortunate fate, Demosthenes found his true calling: He would be the voice of Athens, its great speaker and conscience. He would be successful precisely because of what he'd been through and how he'd reacted to it. He had channeled his rage and pain into his training, and then later into his speeches, fueling it all with a kind of fierceness and power that could be neither matched nor resisted.

Some academic once asked Demosthenes what the three most important traits of speechmaking were. His reply says it all: "Action, Action, Action!"

Sure, Demosthenes lost the inheritance he'd been born with, and that was unfortunate. But in the process of dealing with this reality, he created a far better one—one that could never be taken from him.

But you, when you're dealt a bad hand: What's your response? Do you fold? Or do you play it for all you've got? There's an explosion, metaphoric or otherwise. Are you the guy running toward it? Or running away from it? Or worse, are you paralyzed and do nothing?

This little test of character says everything about us.

And it's sad that so many of us fail—opting away from

action. Because action is natural, innate. You trip and fall right now, your body's instincts protect you. You extend your hands to break your fall so you don't break your face. In a vicious accident, you go into shock but still manage to get your arms up around your face. That's where the term *defensive wounds* comes from. We don't think, we don't complain, we don't argue. We act. We have real strength—more strength than we know.

But in our lives, when our worst instincts are in control, we dally. We don't act like Demosthenes, we act frail and are powerless to make ourselves better. We may be able to articulate a problem, even potential solutions, but then weeks, months, or sometimes years later, the problem is still there. Or it's gotten worse. As though we expect someone else to handle it, as though we honestly believe that there is a chance of obstacles *unobstacle-ing* themselves.

We've all done it. Said: "I am so [overwhelmed, tired, stressed, busy, blocked, outmatched]."

And then what do we do about it? We complain. Distract ourselves. Or treat ourselves. Or sleep in. Or wait.

It feels better to ignore or pretend. But you know deep down that that isn't going to truly make it any better. You've got to act. And you've got to start now.

We forget: In life, it doesn't matter what happens to you or where you came from. It matters what you do with what happens and what you've been given. And the only way you'll do something spectacular is by using it all to your advantage.

People turn shit into sugar all the time—shit that's a lot worse than whatever we're dealing with. We're talking physical disabilities, racial discrimination, battles against over-whelmingly superior armies. But those people didn't quit. They didn't feel sorry for themselves. They didn't delude themselves with fantasies about easy solutions. They focused on the one thing that mattered: applying themselves with gusto and creativity.

Born with nothing, into poverty, strife, or the chaos of decades past, certain types of people were freed from modern notions of fairness or good or bad. Because none of it applied to them. What was in front of them was all they knew—all they had. And instead of complaining, they worked with it. They made the best of it. Because they had to, because they didn't have a choice.

No one wants to be born weak or to be victimized. No one wants to be down to their last dollar. No one wants to be stuck behind an obstacle, blocked from where they need to go. Such circumstances are not impressed by perception, but they are not indifferent—or rather immune—from action. In fact, that's the only thing these situations will respond to.

No one is saying you can't take a minute to think, *Dammit, this sucks.* By all means, vent. Exhale. Take stock. Just don't take too long. Because you have to get back to work. Because each obstacle we overcome makes us stronger for the next one.

But . . .

No. No excuses. No exceptions. No way around it: It's on you.

We don't have the luxury of running away. Of hiding. Because we have something very specific we're trying to do. We have an obstacle we have to lean into and transform.

No one is coming to save you. And if we'd like to go where

THE OBSTACLE IS THE WAY

we claim we want to go—to accomplish what we claim are our goals—there is only one way. And that's to meet our problems with the right action.

Therefore, we can always (and only) greet our obstacles

with energy
with persistence
with a coherent and deliberate process
with iteration and resilience
with pragmatism
with strategic vision
with craftiness and savvy
and with an eye for opportunity and pivotal moments

Are you ready to get to work?

GET MOVING

We must all either wear out or rust out, every one of us.
My choice is to wear out.

—THEODORE ROOSEVELT

Amelia Earhart wanted to be a great aviator. But it was the 1920s, and people still thought that women were frail and weak and didn't have the stuff. Women's suffrage was not even a decade old.

She couldn't make her living as a pilot, so she took a job as a social worker. Then one day the phone rang. The man on the line had a pretty offensive proposition, along the lines of: *We have someone willing to fund the first female transatlantic flight. Our first choice has already backed out. You won't get to actually fly the plane, and we're going to send two men along as chaperones and guess what, we'll pay them a lot of money and you won't get anything. Oh, and you very well might die while doing it.*

You know what she said to that offer? She said yes.

Because that's what people who defy the odds do. That's how people become great at things—whether it's flying or blowing through gender stereotypes. They start. Anywhere. Anyhow. They don't care if the conditions are perfect or if they're being slighted. Because they know that once they get started, if they can just get some momentum, they can make it work.

As it went for Amelia Earhart. Less than five years later she was the first woman to fly solo nonstop across the Atlantic and became, rightly, one of the most famous and respected people in the world.

But none of that would have happened had she turned up her nose at that offensive offer or sat around feeling sorry for herself. None of it could have happened if she'd stopped after that first accomplishment, either. What mattered was that she took the opening and then pressed ahead. She put her foot in the door and then followed with the rest of her body—she didn't let anyone stop her. It wasn't fair that it had to go that way, but it did make her accomplishments all the more impressive.

Life can be frustrating. Oftentimes we know what our problems are. We may even know what to do about them. But we fear that taking action is too risky, that we don't have the experience or that it's not how we pictured it or because it's too expensive, because it's too soon, because we think something better might come along, because it might not work.

And you know what happens as a result? Nothing. We do nothing.

Tell yourself: The time for that has passed. The wind is rising. The bell's been rung. Get started, get moving.

We often assume that the world moves at our leisure. We delay when we should initiate. We jog when we should be running or, better yet, sprinting. And then we're shocked—shocked!—when nothing big ever happens, when opportunities never show up, when new obstacles begin to pile up or the enemies finally get their act together.

Of course they did, we gave them room to breathe. We gave them the chance.

So the first step is: Take the bat off your shoulder and give it a swing. You've got to start to go anywhere.

Now let's say you've already done that. Fantastic. You're already ahead of most people. But let's ask an honest question: Could you be doing more? You probably could—there's always more. At minimum, you could be trying harder. You might have gotten started, but your full effort isn't in it—and that shows.

Is that going to affect your results? No question.

The one thing all fools have in common, Seneca once joked, was that they were *always getting ready to start*. They know they have a problem. They may even know what they have to do about it. They're just going to tackle it *tomorrow*. They're going to start when conditions are more favorable, when all the supplies are here, when they get the go-ahead from their superiors, when they see what other people are going to do first, when they've got some more money saved up.

Sure . . . sure they are.

This procrastination takes many forms—from telling yourself it's impossible to telling yourself victory is guaranteed so you have all the time in the world—but where it leads is the same. Nowhere. Because "I'll do it tomorrow" is one of the most insidious, seductive lies in the world.

While you're sleeping, traveling, attending meetings, or complaining online, the competition is not. The problem is not. Entropy is not. Your doubters, the gatekeepers, the entrenched interests are not.

General James Mattis, a lifelong student of the Stoics, was once asked what keeps him up at night. His answer? "I keep people up at night."

For some reason, these days we tend to downplay the importance of aggression, of taking risks, of barreling forward. It's probably because it's been negatively associated with certain notions of violence or masculinity.

But of course Earhart shows that that isn't true. In fact, on the side of her plane she painted the words, "Always think with your stick forward." That is: You can't ever let up your flying speed. Be deliberate, of course, but you always need to be moving forward.

Don't sit there and complain that you don't have what you want or that this obstacle won't budge. Not when you haven't tried anything yet! Not when you've been passing on opportunities because they're not perfect, not when you've been lamenting your lack of resources, not when you've been hoping this would just resolve itself. Of course you're still in the exact same place. You haven't actually pursued anything!

We talk a lot about courage as a society, but we forget that at its most basic level it's really just taking action—whether that's approaching someone you're intimidated by or deciding to finally crack a book on a subject you need to learn. Just as Earhart did, all the greats you admire started by saying, *Yes, let's go.* And they usually did it in less desirable circumstances than we'll ever suffer.

Just because the conditions aren't exactly to your liking, or you don't feel ready yet, doesn't mean you get a pass. If you want momentum, you'll have to create it yourself, right now, by getting up and getting started.

PRACTICE PERSISTENCE

He says the best way out is always through.
And I agree to that, or in so far
As I can see no way out but through.

—ROBERT FROST

For nearly a year, General Ulysses S. Grant tried to crack the defenses of Vicksburg, a city perched high on the bluffs of the Mississippi, critical to the Confederacy's stranglehold on the most important river in the country. He tried attacking head-on. He tried to go around. He spent months digging a new canal that would change the course of the river. He blew the levees upstream and literally tried to float boats down into the city over flooded land.

None of it worked. "I am very well but much perplexed," Grant wrote to his wife in frustration in March 1863. "Heretofore I have had nothing to do but fight the enemy. This time I have to overcome obstacles to reach him."

All the while, the newspapers chattered. There was an alarming lack of progress. Lincoln had sent a replacement, and the man was waiting in the wings. "The campaign is being badly mismanaged," one general wrote back to Washington. "I fear a calamity before Vicksburg. All Grant's schemes have failed. He knows that he has got to do something or off goes his head."

Despite his place on the chopping block, Grant refused to be rattled, refused to rush or cease. He knew there was a weak spot somewhere. He'd find it or he'd make one.

His next move ran contrary to nearly all conventional military theory. He decided to run his boats past the gun batteries guarding the river—a considerable risk, because once down, they could not come back up. Despite an unprecedented nighttime firefight, nearly all the boats made the run unharmed. A few days later, Grant crossed the river about thirty miles downstream at the appropriately named Hard Times, Louisiana.

Grant's plan was bold: Leaving most of their supplies behind, his troops had to live off the land and make their way up the river, taking town after town along the way. By the time Grant laid siege to Vicksburg itself, the message to his men and his enemies was clear: He would never give up. The defenses would eventually crack. Grant was unstoppable. His victory wouldn't be pretty, but it was inexorable.

If we're to overcome our obstacles, this is the message to broadcast—internally and externally. We will not be stopped by failure, we will not be rushed or distracted by external noise. We will chisel and peg away at the obstacle until it is gone. Resistance is futile.

At Vicksburg, Grant learned two things. First, persistence and pertinacity were incredible assets and probably his main assets as a leader. Second, as is often the result from such dedication, in exhausting all the other traditional options, he'd been forced to try something new. That option—cutting loose from his supply trains and living off the spoils of hostile territory—was a previously untested strategy that the North could now use to slowly deplete the South of its resources and will to fight.

In persistence, he'd not only broken through: In trying it all the wrong ways, Grant discovered a totally new way—the way that would eventually win the war.

Grant's story is not the exception to the rule. It *is* the rule. This is how innovation works.

In 1878, Thomas Edison wasn't the only person experimenting with incandescent lights. But he was the only man willing to test six thousand different filaments—including one made from the beard hair of one of his men—inching closer each time to the one that would finally work.

And, of course, he eventually found it—proving that genius often really is just persistence in disguise. In applying the entirety of his physical and mental energy—in never growing weary or giving up—Edison had outlasted impatient competitors, investors, and the press to discover, in a piece of bamboo, of all things, the power to illuminate the world.

Nikola Tesla, who spent a frustrating year in Edison's lab during the invention of the lightbulb, once sneered that if Edison needed to find a needle in a haystack, he would "proceed at once" to simply "examine straw after straw until he found the object of his search." Well, sometimes that's exactly the right method.

As we butt up against obstacles, it is helpful to picture Grant and Edison. Grant with a cigar clenched in his mouth. Edison on his feet in the laboratory for days straight. Both unceasing, embodying cool persistence and the spirit of the line from the Alfred, Lord Tennyson poem about that other

THE OBSTACLE IS THE WAY

Ulysses, "to strive, to seek, to find." Both, refusing to give up. Turning over in their minds option after option, and trying each one with equal enthusiasm. Knowing that eventually— *inevitably*—one will work. Welcoming the opportunity to test and test and test, grateful for the priceless knowledge this reveals.

The thing standing in your way isn't going anywhere. You're not going to outthink it or outcreate it with some world-changing epiphany. You've got to look at it and the people around you, who have begun their inevitable chorus of doubts and excuses, and say, as Margaret Thatcher famously did: "You turn if you want to. The lady's not for turning."

Too many people think that great victories like Grant's and Edison's came from a flash of insight. That they cracked the problem with pure genius. In fact, it was the slow pressure, repeated from many different angles, the elimination of so many other more promising options, that slowly and surely churned the solution to the top of the pile. Their genius was unity of purpose, deafness to doubt, and the desire to stay at it.

So what if this method isn't as "scientific" or "proper" as others? The important part is that it works.

Working at it *works*. It's that simple. (But again, not easy.)

For most of what we attempt in life, chops are not the issue. We're usually skilled and knowledgeable and capable enough. But do we have the patience to refine our idea? The energy to beat on enough doors until we find investors or supporters? The persistence to slog through the politics and drama of working with a group?

Once you start attacking an obstacle, quitting is not an

option. It cannot enter your head. Abandoning one path for another that might be more promising? Sure, but that's a far cry from giving up. Once you can envision yourself quitting altogether, you might as well ring the bell. It's done.

Consider this mindset:

never in a hurry
never worried
never desperate
never stopping short

As Epictetus once summarized his entire philosophy: *persist* and *resist*. Persist in your efforts. Resist giving in to distraction, discouragement, or disorder.

There's no need to sweat this or feel rushed. No need to get upset or despair. You're not going anywhere—you're not going to be counted out. You're in this for the long haul.

Because when you play all the way to the whistle, there's no reason to worry about the clock. You know you won't stop until it's over—that every second available is yours to use. So temporary setbacks aren't discouraging. They are just bumps along a long road that you intend to travel all the way down.

Doing new things invariably means obstacles. A new path is, by definition, uncleared. Only with persistence and time can we cut away debris and remove impediments. Only in struggling with the impediments that made others quit can we find ourselves on untrodden territory—only by persisting and resisting can we learn what others were too impatient to be taught.

It's okay to be discouraged. It's not okay to quit. To know you want to quit but to plant your feet and keep inching closer until you take the impenetrable fortress you've decided to lay siege to in your own life—that's persistence.

Edison once explained that in inventing, "the first step is an intuition—and comes with a burst—*then* difficulties arise." What set Edison apart from other inventors was tolerance for these difficulties, and the steady dedication with which he applied himself toward solving them.

In other words: It's *supposed* to be hard. Your first attempts *aren't going to work*. It's going to take a lot out of you—but energy is an asset we can always find more of. It's a renewable resource.

Stop looking for an epiphany, and start looking for weak points. Stop looking for angels, and start looking for angles. There are options. Settle in for the long haul and then try each and every possibility, and you'll get there.

When people ask where we are, what we're doing, how that "situation" is coming along, the answer should be clear: We're working on it. We're getting closer. When setbacks come, we respond by working twice as hard.

ITERATE

What is defeat? Nothing but education; nothing but the first step to something better.

—WENDELL PHILLIPS

In Silicon Valley, start-ups don't launch with polished, finished businesses. Instead, they release their "Minimum Viable Product" (MVP)—the most basic version of their core idea with only one or two essential features.

The point is to immediately see how customers respond. And, if that response is poor, to be able to fail cheaply and quickly. To avoid making or investing in a product customers do not want.

As engineers now like to quip: Failure is a feature.

But it's no joke. Failure really can be an asset if what you're trying to do is improve, learn, or do something new. It's the preceding feature of nearly all successes. There's nothing shameful about being wrong, about changing course. Each time it happens we have new options. Problems become opportunities.

The old way of business—where companies guess what customers want from research and then produce those products in a lab, isolated and insulated from feedback—reflects a fear of failure and is deeply fragile in relation to it. If the highly produced product flops on launch day, all that effort was wasted. If it succeeds, no one really knows why or what was responsible for that success. The MVP model, on the other hand, embraces failure and feedback. It gets stronger by failure, dropping the features that don't work, that customers don't find interesting, and then focusing the developers' limited resources on improving the features that do.

In a world where we increasingly work for ourselves, are responsible for ourselves, it makes sense to view ourselves like a start-up—a start-up of one.

And that means changing the relationship with failure. It means iterating, failing, and improving. Our capacity to try, try, try is inextricably linked with our ability and tolerance to fail, fail, fail.

On the path to successful action, we will fail—possibly many times. And that's okay. It can be a good thing, even. Action and failure are two sides of the same coin. One doesn't come without the other. What breaks this critical connection down is when people stop acting—because they've taken failure the wrong way.

When failure does come, ask: *What went wrong here? What can be improved? What am I missing?* This helps birth alternative ways of doing what needs to be done, ways that are often much better than what we started with. Failure puts you in corners you have to think your way out of. It is a source of breakthroughs.

This is why stories of great success are often preceded by epic failure—because the people in them went back to the drawing board. They weren't ashamed to fail, but spurred on, piqued by it. Sometimes in sports it takes a close loss to finally convince an underdog that they've got the ability to compete against that competitor that had intimidated (and beat) them for so long. The loss might be painful, but as Franklin put it, it can also instruct.

When a scientist has a hypothesis and it turns out to be wrong, they're not upset. That's how it's supposed to work! With a business, we shouldn't take failure personally because it's part of the process. If an investment or a new product pays off, great. If it fails, we're fine because we're prepared for it—we didn't invest every penny in that option. And now we have learned something.

Great entrepreneurs are:

never wedded to a position
never afraid to lose a little of their investment
never bitter or embarrassed
never out of the game for long

They slip many times, but they don't fall.

Even though we know that there are great lessons from failure—lessons we've seen with our own two eyes—we repeatedly shrink from it. We do everything we can to avoid it, thinking it's embarrassing or shameful. We fail, kicking and screaming.

Well why would I want to fail? It hurts.

No one would claim otherwise. But can we acknowledge that anticipated, temporary failure certainly hurts less than catastrophic, permanent failure? Like any good school, learning from failure isn't free. The tuition is paid in discomfort or loss and having to start over.

Be glad to pay the cost. There will be no better teacher for your career, for your book, for your new venture. There's a saying about how the Irish ship captain located all the rocks in the harbor—using the bottom of his boat. Whatever works, right?

In the early days of World War II, Erwin Rommel and the Germans made quick work of the British and American forces in North Africa. There was a string of offensives at Cyrenaica, Tobruk, and in Tunisia that led to some of the most astonishing victories in the history of warfare. The Germans' bleak battlefields of North Africa, with its enormous distances, blinding sandstorms, scorching heat, and lack of water, handed the Allies defeat after defeat.

All seemed lost . . . except the Germans were giving the Allies something else in the process: valuable lessons.

In fact, the Allied forces actually chose that disadvantageous battlefield on purpose. Churchill knew that they would have to take their first stand against the Germans somewhere, but to do that and *lose* in Europe would be disastrous for morale.

In North Africa, the British and the Americans learned how to fight the Germans—and early on they learned mostly by failure. But that was acceptable, because they'd anticipated a learning curve and planned for it. They welcomed it because they knew, like Grant and Edison did, what it meant: victory further down the road. As a result, the Allied troops Hitler faced in Italy were far different—far *better*—than those he'd faced in Africa, and the ones he ultimately faced in France and Germany were better still.

The one way to guarantee we don't benefit from failure—to ensure it is a bad thing—is to not learn from it. To continue to try the same thing over and over (which is the definition of insanity for a reason). People fail in small ways all the time. But they don't learn. They don't listen. They don't see the problems that failure exposes. It doesn't make them better.

Thickheaded and resistant to change, these are the types who are too self-absorbed to realize that the world doesn't have time to plead, argue, and convince them of their errors. Soft-bodied and hardheaded, they have too much armor and ego to fail well.

It's time you understand that the world is telling you something with each and every failure and action. It's feedback—giving you precise instructions on how to improve, it's trying to wake you up from your cluelessness. It's trying to teach you something. *Listen.*

Lessons come hard only if you're deaf to them. Don't be.

Make sure that tomorrow, as the poet Longfellow said, finds you farther than today. Further along. Better off. Smarter. More able. That's the approach.

Being able to see and understand the world this way is part and parcel of overturning obstacles. Here, a negative becomes a positive. We turn what would otherwise be disappointment into opportunity. Failure shows us the way—by showing us what *isn't* the way.

FOLLOW THE PROCESS

No one stumbles
All the way to the top
Of Mount Fuji.
Single-mindedly go forward,
Sweeping aside the pebbles in the path.

—AWA KENZO

Coach Nick Saban doesn't actually refer to it very often, but every one of his assistants and players lives by it. They say it for him, tattooing it at the front of their minds and on every action they take, because just two words are responsible for their unprecedented success: The Process.

Saban, who coached the University of Alabama football team—perhaps the most dominant dynasty in the history of college football—for seventeen seasons doesn't focus on what every other coach focuses on, or at least not the *way* they do. He teaches The Process.

Don't think about winning the SEC Championship. Don't think about the national championship. Think about what you needed to do in this drill, on this play, in this moment. That's the process: Let's think about what we can do today, the task at hand.

In the chaos of sport, as in life, process provides us a way. It says: *Okay, you've got to do something very difficult.* Don't focus on that. Instead break it down into pieces. Simply do what you *need* to do *right now.* And do it well. And then move on to the next thing. Follow the process and not the prize.

The road to back-to-back championships is just that, a road. Same goes for a rebuilding year. Or a year or a game that starts off poorly and requires an epic comeback. You travel along a road in steps. Excellence is a matter of steps. Excelling at this one, then that one, and then the one after that. Saban's process is exclusively this—existing in the present, taking it one step at a time, not getting distracted by anything else. Not the other team, not the scoreboard or the crowd.

The process is about finishing. Finishing games. Finishing workouts. Finishing film sessions. Finishing drives. Finishing reps. Finishing plays. Finishing blocks. Finishing the smallest task you have right in front of you and finishing it well.

At one point, Saban had someone study hundreds of thousands of college football downs. The average down was something like seven seconds long. Focus on doing your job for those seven seconds, Saban would say, and then focus on the next seven. That's the process.

Whether it's pursuing the pinnacle of success in your field or simply surviving some awful or trying ordeal, the same approach works. Don't think about the end—think about surviving. Making it from meal to meal, break to break, checkpoint to checkpoint, paycheck to paycheck, one day at a time.

And when you really get it right, even the hardest things

become manageable. Because the process is relaxing. Under its influence, we needn't panic. Even mammoth tasks become just a series of component parts.

This was what the great nineteenth-century pioneer of meteorology, James Pollard Espy, was shown in a chance encounter as a young man. Unable to read and write until he was eighteen, Espy attended a rousing speech by the famous orator Henry Clay. After the talk, a spellbound Espy tried to make his way toward Clay, but he couldn't form the words to speak to his idol. One of his friends shouted out for him: "He wants to be like you, even though he can't read."

Clay grabbed one of his posters, which had the word *CLAY* written on it in big letters. He looked at Espy and said, "You see that, boy?" pointing to a letter. "That's an A. Now you've only got twenty-five more letters to go."

Espy had just been gifted the process. Within a year, he started college.

"Well-being is realized by small steps," Zeno, the founder of Stoicism, once said, "but it's not small thing."

We needn't scramble like we're so often inclined to do when some difficult task sits in front of us. Remember the first time you saw a complicated algebra equation? It was a jumble of symbols and unknowns. But then you stopped, took a deep breath, and broke it down. You isolated the variables, solved for them, and all that was left was the answer.

Do that now, for whatever obstacles you come across. We can take a breath, do the immediate, composite part in front of us—and follow its thread into the next action. Everything in order, everything connected.

When it comes to our actions, disorder and distraction

are death. The unordered mind loses track of what's in front of it—what matters—and gets distracted by thoughts of the future. The process is order, it keeps our perceptions in check and our actions in sync.

It seems obvious, but we forget this when it matters most.

Right now, if someone knocked you down and pinned you to the ground, how would you respond? You'd probably panic. And then you'd push with all your strength to get them off you. It wouldn't work; just using their body weight, they could keep your shoulders against the ground with little effort—while you grew exhausted fighting them.

That's the opposite of the process.

There is a much easier way. First, you don't panic, you conserve your energy. You don't do anything stupid like get yourself choked out by acting without thinking. You focus on not letting it get worse. Then you get your arms up, to brace and create some breathing room, some space. Now work to get on your side. From there you can start to break the hold: Grab an arm, trap a leg, buck with your hips, slide in a knee, and push away.

It'll take some time, but you'll get yourself out. At each step, the person on top is forced to give a little up, until there's nothing left. Then you're free—thanks to the process.

Being trapped is just a position, not a fate. You get out of it by addressing and eliminating each part of that position through small, deliberate actions—not by trying (and failing) to push it away with superhuman strength.

With our business rivals, we rack our brains to think of some mind-blowing new product that will make them irrelevant, and, in the process, we take our eye off the ball. We shy away from writing a book or making a film even though it's our dream because it's so much work—we can't imagine how we get from here to there.

How often do we compromise or settle because we feel that the real solution is too ambitious or outside our grasp? How often do we assume that change is impossible because it's too big? Involves too many different groups? Or worse, how many people are paralyzed by all their ideas and inspirations? They chase them all and go nowhere, distracting themselves and never making headway. They're brilliant, sure, but they rarely execute. They rarely get where they want and need to go.

All these issues are solvable. Each would collapse beneath the process. We've just wrongly assumed that it has to happen all at once, and we give up at the thought of it. We are A-to-Z thinkers, fretting about A, obsessing over Z, yet forgetting all about B through Y.

We want to have goals, yes, so everything we do can be in the service of something purposeful. When we know what we're really setting out to do, the obstacles that arise tend to seem smaller, more manageable. When we don't, each one looms larger and seems impossible. Goals help put the blips and bumps in proper proportion.

When we get distracted, when we start caring about something other than our own progress and efforts, the process is the helpful, if occasionally bossy, voice in our head. It is the bark of the wise, older leader who knows exactly who he is and what he's got to do. It's the voice of an unrattled, laser-focused Ulysses S. Grant at the Battle of the Wilderness settling down a group of generals who had been repeatedly outsmarted and beaten by Robert E. Lee and were terrified it was about to happen again. "Oh, I am heartily tired of hearing about what Lee is going to do," Grant said as he calmly watched the battle that raged around them. "Some of you always seem to think he is suddenly going to turn a double somersault and land in our rear and on both of our flanks at the same time. Go back to your command, and try to think what we are going to do ourselves, instead of what Lee is going to do."

The process is the voice that demands we take responsibility and ownership. That prompts us to *act* even if only in a small way. That we do what's in front of us . . . and then what comes after.

Like a relentless machine, subjugating resistance each and every way it exists, little by little. Moving forward, one step at a time. Subordinate strength to the process. Replace fear with the process. Depend on it. Lean on it. Trust in it.

Take your time, don't rush. Some problems are harder than others. Deal with the ones right in front of you first. Come back to the others later. You'll get there.

The process is about doing the right things, *right now*. Not worrying about what might happen later, or the results, or the whole picture.

DO YOUR JOB, DO IT RIGHT

Whatever is rightly done, however humble, is noble.
(Quidvis recte factum quamvis humile praeclarum.)

—SIR HENRY ROYCE

Long past his humble beginnings, President Andrew Johnson would speak proudly of his career as a tailor before he entered politics. "My garments never ripped or gave way," he would say.

On the campaign trail, a heckler once tried to embarrass him by shouting about his working-class credentials. Johnson replied without breaking stride: "That does not disconcert me in the least; for when I used to be a tailor I had the reputation of being a good one, and making close fits, always punctual with my customers, and always did good work."

Another president, James Garfield, paid his way through college in 1851 by persuading his school, the Western Reserve Eclectic Institute, to let him be the janitor in exchange for tuition. He did the job every day smiling and without a hint of shame. Each morning, he'd ring the university's bell tower to start the classes—his day already having long begun—and stomp to class with cheer and eagerness.

Within just one year of starting at the school he was a

professor—teaching a full course load in addition to his studies. By his twenty-sixth birthday he was the dean.

This is what happens when you do your job—whatever it is—and do it well.

These men went from humble poverty to power by always doing what they were asked to do—and doing it right and with real pride. And doing it better than anyone else. In fact, doing it well because no one else wanted to do it.

Sometimes, on the road to where we are going or where we want to be, we have to do things that we'd rather not do. Often when we are just starting out, our first jobs "introduce us to the broom," as Andrew Carnegie famously put it. There's nothing shameful about sweeping. It's just another opportunity to excel—and to learn.

But you, you're so busy thinking about the future, you don't take any pride in the tasks you're given right now. You just phone it all in, cash your paycheck, and dream of some higher station in life. Or you think, *This is just a job, it isn't who I am, it doesn't matter.*

Of course it does!

What other people think doesn't matter, but everything we do does—whether it's making smoothies while you save up money or studying for the bar. How we step up to hit our last at bat at the end of what's already the greatest game of our career, how we handle our last day in the office, how we push in our chair after a meeting, how we prepare for that little speech we have to give—everything is a chance to do and be your best. Only self-absorbed assholes think they are too good for whatever their current station requires.

Wherever we are, whatever we're doing and wherever we're going, we owe it to ourselves, to our art, to the world to do it well. That's our primary duty. And our obligation. When action is our priority, vanity falls away.

An artist is given many different canvases and commissions in their lifetime, and what matters is that they treat each one as a priority. Whether it's the most glamorous or highest paying is irrelevant. Each project matters, and the only degrading part is giving less than one is capable of giving.

Same goes for us. We will be and do many things in our lives. Some are prestigious, some are onerous, none are beneath us. To whatever we face, our job is to respond with:

hard work
honesty
helping others as best we can

You should never have to ask yourself, *But what am I supposed to do now?* Because you know the answer: Your job. *Your best.*

Whether anyone notices, whether we're paid for it, whether the project turns out successfully—it doesn't matter. We can and always should act with those three traits—no matter the obstacle.

There will never be any obstacles that can ever truly prevent us from carrying out our obligation—harder or easier challenges, sure, but never impossible. Each and every task requires our best. Whether we're facing down bankruptcy and angry customers, or raking in money and deciding how to grow from here, if we do our best we can be proud of our choices and confident they're the right ones. Because we did our job—whatever it is.

Yeah, yeah, I get it. "Obligations" sound stuffy and oppressive. You want to be able to do whatever you want.

But duty is beautiful, and inspiring and empowering.

Steve Jobs even cared about the inside of his products, making sure they were beautifully designed even though the users would never see them. Taught by his father—who finished even the back of his cabinets though they would be hidden against the wall—to think like a craftsman. In every design predicament, Jobs knew his marching orders: Respect the craft and make something beautiful.

Marcus Aurelius's *Meditations* is a beautifully written piece of literature, each sentence, each metaphor seemingly perfect, and done in Greek, no less—not Marcus's native tongue but the language of philosophy. The effort was enormous, clearly painstaking, a fact made all the more remarkable since it was only for himself. It was a private book, never intended to be published!

Every situation is different, obviously. We're not inventing the next iPad or iPhone, but we are making something for someone—even if it's just our own résumé. Every part—especially the work that nobody sees, the tough things we wanted to avoid or could have skated away from—we can treat the same way Jobs and Marcus did: with pride and dedication.

The great psychologist Viktor Frankl, survivor of three concentration camps, found presumptuousness in the age-old question: "What is the meaning of life?" As though it is someone else's responsibility to tell you. Instead, he said, the world is asking *you* that question. And it's your job to answer with your actions.

In every situation, life is asking us a question, and our actions are the answer. When we do things seriously, conscientiously, when we do them well, we're saying: This matters. I matter. Life is meaningful.

It's a way to turn every obstacle into an opportunity. It's a chance to do great work in a crummy situation.

If you see any of this as a burden, you're looking at it the wrong way.

Because all we need to do is those three little duties—to try hard, to be honest, and to help others and ourselves. That's all that's been asked of us. No more and no less.

Sure, the goal is important. But never forget that each individual instance matters, too—each is a snapshot of the whole. The whole isn't certain, only the instances are.

How you do anything is how you can do everything.

We can always act right.

PRACTICE PRAGMATISM

The cucumber is bitter? Then throw it out.
There are brambles in the path? Then go around.
That's all you need to know.

—MARCUS AURELIUS

In 1915, deep in the jungles of Central America, the rising conflict between two rival American fruit companies came to a head. Each desperately wanted to acquire the same five thousand acres of valuable land.

The issue? Two different locals claimed to own the deed to the plantation. In the no-man's-land between Honduras and Guatemala, neither company was able to tell who was the rightful owner so they could buy it from them.

How they each responded to this problem was defined by their company's organization and ethos. One company was big and powerful, the other crafty and cunning. The first, one of the most powerful corporations in the United States: United Fruit. The second, a small upstart owned by Samuel Zemurray.

To solve the problem, United Fruit dispatched a team of high-powered lawyers. They set out in search of every file and scrap of paper in the country, ready to pay whatever it cost to win. Money, time, and resources were no object.

Zemurray, the tiny, uneducated competitor, was outmatched, right? He couldn't play their game. So he didn't. Flexible, fluid, and defiant, he just met separately with both of the supposed owners and bought the land from each of them. He paid twice, sure, but it was *over*. The land was his. Forget the rule book, settle the issue.

This is *pragmatism* embodied. Don't worry about the "right" way, worry about the *right* way. This is how we get things done.

Zemurray always treated obstacles this way. Told he couldn't build a bridge he needed across the Utila River—because government officials had been bribed by competitors to make bridges illegal—Zemurray had his engineers build two long piers instead. And in between reaching out far into the center of the river, they strung a temporary pontoon that could be assembled and deployed to connect them in a matter of hours. Railroads ran down each side of the riverbank, going in opposite directions. When United Fruit complained, Zemurray laughed and replied: "Why, that's no bridge. It's just a couple of little old wharfs."

Sometimes you do it this way. Sometimes that way. Not deploying the tactics you learned in school but adapting them to fit each and every situation. Any way that *works*—that's the motto.

We spend a lot of time thinking about how things are supposed to be, or what the rules say we should do. Trying to get it all perfect. We tell ourselves that we'll get started once the conditions are right, or once we're sure we can trust this or that. When, really, it'd be better to focus on making do with what we've got. On focusing on results instead of pretty methods.

Zemurray never lost sight of the mission: getting bananas across the river. Whether it was a bridge or two piers with a dock in the middle, it didn't matter so long as it got the cargo where it needed to go. When he wanted to plant bananas on a particular plantation, it wasn't important to find the rightful owner of the land—it was to *become* the rightful owner.

As they say in Brazilian jiujitsu, it doesn't matter how you get your opponents to the ground, only that you take them down. Of course, it's a little more complicated than that— there are rules in jiujitsu, just as there are laws and ethics that must constrain us in life. As he got older and more successful, what Zemurray did lose sight of was this, and his legacy is stained by the lengths he went to win.

But us, we have our own mission. We're also in the pinch between the way we wish things were and the way they actually are (which always seems to be a disaster). We're fighting against our own jungles, against unfair or antiquated rules, trying to beat competitors who have far more resources. How far are you willing to go? What are you willing to do about it?

Scratch the complaining. No waffling. No submitting to powerlessness or fear. You can't just run home to Mommy. How are you going to solve this problem? How are you going to get around the rules that hold you back?

Maybe you'll need to be a little more cunning or conniving than feels comfortable. Sometimes that requires ignoring some outdated regulations or asking for forgiveness from management later rather than for permission (which would be denied) right now. But if you've got an important mission, all that matters is that you accomplish it.

At twenty-one, Richard Wright was not the world-famous author he would eventually be. But poor and black, he decided he would read and no one could stop him. Did he storm the library and make a scene? No, not in the Jim Crow South he didn't. Instead, he forged a note that said, "Dear Madam: Will you please let this nigger boy have some books by H. L. Mencken?" (because no one would use that derogatory term about themselves, right?), and checked them out with a stolen library card, pretending they were for someone else.

With the stakes this high, you better be willing to bend the rules or do something desperate or crazy. To thumb your nose at the authorities and say: *What? This is not a bridge. I don't know what you're talking about.* Or, in some cases, giving the middle finger to the people trying to hold you down and blowing right through their evil, disgusting rules.

Pragmatism is not so much realism as flexibility. There are a lot of ways to get from point A to point B. It doesn't have to be a straight line. It's just got to get you where you need to go. *But so many of us spend so much time looking for the perfect solution that we pass up what's right in front of us.*

As Deng Xiaoping once said, "I don't care if the cat is black or white, so long as it catches mice."

The Stoics had their own reminder: "Don't go expecting Plato's Republic."

Because you're never going to find that kind of perfection. Instead, do the best with what you've got. Not that pragmatism is inherently at odds with idealism or pushing the ball forward. The first iPhone was revolutionary, but it still shipped without a copy-and-paste feature or a handful of other features Apple would have liked to have included. Steve Jobs, the supposed perfectionist, knew that at some point, you have to compromise. What mattered was that you got it done and it worked.

Start thinking like a pragmatist: still ambitious, aggressive, and rooted in virtue but also imminently practical and guided by the possible. Not on everything you would like to have, not on changing the world right at this moment, but ambitious enough to get everything you *need*. Don't think small, but make the distinction between the critical and the extra.

Think progress, not perfection.

Under this kind of force, obstacles break apart. They have no choice. Since you're going around them or making them irrelevant, there is nothing for them to resist.

IN PRAISE OF THE FLANK ATTACK

Whoever cannot seek
the unforeseen sees nothing,
for the known way
is an impasse.

—HERACLITUS

The popular image of George Washington in American lore is of a brave and bold general, towering over everything he surveyed, repelling the occupied and tyrannical British. Of course, the true picture is a little less glorious. Washington wasn't a guerrilla, but he was close enough. He was wily, evasive, often refusing to battle.

His army was small, undertrained, undersupplied, and fragile. He waged a war mostly of defense, deliberately avoiding large formations of British troops. For all the rhetoric, most of his maneuvers were pinpricks against a stronger, bigger enemy. Hit and run. Stick and move.

Never attack where it is obvious, Washington told his men. Don't attack as the enemy would expect, he explained, instead, "Where little danger is apprehended, the more the enemy will be unprepared and consequently there is the fairest prospect of success." He had a powerful sense of which minor skirmishes would feel and look like major victories.

His most glorious "victory" wasn't even a direct battle with the British. Instead, Washington, nearly at the end of his rope, crossed the Delaware at dawn on Christmas Day to attack a group of sleeping German mercenaries who may or may not have been drunk.

He was actually better at withdrawing than at advancing—skilled at saving troops that otherwise would have been lost in defeat. Washington rarely got trapped—he always had a way out. Hoping simply to tire out his enemy, this evasiveness was a powerful weapon—though not necessarily a glamorous one.

It's not surprising, then, as the general of the Continental Army and the country's first president, that his legacy has been whitewashed and embellished a little. And he's not the only general we've done it for. The great myth of history, propagated by movies and stories and our own ignorance, is that wars are won and lost by two great armies going head-to-head in battle. It's a dramatic, courageous notion—but also very, very wrong.

In a study of some 30 conflicts comprising more than 280 campaigns from ancient to modern history, the brilliant strategist and historian B. H. Liddell Hart came to a stunning conclusion: In only 6 of the 280 campaigns was the decisive victory a result of a direct attack on the enemy's main army.

Only six. That's 2 percent.

If not from pitched battles, where do we find victory?

From everywhere else. From the flanks. From the unexpected. From the psychological. From drawing opponents out from their defenses. From the untraditional. From anything *but* . . .

As Hart writes in his masterwork *Strategy*:

> *The Great Captain will take even the most hazardous indirect approach—if necessary over mountains, deserts or swamps, with only a fraction of the forces, even cutting himself loose from his communications. Facing, in fact, every unfavorable condition rather than accept the risk of stalemate invited by direct approach.*

When you're at your wit's end, straining and straining with all your might, when people tell you you look like you might pop a vein . . .

Take a step back, then go around the problem. Find some leverage. Approach from what is called the "line of least expectation." The thing no one expects. The thing they thought was impossible. The thing everyone else was afraid to try. The thing that only *you* could do.

What's your first instinct when faced with a challenge? Is it to outspend the competition? Argue with people in an attempt to change long-held opinions? Are you trying to barge through the front door? Because the back door, side doors, and windows may have been left wide open.

Whatever you're doing, it's going to be harder (to say nothing of impossible) if your plan includes defying physics or logic. Instead, think of Grant realizing he had to bypass Vicksburg—not go at it—in order to capture it. Think of Hall of Fame coach Phil Jackson and his famous triangle offense, which is designed to automatically route the basketball *away* from defensive pressure rather than attack it directly.

If we're starting from scratch and the established players have had time to build up their defenses, there is just no way we are going to beat them on their strengths. So it's smarter to not even try, but instead focus our limited resources elsewhere.

Part of the reason why a certain skill often seems so effortless for great masters is not just because they've mastered the process—they really are doing less than the rest of us who don't know any better. They choose to exert only calculated force where it will be effective, rather than straining and struggling with pointless attrition tactics.

As someone once put it after fighting Jigoro Kano, the legendary five-foot-tall founder of judo, "Trying to fight with Kano was like trying to fight with an empty jacket!"

That can be you.

Being outnumbered, coming from behind, being low on funds, these don't have to be disadvantages. They can be gifts. Assets that make us less likely foolishly try a head-to-head attack. These things *force* us to be creative, to find work-arounds, to sublimate the ego and do anything to win besides challenging our enemies where they are strongest. These are the signs that tell us to approach from an oblique angle.

In fact, having the advantage of size or strength or power is often the birthing ground for true and fatal weakness. The inertia of success makes it much harder to truly develop good technique. People or companies who have that size advantage never really have to learn the process when they've been able to coast on brute force. And that works for them . . . until it doesn't. Until they meet you and you make quick work of them with deft and oblique maneuvers, when

THE OBSTACLE IS THE WAY

you refuse to face them in the one setting they know: head-to-head.

We're in the game of little defeating big. Therefore, Force can't try to match Force.

Of course, when pushed, the natural instinct is always to push back. But martial arts teach us that we have to ignore this impulse. We can't push back, we have to *pull* until opponents lose their balance. Then we make our move.

The art of the side-door strategy is a vast, creative space. And it is by no means limited to war, business, or sales.

The great philosopher Søren Kierkegaard rarely sought to convince people directly from a position of authority. Instead of lecturing, he practiced a method he called "indirect communication." Kierkegaard would write under pseudonyms, where each fake personality would embody a different platform or perspective—writing multiple times on the same subject from multiple angles to convey his point emotionally and dramatically. He would rarely tell the reader "do this" or "think that." Instead he would *show* new ways of looking at or understanding the world.

You don't convince people by challenging their longest and most firmly held opinions. You find common ground and work from there. Or you look for leverage to make them listen. Or you create an alternative with so much support from other people that the opposition voluntarily abandons its views and joins your camp.

The way that works isn't always the most impressive. Sometimes it even feels like you're taking a shortcut or fighting unfairly. There's a lot of pressure to try to match people move for move, as if sticking with what works for you is somehow cheating. Let me save you the guilt and self-flagellation: It's not.

You're acting like a real strategist. You aren't just throwing your weight around and hoping it works. You're not wasting your energy in battles driven by ego and pride rather than tactical advantage.

Believe it or not, *this* is the hard way. That's why it works.

Remember, sometimes the longest way around is the shortest way home.

USE OBSTACLES AGAINST
THEMSELVES

—————

Wise men are able to make a fitting use even
of their enmities.

—PLUTARCH

Gandhi didn't fight for independence for India. The British Empire did all of the fighting—and, as it happens, all of the losing.

That was deliberate, of course. Gandhi's extensive satyagraha campaign and civil disobedience show that action has many definitions. It's not always moving forward or even obliquely. It can also be a matter of positions. It can be a matter of taking a stand.

Sometimes you overcome obstacles not by attacking them but by withdrawing and letting them attack you. You can use the actions of others against themselves instead of acting yourself.

Weak compared to the forces he hoped to change, Gandhi leaned into that weakness, exaggerated it, made himself more vulnerable to it. He said to the most powerful occupying military in the world, *I'm marching to the ocean to collect salt in direct violation of your laws.* He was provoking them—*What are you going to do about it? There is nothing wrong with what we're doing*—knowing that it placed authorities in an impossible dilemma: Enforce a bankrupt policy or abdicate. Within that framework, the military's enormous strength is neutralized. Its very usage is counterproductive.

Martin Luther King Jr., taking Gandhi's lead, told his followers that they would meet "physical force with soul force." In other words, they would use the power of opposites. In the face of violence they would be peaceful, to hate they would answer with love—and in the process, they would expose those attributes as indefensible and evil.

Opposites work. Nonaction can be action. It uses the power of others and allows us to absorb their power as our own. Letting them—or the obstacle—do the work for us.

Just ask the Russians, who defeated Napoleon and the Nazis not by rigidly protecting their borders but by retreating into the interior and leaving the winter to do their work on the enemy, bogged down in battles far from home.

Is this an action? You bet it is.

Perhaps your enemy or obstacle really is insurmountable—as it was for many of these groups. Perhaps in this case, you haven't got the ability to win through attrition (persistence) or you don't want to risk learning on the job (iteration). Okay. You're still a long way from needing to give up.

It is, however, time to acknowledge that some adversity might be impossible for you to defeat—no matter how hard you try. Instead, you must find some way to use the adversity, its energy, to help yourself.

Before the invention of steam power, boat captains had an ingenious way of defeating the wickedly strong current of the Mississippi River. A boat going upriver would pull alongside a boat about to head downriver, and after wrapping a rope around a tree or a rock, the boats would tie themselves to each other. The second boat would let go and let the river take it downstream, slingshotting the other vessel upstream.

The actress Kate Winslet, a seven-time Academy Award nominee despite lacking any classical training, once explained that her secret on camera was to ask herself the question, "What can I get for free?" Meaning, if she's tired, she uses that in the character. If she's nervous, she puts that into the character. If her arm hurts or her feet are sore, same thing. Instead of thinking, "I can't because . . . ," she takes the same stress, the same factors, the same difficulties and thinks, "What can I do because . . ."

Instead of fighting the obstacle, you try to use its energy to your advantage—you see what you can get for free from it.

That they underestimate you? That they attacked you and made you sympathetic? That they ignored you entirely? That the tough market has eliminated a lot of the competition? These are all things you've gotten for free, things that direct us toward various strategies, things we can be thankful for and use.

There is a famous story of Alexander the Great and a famously difficult horse named Bucephalus—a horse that even his father, King Philip II of Macedon, could not break. While others had tried sheer force and whips and ropes, a young Alexander succeeded by lightly mounting and simply hanging onto the racing and wild animal until the horse was calm. Having exhausted himself, Bucephalus finally submitted to his rider's influence. Alexander, having taken Bucephalus's energy and used it against him, would ride into battle on that faithful horse for the next twenty years.

Now what of your obstacles?

Yes, sometimes we need to learn from Amelia Earhart and just take action. But we also have to be ready to see that restraint might be the best action for us to take. Gandhi's campaign against bigotry and the British lasted for decades—more often than not, he was reining in his supporters instead of spurring them toward some decisive action. He understood it would take time for the British to beat themselves, for public opinion to be changed by each mistake he baited them into.

Sometimes in your life you need to have patience—wait for temporary obstacles to fizzle out. Let two jousting egos sort themselves out instead of jumping immediately into the fray. Sometimes a problem needs less of you—fewer people period—and not more.

When we want things too badly we can be our own worst enemy. In our eagerness, we strip the very screw we want to turn and make it impossible to ever get what we want. We spin our tires in the snow or mud and dig a deeper rut—one that we'll never get out of.

We get so consumed with moving forward that we forget that there are other ways to get where we are heading. It doesn't naturally occur to us that standing still—or in some cases, even going backward—might be the best way to advance. Don't just do something, stand there!

We push and push. We're pushing to get a raise, a new client, to prevent some exigency from happening. In fact, the best way to get what we want might be to reexamine those desires in the first place. Or it might be to aim for something else entirely, and use the impediment as an opportunity to explore a new direction. In doing so, we might end up creating a new venture that replaces our insufficient income entirely. Or we might discover that in ignoring clients, we attract more—finding that they want to work with someone who does not so badly want to work with them. Or we rethink that disaster we feared (along with everyone else) and come up with a way to profit from it when and if it happens.

We wrongly assume that moving forward is the only way to progress, the only way we can win. Sometimes, staying put, going sideways, or moving backward is actually the best way to eliminate what blocks or impedes your path.

There is a certain humility required in the approach. It means accepting that the way you originally wanted to do things is not possible. You just haven't got it in you to do it the "traditional" way. But so what?

What matters is whether a certain approach gets you to where you want to go. And let's be clear, using obstacles against themselves is very different from doing nothing. Passive resistance is, in fact, incredibly active. But those actions come in the form of discipline, self-control, fearlessness, determination, and grand strategy.

The great strategist Saul Alinsky believed that if you "push a negative hard enough and deep enough it will break through into its counterside." Every positive has its negative. Every negative has its positive. The *action* is in the pushing through—all the way through to the other side. *Making* a negative into a positive.

This should be great solace. It means that very few obstacles are ever too big for us. Because that bigness might in fact be an advantage. Because we can use that bigness against the obstacle itself. Remember, a castle can be an intimidating, impenetrable fortress, or it can be turned into a prison when surrounded. The difference is simply a shift in action and approach.

We can use the things that block us to our advantage, letting them do the difficult work for us. Sometimes this means leaving the obstacle as is, instead of trying so hard to change it.

The harder Bucephalus ran, the sooner he got tired out. The more vicious the police response to civil disobedience, the more sympathetic the cause becomes. The more they fight, the easier it becomes. The harder you fight, the less you'll achieve (other than exhaustion).

So it goes with our problems.

CHANNEL YOUR ENERGY

When jarred, unavoidably, by circumstance, revert at once to yourself, and don't lose the rhythm more than you can help. You'll have a better grasp of harmony if you keep going back to it.

—MARCUS AURELIUS

As a tennis player, Arthur Ashe was a beautiful contra-diction. To survive segregation in the 1950s and 1960s, he learned from his father to mask his emotions and feel-ings on the court. No reacting, no getting upset at missed shots, and no challenging bad calls. Certainly, as a black player he could not afford to show off, celebrate, or be seen as trying too hard.

But his actual form and playing style was something quite different. All the energy and emotion he had to suppress was channeled into a bold and graceful playing form. While his face was controlled, his body was alive—fluid, brilliant, and all over the court. His style is best described in the epi-thet he created for himself: "physically loose and mentally tight."

For Arthur Ashe, this combination created a nearly un-beatable tennis game. As a person he'd control his emotions, but as a player he was swashbuckling, bold, and cool. He dove for balls and took—and made—the kind of shots that made other players gasp. He was able to do this because he was free. He was free where it mattered: inside.

Other players, free to celebrate, free to throw tantrums or glower at refs and opponents, never seemed to be able to handle the pressure of high-stakes matches the way Ashe could. They often mistook Ashe as inhuman, as bottled up. Feelings need an outlet, of course, but Ashe deployed them to fuel his explosive speed, in his slams and chips and dives. In the abandon with which he played, there was none of the quiet prudence with which he composed himself.

Adversity can harden you. Or it can loosen you up and make you better—if you let it.

Rename it and claim it, that's what Ashe did—as have many other black athletes. The boxer Joe Louis, for example, knew that racist white boxing fans would not tolerate an emotional black fighter, so he sublimated all displays behind a steely, blank face. Known as the Ring Robot, he greatly intimidated opponents by seeming almost inhuman. He took a disadvantage and turned it into an unexpected asset in the ring.

Taylor Swift has been famous since she was a teenager, yet there are no videos or stories of her losing her temper in public, there are no real scandals, no gaffes or stupid comments. This is not because she's an unfeeling person. If anything, her music reveals her to be quite emotional, even impulsive—falling in love, feeling mistreated, having body image issues. But that's the point—those things are expressed in the music, not in interviews, not in destructive behavior.

What Swift has done is channel those feelings into a place

where it serves her, artistically and as a businesswoman. In the fight for control over her masters, she could have thrown a fit. She could have spent years battling in court. She could have tried to raise millions of dollars to buy them herself. She could have let her frustrations sour her on supporting her back catalog, even sap her creativity with new music.

Instead, in a career-defining moment, she threw herself into rerecording every single one of her first six albums, rereleasing each with new artwork, new songs, and a new marketing campaign. We can imagine her smirking, like Zemurray, at the hedge fund who shelled out the money for her old masters as she matched her songs note for note. "What do you mean? These are totally new recordings. Don't you see, the title says (Taylor's Version) now?"

She not only wrested back control of her music but the constant stream of releases that followed—eras and eras of it—catapulted her into a level of popular consciousness that few entertainers have ever reached. Her Eras Tour, which grossed more than a *billion* dollars, was made possible because a new generation discovered her music, and it was fueled by the massive amounts of attention that the relaunches of her albums have generated. On top of all that, she made herself the underdog in the process! It was career jiujitsu and public relations jiujitsu without parallel.

We all have our own constraints to deal with—rules and social norms we're required to observe that we'd rather not. Dress codes, protocols, procedures, legal obligations, and company hierarchies that are all telling us how we have to behave. Think about it too much and it can start to feel oppressive, even suffocating. If we're not careful, this is likely to throw us off our game.

Instead of giving in to frustration, we can put it to good use. It can power our actions, which, unlike our disposition, become stronger and better when loose and bold. While others obsess over observing the rules, we're subtly undermining them and subverting them to our advantage. Think water. When dammed by a man-made obstacle, it does not simply sit stagnant. Instead, its energy is stored and deployed, fueling the power plants that run entire cities.

Toussaint Louverture, the former Haitian slave turned general, so exasperated his French enemies that they once remarked: "*Cet homme fait donc l'ouverture partout*" ("This man makes an opening everywhere"). He was so fluid, so uncontainable, he was actually given the surname Louverture, meaning "the opening." It makes sense. Everything in his life had been an obstacle, and he turned as many of his experiences as he could into openings. His circumstances had trained him to be wily, relentless, to go where others could not go. And when his obstacles were politics or mountains and Napoleon himself, he wasn't rattled—he just got to work.

And yet we feel like going to pieces when our setup for a presentation isn't perfect (instead of throwing it aside and delivering an exciting talk without notes). We stir up gossip with our coworkers (instead of pounding something productive out on our keyboards). We act out instead of *act.*

But think of an athlete "in the pocket," "in the zone," "on a streak," and the seemingly insurmountable obstacles that fall in the face of that effortless state. Enormous deficits collapse, every pass or shot hits its intended target, fatigue melts away. Those athletes might be stopped from carrying out this or that action, but not from their goal. External factors influence the path, but not the direction: forward.

What setbacks in our lives could resist that elegant, fluid, and powerful mastery?

To be physically and mentally loose takes no talent. That's just recklessness. (We want right action, not action *period*.) To be physically and mentally tight? That's called anxiety. It doesn't work, either. Eventually we snap. But physical looseness combined with mental restraint? That is powerful.

It's a power that drives our opponents and competitors nuts. They think we're toying with them. It's maddening—like we aren't even trying, like we've tuned out the world. Like we're immune to external stressors and limitations on the march toward our goals.

Because we are.

SEIZE THE OFFENSIVE

The best men are not those who have waited for chances—
but taken them, besieged the chance, conquered the
chance, and made the chance their servitor.

—E. H. CHAPIN

In the spring of 2008, Barack Obama's presidential candidacy was imperiled. A race scandal involving inflammatory remarks by his pastor, Reverend Jeremiah Wright, threatened to unravel his campaign—to break the thin bond he'd established between black and white voters at a critical moment in the primaries.

Race, religion, demographics, and controversy emulsified into one. It was the kind of political disaster that political campaigns do not survive, leaving most candidates so paralyzed by fear that they defer taking action. Their typical response is to hide, ignore, obfuscate, or distance themselves.

Even those who dislike Obama can't help but be impressed with what happened next. He turned one of the lowest moments in his campaign into a surprise offensive.

Against all advice and convention, he decided that he would take action and that this negative situation was actually a "teachable moment." Obama channeled the attention and energy swirling around the controversy to draw a national audience and speak directly to the American people of the divisive issue of race.

This speech, known today as the "A More Perfect Union" speech, was a transformative moment. Instead of distancing himself, Obama addressed everything directly. In doing so, he not only neutralized a potentially fatal controversy but created an opportunity to seize the electoral high ground. Absorbing the power of that negative situation, his campaign was instantly infused with an energy that propelled it into the White House.

If you think it's simply enough to take advantage of the opportunities that arise in your life, you will fall short of greatness. Anyone sentient can do that. What you must do is learn how to press forward precisely when everyone around you sees disaster.

It's at the seemingly bad moments, when people least expect it, that we can act swiftly and unexpectedly to pull off a big victory. While others are arrested by discouragement, we are not. We see the moment differently, and act accordingly.

Ignore the politics and focus on the brilliant strategic advice that Obama's adviser Rahm Emanuel once gave him. "You never want a serious crisis to go to waste," he said. "Things that we had postponed for too long, that were long-term, are now immediate and must be dealt with. [A] crisis provides the opportunity for us to do things that you could not do before."

If you look at history, some of our greatest leaders used shocking or negative events to push through much-needed reforms that otherwise would have had little chance of passing. We can apply that in our own lives.

You always planned to do something. Write a screenplay. Travel. Start a business. Approach a possible mentor. Launch a movement.

Well, now something has happened—some disruptive event like a failure or an accident or a tragedy. *Use it.*

Perhaps you're stuck in bed recovering. Well, now you have time to write (Ian Fleming wrote *Chitty Chitty Bang Bang* from a hospital bed where a doctor had told him that working on another James Bond novel would be too taxing). Perhaps your emotions are overwhelming and painful because you've just had your heart broken. This is material. You lost your job? That's awful, but now you can travel unencumbered. Your kid just got in trouble? You have a moment where you might be able to finally reach them. You're having a problem? Now you know exactly what to approach that mentor about. Seize this moment to deploy the plan that has long sat dormant in your head. Every chemical reaction requires a catalyst. Let this be yours.

Ordinary people shy away from negative situations, just as they do with failure. They do their best to avoid trouble. What great people do is the opposite. They are their best in these situations. They turn personal tragedy or misfortune— really anything, everything—to their advantage.

But this crisis in front of you? You're wasting it feeling sorry for yourself, feeling tired or disappointed. You forget: Life speeds on the bold and favors the brave.

We sit here and complain that we're not being given opportunities or chances. But we are.

At certain moments in our brief existences we are faced with great trials. Often those trials are frustrating, unfortunate, or unfair. They seem to come exactly when we think we need them the least. The question is: Do we accept this as an exclusively negative event, or can we get past whatever negativity or adversity it represents and mount an offensive? Or more precisely, can we see that this "problem" presents an opportunity for a solution that we have long been waiting for?

The writer Julia Baird tells the story of her lowest point. She was heartbroken. She was sick. She was tired. She sought out help from a therapist, where she found herself saying out loud, "I just don't know how I am going to get through this."

This is why we seek help, why we ask for advice, why we don't just pretend like some lowercase-stoic that we're doing just fine when we're not. Because there, pouring her feelings out, Julia got an insight from her therapist that changed her life. "It is now that everything that you have been given in your life matters," her therapist explained. "This is what you draw on. Your parents, your friends, your work, your books, everything you have ever been told, everything you have ever learned, this is when you use that."

In many battles, as in life, the two opposing forces will often reach a point of mutual exhaustion. It's the one who rises the next morning after a long day of fighting and rallies, instead of retreating—the one who says, *I intend to attack and whip them right here and now*—who will carry victory home. Napoleon described war in simple terms: Two armies are two bodies that clash and attempt to frighten each other. At impact, there is a moment of panic and it is *that moment* that the superior commander turns to his advantage. Great commanders have what's known in German as *Fronterfahrung*, a sixth sense for the decisive point in battle. This acute ability to feel—even in the heat of the moment—the precise instant when going on the offensive would be most effective. You have to feel it . . . and then act on it!

This is what Obama did. Not shirking, not giving in to exhaustion despite the long neck-and-neck primary. But rallying at the last moment. Transcending the challenge and reframing it, triumphing as a result of it. He turned an ugly incident into that "teachable moment," and one of the most profound speeches on race in our history.

The obstacle is not only turned upside down but used as a catapult.

PREPARE FOR
NONE OF IT TO WORK

You are invincible if nothing outside the will can
disconcert you.

—EPICTETUS

Perceptions can be managed. Actions can be directed.
We can always think clearly, respond creatively. Look
for opportunity, seize the initiative.

What we can't do is control the world around us—not as
much as we'd like to, anyway. We might perceive things well,
then act rightly, and fail anyway.

Run it through your head like this: Nothing can ever prevent us from trying. Ever.

All creativity and dedication aside, after we've tried, *some*
obstacles may turn out to be impossible to overcome. Some
actions are rendered impossible, some paths impassable.
Some things are bigger than us. Some problems just keep
happening.

We think it would be wonderful if life went our way, if every action succeeded, but it's to our advantage that this isn't
how it works. As Emerson said, a person whose life is cush-
ioned falls asleep. But when we are "pushed, tormented, defeated," a man "has a chance to learn something; he has been

put on his wits, on his manhood; he has gained facts; learns his ignorance; is cured of the insanity of conceit; has got moderation and real skill."

We can turn every obstacle upside down, too, simply by using it as an opportunity to practice some other virtue or skill—even if it is just learning to accept that bad things happen, or practicing humility.

It's an infinitely elastic formula: In every situation, that which blocks our path actually presents a new path with a new part of us. If someone you love hurts you, there is a chance to practice forgiveness. If your business fails, now you can practice acceptance. If there is nothing else you can do for yourself, at least you can try to help others.

Everything is a chance to do our best, to be our best.

Just our best, that's it. Not the impossible.

We must be willing to roll the dice and lose. Prepare, at the end of the day, for none of it to work.

Anyone in pursuit of a goal comes face-to-face with this time and time again. Sometimes, no amount of planning, no amount of thinking—no matter how hard we try or patiently we persist—will change the fact that some things just aren't going to work.

The world could use fewer martyrs.

We have it within us to be the type of people who try to get things done, try with everything we've got, and, whatever verdict comes in, are ready to accept it instantly and move on to whatever is next.

Is that you? Because it can be.

PART III

Will

WHAT IS WILL? Will is our internal power, which can never be affected by the outside world. We orient our mind, we take action, but all this is dependent on will. Placed in some situation that seems unchangeable and undeniably negative, we determine what we'll be able to do and how we'll do it, whether we can turn it into a breakthrough, a learning experience, a humbling experience, a chance to provide comfort to others. That's will *power*. But that needs to be cultivated. We must prepare for adversity and turmoil, we must learn the art of acquiescence and practice cheerfulness even in dark times. Too often people think that will is how bad we want something. There is also surrender in our strength. Try "God *willing*" over "the will to win" or "*willing* it into existence," for even those attributes can be broken. True will is quiet humility, resilience, and flexibility; the other kind of will is weakness disguised by bluster and ambition. See which lasts longer under the hardest of obstacles.

THE DISCIPLINE OF THE WILL

B ecause he has become more myth than man, most people are unaware that Abraham Lincoln battled crippling depression his entire life. Known at the time as *melancholy*, his depression was often debilitating and profound—nearly driving him to suicide on two separate occasions.

His penchant for jokes and bawdy humor, which we find more pleasant to remember him for, was in many ways the opposite of what life must have seemed like to him during his darker moments. Though he could be light and joyous, Lincoln suffered periods of intense brooding, isolation, and pain. Inside, he struggled to manage a heavy burden that often felt impossible to lift.

Lincoln's life was defined by enduring and transcending great difficulty. Growing up in rural poverty with an abusive father, the devastating death of his mother while he was still a child, educating himself, teaching himself the law, losing the woman he loved as a young man, practicing law in a small country town, experiencing multiple defeats at the ballot box as he made his way through politics, and, of course, the bouts of depression, which at the time were not understood or appreciated as a medical condition. All of these were impediments that Lincoln reduced with a kind of prodding, gracious ambition and smiling, tender endurance.

Lincoln's personal challenges had been so intense that he came to believe they were destined for him in some way, and that the depression, especially, was a unique experience that prepared him for greater things. He learned to endure all this, articulate it, and find benefit and meaning from it.

And he hated how people missed what a fundamental part of life this was. Too many biographies of the greats of history, Lincoln once complained to a friend, "are all alike." They were interchangeable and altogether uninteresting, if not outright "false and misleading," he explained, "never once hinting at failures and blunders" that characterize the human experience and history. It was these obstacles and difficulties, mistakes and disasters that actually taught the person something on their path to greatness, and thus instruct the reader. His own experience clued him in to the fact that this is where the lessons were—not in the good times, not when everything went as planned.

For all of Lincoln's political career, slavery was a dark cloud that hung over our entire nation, a cloud that portended an awful storm. Some ran from it, others resigned themselves to it or became apologists, and still others enriched themselves by it, giving themselves over to its evil. Most assumed it meant the permanent breakup of the Union—or worse, the end of the world as they knew it.

It came to be that every quality produced by Lincoln's personal journey was exactly what was required to lead the nation through its own journey and trial. Unlike other politicians, he was not tempted to lose himself in petty conflict and distractions—he could not be sanguine, he could not find it in his heart to hate like others would. His own experience with suffering drove his compassion to allay it in others. He was patient because he knew that difficult things took time. Above all, he found purpose and relief in a cause bigger than himself and his personal struggles.

The nation called for a leader of magnanimity and force of purpose—it found one in Lincoln, a political novice who was a practitioner of what he called "cold, calculating, unimpassioned reason." Molded by his self-education and his own "severe experience," as he described it, no one was more well-suited to lead the nation through one of its most difficult and painful trials: the Civil War.

As crafty and ambitious and smart as he was, Lincoln's real strength was his will: the way he was able to resign himself to an onerous task without giving in to hopelessness, the way he could contain both humor and deadly seriousness, the way he could use his own private turmoil to teach and help others, the way he was able to rise above the din and see politics *philosophically.* "This too shall pass" was Lincoln's favorite saying, one he once said was applicable in any and every situation one could encounter.

To live with his depression, Lincoln had developed a strong inner fortress that girded him. And in 1861 it again gave him what he needed in order to endure and struggle through a war that was about to begin. Over four years, the "fiery trial" of the Civil War was to become nearly incomprehensibly violent, and Lincoln, who'd attempted at first to prevent it, would fight to win justly, and finally try to end it with "malice towards none." Admiral David Porter, who was with Lincoln in his last days, described it as though Lincoln "seemed to think only that he had an unpleasant duty to perform" and set himself to "perform it as smoothly as possible."

We should count ourselves lucky to never experience such a duty, or be required, as Lincoln had been, to hold and be able to draw from our personal woe in order to surmount it. But we certainly can and must learn from his poise, his courage, and his unrelenting sense of justice.

Clearheadedness and action are not always enough, in politics or in life. Some obstacles are beyond a snap of the fingers or novel solution. It is not always possible for one person to rid the world of a great evil or stop a country bent toward conflict. Of course, we try—because it *can* happen. But we should be ready for it not to. And we need to be able to find a greater purpose in this suffering and handle it with firmness and forbearance.

This was Lincoln: always ready with a new idea or innovative approach—whether it was sending a supply boat instead of reinforcements to the troops besieged at Fort Sumter, or timing the Emancipation Proclamation with a Union victory at Antietam to back it with the appearance of strength, or having the political pragmatism to pass the Thirteenth Amendment, which ended chattel slavery in America forever. Lincoln was a dreamer. He had big hopes, but he was also always equally prepared for the worst. He understood the flaws of humanity, of the nation, yet he was also prepared to make the best of the worst.

Leadership requires determination and energy. And certain situations, at times, call on leaders to marshal that determined energy simply to endure. To provide strength in terrible times. Because of what Lincoln had gone through, because of what he'd struggled with and learned to cope with in his own life, he was able to lead. To hold a nation, a cause, an effort together.

This is the avenue for the final discipline: the Will. If Perception and Action were the disciplines of the mind and the body, then Will is the discipline of the heart and the soul. The will is the one thing we control completely, always. Whereas you can *try* to mitigate harmful perceptions and give 100 percent of your energy to actions, those attempts can be thwarted or inhibited. The will is different, because it is within you.

Will is fortitude and wisdom—not just about specific obstacles but about life itself and where the obstacles we are facing fit within it. It gives us ultimate strength. As in: the strength to endure, contextualize, and derive meaning from the obstacles we cannot simply overcome (which, as it happens, is the way of flipping the unflippable).

Even in his own time, Lincoln's contemporaries marveled at the calmness, the gravity, and the compassion of the man. "In weaker hands such a Cabinet would have been a hot-bed of strife," his aides remarked of his so-called team of rivals, "under him it became a tower of strength." He could and would work with anyone. He liked to be disagreed with and received feedback well. He didn't take things personally. He forgave quickly and easily. "His own spirit had already been through the fiery trial of resentment," they observed, which made him always quick with a smile, with a solution, with a reassurance.

Today, those qualities seem almost godlike—almost superhuman. He had this sense of what needed to be done. As though he were above or beyond the bitter divisions that weighed everyone else down. As though he were from another planet.

In a way, he was. Or at least he had traveled from somewhere very far away, somewhere deep inside himself, from where others hadn't. Schooled in suffering, to quote Virgil, Lincoln learned "to comfort those who suffer too." This, too, is part of the will—to think of others, to make the best of a terrible situation that we tried to prevent but could not, to deal with fate with cheerfulness and compassion.

Lincoln's words went to the people's hearts because they came from his, because he had access to a part of the human experience that many had walled themselves off from. His personal pain was an advantage.

Lincoln was strong and decisive as a leader. But he also embodied the Stoic maxim: *sustine et abstine*. Bear and forbear. Acknowledge the pain but trod onward in your task. Had the war gone on even longer, Lincoln would have led his people through it. Had the Union lost the Civil War, he'd have known that he'd done everything he could in pursuit of victory. More important, if Lincoln had been defeated, he was prepared to bear whatever the resulting consequences with dignity and strength and courage. Providing an example for others, in victory or in defeat—whichever occurred.

With all our modern technology has come the conceited delusion that we control the world around us. We're convinced that we can now, finally, control the uncontrollable.

Of course that is not true. It's highly unlikely we will ever get rid of all the unpleasant and unpredictable parts of life. One needs only to look at history to see how random and vicious and awful the world can be. The incomprehensible happens all the time.

Although we should add that Lincoln's life was not all

darkness. Sure, he battled depression and saw the "mighty scourge of war," but he also was a doting, loving father. He really did tell hilarious stories, and he was notorious for his jokes. "With this fearful strain that is upon me, day and night," he once explained to his cabinet after he read aloud to them several chapters from one of his favorite books, "if I did not laugh, I should die." His youthful atheism was transformed into a deep kind of spirituality as he aged, giving him the perspective and the wisdom and the will he needed to endure. It allowed him to find happiness in and through all situations, in all things.

Life will cut you open like a knife. When that happens— at that exposing moment—the world gets a glimpse of what's truly inside you. So what will be revealed when you're sliced open by tension and pressure? Iron? Or air? Or *bullshit*?

As such, the will is the critical third discipline. We can think, act, and finally *adjust* to a world that is inherently unpredictable. The will is what prepares us for this, protects us against it, and allows us to thrive and be happy in spite of it. It is also the most difficult of all the disciplines. It's what allows us to stand undisturbed while others wilt and give in to disorder. Confident, calm, and ready to work regardless of the conditions. *Will*ing and able to continue, even during the unthinkable, even when our worst nightmares have come true.

It's much easier to control our perceptions and emotions than it is to give up our desire to control other people and events. It's easier to persist in our efforts and actions than to endure the uncomfortable or the painful. It's easier to think and act than it is to practice wisdom.

These lessons come harder but are, in the end, the most

critical to wresting advantage from adversity. In every situation, we can

Always prepare ourselves for more difficult times.
Always accept what we're unable to change.
Always manage our expectations.
Always persevere.
Always learn to love our fate and what happens to us.
Always protect our inner self, retreat into ourselves.
Always submit to a greater, larger cause.
Always remind ourselves of our own mortality.

And, of course, prepare to start the cycle once more.

BUILD YOUR INNER CITADEL

If thy faint in the day of adversity, thy strength is small.

—PROVERBS 24:10

By age twelve, Theodore Roosevelt had spent almost every day of his short life struggling with horrible asthma. Despite his privileged birth, his life hung in a precarious balance—the attacks were an almost nightly near-death experience. Tall, gangly, and frail, the slightest exertion would upset the entire balance and leave him bedridden for weeks.

One day his father came into his room and delivered a message that would change the young boy's life: "Theodore, you have the mind but haven't got the body. I'm giving you the tools to make your body. It's going to be hard drudgery and I think you have the determination to go through with it."

You'd think that would be lost on a child, especially a fragile one born into great wealth and status. But according to Roosevelt's younger sister, who witnessed the conversation, it wasn't. His response, using what would become his trademark cheerful grit, was to look at his father and say with determination: *"I'll make my body."*

At the gym that his father built on the second-floor porch,

young Roosevelt proceeded to work out feverishly every day for the next five years, slowly building muscle and strengthening his upper body against his weak lungs and for the future. By his early twenties the battle against asthma was essentially over. He'd worked—almost literally—that weakness out of his body.

That gym work prepared a physically weak but smart young boy for the uniquely challenging course on which the nation and the world were about to embark. It was the beginning of his preparation for and fulfillment of what he would call "the Strenuous Life."

And for Roosevelt, life threw a lot at him: He lost a wife and his mother in rapid succession, faced powerful, entrenched political enemies who despised his progressive agenda, was dealt defeat in elections, witnessed a nation embroiled in foreign wars, and survived nearly fatal assassination attempts. But he was equipped for it all because of his early training and because he kept at it every single day.

Are you similarly prepared? Could you actually handle yourself if things suddenly got *worse*?

We take weakness for granted. We assume that the way we're born is the way we simply are, that our disadvantages are permanent. And then we atrophy from there.

That's not necessarily the best recipe for the difficulties of life.

Not everyone accepts their bad start in life. They remake their bodies and their lives with activities and exercise. They prepare themselves for the hard road. Do they hope they never have to walk it? Sure. But they are prepared for it in any case.

Are you?

Nobody is born with a steel backbone. We have to forge that ourselves.

We craft our spiritual strength through physical exercise, and our physical hardiness through mental practice (*mens sana in corpore sano*—sound mind in a strong body).

This approach goes back to the ancient philosophers. Every bit of the philosophy they developed was intended to reshape, prepare, and fortify them for the challenges to come. Many saw themselves as mental athletes—after all, the brain is as active as any other tissue. It can be built up and toned through the right exercises. Over time, their muscle memory grew to the point that they could intuitively respond to every situation. Especially obstacles.

It is said of the Jews, deprived of a stable homeland for so long, their temples destroyed, and their communities in the Diaspora, that they were forced to rebuild not physically but within their minds. The temple became a metaphysical one, located independently in the mind of every believer. Each one—wherever they'd been dispersed around the world, whatever persecution or hardship they faced—could draw upon it for strength and security.

Consider the line from the Haggadah: "In every generation a person is obligated to view himself as if he were the one who went out of Egypt."

During Passover Seder, the menu is bitter herbs and unleavened bread—the "bread of affliction." Why? In some ways, this taps into the fortitude that sustained the community for generations. The ritual not only celebrates and honors Jewish traditions but prompts those partaking in the feast to visualize and possess the strength that has kept them going.

This is strikingly similar to what the Stoics called the Inner Citadel, that fortress inside of us that no external adversity can ever break down. An important caveat is that we are not born with such a structure; it must be built and actively reinforced. During the good times, we strengthen ourselves and our bodies so that during the difficult times, we can depend on it. We protect our inner fortress so it may protect us.

To Roosevelt, life was like an arena and he was a gladiator. In order to survive, he needed to be strong, resilient, fearless, ready for anything. And he was willing to risk great personal harm and expend massive amounts of energy to develop that hardiness.

You'll have far better luck toughening yourself up than you ever will trying to take the teeth out of a world that is—at best—indifferent to your existence. Whether we were born weak like Roosevelt or we are currently experiencing good times, we should always prepare for things to get tough. In our own way, in our own fight, we are all in the same position Roosevelt was in.

No one is born a gladiator. No one is born with an Inner Citadel. If we're going to succeed in achieving our goals despite the obstacles that may come, this strength in will must be built.

To be great at something takes practice. Obstacles and adversity are no different. Though it would be easier to sit back and enjoy a cushy modern life, the upside of preparation is that we're not disposed to lose all of it—least of all our heads—when someone or something suddenly messes with our plans.

It's almost a cliché at this point, but the observation that the way to strengthen an arch is to put weight on it—because it binds the stones together, and only with tension does it hold weight—is a great metaphor.

The path of least resistance is a terrible teacher. We can't afford to shy away from the things that intimidate us. We don't need to take our weaknesses for granted.

Are you okay being alone? Are you strong enough to go a few more rounds if it comes to that? Are you comfortable with challenges? Does uncertainty bother you? How does pressure feel?

Because these things *will* happen to you. No one knows when or how, but their appearance is certain. And life will demand an answer. You chose this for yourself, a life of doing things. Now you better be prepared for what it entails.

It's your armor plating. It doesn't make you invincible, but it helps prepare you for when fortune shifts . . . and it always does.

ANTICIPATION
(THINKING NEGATIVELY)

> In the meantime, cling tooth and nail to the following
> rule: not to give in to adversity, not to trust prosperity,
> and always take full note of fortune's habit of behaving
> just as she pleases.

—SENECA

A CEO calls her staff into the conference room on the eve of the launch of a major new initiative. They file in and take their seats around the table. She calls the meeting to attention and begins: "I have bad news. The project has failed spectacularly. Tell me what went wrong."

What?! But we haven't even launched yet . . .

That's the point. The CEO is forcing an exercise in hindsight—in advance. She is using a technique designed by psychologist Gary Klein known as a *premortem*.

In a *post*mortem, doctors convene to examine the causes of a patient's unexpected death so they can learn and improve for the next time a similar circumstance arises. Outside of the medical world, we call this a number of things—a debriefing, an exit interview, a wrap-up meeting, a review—but whatever it's called, the idea is the same: We're examining the project in hindsight, after it happened.

A premortem is different. In it, we look to envision what could go wrong, what will go wrong, in advance, before we start. Far too many ambitious undertakings fail for preventable reasons. Far too many people don't have a backup plan because they refuse to consider that something might not go exactly as they wish.

Your plan and the way things turn out rarely resemble each other. What you think you deserve is also rarely what you'll get. Yet we constantly deny this fact and are repeatedly shocked by the events of the world as they unfold.

It's ridiculous. Stop setting yourself up for a fall.

No one has ever said this better than Mike Tyson, who, reflecting on the collapse of his fortune and fame, told a reporter, "If you're not humble, life will visit humbleness upon you."

If only more people had been thinking worst-case scenario at critical points in our lifetimes, the tech bubble, Enron, 9/11, the invasion of Iraq, the withdrawal from Afghanistan, and the real estate bubble might have been avoidable, or might have gone very differently.

How many people were surprised by the pandemic? No one wanted to consider what could happen, and the result? Catastrophe. And then, despite the humbling of such an event, people talked with such naivete about "things going back to normal," as if what had happened wasn't normal, hadn't happened before, and wouldn't happen again.

Today, the premortem is increasingly popular in business circles, from start-ups to Fortune 500 companies and the *Harvard Business Review*—and for good reason. But like all great ideas, it is actually nothing new. The credit goes to the Stoics. They even had a better name: *premeditatio malorum* (premeditation of evils).

Whether Seneca was traveling or giving a speech or enacting some policy while serving as consul, he would begin by reviewing or rehearsing his plan. Then he would go over, in his head (or in writing), the things that could go wrong or prevent it from happening: a storm could arise, the captain could fall ill, the ship could be attacked by pirates. The audience could boo or hiss. The policy could face delays.

"Nothing happens to the wise man against his expectation," he wrote to a friend. "Nor do all things turn out for him as he wished but as he reckoned—and above all he reckoned that something could block his plans." Torture, war, exile, shipwreck—these things must be front of mind, Seneca said (and, indeed, most of them happened to him). What was utterly unacceptable for a leader to say, he wrote, referencing a rule by a great military commander, was "I did not think that would happen."

If it can happen, it will. Are you ready for when it happens to *you*?

Always prepared for disruption, always working that disruption into our plans. Fitted, as they say, for defeat or victory. And let's be honest, a pleasant surprise is a lot better than an unpleasant one.

What if . . .

Then I will . . .

What if . . .

Instead I'll just . . .

What if . . .

No problem, we can always . . .

And in the case where nothing could be done, the Stoics would use it as an important practice to do something the rest of us too often fail to do: manage expectations. Because sometimes the only answer to "What if . . ." is, *It will suck but we'll be okay. We'll endure it. We won't be broken by it.*

Your world is ruled by external factors. Promises aren't kept. You don't always get what is rightfully yours, even if you earned it. Not everything is as clean and straightforward as the games they play in business school. "Offer a guarantee and disaster threatens" went the inscription at the Oracle of Delphi.

Be humble. Be prepared.

Every plan, every project must make concessions to reality. We are all dependent on other people. Not everyone can be counted on like you can (though, let's be honest, we're all our own worst enemy sometimes). And that means people are going to make mistakes and screw up your plans—not always, but a lot of the time.

If this comes as a constant surprise each and every time it occurs, you're not only going to be miserable, you're going to have a much harder time accepting it and moving on to attempts number two, three, and four. The only guarantee, ever, is that *things will go wrong.* The only thing we can use to mitigate this is anticipation. Because the only variable we control completely is ourselves.

Common wisdom provides us with the maxims:

Beware the calm before the storm.
Hope for the best, prepare for the worst.
The worst is yet to come.
It gets worse before it gets better.
It always takes longer than you expect . . . even when
    you take this into account.

The world might call you a pessimist. Who cares? It's far better to seem like a downer than to be blindsided or caught off guard. It's better to meditate on what could happen, to probe for weaknesses in our plans, so those inevitable failures can be correctly perceived, appropriately addressed, or simply endured.

Then, the real reason we won't have any problem thinking about bad luck is because we're not afraid of what it portends. We're prepared in advance for adversity—it's other people who are not. In other words, this bad luck is actually a chance for us to make up some time. We're like runners who train on hills or at altitude so they can beat the runners who expected the course would be flat.

Anticipation doesn't magically make things easier, of course. But we are prepared for them to be as hard as they need to be, as hard as they actually are. It's certainly better to learn a lesson during the premortem than during the postmortem (usually those lessons are good for everyone else . . . not so much us if we're dead!).

As a result of our anticipation, we understand the range of potential outcomes and know that they are not all good (they rarely are). We can accommodate ourselves to any of them. We understand that it could possibly all go wrong. And now we can get back to the task at hand.

You know you want to accomplish X, so you invest time, money, and relationships into achieving it. About the worst thing that can happen is not something going wrong but something going wrong and catching you by surprise. Why? Because unexpected failure is discouraging and being beaten back hurts.

But the person who has rehearsed in their mind what

could go wrong will not be caught by surprise. The person ready to be disappointed won't be. They will have the strength to bear it. They are not as likely to get discouraged or to shirk from the task that lies before them, or make a mistake in the face of it.

You know what's better than building things up in your imagination? Building things up in real life. Of course, it's a lot more fun to build things up in your imagination than it is to tear them down. But what purpose does that serve? It only sets you up for disappointment. Chimeras are like bandages—they hurt only when torn away.

With anticipation, we have time to raise defenses, or even avoid them entirely. We're ready to be driven off course because we've plotted a way back. We can resist going to pieces if things didn't go as planned. With anticipation, we can endure.

We are prepared for failure and ready for success.

THE ART OF ACQUIESCENCE

The Fates guide the person who accepts them and
hinder the person who resists them.

—CLEANTHES

In 1922, a young, struggling, starving artist named Ernest Hemingway was trying to make his way as a writer in France. His wife, Hadley, traveling to meet him and a well-known editor, packed up all the writing Hemingway had accumulated in their tiny, unheated apartment—manuscripts, short stories, poetry, and an unfinished novel.

As Hadley waited during a stopover at the Gare de Lyon train station, her bag went missing. Was it stolen? Did she forget where she left it? It doesn't matter. It was an enormous, nearly unbearable loss. Years of work had been lost in an instant, impossible to recover.

Of course, you know the end of Hemingway's story and can probably guess how this "obstacle" contributed to it. Hemingway would go on to be one of the greatest writers of his generation. The loss of his back catalog forced him to start fresh, partly driving him to reinvent his literary style.

But no one gets there *right away*. "I suppose you heard about the loss of my Juvenilia?" Hemingway wrote in a letter to the writer Ezra Pound. "You, naturally, would say, 'Good' etc. But don't say it to me. I ain't yet reached that mood. I worked three years on the damn stuff."

It's a certifiable fact that most of what we despair over and resist turns out to be good for us. We change because of it, respond to it. Still, that doesn't change the heartbreak. It doesn't change the moment.

It doesn't change the fact that in order to be able to respond, to move on, to see the "good," we have to begin with *acceptance*. And that acceptance takes time. It is no small thing.

It took time for Hemingway to accept what had happened, to reach that mood . . . but then again, not too much time. Within a few weeks he was writing again. Within a few months, the wound was no longer so raw. Within a few years, he would actually fictionalize the experience in one of his short stories. "I could see already," he has the man who lost a manuscript say, "as you begin to see clearly over the water when a rainstorm lifts on the ocean as the wind carries it out to sea, that I could write a better novel."

The skateboarder Tony Hawk began his professional career at age fourteen, essentially when he was still a child. He was so much smaller than the other skaters, so small generally, that getting air off the ramp was difficult. This was frustrating, difficult, unfair even. Only after Hawk accepted that he simply could not do what the bigger skaters could naturally, easily do was he able to invent his own way of doing it—ollieing as he left the lip of the pool—to compensate.

This little innovation did more than help Tony Hawk level the playing field. It revolutionized the entire sport.

It doesn't always feel that way, but constraints in life are a good thing. Especially if we can accept them and let them

THE OBSTACLE IS THE WAY

direct us. They push us to places and to develop skills that we'd otherwise never have pursued. Would we rather have everything? Sure, but that isn't up to us.

It's easy to observe that people who are deprived of one of their senses often find that others are heightened. But imagine being Thomas Edison and losing your hearing as a young boy. Imagine actually being Helen Keller, who was deaf *and* blind. They had to wrestle with this cruel deprivation first, come to terms with it, and then bravely move through life without these senses.

Acceptance, too, often feels like resignation to us, especially when we are young, ambitious, and determined.

I can't just give up! I want to fight!

You know you're not the only one who has to accept things you don't necessarily like, right? It's part of the human condition.

If someone we knew took traffic signals personally, we would judge them insane. If we met someone who was fighting gravity or the sunset, we'd pity them.

Life deals us unavoidable, inalterable things. It tells us to come to a stop here. Or that some intersection is blocked or that a particular road has been rerouted through an inconvenient detour. We can't argue or yell this problem away. We must simply accept it.

That is not to say we allow it to prevent us from reaching our ultimate destination. But it does change the way we travel to get there and the duration of the trip.

When a doctor gives you orders or a diagnosis—even if it's the opposite of what you wanted—what do you do? You accept it. You don't have to like or enjoy the treatment, but you know that denying it only delays the cure.

After you've distinguished between the things that are up to you and the things that aren't (*ta eph'hemin, ta ouk eph'hemin*), and the break comes down to something you don't control . . . you've got only one option: *acceptance.*

The shot didn't go in.

The stock went to zero.

The weather disrupted the shipment.

Say it with me: *C'est la vie. It's all fine.*

You don't have to like something to master it—or to use it to some advantage. When the cause of our problem lies outside of us, we are better for accepting it and moving on. For ceasing to kick and fight against it, and coming to terms with it. The Stoics have a beautiful name for this attitude. They call it the Art of Acquiescence.

Let's be clear, that is not the same thing as giving up. This has nothing to do with action—this is for the things that are immune to action. It is far easier to talk of the way things should be. It takes toughness, humility, and will to accept them for what they actually are. It takes a real man or woman to face necessity.

All external events can be equally beneficial to us because we can turn them all upside down and make use of them. They can teach us a lesson we were reluctant to otherwise learn.

For instance, in 2006 a long-term hip injury finally caught up with Lakers coach Phil Jackson, and the surgery he had to fix it severely limited his courtside movement. Relegated to a special captain's-style chair near the players, he couldn't pace the sideline or interact with the team the same way. Initially, Jackson was worried this would affect his coaching. In fact, sitting back on the sideline above the rest of the bench *increased* his authority. He learned how to assert himself without ever being overbearing the way he'd been in the past.

But to get these unexpected benefits we first have to accept the unexpected costs—even though we'd rather not have them in the first place.

Unfortunately, we are often too greedy to do this. We instinctively think about how much better we'd like any given situation to be. We start thinking about what we'd rather have. Rarely do we consider how much worse things could have been.

And things can *always* be worse. Not to be glib, but the next time you:

> *Lost money?*
> Remember, you could have lost a friend.
> *Lost that job?*
> What if you'd lost a limb?
> *Lost your house?*
> You could have lost *everything*.

Yet we squirm and complain about what was taken from us. We still can't appreciate what we have.

Some of this entitlement is new, a product of a world where we can beam documents around the globe in nanoseconds, chat in high-definition video with anyone anywhere, travel at thirty thousand feet and six hundred miles per hour, predict the weather down to the minute. We have internalized the assumption that nature has been domesticated and submits to our every whim. Of course it hasn't.

We haven't conquered anything. The world is far more powerful than we are.

The ancients (and the not so ancients) used the word *fate* far more frequently than us because they were better acquainted with and exposed to how capricious and random the world could be. Events were considered to be the "will of the Gods." The Fates were forces that shaped our lives and destinies, often not with much consent.

Letters used to be signed *Deo volente*—God willing. Because who knew what would happen?

Think of George Washington, putting everything he had into the American Revolution, and then saying, "The event is in the hand of God." Or Eisenhower, writing to his wife on the eve of the Allied invasion at Sicily: "Everything we could think of have been done, the troops are fit, everybody is doing his best. The answer is in the lap of the gods." These were not guys prone to settling or leaving the details up to other people—but they understood ultimately that what happened would happen. And they'd go from there.

It's time to be humble and flexible enough to acknowledge the same in our own lives. That there is always someone or something that could change the plan. And that person is not us. As the saying goes, "Man proposes but God disposes."

As fate would have it.
Heaven forbid.
Nature permitting.
Murphy's Law.

Whatever version you prefer, it's all the same. Not that much has changed between their time and ours—they were just more cognizant of it.

Look: If we want to use the metaphor that life is a game,

THE OBSTACLE IS THE WAY

it means playing the dice or the chips or the cards where they fall. Play it where it lies, as a golfer would say.

But to do that, first you have to accept. And the quicker you accept, the better you can play.

The way life *is* gives you plenty to work with, plenty to leave your imprint on. Taking people and events as they are is quite enough material already. Follow where the events take you, like water rolling down a hill—it always gets to the bottom eventually, doesn't it?

Because (a) you're robust and resilient enough to handle whatever occurs, (b) you can't do anything about it anyway, and (c) you're looking at a big-enough picture and long-enough timeline that whatever you have to accept is still only a negligible blip on the way to your goal.

We're indifferent and that's not a weakness.

As Francis Bacon once said, nature, in order to be commanded, must be obeyed.

LOVE EVERYTHING
THAT HAPPENS: *AMOR FATI*

My formula for greatness in a human being is *amor fati*:
that one wants nothing to be different, not forward, not
backward, not in all eternity. Not merely bear what is
necessary, still less conceal it . . . but love it.

—NIETZSCHE

At age sixty-seven, Thomas Edison returned home early
one evening from another day at the laboratory. Shortly
after dinner, a man came rushing into his house with urgent
news: A fire had broken out at Edison's research and production campus a few miles away.

Fire engines from eight nearby towns rushed to the scene,
but they could not contain the blaze. Fueled by the strange
chemicals in the various buildings, green and yellow flames
shot up six and seven stories, threatening to destroy the entire empire Edison had spent his life building.

Edison calmly but quickly made his way to the fire, through
the now hundreds of onlookers and devastated employees,
looking for his son. "Go get your mother and all her friends,"
he told his son with childlike excitement. "They'll never see
a fire like this again."

What?!

"Don't worry," Edison calmed him. "It's all right. We've just got rid of a lot of rubbish."

That's a pretty amazing reaction. But when you think about it, there really was no other response.

What should Edison have done? Wept? Gotten angry? Quit and gone home?

What, exactly, would that have accomplished?

You know the answer now: nothing. So he didn't waste time indulging himself. To do great things, we need to be able to endure tragedy and setbacks. We've got to love what we do and all that it entails, good and bad. We have to learn to find joy in every single thing that happens.

Of course, there was more than just a little "rubbish" in Edison's buildings. Years and years of priceless records, prototypes, and research were turned to ash. The buildings, which had been made of what was supposedly fireproof concrete, had been insured for only a fraction of their worth. Thinking they were immune to such disasters, Edison and his investors were covered for about a third of the damage.

As he looked at the flames, he was reminded of Kipling's line to treat triumph and disaster the same. He had known incredible success. Now he was once again meeting with failure and loss and heartbreak. But he chose to be invigorated by it. As he told a reporter the next day, he wasn't too old to make a fresh start. "I've been through a lot of things like this. It prevents a man from being afflicted with ennui."

Within about three weeks, the factory was partially back up and running. Within a month, its men were working two shifts a day churning out new products the world had never seen. Despite a loss of almost $1 million dollars (more than $31 million in today's dollars), Edison would marshal enough energy to make nearly $10 million dollars in revenue that year ($300-plus million today). He suffered a spectacular disaster, but he turned it into a spectacular final act.

The next step after we discard our expectations and *accept* what happens to us, after understanding that certain things—particularly bad things—are outside our control, is this: loving whatever happens to us and facing it with unfailing cheerfulness.

It is the act of turning what we *must* do into what we *get* to do.

We put our energies and emotions and exertions where they will have real impact. This is that place. We will tell ourselves: *This is what I've got to do or put up with? Well, I might as well be happy about it.*

Here's an image to consider: the great boxer Jack Johnson in his famous fifteen-round brawl with Jim Jeffries. Jeffries, the Great White Hope, called out of retirement like some deranged Cincinnatus to defeat the ascendant black champion. And Johnson, genuinely hated by his opponent and the crowd, still enjoyed every minute of it. Smiling, joking, playing the whole fight.

Why not? There's no value in any other reaction. Should he hate them for hating him? Bitterness was their burden and Johnson refused to pick it up.

Not that he simply took the abuse. Instead, Johnson designed his fight plan around it. At every nasty remark from Jeffries's corner, he'd give his opponent another lacing. At every low trick or rush from Jeffries, Johnson would quip and beat it back—but never lose his cool. And when one well-placed blow opened a cut on Johnson's lip, he kept smiling—a gory, bloody, but nevertheless cheerful smile. Every round, he got happier, friendlier, as his opponent grew enraged and tired, eventually losing the will to fight.

In your worst moments, picture Johnson: always calm, always in control, genuinely loving the opportunity to prove himself, to perform for people, whether they wanted him to succeed or not. Each remark bringing the response it deserved and no more—letting the opponent dig his own grave. Until the fight ended with Jeffries on the floor and every doubt about Johnson silenced.

As Jack London, the famous novelist, reported from ringside seats:

> *No one understands him, this man who smiles. Well, the story of the fight is the story of a smile. If ever a man won by nothing more fatiguing than a smile, Johnson won today.*

You can't beat a man who doesn't stop smiling, who takes the worst you could throw at him and eats it up.

We can strive to be like that, not just gritting our teeth and bearing it but *showing our teeth in a big old grin*. Nothing is more frustrating to the people or impediments attempting to frustrate *us*.

As the Stoics commanded themselves: Cheerfulness in all situations, especially the bad ones. Who knows where Edison and Johnson learned this, but they clearly did.

Learning not to kick and scream about matters we can't control is one thing. Indifference and acceptance are certainly better than disappointment or rage. Very few understand or practice that art. But it is only a first step. Better than all of that is love for *all* that happens to us, for every situation.

The goal is:

Not: *I'm okay with this.*
Not: *I think I feel good about this.*
But: *I feel great about it.*
Because if it happened, then it was meant to happen, and I am glad that it did when it did. I am meant to make the best of it.

And proceed to do exactly that.

We don't get to choose what happens to us, but we can always choose how we feel about it. And why on earth would you *choose* to feel anything but good? We can choose to render a good account of ourselves. If the event must occur, *amor fati* (a love of fate) is the response.

Don't waste a second looking back at your expectations. Face forward, and face it with a smug little grin.

It's important to look at Johnson and Edison because they weren't passive. They didn't simply roll over and tolerate adversity. They accepted what happened to them. They *liked* it.

It's a little unnatural, I know, to feel gratitude for things we never wanted to happen in the first place. But we know, at this point, the opportunities and benefits that lie within adversities. We know that in overcoming them, we emerge stronger, sharper, empowered. There is little reason to delay these feelings. To begrudgingly acknowledge later that it was for the best, when we could have felt that in advance because it was inevitable.

You love it because it's all fuel. And you don't just want fuel. You need it. You can't go anywhere without it. No one or no thing can. So you're grateful for it.

That is not to say that the good will always outweigh the bad. Or that it comes free and without cost. But there is always some good—even if only barely perceptible at first—contained within the bad.

And we can find it and be cheerful because of it.

PERSEVERANCE

Anybody can rise to meet a crisis and face a crushing
tragedy with courage, but to meet the petty hazards of
the day with a laugh—I really think that requires spirit.

—JEAN WEBSTER

Odysseus leaves Troy after ten long years of war destined
for Ithaca, for home. If only he knew what was ahead
of him: ten more years of travel. That he'd come so close to
the shores of his homeland, his queen and young son, only
to be blown back again.

That he'd face storms, temptation, a Cyclops, deadly whirl-
pools, and a six-headed monster. Or that he'd be held cap-
tive for seven years and suffer the wrath of Poseidon. And,
of course, that back in Ithaca his rivals were circling, trying
to take his kingdom and his wife.

How did he get through it? How did the hero make it
home despite it all?

Creativity, of course. And craftiness and leadership and
discipline and courage.

But above all: perseverance.

That was Odysseus standing at the gates of Troy, trying

everything before the success of the Trojan horse. Persistence. Everything directed at one problem, until it breaks.

But a ten-year voyage of trials and tribulations. Of disappointment and mistakes without giving in. Of checking your bearings each day and trying to inch a little closer to home—where you'll face a whole other host of problems once you arrive. Ironhearted and ready to endure whatever punishment the Gods decide you must, and to do it with courage and tenacity in order to make it back to Ithaca? That's more than persistence, that's *perseverance*.

A hard term as prime minster, that's persistence. Seven decades as queen, serving as Queen Elizabeth II did without complaint? That's perseverance. Ulysses S. Grant across the river from Vicksburg, fighting to take it back from the Confederacy? That's persistence. Edison painstakingly trying every filament until he gets the lightbulb, that's persistence. Grant clawing his way out of poverty, into sobriety, fighting all those horrible battles in that long war, then the fight of Reconstruction, then finding out every penny he had was swindled by a Wall Street fraud, rushing to write his memoirs as he died of cancer in order to leave his family something to live on?

Perseverance.

If persistence is attempting to solve some difficult problem with dogged determination and hammering until the break occurs, then plenty of people can be said to be persistent. But perseverance is something larger. It's the long game. It's about what happens not just in round one but in round two and every round after—and then the fight after that and the fight after that, until the end.

The Germans have a word for it: *Sitzfleisch*. Staying power. Winning by sticking your ass to the seat and not leaving until after it's over.

Life is not about one obstacle, but *many*. What's required of us is not some shortsighted focus on a single facet of a problem, but simply a determination that we *will* get to where we need to go, somehow, someway, and nothing will stop us.

We will overcome every obstacle—and there will be many in life—until we get there. Persistence is an action. Perseverance is a matter of will. One is energy. The other, *endurance*.

And, of course, they work in conjunction with each other. That Tennyson line in full:

> *Made weak by time and fate, but strong in will*
> *To strive, to seek, to find, and not to yield*

Persist and *resist*.

Throughout human history, there have been many strategies for overcoming the seemingly endless problems that affect us as individuals and as a group. Sometimes the solution was technology, sometimes it was violence, sometimes it was a radical new way of thinking that changed everything.

We've looked at a lot of those examples. But across the board, one strategy has been more effective than all the others, and it is responsible for far more than anything else. It works in good situations and in bad situations, dangerous situations and seemingly hopeless situations.

When Antonio Pigafetta, the assistant to Magellan on his trip around the world, reflected on his boss's greatest and most admirable skill, what do you think he said? It had nothing to do with sailing. The secret to his success, Pigafetta said, was Magellan's ability to endure hunger better than the other men. But of course it was also his ability to be calm under pressure, to endure freezing cold and searing heat and monotony and loneliness, to put down mutinies, to use disasters as a chance to consolidate his command, to teach and to learn. He was Shackleton before Shackleton: *Fortitudine vincimus*. By endurance we conquer.

There are far more failures in the world due to a collapse of will than there will ever be from objectively conclusive external events.

Perseverance. Force of purpose. Indomitable will. Those traits were once uniquely part of the American DNA. But they've been weakening for some time. As Emerson wrote in 1841,

> *If our young men miscarry in their first enterprises, they lose all heart. If the young merchant fails, men say he is ruined. If the finest genius studies at one of our colleges, and is not installed in an office within one year afterwards in the cities or suburbs of Boston or New York, it seems to his friends and to himself that he is right in being disheartened, and in complaining the rest of his life.*

Think of what he'd say about us now. What would he say about you?

We whine and complain and mope when things don't go our way. We're crushed when what we were "promised" is revoked—as if that's not allowed to happen. Instead of doing much about it, we sit at home and play video games or travel or worse, pay for more school with more loan debt that will never be forgiven. And then we wonder why it isn't getting any better.

We'd be so much better following the lead of Emerson's counterexample. Someone who is willing to try not one thing but "tries all the professions, who teams it, farms it, peddles, keeps a school, preaches, edits a newspaper, goes to Congress, buys a township, and so forth, in successive years, and always, like a cat, falls on his feet."

This is perseverance. And with it, Emerson said, "with the exercise of self-trust, new powers shall appear." The good thing about true perseverance is that it can't be stopped by anything besides death. To quote Beethoven: "The barriers are not erected which can say to aspiring talents and industry, Thus far and no farther."

We can go around or under or backward. We can decide that momentum and defeat are not mutually exclusive—we can keep going, advancing, even if we've been stopped in one particular direction.

Our actions can be constrained, but our will can't be. Our plans—even our bodies—can be broken. But belief in ourselves? No matter how many times we are thrown back, we alone retain the power to decide to go once more. Or to try another route. Or, at the very least, to accept this reality and decide upon a new aim.

Determination, if you think about it, is invincible. Nothing other than death can prevent us from following Churchill's old acronym: KBO. Keep Buggering On.

Despair? Who has time? Who can afford it? Too many people are counting on you to keep going.

We don't control the barriers or the people who put them there. But we control ourselves—and that is sufficient.

The true threat to determination, then, is not what happens to us, but us ourselves. Why would you be your own worst enemy?

Hold on and hold steady.

SOMETHING BIGGER
THAN YOURSELF

—

A man's job is to make the world a better place to live in,
so far as he is able—always remembering the results will
be infinitesimal—and to attend to his own soul.

—LEROY PERCY

A United States Navy fighter pilot named James Stock-dale was shot down in North Vietnam in 1965. As he
drifted back down to earth after ejecting from his plane, he
spent those few minutes contemplating what awaited him
down below. Imprisonment? Certainly. Torture? Likely. Death?
Possibly. Who knew how long it would all take, or if he'd ever
see his family or home again.

But the second Stockdale hit the ground, that contempla-tion stopped. He wouldn't dare think about *himself*. See, he
had a mission.

During the Korean War over a decade earlier, individual
self-preservation showed its ugly side. In the terrible, freez-ing prison camps of that war, it had very much become every
American soldier for himself. Scared to death, the survival
instincts of American prisoners of war kicked in so over-whelmingly that some ended up fighting and even killing

one another simply to stay alive, rather than fighting against their captors to survive or escape.

Stockdale (then a commander), aware that he would be the highest-ranking Navy POW the North Vietnamese had ever captured, knew he couldn't do anything about his fate. But as a commanding officer, he could provide leadership and support and direction to his fellow prisoners (who included future senator John McCain). He could change *that* situation and not let history repeat itself—this would be his cause, and he would help his men and lead them. Which is exactly what he proceeded to do for more than seven years; two of which were spent wearing leg irons in solitary confinement.

Stockdale didn't take his obligation as a commander lightly. He went so far as to attempt suicide at one point, not to end his suffering but to send a message to the guards. Other soldiers in the war effort had given their lives. He would not disgrace them or their sacrifice by allowing himself to be used as a tool against their common cause. He would rather hurt himself than contribute—even against his will—to hurting or undermining others. He proved himself formidable to whatever physical harm his captors threatened him with.

But he was human. And he understood that his men were, too. The first thing he did was throw out any idealistic notions about what happens to a soldier when asked to give up information under hours of torture. So he set up a network of support inside the camp, specifically to help soldiers who felt ashamed for having broken under the pressure. We're in this together, he told them. He gave them a watchword to remind them: U.S.—Unity over Self.

John McCain in his own cell nearby responded in essentially the same way and was able to endure indescribable torture for the same reasons. Hoping to stain the McCain family's prestigious military legacy and the United States, the Vietcong repeatedly offered McCain the opportunity to abandon his fellow prisoners and return home. He refused the special treatment. He would not undermine the cause, despite self-interest. He stayed and was tortured—by choice.

These two men were not zealots for the cause—they certainly had their own doubts about the war in Vietnam. But their cause was their men. They cared about their fellow prisoners and drew great strength by putting their well-being ahead of their own.

Hopefully, you will not find yourself in a POW camp anytime soon. But we are in our own tough economic times—in fact, they can sometimes feel downright desperate.

You're young, you didn't cause this, it isn't your fault. We all got screwed. This only makes it easier to lose our sense of self, to say nothing of our sense of others. To think—if only privately—*I don't care about them, I've got to get mine before it's too late.*

Especially when the leaders in your supposed community make it clear that that is exactly how they feel about you when it comes down to the crunch. But no, ignore that. It is in this moment that we must show the true strength of will within us.

A few years ago, in the middle of the financial crisis, the artist and musician Henry Rollins managed to express this deeply human obligation better than millennia of religious doctrine ever have:

People are getting a little desperate. They might not show their best elements to you. You must never lower yourself to being a person you don't like. There is no better time than now to have a moral and civic backbone. To have a moral and civic true north. This is a tremendous opportunity for you, a young person, to be heroic.

Not that you need to martyr yourself. See, when we focus on others, on helping them or simply providing a good example, our own personal fears and troubles will diminish. With fear or heartache no longer our primary concern, we don't have time for it. Shared purpose gives us strength.

The desire to quit or compromise on principles suddenly feels rather selfish when we consider the people who would be affected by that decision. When it comes to obstacles and whatever reactions they provoke—boredom, hatred, frustration, or confusion—just because you feel that way doesn't mean everyone else does.

Sometimes when we are personally stuck with some intractable or impossible problem, one of the best ways to create opportunities or new avenues for movement is to think: *If I can't solve this for myself, how can I at least make this better for other people?* Take it for granted, for a second, that there is nothing else in it for us, nothing we can do for ourselves. How can we use this situation to benefit *others?* How can we salvage some good out of this? *If not for me, then for my family or the others I'm leading or those who might later find themselves in a similar situation.*

What doesn't help anyone is making this all about you, all the time. *Why did this happen to me? What am I going to do about this?*

You'll be shocked by how much of the hopelessness lifts

when we reach that conclusion. Because now we have something to *do*. Like Stockdale, now we have a mission. In the light of blinding futility, we've got marching orders and things that must be done.

Stop making it harder on yourself by thinking about *I, I, I*. Stop putting that dangerous "I" in front of events. *I* did this. *I* was so smart. *I* had that. *I* deserve better than this. No wonder you take losses personally, no wonder you feel so alone. You've inflated your own role and importance.

Start thinking: *Unity over Self. We're in this together.*

Even if we can't carry the load all the way, we're going to take a crack at picking up the heavy end. We're going to be of service to others. Help ourselves by helping them. Becoming better because of it, drawing purpose from it.

Whatever you're going through, whatever is holding you down or standing in your way, can be turned into a source of strength—by thinking of people other than yourself. You won't have time to think of your own suffering because there are other people suffering and you're too focused on them.

Pride can be broken. Toughness has its limits. But a desire to help? No harshness, no deprivation, no toil should interfere with our empathy toward others. Compassion is always an option. Camaraderie as well. That's a power of the will that can never be taken away, only relinquished.

Stop pretending that what you're going through is somehow special or unfair. Whatever trouble you're having—no matter how difficult—is not some unique misfortune picked out especially for you. It just is what it is.

This kind of myopia is what convinces us, to our own detriment, that we're the center of the universe. When really, there is a world beyond our own personal experience filled with people who have dealt with worse. We're not special or unique simply by virtue of being. We're all, at varying points in our lives, subject to random and often incomprehensible events.

Reminding ourselves of this is another way of being a bit more selfless.

You can always remember that a decade earlier, a century earlier, a millennium earlier, someone just like you stood right where you are and felt very similar things, struggling with the very same thoughts. They had no idea that you would exist, but you know that they did. And a century from now, someone will be in your exact same position once more.

Embrace this power, this sense of being part of a larger whole. It is an exhilarating thought. Let it envelop you. We're all just humans, doing the best we can. We're all just trying to survive, and in the process, inch the world forward a little bit.

Help your fellow humans thrive and survive, contribute your little bit to the universe before it swallows you up, and be happy with that. Lend a hand to others. Be strong for them, and it will make you stronger.

MEDITATE ON YOUR MORTALITY

When a man knows he is to be hanged in a fortnight,
it concentrates his mind wonderfully.

—SAMUEL JOHNSON

In late 1569, a French nobleman named Michel de Montaigne was given up as dead after being flung from a galloping horse.

As his friends carried his limp and bloodied body home, Montaigne watched life slip away from his physical self, not traumatically but almost flimsily, like some dancing spirit on the "tip of his lips." Only to have it return at the last possible second.

This sublime and unusual experience marked the moment Montaigne changed his life. Within a few years, he would be one of the most famous writers in Europe. After his accident, Montaigne went on to write volumes of popular essays, serve two terms as mayor, travel internationally as a diplomat, and serve as a confidante of the king.

It's a story as old as time. Man nearly dies, he takes stock, and emerges from the experience a completely different, and better, person.

And so it was for Montaigne. Coming so close to death energized him, made him curious. No longer was death something to be afraid of—looking it in the eyes had been a relief, even inspiring.

Death doesn't make life pointless, but rather purposeful. And, fortunately, we don't have to nearly die to tap into this energy.

In Montaigne's essays, we see proof of the fact that one can meditate on death—be well aware of our own mortality—without being morbid or a downer. In fact, his experience gave him a uniquely playful relationship with his existence and a sense of clarity and euphoria that he carried with him from that point forward. This is encouraging: It means that embracing the precariousness of our own existence can be exhilarating and empowering.

Our fear of death is a looming obstacle in our lives. It shapes our decisions, our outlook, and our actions.

But for Montaigne, for the rest of his life, he would dwell and meditate on that moment, re-creating the near-death experience as best he could. He studied death, discussing it, learning of its place in other cultures. For instance, Montaigne once wrote of an ancient drinking game in which participants took turns holding up a painting of a corpse inside a coffin and toasting to it: "Drink and be merry for when you're dead you will look like this."

As Shakespeare wrote in *The Tempest* not many years later, as he himself was growing older, "Every third thought shall be my grave."

Every culture has its own way of teaching the same lesson: *Memento mori*, the Romans would remind themselves. Remember you are mortal.

It seems weird to think that we'd forget this or need to be reminded of it, but clearly we do.

Part of the reason we have so much trouble with acceptance is because our relationship with our own existence is totally messed up. We may not say it, but deep down we act and behave like we're invincible. Like we're impervious to the trials and tribulations of mortality. *That stuff happens to* other *people, not to* ME. *I have plenty of time left.*

We forget how light our grip on life really is.

Otherwise, we wouldn't spend so much time obsessing over trivialities, or trying to become famous, make more money than we could ever spend in our lifetime, or make plans far off in the future. All of these are negated by death. All these assumptions presume that death won't affect us, or at least, not when we don't want it to. The paths of glory, Thomas Gray wrote, lead but to the grave.

Without exception.

It doesn't matter who you are or how many things you have left to be done, somewhere there is someone who would kill you for a thousand dollars or for a vial of crack or for getting in their way. A car can hit you in an intersection and drive your teeth back into your skull. That's it. It will all be over. Today, tomorrow, someday soon.

It's a cliché question to ask, *What would I change about my life if the doctor told me I had cancer?* After our answer, we inevitably comfort ourselves with the same insidious lie: *Still, good thing I don't have cancer.*

But we do. The diagnosis is terminal for all of us. A death sentence has been decreed. The doctor knew for certain that your days were numbered the moment you came out of your mother. Today, no matter how old we are, probability is eating away at the chances that we'll be alive tomorrow; something is coming and you'll never be able to stop it. Be ready for when that day comes.

Some things are up to us, some are not. Death is not one of those things—besides watching what we eat and not being stupidly reckless, it is not in our control how long we will live or what will come and take us from life.

This awareness of mortality can create real perspective and urgency. It doesn't need to be depressing. It can be invigorating. Instead of denying—or worse, fearing—our mortality, we can embrace it.

Reminding ourselves each day that we will die helps us treat our time as a gift. Someone on a deadline doesn't indulge themselves with attempts at the impossible, they don't waste time complaining about how they'd like things to be. They don't take people for granted, they are grateful for everything.

They figure out what they need to do and do it, fitting in as much as possible before the clock expires. They figure out how, when that moment strikes, to say, *Of course, I would have liked to last a little longer, but I made a lot of out what I was already given so this works, too.*

There's no question about it: Death is the most universal of our obstacles. It's the one we can do the least about. At the very best, we can hope to delay it—and even then, we'll still succumb eventually.

But that is not to say it is not without value to us while we are alive. In the shadow of death, prioritization is easier. As are graciousness and appreciation and principles. Everything falls in its proper place and perspective. Why would you do the wrong thing? Why feel fear? Why let yourself and others down? Life will be over soon enough; death chides us that we may as well do life right.

We can learn to adjust and come to terms with death— this final and most humbling fact of life—and find relief in the understanding that there is nothing else nearly as hard left.

And so, if even our own mortality can have some benefit, how dare you say that you can't derive value from each and every other kind of obstacle you encounter?

PREPARE TO START AGAIN

Live on in your blessings, your destiny's been won.
But ours calls us on from one ordeal to the next.

—VIRGIL

The great law of nature is that it never stops. There is no end. Just when you think you've successfully navigated one obstacle, another emerges.

But that's what keeps life interesting. And as you're starting to see, that's what creates opportunities.

Life is a process of breaking through these impediments— a series of fortified lines that we must break through.

Each time, you'll learn something. Each time, you'll develop strength, wisdom, and perspective. Each time, a little more of the competition falls away. Until all that is left is you: the best version of you.

As the Haitian proverb puts it: Behind mountains are more mountains.

Elysium is a myth. One does not overcome an obstacle to enter the land of no obstacles.

On the contrary, the more you accomplish, the more things will stand in your way. There are always more obstacles, bigger challenges. You're always fighting uphill. Always against the wind. Get used to it and train accordingly.

Knowing that life is a marathon and not a sprint is important. Conserve your energy. Understand that each battle is only one of many and that you can use it to make the next one easier. More important, you must keep them all in *real* perspective.

Passing one obstacle simply says you're worthy of more. The world seems to keep throwing them at you once it knows you can take it. Which is good, because we get better with every attempt.

Never rattled. Never frantic. Always hustling and acting with creativity. Never anything but deliberate. Never attempting to do the impossible—but everything up to that line.

Simply flipping the obstacles that life throws at you by improving in spite of them, because of them.

And therefore no longer afraid. But excited, cheerful, and eagerly anticipating the next round.

FINAL THOUGHTS

The Obstacle Becomes the Way

L ate in his reign, sick and possibly near death, Marcus Aurelius received surprising news. His old friend and most trusted general, Avidius Cassius, had rebelled in Syria. Having heard the emperor was vulnerable or possibly dead, the ambitious general had decided to declare himself Caesar and forcibly seize the throne.

It was another crisis in what had been nearly two decades of unending adversity, in a life that had been more painful than privileged. Floods. A plague. A debilitating stomach ailment. Years at war. He had buried six children.

At some point, at another funeral, as he spent another night far from home, as he wept over the ceaseless death toll from disease and pestilence, he must have thought: *Haven't I given enough? When will this end? What's the point?*

So Marcus could have been angry. Not just at Cassius but at the gods. At fortune, at fate. Marcus, one historian would write in the early third century, "did not have the good fortune that he deserved . . . and for almost his whole reign was involved in a series of troubles."

History would have forgiven him for wanting to avenge this enemy, for taking all his rage and frustration out on this man who had betrayed him, who threatened his life, his family, and his legacy. Instead, Marcus did nothing—going as far as to keep the news secret from his troops, who might have been enraged or provoked on his behalf—but waited to see if Cassius would come to his senses.

The man did not. And so Marcus Aurelius called a council of his soldiers and made a rather extraordinary announcement. They would march against Cassius and obtain the "great prize of war and of victory." But of course, because it was Marcus, this war prize was something wholly different.

They would capture Cassius and endeavor not to kill him, but "forgive a man who has wronged one, to remain a friend to one who has transgressed friendship, to continue faithful to one who has broken faith."

It's been said that Stoicism is a depressing, resigned philosophy. Nothing disproves this more than the actual life of Marcus Aurelius. How did he even get out of bed in the morning? Where did he find the strength to be compassionate, to even care at all after what had happened to him? Where did the hope come from, the belief that any of it mattered? From his Inner Citadel, that's where.

Acting quickly—rightly and firmly—Marcus ordered troops to Rome to calm the panicking crowds and then set out to do what must be done: protect the empire, put down a threat. He not only wasn't blind with rage, he was intent on meeting this challenge as he'd met his earlier ones—as an opportunity to grow and learn and teach. As he explained to his men, there was good that could come of this awful situation that they had not wanted, that they could "settle this affair well and show to all mankind that there is a right way to deal even with civil wars."

The obstacle becomes the way.

Of course, as so often happens, even the most well-intentioned plans can be interrupted by others. For both Cassius and Marcus, their destiny was changed when a lone assassin struck Cassius down in Egypt, three months later. His dream of empire ended right there. Marcus's initial hope to be able to forgive, in person, his betrayer ended as well.

But this itself created a better opportunity—the opportunity to practice forgiveness on a significantly larger scale. The Stoics liked to use the metaphor of fire. Writing in his journal, Marcus once reminded himself that "when the fire is strong, it soon appropriates to itself the matter which is heaped on it, and consumes it, and rises higher by means of this very material."

The unexpected death of his rival, the man whom Marcus had been deprived of granting clemency to, was this metaphor embodied. Marcus would now forgive essentially *everyone* involved. He wouldn't take any of it personally. He'd be a better person, a better leader for it.

Arriving in the provinces shortly after the death of Cassius, Marcus refused to put any coconspirators to death. He declined to prosecute any of the senators or governors who had endorsed or expressed support for the uprising. And when other senators insisted on death sentences for their peers associated with the rebellion, he wrote them simply: "I implore you, the senate, to keep my reign unstained by the blood of any senator. May it never happen."

The obstacle becomes the way, becomes the way.

Forever and ever and ever.

There is a kind of pine tree whose seeds can only germinate when they are subjected to temperatures impossible to achieve in daily life. It's only a forest fire, which seems destructive and merciless and awful, that can unlock this tree's ability to spawn and grow.

Marcus Aurelius would not have known about this tree, but he did know that fire itself is a similar metaphor, observing that flame turns whatever is put in front of it into fuel, transforming raw materials into heat and brightness. As a person and as a leader, he didn't deserve the adversity that life dealt him, but he met it well. He used it. He used it to become *Marcus Aurelius*. As that ancient historian would write, "I for my part admired him all the more for this very reason, that amid unusual and extraordinary difficulties he both survived himself and preserved the empire."

"It's unfortunate that this happened to me," Marcus would himself write in *Meditations*. "No," he says, correcting his initial perception. "It's *fortunate* that this has happened and I've remained unharmed by it—not shattered by the present or frightened of the future. It could have happened to anyone. But not everyone could have remained unharmed by it."

Yes, it's unlikely that anyone is going to make an armed run at our throne anytime soon. Let us hope that we don't have to be touched with fire. Ideally, your obstacles will not be so life-and-death . . . but they may be. Our rivals will steal our business. Markets will crash. Things will break. We will be hurt. Forces will try to hold us back. Bad stuff will happen.

We can turn even this to our advantage. Always.

It is an opportunity. Always.

It can unlock something in us, something that normal circumstances could not.

And if our only option—as was the case with Marcus—because of someone else's greed or lust for power, is simply to be a good person and practice forgiveness? Well, that's still a pretty good option.

This, you've surely noticed, is the pattern in every one of the stories in this book.

Something stands in someone's way. They stare it down, they aren't intimidated. Leaning into their problem or weakness or issue, they give everything they have, mentally and physically. Even though they did not always overcome it in the way they intended or expected, each individual emerged better, stronger.

What stood in the way became the way. What impeded action in some way advanced it.

It's inspiring. It's moving. It's an art we need to bring to our own lives.

Not everyone looks at obstacles—often the same ones you and I face—and sees reason to despair. In fact, they see the opposite. They see a problem with a ready solution. They see a chance to test and improve themselves.

Nothing stands in their way. Rather, everything guides them on the way.

It is so much better to be this way, isn't it? There is a lightness and a flexibility to this approach that seem very different from how we—and most people—choose to live. With our disappointments and resentments and frustrations.

We can see the "bad" things that happen in our lives with gratitude and not with regret because we turn them from disaster to real benefit—from defeat to victory.

Fate doesn't have to be fatalistic. It can be destiny and freedom just as easily.

There is no special school that these individuals attended (aside from, for many, a familiarity with the ancient wisdom of Stoicism). Nothing that they do is out of reach for us. Rather, they have unlocked something that is very much within each and every person. Tested in the crucible of adversity and forged in the furnace of trial, they realized these latent powers—the powers of perception, action, and the will.

With this triad, they:

First, see clearly.
Next, act correctly.
Finally, endure and accept the world as it is.

Perceive things as they are, leave no option unexplored, then stand strong and transform whatever can't be changed. And they all feed into one another: Our actions give us the confidence to ignore or control our perceptions. We prove and support our will with our actions.

To be sure, no one is saying you've got to do it all at once. There's a saying in Latin: *Vires acquirit eundo* (We gather strength as we go). That's how it works. That's our motto.

In mastering these three disciplines we have the tools to flip any obstacle upside down. We are worthy of any and every challenge.

Of course, it is not enough to simply read this or say it.

We must practice these maxims, rolling them over and over in our minds and acting on them until they become muscle memory.

So that under pressure and trial we get better—become better people, leaders, and thinkers. Because those trials and pressures will inevitably come. And they won't ever stop coming.

But don't worry, you're prepared for this now, this life of obstacles and adversity. You know how to handle them, how to brush aside obstacles and even benefit from them. You understand the process.

You are schooled in the art of managing your perceptions and impressions. Like Rockefeller, you're cool under pressure, immune to insults and abuse. You see opportunity in the darkest of places.

You are able to direct your actions with energy and persistence. Like Demosthenes, you assume responsibility for yourself—teaching yourself, compensating for disadvantages, and pursuing your rightful calling and place in the world.

You are iron-spined and possess a great and powerful will. Like Lincoln, you realize that life is a trial. It will not be easy, but you are prepared to give it everything you have regardless, ready to endure, persevere, and inspire others.

The names of countless other practitioners escape us, but they dealt with the same problems and obstacles. This philosophy helped them navigate those successfully. They quietly overcame what life threw at them and, in fact, thrived because of it.

They were nothing special, nothing that we are not just as capable of being. What they did was simple (simple, not easy). But let's say it once again just to remind ourselves:

See things for what they are.
Do what we can.
Endure and bear what we must.

What blocked the path now is a path.
What once impeded action advances action.
The Obstacle is the Way.

POSTSCRIPT

You're Now a Philosopher. Congratulations.

⁓

To be a philosopher is not merely to have subtle thoughts, nor even to found a school . . . it is to solve some of the problems of life, not only theoretically, but practically.

—HENRY DAVID THOREAU

You now join the ranks of Marcus Aurelius, Cato, Seneca, Thomas Jefferson, James Stockdale, Epictetus, Theodore Roosevelt, George Washington, and many others.

These men, among countless others, explicitly practiced and studied Stoicism—we know this for a fact. They were not academic—they were action-oriented. Marcus Aurelius was emperor of the most powerful empire in the history of the world. Cato, the moral example for many philosophers, never wrote down a word but defended the Roman republic with Stoic bravery until his defiant death. His daughter, Porcia, was steeped in the same ideas and it was her iron will and courage that allowed her husband, Brutus, to finish the job in the fight against Julius Caesar's tyranny.

Epictetus, the lecturer, had no cushy tenure—he was a former slave. Both he and Seneca had to navigate the surreal and terrifying world of Nero's regime.

Frederick the Great was said to ride with the works of the

Stoics in his saddlebags because they could, in his words, "sustain you in misfortune." Montaigne had a line from Epictetus carved into the beam above the study in which he spent most of his time. George Washington was introduced to Stoicism by his neighbors at age seventeen, then he put on a play about Cato to inspire his men in that dark winter at Valley Forge.

When Thomas Jefferson died, he had a copy of Seneca on his nightstand. The economist Adam Smith's theories on the interconnectedness of the world—capitalism—were significantly influenced by the Stoicism he'd studied as a schoolboy under a teacher who'd translated the works of Marcus Aurelius. Eugène Delacroix, the renowned French Romantic artist (known best for his painting *Liberty Leading the People*) was a practicing Stoic, referring to it as his "consoling religion." Toussaint Louverture, himself formerly enslaved and who challenged an emperor, read and was deeply influenced by the works of Epictetus. The political thinker John Stuart Mill wrote of Marcus Aurelius and Stoicism in his famous treatise *On Liberty*, calling it "the highest ethical product of the ancient mind."

Thomas Wentworth Higginson, a translator of Epictetus, not only led black troops in the Civil War but was a fervent advocate for women's rights, helping to publish the poetry of Emily Dickinson. The writer Ambrose Bierce, another decorated Civil War veteran and contemporary of Mark Twain and H. L. Mencken, used to recommend Seneca, Marcus Aurelius, and Epictetus to aspiring writers who wrote to him, saying they'd teach them "how to be a worthy guest at the table of the gods." Theodore Roosevelt, after his presidency, spent five months exploring (and nearly dying in) the jungles of the Amazon, and of the eight books he brought on the journey, two were Marcus Aurelius's *Meditations* and Epictetus's *Enchiridion*.

Beatrice Webb, the English social reformer who invented the concept of collective bargaining, recalled the *Meditations* fondly in her memoirs as a "manual of devotion." The Percys, the famous Southern political, writing, and planting dynasty (LeRoy Percy, United States senator; William Alexander Percy, *Lanterns on the Levee*; and Walker Percy, *The Moviegoer*) who saved thousands of lives during the flood of 1927, were well-known adherents to the works of the Stoics, because, as one of them wrote, "when all is lost, it stands fast."

In 1908, the banker, industrialist, and senator Robert Hale Ives Goddard donated an equestrian statue of Marcus Aurelius to Brown University. Eighty or so years after Goddard's donation, the Soviet poet, dissident, and political prisoner Joseph Brodsky wrote in his famous essay on the original version of that same statue of Marcus Aurelius in Rome that "if *Meditations* is antiquity, it is we who are the ruins." Like Brodsky, James Stockdale spent time imprisoned against his will—seven and a half years in a Vietcong prison camp, to be exact. And as he parachuted from his plane, Stockdale said to himself, "I'm leaving the world of technology and entering the world of Epictetus."

Today, Bill Clinton rereads Marcus Aurelius every single year. Wen Jiabao, the former premier of China, claims that *Meditations* is one of two books he travels with and that he has read it more than one hundred times over the course of his life. Bestselling author and investor Tim Ferriss refers to Stoicism as his "operating system"—and, in the tradition of those who came before him, has successfully driven its adoption throughout Silicon Valley. General James Mattis has carried *Meditations* with him on deployments all over the world. Hall of Famers like Tony Gonzalez, Dont'a Hightower, Rory McIlroy, Manu Ginóbili, Carli Lloyd, and Chris Bosh have all read the Stoics. So have actors like Zooey Deschanel and musicians like Camila Cabello and Randy Blythe, along with comedians and elected officials that you know and admire.

You might not see yourself as a "philosopher," but then again, neither did or do most of these men and women. By every definition that counts, however, they were. And now you are, too. You are a person of action. And the thread of Stoicism runs through your life just as it did through theirs—just as it has for all of history, sometimes explicitly, sometimes not.

Philosophy is more than something you read about. It's something you think about, journal about, talk about, teach, and apply. The essence of philosophy is action—in making good on the ability to turn the obstacle upside down with our minds. Understanding our problems for what's within them and their greater context. To see things *philosophically* and *act* accordingly.

As I tried to show in this book, countless others have embodied the best practices of Stoicism and philosophy without even knowing it. These individuals weren't writers or lecturers, they were doers—like you.

Over the centuries, though, this kind of wisdom has been taken from us, co-opted and abstracted by academics (when they weren't ignoring it all together, dismissing Stoicism as "self-help"). They deprived us of philosophy's true use: as an operating system for the difficulties and hardships of life.

Philosophy was never just what happened in the classroom. It was a set of lessons from the battlefield of life.

The Greek translation for the title of *Enchiridion*—Epictetus's famous work—means "close at hand," or as some have said, "in your hands." That's what the philosophy was meant for: to be in your hands, to be an extension of you. A defense against attacks, a tool to use in situations big and small. Not something you read once and put up on a shelf. It was meant, as Marcus once wrote, to make us boxers instead of fencers—to wield our weaponry, we simply need to close our fists.

Hopefully, in some small way, this book has translated those lessons and armed you with them.

Now you are a philosopher and a person of action. And that is not a contradiction.

**Interested in learning
even more about Stoicism?**

Visit
DailyStoic.com/email
to sign up for a daily email,
engage in discussion, get advice,
and more.

ACKNOWLEDGMENTS

A decade later, I have many more people to thank but also am reluctant to tweak the acknowledgments I was compelled to write when I first finished this book. So much has changed (circumstances, myself, and some of the people mentioned below) but my gratitude has grown. It was Dr. Drew Pinsky, of all people, who introduced me to Stoicism. I was in college and I was invited to a small, private summit of college journalists that Dr. Drew, then the host of *Loveline*, was hosting. After it ended, he was standing in the corner and I cautiously made my way over to nervously ask if he had any book recommendations. He said he'd been studying a philosopher named Epictetus and that I should check it out.

I went back to my hotel room and ordered the book on Amazon along with another, *Meditations* by Marcus Aurelius. Marcus Aurelius, translated by Gregory Hays, arrived first. My life has not been the same since.

I want to thank Samantha, my girlfriend (now wife), whom I love more than anyone. We'd only been dating a few weeks, but I knew she was special when she went out and bought this book *Meditations*, the book I had been raving about. She deserves extra credit if only for enduring my many private and admittedly unstoic moments over the years. Thank you for coming on the many walks with me where I thought out loud. I want to thank my dog, Hanno—not that she is reading this—because she is a constant reminder of living in the present and of pure and honest joy. (RIP.)

The book you've just read would not have been possible without Nils Parker, whose editing and long talks shaped it. It would not exist without Stephen Hanselman, my agent who pushed for it, and my editor, Niki Papadopoulos, who believed in it and fought for what was a radical departure from my first book. Thanks to Adrian Zackheim for giving me my shot and providing a home for me as a writer at Portfolio.

I need to thank my master teacher and mentor Robert Greene, who not only subsidized my reading of many of the books I used as sources but taught me the art of crafting a message and a book. His notes on my drafts were invaluable.

Thanks to Aaron Ray. Thanks to Tim Ferriss for encouraging me to write about Stoicism for his site back in 2009 and for our long talk in Amsterdam, which provided great additions to the book.

I owe Jimmy Soni and Rob Goodman for their excellent notes (and book on Cato), Shawn Coyne for his suggestion of a three-part structure, Brett Mckay of ArtofManliness.com for his book recommendations, and Matthias Meister for his insight and instruction in BJJ. Thanks to Garland Robinette, Amy Holiday, Brent Underwood, and Michael Tunney, for their thoughts and feedback. Thanks to /r/Stoicism on Reddit, a great community who answered my questions and provoked many more.

In addition to the sources, I want to give profound thanks to the many other people and writers who exposed me to the stories and bits of wisdom in this book—I transferred much of it to my commonplace book and was so awed by the lessons that I didn't always record attribution. I very much see this book as a collection of the thoughts and actions of people better and smarter than me. I hope you read it the same way and attribute any credit deserved accordingly.

I must thank the National Arts Club, the Los Angeles Athletic Club, the New York Public Library, the libraries at the University of California, Riverside, The Painted Porch, and a bunch of different Starbucks and airplanes where I wrote or researched this book.

THE STOIC READING LIST

Stoicism is perhaps the only "philosophy" where the original, primary texts are actually cleaner and easier to read than anything academics have written afterward. Which is awesome because it means you can dive into the subject and go straight to the source. I firmly believe everyone is capable of reading these very accessible writers. Below are my recommendations both on specific translations and then some additional texts worth looking at.

Meditations **by Marcus Aurelius (Modern Library).** There is one translation of Marcus Aurelius to read and that is Gregory Hayes's amazing edition for the Modern Library. Everything else falls sadly short. His version is completely devoid of any "thous," "arts," and "shalls." It's beautiful and haunting. I've recommended this book to literally thousands of people at this point. Buy it. Change your life. A few years ago, I bought the rights for a leather edition myself so I could have one that stands the test of time. You can grab it at DailyStoic.com/Meditations.

Letters from a Stoic by **Seneca** (see also: *On the Shortness of Life*). Both these translations by Penguin are fantastic. Seneca or Marcus are the best places to start if you're looking to explore Stoicism. Seneca seems like he would have been a fun guy to know—which is unusual for a Stoic. I suggest starting with *On the Shortness of Life* (a collection of short essays) and then moving to his book of letters (which are really more like essays than true correspondence).

Discourses by **Epictetus (Penguin).** Personally, I prefer the Penguin translations, but I've tried a handful of others and found the differences to be relatively negligible. Of the big three, Epictetus is the most preachy and least fun to read. But he will also from time to time express something so clearly and profoundly that it will shake you to your core.

The above translations were the ones I used for this book.

OTHER BOOKS AND AUTHORS

The great modern scholar of Stoicism is Pierre Hadot. While all the other academics and popularizers of Stoicism mostly miss the point or needlessly complicate things, Hadot clarifies. His interpretation of Marcus Aurelius in the book *The Inner Citadel*—that Marcus was not writing some systemic explanation of the universe but creating a set of practical exercises the emperor was actually practicing himself—was a huge leap forward. His book *Philosophy as a Way of Life* explains how philosophy has been wrongly interpreted as a thing people talk about rather than something that people do. If you really want to dive into practical philosophy, Hadot is the guy to read. (Also his translations of Seneca, Marcus Aurelius, and Epictetus—which he does for himself from the originals in his analysis—are quite good.) I also recommend Donald Robertson's biography *Marcus Aurelius: The Stoic Emperor,* James Romm's *Dying Every Day,* and Emily Wilson's *Seneca: A Life.*

READING RECOMMENDATIONS

This book and its stories were a result of the books I've been fortunate enough to come across in my life. Each month I distill what I read into a short email of book recommendations, which I send to my network of friends and connections. The list started as about forty people and is now received and read by two hundred thousand people from all over the world. All in all, I've recommended, discussed, and chatted about more than a thousand books with these fellow readers in the last five years.

If you'd like to join us and get these recommendations, sign up at RyanHoliday.net/Reading-Newsletter.

LET'S CONNECT!

If you'd like to continue the conversation about turning obstacles into opportunities, or learn about any of Ryan's other books, you can contact Ryan at:

Online: RyanHoliday.net/Reading-Newsletter
Facebook, Instagram, and Twitter: @RyanHoliday

To bring *The Obstacle is the Way*, Stoicism, or Ryan Holiday to your organization—as Google, the Texas Rangers, the University of Alabama (Football), HSBC, and the United States Marine Corps have—please go to RyanHoliday.net/Speaking

To purchase bulk copies of *The Obstacle is the Way* and Ryan's other books at a discount for large groups or organizations, please reach out to the Painted Porch Bookshop at paintedporchbookshop@gmail.com.

Thanks for reaching out!

By Ryan Holiday

Also by Ryan Holiday and Stephen Hanselman

RyanHoliday.net
DailyStoic.com